Religion in the Secular Age

Wiener Reihe

―

Themen der Philosophie

Herausgegeben von
Cornelia Klinger, Herta Nagl-Docekal,
Ludwig Nagl und Alexander Somek

Band 22

Religion in the Secular Age

Perspectives from the Humanities

Edited by
Herta Nagl-Docekal and Waldemar Zacharasiewicz

DE GRUYTER

ISBN 978-3-11-221538-8
e-ISBN (PDF) 978-3-11-124787-8
e-ISBN (EPUB) 978-3-11-124869-1
ISSN 2363-9237

Library of Congress Control Number: 2023935967

Bibliographic information published by the Deutsche Nationalbibliothek
The Deutsche Nationalbibliothek lists this publication in the Deutsche Nationalbibliografie;
detailed bibliographic data are available on the internet at http://dnb.dnb.de.

© 2025 Walter de Gruyter GmbH, Berlin/Boston
This volume is text- and page-identical with the hardback published in 2023.
Cover image: Grafik © Bernd Ganser-Lion ganserlion.com
Printing and binding: CPI books GmbH, Leck

www.degruyter.com

Table of Contents

Acknowledgements —— IX

Herta Nagl-Docekal and Waldemar Zacharasiewicz
Introduction: Religion in the Secular Age —— 1

Part I **Post-Kantian Approaches to Religion**

Irene Kajon
God as the Infinite: Martin Buber's Interpretation of Kant's Concept of Religion —— 21

Sami Pihlström
(Secular) Theodicy, Antitheodicy, and the Critique of Meaning: Pragmatist Reflections —— 35

Ludwig Nagl
Beyond Dogmatic Scientism: Hilary Putnam on Religious Faith —— 53

Ruth Abbey
Angles and Angels: Charles Taylor and Steven Pinker on Moral Progress in History —— 69

Part II **Religion in Critical Theory and Deconstruction**

Brendan Moran
Benjamin's Time of Healing: The Messianic as Remembrance, Happiness, and Justice —— 89

Herta Nagl-Docekal
Re-considering the Distinction between Atheists and Believers, or: Max Horkheimer's Reading of Kant —— 109

Maureen Junker-Kenny
Defining What is "Extraterritorial": Religion and Utopia in Habermas and Ricœur — 123

John D. Caputo
Secularizing Both Religion and Reason: Upending the Secular/Religious Distinction — 141

Getrude Postl
***This Incredible Need to Believe:* Julia Kristeva's Reinvention of Secular Humanism at the Crossroad of Religion, Psychoanalysis, and Politics — 151**

Part III Religion in U.S. Literature and Politics in a Global Context

Waldemar Zacharasiewicz
Critical Perspectives on Self-Sufficing Humanism in Southern Fiction — 165

Charles Reagan Wilson
The Southern Civil Religion: The Intermingling of the Sacred and the Secular in the American South — 179

Michael Hochgeschwender
Catholicism in Defense? Roman Catholic Answers to the Quest for Modernity — 193

Manfred Siebald
Competing Quests for a Hidden God in John Updike's *Roger's Version* — 223

Carmen Birkle
Science and Religion in U.S.-American Pandemic Literature — 237

Part IV Re-Framing Theological Issues and Individual Convictions

William Sweet
Philosophical Pluralism and Religious Faith in a Secular Age —— 257

Klaus Viertbauer
Religious Convictions and Public Reason: On the Way to a Two-Stage Epistemology of Religion —— 279

Christoph Irmscher
Scientists Who Believe: From Louis Agassiz to Katharine Hayhoe —— 297

David Staines
Northrop Frye and Marshall McLuhan: Two Canadian Christian Thinkers —— 307

Part V Religion in Poetry, Music and Visual Media

Alois Woldan
Religious Aspects of Ukrainian Poetry – The Case of Vasyl' Stus —— 321

Federico Celestini
Gustav Mahler's Symphonic Transcendence and Its Counterparts —— 337

Jörg Türschmann
Serial Baroque in the TV Show *American Gods* —— 349

List of Contributors —— 361

Index of Authors —— 367

Index of Subjects —— 371

Acknowledgements

The present volume is based on papers that were presented (partly online) at an international conference entitled "Religion in the Secular Age", held in Vienna on 24–26 March 2022, which was convened by the members of the commission established by the Austrian Academy of Sciences on "The North Atlantic Triangle: Social and Cultural Exchange between Europe, the USA and Canada". In a long series of previous conferences and workshops, this commission had invited scholars from both sides of the Atlantic, representing a variety of disciplines of the humanities, to undertake a joint exploration of two major fields of interest. The first was the reciprocal adoption and transformation of key ideas from overseas, typically initiated and facilitated by personal contacts and collaboration. The volumes *Transatlantic Elective Affinities: Traveling Ideas and Their Mediators* (Zacharasiewicz/Nagl-Docekal 2021) and *Narratives of Encounters in the North Atlantic Triangle* (Zacharasiewicz/Staines 2015) – as well as a number of other books – document this research. The second field focused on shared cultural phenomena, ranging from challenges created by the rapidly changing living conditions in the contemporary world to the aesthetics of the cinematic experience. The first field is documented in the volume *Artificial Intelligence and Human Enhancement. Affirmative and Critical Approaches in the Humanities* (Nagl-Docekal/Zacharasiewicz 2022), while an international symposium in the second field, convened in Vienna by The North Atlantic Triangle Commission, is presented in *Ein Filmphilosophie-Symposium mit Robert B. Pippin: Western, Film Noir und das Kino der Brüder Dardenne* (Nagl/Zacharasiewicz 2016). Important current issues will be discussed in the forthcoming collection of papers presented at the international conference held in Vienna on 18–20 November 2021, "Polarization in the North Atlantic Triangle" (Zacharasiewicz/Birkle/Prisching), and at the international conference with the topic "Images of War," scheduled for 18–20 October 2023.

The Austrian Academy of Sciences provided the funds needed to enable the invitation of scholars from abroad and overseas and covered the costs of the technical team in charge of the online presentation of the conference. Additional support was granted by the Otto Mauer Fund, the Canadian Embassy to Austria, the City of Vienna and the Society for the Promotion of North America Studies at the University of Vienna. The task of formatting and proofreading the manuscripts was undertaken by Stefanie Pointl, which is here gratefully acknowledged.

Herta Nagl-Docekal and Waldemar Zacharasiewicz
Introduction: Religion in the Secular Age

When Jürgen Habermas was awarded the Peace Prize of the German Bookdealers in 2001, he noted in his acceptance speech – *"Glauben und Wissen* (Faith and Knowledge)" – that the contemporary societies "need to expect the perseverance of religious communities in the context of an increasingly secularized environment"[1]. The notion "secular" refers here to a process that has characterized modernity: the irreversible severance of core segments of public life from religious ties. Today, public spheres such as constitution and law, the sciences, art and education are all based on specific criteria of argumentative legitimation.

The title of the present book alludes to Charles Taylor's masterpiece *A Secular Age*, published in 2007, which focuses on the fact that, in our time, "faith, even for the staunchest believer, is one human possibility among others."[2] Elaborating a complex reflection, Taylor first notes that we all share "the immanent frame" that is constituted by the insight that the various structures we live in are part of a "natural, or this-worldly order which can be understood in its own terms, without reference to the 'supernatural' or 'transcendent'". He emphasizes that "this order of itself leaves the issue open, whether, for purposes of ultimate explanation, [...] or final sense-making, we might have to invoke something transcendent"[3]. The central thesis of this book is that we need to face the fact that "the whole culture experiences cross pressures, between the draw of the narratives of closed immanence on one side, and the sense of their inadequacy on the other, strengthened by encounter with existing milieus of religious practice"[4]. Taylor's own approach is revealed as he raises doubts whether the longing for human "fullness"[5] that believers as well as non-believers share could be captured appropriately within the limits of "closed immanence".

In the recent debate, one crucial question has been this: What does it mean for human beings whose living conditions are defined by the principles of modernity – who do, for instance, identify with the idea of the liberal constitutional state, and to whom it is a matter of course to consider results of research in their decision

---
[1] Jürgen Habermas, *Glauben und Wissen*. Frankfurt: Suhrkamp (Sonderdruck edition suhrkamp) 2001, 13 (trans. Herta Nagl-Docekal).
[2] Charles Taylor. *A Secular Age.* Cambridge, MA, and London, UK: The Belknap Press of Harvard UP 2007, 3.
[3] Taylor 2007, 594.
[4] Taylor 2007, 595.
[5] Taylor 2007, 600–607.

making – to be religious believers? Is it possible for people today to avoid the following dichotomy: to either adhere, like many conventional believers, to a premodern theological conception of "ordo" that clearly contradicts the secularized conditions, or to consider themselves "enlightened" in the sense of regarding religion *toto genere* as obsolete? The most contested concept in this debate has been "reason": As the widely accepted scientific understanding of that term implies the view that religious convictions represent the "other of reason," employing an "extraterritorial"[6] language, the question arises whether believers and, indeed, converts are required to perform a *sacrificium intellectus*, or whether the concept "reason" rather allows for a more comprehensive definition. Along this line of thought the question arises whether, or how, a mutual enrichment of faith and knowledge might be possible today. In which way could views based on religion contribute to enhancing the differentiation and sensitivity of public discourse?

It seems obvious that these issues, which concern the fundamental question whether the human existence ultimately might make sense, do not belong exclusively to the domain of theology. This volume assembles a variety of approaches to these issues representing the perspective of diverse fields of the humanities; the contributions cover reflections ranging from philosophy – including American pragmatism, critical theory, Jewish philosophy and deconstruction – through studies of US and Canadian literature and modern history as well as media studies, to contemporary theology, musicology, and Slavic poetry.

Part 1: *Post-Kantian Approaches to Religion* begins with an essay by *Irene Kajon*, "God as the Infinite: Martin Buber's Interpretation of Kant's Concept of Religion", who examines whether there might be an understanding of religion that fits our secular age. She draws attention to the way in which Martin Buber employs Kant's concept of "antinomy" as he explains "how we, finite beings with all our weaknesses and fragilities, nevertheless come into positive contact with the infinite or eternal". Introducing Buber's reflections on the "nearness-distance" between humans and the divine, Kajon highlights his view that the core of Kant's thinking lies in the thesis that human beings encounter "a God whom they conceive as a Subject who acts with goodness and justice in the world". As she explains, this reading of Kant provides the basis of Buber's claim that there exists a dialogical relationship between the human being and God, as elaborated in his *I and Thou*. The very essence of this relationship is the sphere of ethics: eternity becomes a "Presence" when we encounter other "Thou"s: God is the medium (*Mittlertum*) of all our relations (*Beziehungen*) in the world. Underscoring Buber's view

---

6 Cf., for instance, Jürgen Habermas. *Between Naturalism and Religion*. Cambridge, UK, and Malden, MA: Polity 2008, 130, 142.

that this concept of God "could perhaps be accepted by both believers and non-believers in our secular societies," Kajon addresses a topic that is also discussed in some other essays in the present volume. Non-believers, she suggests, might acknowledge that Buber offers a new perspective on religion – most notably, by provoking the question which understanding of the term "religion" might be most appropriate for our time. She advocates reading this word, rather than with traditional references to "relegere" (Cicero) or religare (Lactantius), with the Hebrew term "da'al" in mind, which means *"ligare"*: a term that "means not only to connect, but – taking into consideration the term *legati* – also to entrust: human beings are charged to act in the world as if they were messengers of the Infinite".

One most pressing moral issue is addressed in the essay – "(Secular) Theodicy, Antitheodicy, and the Critique of Meaning: Pragmatist Reflections" – by *Sami Pihlström*, who deals with the grave evil marking the history of humankind, as experienced, in particular, in the horrendous suffering caused by the totalitarian political systems of the twentieth century. His focus is on the concept of "theodicy" that philosophers of religion[7] have introduced to signify theories seeking to morally excuse God's allowing the world to contain such pointless pain. As he highlights the "theodicist tendency to view suffering as (necessarily) meaningful in some deeper [...] sense", he notes that such thoughts are expressed not exclusively in religious but also in metaphysical and secular terms. In contrast, the essay elaborates an "antitheodicist critique" that challenges "the pursuit of meaning(fulness) [...] associated with theodicies". This "project of defending antitheodicism", Pihlström claims, "is crucially based on broadly Kantian premises".[8] He provides a specific argumentative edge, however, by emphasizing that "antitheodicism is a normative view according to which we *should not* approach the problem of evil and suffering by offering, or expecting others to offer, theodicies". In other words, "antitheodicism urges us to ethically acknowledge the victim's experiences of the meaninglessness of their suffering". Discussing the search for meaningfulness, Pihlström pays particular attention to the diversity of reactions to the extreme suffering of the Holocaust. His survey culminates in the thesis that what is needed today is "a philosophical and ethical critique of the very project of meaning-making", based on the insight that we rather need to carefully reflect on the way in

---

[7] The term was first brought to the fore by Gottfried Wilhelm Leibniz in his *Essais de theodicée sur la bonté de Dieu, la liberté de l'homme et l'origine du mal* (Amsterdam 1710).

[8] Cf. Immanuel Kant, "On the miscarriage of all philosophical trials in theodicy". Immanuel Kant, *Religion and Rational Theology*, trans. Allen W. Wood and George di Giovanni. Cambridge, UK: Cambridge UP, 1996, 24–37. Pihlström's essay also refers to Kant's Third Critique: *Critique of the Power of Judgment*. Cambridge, UK: Cambridge UP 2000.

which "we respond to the evil and suffering around us". In this manner, Pihlström pleads for an antitheodicism that is defined "as a thoroughly humanistic project," while emphasizing that this ethical critique of theodicist views "is *not* directed at God and does not even have to take any stand whatsoever regarding the question concerning God's existence". He suggests adopting a pragmatic critique of meaning, inspired by classical American pragmatism, especially William James. The essay concludes with a caveat, however, as Pihlström argues that pragmatist antitheodicism must be aware of the potential problem of a "return" of theodicism.

The relevance of American pragmatism and of Martin Buber for today's discourse on religion in a secular age is addressed again, albeit from a different angle, in the essay "Beyond Dogmatic Scientism: Hilary Putnam on Religious Faith" by *Ludwig Nagl*. The introductory segment of this essay highlights, with reference to John Rawls and Charles Taylor, that modern states, unlike traditional ones, are decoupled from a (substantial) religious legitimation. In modern societies, Nagl notes, religious faith has thus attained, as William James argues, the status of an "option". The main focus is then on the way in which Hilary Putnam's thoughts on religion have evolved since the 1970s. Nagl first recounts Putnam's neo-pragmatic critique of the self-sufficiency of "dogmatic scientism", pointing out that the Harvard philosopher investigated, "with reference to Wittgenstein, Dewey and James, the complex question whether our secularistically configured democratic culture inevitably leads us to a world-view that is *in toto* immanence-focused". Putnam argues that we can "keep the 'immanent frame' open to what lies beyond the observable", and thus makes room for the "hypothesis" of religious belief. As Nagl explains, these thoughts are elaborated "in a Kant-informed, post-Kantian manner" that supports "a non-relativistic, affirmative interpretation of religion which at the same time is sensitive to pluralism." In its main section, Nagl's essay focuses on Putnam's book *Jewish Philosophy as a Guide to Life. Rosenzweig, Buber, Levinas, Wittgenstein* (2008), drawing attention to Putnam's thesis that religious faith remains an abstract "object of description and control" as long as it has not become personal: "Religions are communal and have long histories, but religion is also a personal matter or it is nothing." From this perspective, a theistically configured image of the Absolute, which implies a practical, motivating force, is for Putnam "far more valuable than any metaphysical concept of an impersonal God, let alone a God who is 'totally other'." It is in this context that Putnam discusses Buber's reflections on the basic words I-You, which are focused on an "ultimate You". As Nagl highlights, Putnam summarizes these reflections in the following two theses, which, while avoiding anthropomorphism, are at the same time person-related: firstly, "it is impossible to describe God, or to theorize about him"; and secondly, "what one can do is speak *to* God, or rather to enter into an 'I-You' relation with God". – The final part of the essay takes a look at Putnam's defense of religious pluralism in his essay "Let's Stop Using the Notion of 'Idolatry'".

The essay "Angles and Angels: Charles Taylor and Steven Pinker on Moral Progress in History" by *Ruth Abbey* refers primarily to Taylor's paper "History of ethical growth", first presented to the Czech Christian Academy in 2021. Summarizing Taylor's thesis that human history has been shaped by "a drive to ethical ascent", Abbey underscores his reference to the concept of the Axial Age, as conceived by Karl Jaspers"[9]. As she points out, "Taylor detects two key features in this watershed in humanity's history of ethical growth": the first is that these teachings "offered new ideals of the human which were genuinely universal," the second is that no single tradition could capture the full gamut of this growth; rather, Taylor argues, we find here "the germ of what we now recognize as the ecumenical sources of ethical growth: this is not sustained and furthered alone by any one spiritual source." With regard to the criterion Taylor applies in order to support his claim of a continued, although very gradual, ethical growth across history, Abbey notes that "the reduction of violence turns out to be central to Taylor's account". With regard to this key concern, she suggests relating Taylor's approach to Steven Pinker's thoughts on that matter, elaborated in his book *The Better Angels of our Nature: Why Violence has Declined* (2011). Thus her essay arranges a confrontation between the two authors, guided by the claim that "there are a number of ways in which Taylor's developing ideas about moral growth in history could profit from an encounter with Pinker's work". Specifying the difference between the two authors, Abbey notes "what really divides Taylor and Pinker is the status of religious belief in modernity. Pinker self-defines as a Jewish atheist," who qualifies "as one who is content to live the immanent frame in a closed way, not feeling any lack or shortcoming in the absence of personal religious belief". In contrast, "as a religious believer, Taylor strives to persuade that the immanent frame can be lived in an open way that is amenable to the experience of transcendence." Discussing this cleavage, Abbey addresses the question whether the perceived distance between those who are and those who are not religious is indeed warranted. She suggests recalling Taylor's view, elaborated in *A Secular Age*, that "when it comes to understanding fullness, we need 'a conversation between a host of different positions, religious, nonreligious, anti-religious'", and she argues that this view should also apply to the shared dilemma "how to make sense of violence". Furthermore, Abbey claims, "engaging with Pinker would exemplify and extend the ecumenism that Taylor identifies and values about the Axial Age".

---

[9] Cf. Karl Jaspers, *Vom Ursprung und Ziel der Geschichte*. München/Zürich 1949.

Part 2: *Religion in Critical Theory and Deconstruction* explores approaches to religion that were elaborated in the context of schools of thought that dominated the 20th century intellectual discourse across the globe. The first two articles represent the diversity of theories articulated against the background of the Marxist tradition. The essay "Benjamin's Time of Healing: The Messianic as Remembrance, Happiness and Justice" by *Brendan Moran* focuses on the way in which Walter Benjamin challenges the common view "that past injustice is complete (over and done with, so to speak)" in terms of the "messianic time". "Benjamin draws upon the motif of the Last Judgement insofar as this motif attests to the time that heals with the justice of release from imposed fate", claiming that, in messianic time, "happiness and justice converge in the hope that finds healing as the breaking of an ostensible fate." While citing Benjamin's view "that the sole irrevocable significance of notions of God, and of God's remembrance, is that there is always something beyond the meaning ascribed by humans", Moran underscores that Benjamin, however, "does *not* say that he *believes* in the Last Judgement." Thus he draws attention to Benjamin's way of entrusting the (ideal of the) historical materialist with the messianic task: "theology is conceived by Benjamin as integral to historical materialism. Without messianism, the legacy of hope for healing is more likely to be diminished in scientistic and brutal versions of Marxism"; accordingly, Benjamin blames the latter versions of Marxism for tending "to legitimize the purported necessity for certain sufferings and deaths". In contrast, the concept of messianic time, as described in Benjamin's *On the Concept of History*, claims that it is the people of the present day "who are the hope of past generations". Having summarized these key reflections, Moran makes it his task to reveal their subtle implications and to explain their connections with the work of other authors representing Jewish thought. He suggests, for instance, that an anticipation of Benjamin's concept of time can be found in Hermann Cohen's *Religion of Reason out of the Sources of Judaism* (1919), as "Cohen refers to 'the overcoming of the person of the Messiah' and 'the dissolution of the personal image [*Sinnbild*] in the pure notion of time'." Moran also argues that Benjamin "is not far from one of Scholem's many accounts of *tikkun* – mending" which does not associate this term with "someone divine entrusted with 'redemption' (*Erlösung*)"; as Scholem shows in "Kabbalah and Myth," *tikkun* rather pertains to "'your deed and mine' as a possible 'guarantor' of the 'restitution of all things' [*Restitution aller Dinge*]." Demonstrating further convergences that include the work of Franz Kafka, Karl Kraus and Jacques Derrida, Moran manages to invoke the image of a complex web of thoughts.

A significantly different way of addressing religion against a Marxist background is discussed in the essay "Re-considering the Distinction between Atheists and Believers, or: Max Horkheimer's Reading of Kant" by *Herta Nagl-Docekal*, which focuses on one of the founders of the Frankfurt School. The essay refers primarily to the conversation with Horkheimer on the occasion of his seventy-fifth birthday, published in *Der Spiegel* in January 1970, in which Horkheimer advocated a "theology of hope", challenging the common Marxist expectation that humans will eventually be able to overcome their pains by means of establishing just socio-economic conditions. Insisting on the unsurmountable finiteness of humans, Horkheimer raises the issue of the meaning of life in a radical manner, Nagl-Docekal shows. As he refers in particular "to the heinous crimes committed under the totalitarian regimes of the twentieth century, Horkheimer claims that, facing the tremendous pain that has been inflicted on innocent people, we find ourselves unable to accept the idea that there might be no ultimate 'sense'". Thus, "we feel a longing that the murderer must not triumph over the innocent victim" – a longing that indicates our hope "that the injustice which characterizes our world [...] may not represent the final verdict." As Nagl-Docekal highlights, Horkheimer contends that this rudimentary "theology of hope" is shared by all people, arguing that a "desire for the totally other" is known even to atheists. He adds, however, that this desire does not represent a transition into an explicit religious conviction. Nagl-Docekal emphasizes the convergence of Horkheimer's thoughts with Kant's thesis that "the purely moral religion", as distinguished from the plurality of historical churches, is shared by atheists as well as believers. In her search for further arguments that may underpin the claim that humans share a longing for transcending their finiteness, she turns to Hegel. While Kant and Horkheimer refer to morality and justice, she notes, Hegel's concept of love draws attention to the way in which utmost grief over the loss of a beloved person gives rise to hope for a reunion in another world. Finally, the essay discusses the question whether, under the contemporary economic and technological conditions, humans may be about to lose their intuition for understanding the ultimate meaning of their lives. Nagl-Docekal cites Horkheimer's anticipation of "the totally administered world" that is bound to have a devastating impact, confronting both believers and non-believers with the "eclipse of reason" that causes "spiritual misery". The final section of her essay adds that, about twenty years after Horkheimer's *Spiegel* conversation, Charles Taylor, in *A Secular Age*, voiced similar concerns, warning that we might be doomed to encounter the "suffocation of the spirit".

A recent approach to religion that represents far-reaching transformations of the thinking of the Frankfurt School is taken up by *Maureen Junker-Kenny* in her essay "Defining what is 'extraterritorial': Religion and Utopia in Habermas and Ricoeur". Her focus is first on Habermas's major work, *Auch eine Geschichte der Philosophie* (2019), which presents an "in-depth reconstruction of the development towards post-metaphysical thinking made possible by the encounter of Greek philosophy with biblical monotheism", concluding with a re-confirmation of Habermas's earlier position that religion is "extraterritorial", while "'reason' prevails as a 'secular' power on its own". Junker-Kenny's account underscores that Habermas, while reconstructing this process of detachment, attributes to religion a genuine potential, as, "from its foundation in ritual, religion is deemed capable of offering inspiring resources that support self-reflection and renew the dwindling motivation for solidarity. Its position outside the realm of reason thus harbors a heuristic potential for detecting and addressing problematic directions." More precisely, she notes, Habermas considers religion as "not simply 'irrational'," albeit "extraterritorial," "opaque" and "profoundly alien to discursive thought". The key concern of the essay is to examine the plausibility of this perception by comparing and contrasting it with Paul Ricoeur's approach. Unlike Habermas, who focuses on major turning points in Christian theology that have shaped European thinking, Ricoeur treats "religion" mainly as it appears in the foundational scriptures of religious traditions, with a special focus on Hebrew and Christian biblical texts, Junker-Kenny points out. "The new dimension its genres open up is accessed under the rubric of the 'poetic'." In contrast to the "otherness" of ritual in Habermas's division of the field, "religious scriptures are part of the symbolic mediations through which humans access reality". Junker-Kenny addresses the relevance Ricoeur attributes to the imaginative power of "utopia", which "serves as the counterpole to established conceptions of social and political life". In this context, she explains, he employs the term "extraterritorial" in a way that is clearly distinct from Habermas's usage: while, for Ricoeur, utopias present what is "extraterritorial" to the existing social order, as they envisage what is radically new to their current context, "they are seen at the same time as drawing on symbolic resources projecting a fulfilling life, and on memories of the hopes of past struggles which did not come to pass". Paying particular attention to the way in which the two authors differ in the evaluation of Kant's philosophy of religion, Junker-Kenny cites Ricoeur's defense of the link between religion and hope provided in Kant's doctrine of postulates: "Kant explicitly brings religion to the question 'What can I hope for?' I do not know any other philosopher who has defined religion exclusively with that question." With reference to the fact that the postulates are anchored in practical reason, she emphasizes Ricoeur's insistence that Kant "keeps a space within reason for a transcendence which cannot be proven but assumed without verging into the irrational".

The imaginative power of humans is also of central significance for *John D. Caputo*, whose essay "Secularizing both Religion and Reason: Upending the Secular/Religious Distinction" represents the specific approach taken in "postmodern theory" by means of "deconstruction". Emphasizing that the key concern is to dismiss the "classical" idea of a "transcendent God", he advocates "the beginning of another and radical post-theistic theology" that he defines in the following way:

"To say God does not exist, is to say, God insists, God calls – and it is up to us to respond", which means "putting the burden of the response […] on us" with the implication that "we may or may not respond". In the first paragraphs of the essay Caputo refers to the German Lutheran theologians Dietrich Bonhoeffer, Karl Barth and Paul Tillich, whose proposals for a "religionless Christianity" and a religion that has abandoned "supernaturalism" he deems to be only "one step away" from a postmodern approach. Suggesting a more consequent mode of proceeding, the main sections of the essay explain that two moves of "suspension" are required in order to make room for post-theistic theology: first, "the suspension of the supernatural attitude", secondly "the suspension of the transcendental attitude". Through the first move "religion is translated without remainder into the world", so that the distinction between the religious and secular "looks more like the distinction between poetry and prose". From this perspective, Caputo claims, theology is "better understood as theopoetics, where the logos of theology is weakened into a poetics". The second suspension challenges Kant's concept of pure reason that Caputo blames for its transcendental pretense of having "kept itself pure of empirical contact". Arguing that "transcendentalism (masquerading as 'reason') and supernaturalism (masquerading as 'faith') share a *common otherworldliness*, a common degradation or distortion of the *saeculum*", Caputo claims that both need to "come down to earth", to live "in the saeculum". He adds, "I am trying to 'secularize' both religion and reason", that is, "I am trying to embody religion in the world", so that "the so-called secular culture can be seen to be permeated with religious motifs and religion can be seen to be an intrinsically cultural form of life." Addressing the issue "whether religion has a future", Caputo concludes that "it is time to move on and look for other ways to address the mystery of our lives".

An emphatic refusal to accept the separation of the religious and the secular is also discussed in the essay "'This Incredible Need to Believe': Julia Kristeva's Reinvention of Secular Humanism at the Crossroad of Religion, Psychoanalysis, and Politics" by *Gertrude Postl*. Focusing on Julia Kristeva's *This Incredible Need to Believe*, this paper examines the way in which Kristeva counters the evils of secularized Western societies. "In her view", Postl notes, "we live in a society of the spectacle […], a culture dominated by media images, commodity exchange, and the superficiality of entertainment. Art and literature have lost their meaning, immediate satisfaction is the goal". Examining Kristeva's response, Postl points out that she locates this loss "in the failure to recognize a prelinguistic 'need to believe'", that is a need that "has always been with us; it is built into the psychic development of early subject formation, it becomes the foundation for the speaking being itself, a 'prepolitical and prereligious need'". Kristeva's claim that "traces for this 'need to believe' may be encountered in two related areas: psychoanalysis and the psychoanalytic process on the one hand, language, literature, and art on the other" informs the two main parts of Postl's essay. As to the first area, Kristeva argues that there exist significant affinities between (Christian) faith and psychoanalytic theory, noting "Religions, in short, seem to be a recognition of what Freud calls *das höhere Wesen im Menschen*, 'the higher side of man' in which the subject's freedom is inscribed". Based on her specific conception of psychoanalysis, Kristeva describes the sacred, the divine, in terms of the human transition from a prelinguistic state to the realm of signification, claiming "not to eradicate the sacred but to rediscover it in the very depth of language". – Regarding the second area, Kristeva's notion of the sacred source of art and literature, Postl focuses on the way in which the subjective belief of the early stages of subject formation is related to Kristeva's concept of 'intimate revolt' that provides the basis for her proposed 'radical reformation of humanism' and its political implications: "Intimate revolt is a response to the failure of secularized Enlightenment humanism, which focused too strongly on a disembodied form of reason". On this basis, Kristeva pleads for a "'radical reformation of humanism' which, in her view, means a humanism freed not only from metaphysical dichotomies but also from its seeming rejection of religion". Emphasizing the political potential of these thoughts, Postl points out Kristeva's thesis that literature and art, together with psychoanalysis, "offer themselves as laboratories of new forms of humanism" which allow us "to confront the new barbarities of automation".

Part 3: *Religion in US Literature and Politics in a Global Context* begins with the essay "Critical Perspectives on Self-Sufficing Humanism in Southern Fiction" by *Waldemar Zacharasiewicz*. Few modern US American authors were as widely read in philosophical reflections and treatises as Walker Percy, whose relatively late successful entry into the literary scene mirrors his intense reading of S. Kierkegaard, of the early pragmatist philosopher Charles Sanders Peirce and of existentialist thinkers, such as Gabriel Marcel and Albert Camus. As Zacharasiewicz shows, several of Percy's novels exhibiting dystopian features demonstrate the conflict between modern agnostics and complacent behaviorists or hedonistic scientists, on the one hand, and seekers investing emotionally in a religious vision. Like the fiction of Percy's fellow Southern writer Flannery O'Connor, who was preoccupied with the dramatic clash between fundamentalist Christians and arrogant deniers of an inexplicably mysterious – transcendent – dimension, Percy's narratives offer Charles Taylor in his magisterial study of the shortcomings of a self-sufficing humanism in *The Secular Age* significant examples in modern literature which take the reader beyond such a restricted attitude. In two dystopias Percy – in line with Kierkegaard's exposure of a merely aesthetic stance – links the grave ethical problems of several of his characters with the alleged/ presumptive hedonistic aspects of Viennese musical culture, and alludes to the inhumane actions of ostensibly sophisticated aesthetes in Nazi Germany (including annexed Austria). All this adds a very personal note and some topicality to his fiction.

While the fiction by these two Catholic authors from the American South reflects to some extent the collective experience of Southerners of defeat in the Civil War and a rejection of the hyper-optimistic embrace of the American Dream in the rest of the country, *Charles R. Wilson's* historical survey – "The Southern Civil Religion: The Intermingling of the Sacred and the Secular in the American South" – traces the emergence of the regional southern variant of the American "civil religion", the religious nationalism manifest in the public rituals in the USA. This was developed in the late nineteenth century by the white Evangelical Protestants dominant in the South, who came to celebrate the military and political leaders of the defeated Confederacy and their devotion to the "lost cause". The essay shows how they turned public spaces, soon studded with monuments, into the arena for quasi-religious rituals, blending the sacred and the secular when affirming white supremacy and excluding African Americans in Southern communities. But Wilson draws attention also to the adoption of a variant of this civil religion, offering a hagiography of deceased leaders by the spokespersons of the civil rights movement, especially by Martin Luther King and other activists of the formerly marginalized ethnic and cultural group.

Wilson's scrutiny of the application of the paraphernalia of religious practices in the American South in the late 19th century is followed by a very detailed study of the complexities of the opposition of Catholic clergy and theologians to the strong secular influences which threatened to marginalize the Catholic church in the course of the nineteenth century. *Michael Hochgeschwender's* essay "Catholicism in Defense? The Critique of Modernity in Catholic Neo-Scholastics" explains that, modifying philosophical practices of the Middle Ages, the proponents of neo-scholastic concepts developed ideas which distanced them from the advocates of liberalism and linked them with the strong movement of "ultramontanism" in an era in which the papacy was under siege by nationalist movements in Italy and defended its stance through pronouncements at the Vatican Council. The bulk of the essay considers the complex arguments in which theologians, often with great reservations concerning democracy, challenged modern trends and were involved in culture wars, especially in Bismarck's Prussia. It examines the different directions in which two influential theologians, the Jesuit H. Pesch and the Dominican A. M. Weiss, tried to lead society. The former is shown to have been a "social realist" with training in political economics and interested in social reform, and a sharp opponent of Manchester capitalism and liberalism, while the latter was a "social romanticist" who disseminated concepts favoring a paternalistic attitude in society, which eventually led to the establishment of a "Ständestaat" in twentieth century Austria. The complex picture of the development of the Catholic church in the USA, where its adherents were for decades excluded from positions of responsibility, includes hints at the replacement of "Gentlemen Catholics" by more reform-oriented Irish immigrants, as well as the indirect influence of the ideas of H. Pesch on John A. Ryan, and more democratic practices in the church. The essay also refers to the later marginalization of the so-called "Americanism" by the religious authorities.

The following essay by *Manfred Siebald* – "Competing Quests for a Hidden God in John Updike's *Roger's Version*" – examines one of the trio of novels by the modern US American fiction writer John Updike which through the complex intertextual relationship(s) of their characters with the protagonists in Nathaniel Hawthorne's mid-nineteenth century masterpiece *The Scarlet Letter* evoke an image of the progress of secularization in (formerly Puritan) New England. In this novel, *Roger's Version*, major obstacles to faith in contemporary American society, the apparent invisibility of God and the dramatic advances of science, which has explained so much formerly deemed mysterious, are presented in the interaction of two characters linked through their names to Hawthorne's romance: Roger Lambert, a cynical former minister, originally a disciple of the Protestant theologian Karl Barth and an adherent of his assertion of God's inscrutability, but now an immoral figure who commodifies religion and exhibits numerous contradictions, and Dale Kohler, an ostensible believer, who as a computer nerd is eager to prove God's existence technologically. The obvious failure of this project and the wavering of the convictions of both figures, which seem also to reflect Updike's own pronounced radical religious uncertainty, and the immoral conduct of the two protagonists may arguably be read as a negative assessment of the decline of religion in secularized modern America, a process which had begun much earlier in the late eighteenth and nineteenth centuries.

The rejection of organized religion despite a yearning for spirituality shapes the conduct of the protagonists, all scientists, in the trio of modern American novels set in times of multiple crises examined by *Carmen Birkle* in her essay "Science and Religion in U.S.-American Pandemic Literature". These novels were written before the COVID-19 pandemic: Robert Cook's *Pandemic* (2018), Lawrence Wright's *The End of October* (2020) and Connie Willis's *Doomsday Book* (1992). While Cook's novel about the serial deaths of patients who had received organ transplantations includes features of a detective novel and exposes the narrowmindedness of fundamentalist Christians, who readily see such deaths as God's punishment for immoral behavior, Wright's dystopian novel traces the complex evolution of attitudes to religious beliefs, especially in the central protagonist, a medical expert and epidemiologist: Henry Parsons studies the spread of a genuine pandemic from a camp in Indonesia through the Muslim hajj to Mecca, and witnesses the reaction of a religious Muslim medical man and leading politician to this terrible emergency, and then, in his American family, the response of his wife, who succumbs to the pandemic. While the brutal experiments of a German scientist with Indigenous people and then globally, echo earlier hetero-stereotypes of unscrupulous evil Teutonic actors (but possibly also the action of Crake in Margaret Atwood's *Oryx and Crake*), Henry's secular humanist ethics, which enables him to discover the origin and spread of the virus from the Arctic circle to Indonesia, cause the recognition of his genuine humanity by his religious Indonesian colleague; his medical skills make it possible for him and other inoculated individuals to survive the global pandemic, waiting in a submarine until the pandemic ends. Willis's dystopia, set in 2054, adopts the scheme of time travel, taking a young historian, Kivrin Engle, back to the time of the Black Death in an English village as a result of some incorrect application. After having been infected with a virus which spread (in Oxford) after its dissemination following archeological digging in the present, and after having recovered in the Middle Ages, the time traveler is interpreted as a saint and messenger from God by a clergyman. He is confronted with the Black Death killing the villagers and converses with her until he himself becomes a victim of the plague, while Kivrin herself, as a convinced agnostic, is ready to return via the "net" to her mentor, the history professor back in Oxford, who critically observes the conduct of the people and their religious ministers during the contemporary pandemic, which reminds him of the Spanish flu epidemic of 1918.

Part 4: *Re-framing Theological Issues and Individual Convictions* presents, in the first section, two innovative contributions from the field of Roman Catholic theology, both providing reasons for challenging the widely shared view that religious language ought to be excluded from secular public political discourse. *William Sweet*, whose paper is titled "Philosophical Pluralism and Religious Faith in a Secular Age", suggests focusing first on the pluralism that has evolved in the discipline of philosophy in recent times. As he explains, "philosophical pluralism reflects general (secular) values such as equality, inclusiveness/openness, fairness, comprehensiveness and justice, and this leads to the inclusion of [...] marginalized philosophies and philosophers". Sweet's key proposition is that the inclusiveness of philosophy may serve as a model for dealing with the expression of religious convictions in the public sphere. Specifying four reasons why such expression does "fit in a pluralistic, open, secular context", he argues, for instance, that "just as philosophers are curious about new or marginalized philosophies, there should be a genuine, secular, pluralistic curiosity in the public sphere about the faith and the beliefs of those of religious faith". More specifically, Sweet claims that granting a place for religious expression in public discourse is not only consistent with secular values but is also required "alongside the range of expressions of ethnicity, culture, tradition, sexual orientation, and so on, present in a pluralistic society". Seeking to support this proposal, the final part of the essay addresses four likely objections to it, including the thesis that "it is only when there are shared standards for discussion," such as publicly observable evidence, that we can have a "level playing field"; Sweet counters these objections with the argument that such standards would require excluding many other "comprehensive ethical views and beliefs" from the public sphere.

Plurality is also a key concern in *Klaus Viertbauer's* essay "Religious Convictions and Public Reason: On the Way to a Two-Stage Epistemology of Religion". The first part summarizes three distinct concepts that have dominated the discourse on the place of religion in the context of a secular society: civil religion, laicism, and secularization. Viertbauer describes these concepts as being based on key paradigms of modern political philosophy, linking civil religion to communitarianism, laicism and secularization to liberalism. Pointing out their embeddedness in specific national contexts, he labels civil religion as the American, laicism as the French, and secularization as the German model. With reference to Robert N. Bellah and Michael Walzer, Viertbauer deems the communitarian approach unsuitable for current Western societies, where religious communities can no longer be concisely identified with whole civic groups. In contrast, he explains the merits of the liberal perspective, highlighting John Rawls' emphasis on religious plurality. Specifying the two variants of the liberalist approach, he explains that laicism is oriented toward negative religious freedom, while secularization is oriented toward positive religious freedom. The second part suggests approaching these issues in terms of epistemology. Viertbauer argues that two distinct modes of understanding religious conviction need to be distinguished. The first is constituted by believers who consider their convictions as "a worldview that is not simply one perspective among others, but rather provides an interpretive framework within which the other bodies of knowledge about the world can develop their reality-defining power in the first place." This perception, he claims, "poses a serious problem for liberal democracy", as religious communities threaten to stand monolithically opposite both one another and the state. The second mode, which is committed to modern society's pluralism, views religious belief as "a form of life". Viertbauer emphasizes the relevance of Jürgen Habermas's thesis that believers need not be excluded from public debate, provided they follow the rules of liberal interaction, for instance by accepting that the members of other religious groups must be treated as equal partners in discourse, and by acknowledging that the principles of the constitutional state are based on profane morality rather than religious doctrines. On this basis, Viertbauer pleads for a "paradigm shift", arguing that believers need to transform their religious convictions from a worldview into a form of life, understanding their religiosity as one form of life among many.

The essay "Scientists Who Believe" by *Christoph Irmscher* takes its departure from his extensive research for his monograph on the Swiss polymath and immensely influential nineteenth century Harvard biology professor Louis Agassiz, one of Charles Darwin's chief opponents and of the latter's rejection of belief in a benevolent deity. Irmscher comments on one of Agassiz's ms. notes, which rejects the psalmist's humility in the face of the cosmos in Psalm 8, and stresses the pride of the scientist, who demonstrated the achievements and progress of human science by referring to the French astronomer Le Verrier, who merely through mathematical deductions had been able to confirm the existence and location of the planet Uranus as the cause of irregularities in the motion of Neptune. While Agassiz may thus be read as an advocate of conversion to science rather than to the Christian religion, the two contemporary American scientists who profess their belief are the prominent physician-geneticist Francis S. Collins and the climate scientist Katharine Hayhoe. The former, who was a leader in the Human Genome Research and for thirteen years director of the National Institutes of Health, in a widely published bestseller *The Language of God* (2006) shared his personal conviction that there are plausible arguments for the existence of God, and that belief is thus the result of a rational choice. While Collins's appreciation of the Moral Law positively regulating human behavior provides arguments supporting belief, his trust in the evolution of the cosmos offers a basis for making science and belief compatible. Through her role in the Evangelical Environmental Network, Katharine Hayhoe works as a scientist and activist with a mission for the ecological survival of the world, but has to struggle with "the anti-science attitude" among many evangelical Christians. She can, however, draw on the Biblical concept of man's stewardship of the Earth, as her recent personal confession and narrative of her encounters with her audiences in *Saving Us: A Climate Scientist's Case for Hope and Healing in a Divided World* (2021) shows.

David Staines's essay on "Two Canadian Christian Thinkers" stands out among the contributions to this volume through its very personal touch, as he was intimately familiar with the two celebrated but very different professors teaching in Toronto's colleges, who were also mentors and paternal friends of his: Northrop Frye, an ordained United Church minister, early rebelled against the fundamentalism of his mother and distanced himself from Christian tenets; but his influential development of myth criticism from his first study of William Blake onwards and recurrent references to the Bible as the archetype of Western culture culminated in his comprehensive studies of its text from the angle of literary criticism in *The Great Code: the Bible and Literature* (1982) and *Words with Power: Being a Second Study of "The Bible and Literature"* (1990). He has been credited with having made a religion of literature. Marshall McLuhan, by contrast, in the course of his academic career in several American universities, among them the Jesuit St. Louis

University, was originally a conservative critic who converted to Catholicism and became a regular communicant; but in his trail-blazing studies of popular culture (*The Mechanical Bride*; *The Gutenberg Galaxy*; *Understanding Media*), which were intended to reach generations of his students, earned him the reputation of being a visionary theorist with a rare understanding of contemporary social reality, he avoided any overt reference to the religious basis of his personal identity. In these very different ways the two celebrated Canadian intellectuals, who did not accept many academic offers to move elsewhere, represented significant aspects of religion in the secular present.

Part 5: *Religion in Poetry, Music and Visual Media* is devoted to the presence of religious themes in literature and the arts. It opens with *Alois Woldan's* essay "Religious Aspects of Ukranian Poetry – the Case of Vasyl' Stus" that analyses the poetry of Vasyl Stus, who died as an imprisoned dissident in a Soviet labor camp. His numerous lyrics, which were collected only after Ukraine's achievement of independence, reflect his personal sense of a patriotic mission closely linked to the religious tradition of his country saddled with the anti-religious ideology of the Soviet era. The intense experience of the personal ordeal is expressed by the lyrical speaker with the help of liturgical forms and biblical phrases; he includes images of destroyed churches in Kyiv and dwells on the suffering of the prophetic individual in a world dominated by evil forces. The existential crisis of the courageous victim of barbarous repression and persecution takes the speaker to the limits of endurance and occasionally evokes images of wrestling with a seemingly passive God in a quarrel as godlike evil powers dominate the world.

The sphere of music is addressed by *Federico Celestini* whose essay "Gustav Mahler's Symphonic Transcendence and its Counterparts" investigates the sources of and inspirations for Gustav Mahler's symphonic representation and adaptation of religious concepts. He discovers them in the composer's indebtedness to Siegfried Lipiner's poetry and criticism, thus drawing attention to this respected younger contemporary of Richard Wagner and Friedrich Nietzsche. The essay initially dwells on Lipiner's early lecture on "the religious renewal in the present age" and on his poem *The Unbound Prometheus*, and reflects on his continuing focus on religious themes. It illustrates the continuing use of biblical elements and stresses his combination of art and a pantheistic form of religion, which shapes his concept of the tragedy, showing his increasing distance from Nietzsche, whose thoughts he had earlier fused with Schopenhauer's and Wagner's. Celestini underlines Lipiner's stress on the human desire for transcendence, before explicating in detail the transfer of some of Lipiner's inspiring ideas in the symphonies of his admirer Gustav Mahler, which develop the model of Beethoven's great symphonies, and offer symphonic narratives (especially in the first and third symphonies), including moments of "tragic collapse" followed by a "breakthrough", and in the finale a concluding jubilant apotheosis.

Another very specific variant of the contemporary secular attitude to religious concepts is analyzed in *Jörg Türschmann's* essay "Serial Baroque in the TV Show American Gods" that analyzes the American TV show *American Gods*, which, in its limited run of three seasons, presented the dramatized encounter between gods from the old world and new gods in the form of allegorical figures. Türschmann relates this combination to the inclusion of such personifications in late medieval and Baroque literature before discussing the neo-baroque actualization of this received mode in the appearance of old gods in the guise of migrants to America who are met in a "road trip" by contemporary deities of globalization, new technologies and new media. Various stages of American history, which are rendered in several episodes, prompt reflections on the strategic use of metalepsis in the contemporary film genre, which in this series does not, however, explode the illusion, but accepts the reality of the gods, with the old gods struggling for supremacy with the new divinities. Türschmann also speculates on the reasons for the favorable reception of this TV show in the Balkans and in Turkey, and relates this phenomenon to the important role of religion in their societies, which differ from western countries in which secularization has progressed much further.

Part I Post-Kantian Approaches to Religion

Irene Kajon
God as the Infinite: Martin Buber's Interpretation of Kant's Concept of Religion

Abstract: According to Cicero (106–43 BCE), *religio* comes from the verb *relegere* which means to collect, to repeat, with reference to the cult (*De natura deorum*, II, 70–72). Instead, for the Church Father Lactantius (250–327), *religio* comes from the verb *religare*, i.e. to connect, because it indicates the relationship between human beings and the true God whom we can know and worship (*Divinae Institutiones*, IV, 28). Neither meaning of *religio*, cult or a peculiar knowledge, fits into our secular age: the first because people no longer feel the value of traditional rites; the second because in modern philosophy, from Hume and Kant onwards, human reason is recognized as incapable of knowing God. Is a third path perhaps possible? Martin Buber, interpreting Kant's thought, refers to God as the Infinite: God is an eternal Thou, who acts in accordance with goodness and justice. This concept of God, implying ethical measures for our private and public life, could perhaps be accepted by both believers and non-believers in our secular societies. Hence religion has a new meaning.

1 About the Term *Religio*

The Latin term *religio* is the root of the English word *religion*. Many other European languages use the same root to compose a similar word: we use, for example, the German term *Religion*, the French *religion*, the Spanish *religión*, the Russian *religiya* in our everyday conversation. But this term is not univocal. It comes from the Latin word *religio*, which has two different meanings according to its root. Cicero (106–43 BCE) provided an etymology of *religio*. So he writes in *De natura deorum*:

> Qui [...] omnia quae ad cultum deorum pertinerent diligenter retractarent et tamquam relegerent, <hi> sunt dicti religiosi ex relegendo ut elegantes ex eligendo ex diligendo diligentes ex intellegendo intellegentes (Cicero, II 72, 192).

> Those [...] who carefully reviewed and so to speak retraced all the lore of ritual were called 'religious' from *relegere* (to retrace or re-read), like 'elegant' from *eligere* (to select), 'diligent' from *diligere* (to care for), 'intelligent' from *intellegere* (to understand) (ibid., 193).

Cicero ascribes to the word *religio* a meaning that corresponds exactly to the conception then current in Rome regarding the proper attitude one was to assume towards the gods: those who follow scrupulously the ceremonies established by tradition (*relegunt* – from *relegere*) are deemed religious. *Religio* in the Roman world is expressed through the link between past and present: *religio* consists of liturgical practices in pre-determined times and places, either to be held in certain seasons of the year or on certain set occasions, or, in the case of events that were unexpected, to be introduced but without breaking the rules that allow continuity between generations.

In the Christian world it was the Church Father Lactantius (250–327) who, in disputing Cicero's conception of *religio*, dwelt on the term's etymology. In book four, entitled *De vera sapientia et religione*, of his *Divinae Institutiones*, Lactantius writes:

> Hac [...] conditione gignimur, ut generanti nos deo justa et debita obsequia praebeamus, hunc solum noverimus, hunc sequamur. Hoc vinculo pietatis obstricti deo et religati sumus: unde ipsa religio nomen accepit, non ut Cicero interpretatus est a relegendo (Lactantius, IV 28, 388–89).
>
> We were created so that we might offer the right and proper signs of submission to the God who has created us, that we might know Him only and follow Him only. With this bond of piety we are subjugated and bound (*religati*) to God; religion received its name from this and not, as Cicero interpreted it, from re-read (*relegendo*) (my tr.).

Lactantius, unlike Cicero, does not regard behaviour as fundamental to *religio*, but knowledge of the true God. The God that Lactantius appeals to is the God who enters into relation with the individual and ensures his salvation. Religion owes its name not to the mind going back over what has been already done, to *relegere*, but to being bound to a God who made Himself known to men by coming into the world, to *religare*. What is essential to *religio* are truth, as a state of things revealed to men, and the relation between man and God. *Religio* means a bond: God will save man if he believes in Him and follows Him.

Now, in our secular age, we cannot anymore take the term *religio* in these old meanings. We do not respect the ancient ceremonies as in the past. The secular age is directed to the future, we praise youth much more than old age, and we do not understand anymore many things that the traditions transmit to us. We renew the *querelle des anciens et des modernes* simply often giving the victory to the moderns without reflecting enough about what characterizes modernity, differently from those who in the seventeenth and eighteenth centuries defended science against myth, modern style against the classic forms (*La querelle* 2001). But also the other meaning of *religio*, which refers to the link between human beings and God, according to the Christian doctrine, is no more maintained: after Hume and Kant most of the modern thinkers have a suspicious attitude towards any metaphysics. Could we really believe in teachings which refer to God's being? Or is not perhaps the negative theology the theology which in our days dominates the culture? As Franz Rosenzweig recognized in his *Stern der Erlösung* [*Star of Redemption*] (1921), negative theology and atheism are closely connected.

It seems to me that another sense of the term *religion* is possible. I would no longer link its root to *relegere* or *religare*, but – translating it in the Hebrew term *da'at* (listening to commandments and practicing them) – to *ligare: legati* means in Latin the ambassadors, those who represent the will of a superior and act in his name. In this case this person is God. Buber, as we shall see, maintains precisely this meaning of religion. I would like to show how Buber is close to Kant when offering this concept of *religio*. But before I come to this topic, I would like to recall how difficult it was for Kant to ponder the relationship between ethics and religion, between human beings and God. Interpreting Kant, Buber gave a solution to this difficulty.

2 The *Summum Bonum* in the *Critique of Practical Reason*

In the Third Part of the *Grundlegung zur Metaphysik der Sitten* [*Groundwork of the Metaphysics of Morals*] (1785) Kant tries to justify the moral law, i. e. to prove its ideal existence, escaping the vicious circle which consists in founding autonomy on the moral law, and the moral law on autonomy, by recalling human participation in the *mundus intelligibilis*. In the *Kritik der praktischen Vernunft* [*Critique of Practical Reason*] (1788), by contrast, Kant rejects this justification because he realizes that it is impossible to base a reality – the moral law which by itself moves to moral actions – on an idea of pure reason whose reality we cannot prove. The moral law, Kant recognizes in the section devoted to the *Deduktion* of the principles of the pure practical reason, is a *Faktum* in our reason, and therefore it needs no defense at all: if we tried such a defense, we would deny its unconditioned character and make practical reason dependent on theoretical reason. On the contrary, it is on this *Faktum* that we can found the *Wirklichkeit*, effective reality, of the intelligible world. Kant offers this foundation in the last part of his work, whose title is "Dialectic of pure practical reason". In this part Kant describes how reason always tries to arrive at the Absolute. When reason is pure theoretical reason, it tries to identify thinking and knowing, thinking and being; when reason is pure practical reason, it tries to identify *noumena* and *phenomena*, moral law and the course of the world, virtue and happiness. Kant gives the name of *summum bonum* to this highest object of the good will when the good will looks at the unification of morality and natural inclinations as two different elements. Certainly, the moral law should be the only *Bestimmungsgrund*, the ground of determination, of the pure will: if the highest good were this *Bestimmungsgrund*, the good will would be impure, influenced by the sensible world, or *Sein*, Being, rather than only by *Sollen*, the Ought to Be. But, according to Kant, if the *Bestimmungsgrund* of the will is the moral law, then it is not only natural, but also legitimate to strive for the highest good. However, if in the *summum bonum* virtue and happiness do not have an analytical relation, but only a synthetic one, then their unification will not be possible in this world, so full of unhappy righteous human beings, but only in a world which will be beyond this world. Only immortal souls are able to be virtuous and blissful in a kingdom whose God is the guarantor: only there will there be a perfect harmony between merits and happiness, morality and sensibility, the individual's longing and moral universality. Religion is not an illusion: it is important to maintain these propositions, which are founded on a rational faith dependent on ethics, as postulates if we intend to support the validity of the moral law itself.

In the conclusion of the *Elementarlehre* of the *Critique of Practical Reason* Kant writes that it is a good thing that human beings are not able to demonstrate the postulates concerning the immortality of the soul and God, and therefore the reality of the *mundus intelligibilis:* if this were the case, everybody would be obedient to the moral law only out of hope or fear, and not out of a pure moral intention. Theoretical doubt about unconditioned objects makes the moral intention pure and always alive in this world. But, on the other side, without hope and fear the moral intention would be weak and fragile. Kant grounds religion on the moral philosophy that he builds on the concept of moral law: without this basis religion would be useless. But it is also true that for him ethics, if detached from religion, would be abstract, without practical effects. However, is it possible to give force to religious postulates through a moral law which – if considered in itself – does not have a true real force?

3 Humanity as the Last End in the *Critique of Judgment*

In his *Kritik der Urtheilskraft* [*Critique of Judgment*] (1790) Kant gives a new solution to the religious question compared to the response he had offered in his *Critique of Practical Reason*. While in the preceding *Critique* he considers the dualism of *mundus sensibilis* and *mundus intelligibilis* as the basis of his arguments and elaborations, and for this reason he keeps the transcendence of the *summum bonum* with regard to nature and history, although the process for arriving at it already begins on earth, in the *Critique of Judgment*, dedicated to art and to nature as if nature were the result of an artistic will, and therefore teleologically ordered, the *summum bonum* takes the form of a final perfection which regards precisely this world. The *summum bonum* now has a communitarian aspect whereas before it had an individualistic appearance as it referred to the souls, which will also live after the death of their bodies. The realization of humanity as an intelligible Subject in the sensible world – a hope which requires faith in God's moral will and in His creative activity – is the final aim: reflexive judgments give us this idea of a last accomplishment of Being according to which we should work in our existence.

Thus in the *Critique of Judgment* Kant introduces a new way to justify our rational faith in God: God is not only the guarantor of the correspondence between virtue and happiness in another world, but also the Creator of a world which has a finality. When human beings pronounce their aesthetic and teleological judgments, they certainly have God as their example and model: they consider the particular as if it were a harmonious part of a meaningful whole and they feel a contemplative pleasure in such judgments. While for God there is no difference between subjectivity and reality – human reason has the idea of an intuitive intellect which embraces the entire being, and human will has the idea of a holy will which will never be countered by nature – for human beings this difference remains: they use their faculty of judgment as if there were a profound order in things themselves, but they know that the use of this faculty has only a regulative, not a constitutive value, and does not form any objectivity.

From this perspective one can deduce two themes that are discussed in the *Critique of Judgment*. One of them is the impossibility for human thinking, which belongs to a finite being, to embrace the All, God, the Totality: hence the importance of the *ästhetische Idee*, which is able to point out or evoke an unconditioned idea that reason cannot determine exactly, as well as of the sublime which – unlike the beautiful, the expression of a complete harmony between form and content – shows the difference between form and an infinite content. The other theme is the question of theodicy: theodicy cannot be grounded on a philosophical doctrine, but only on a faith that, notwithstanding all the evils in human life and in the world, is able to find an order in Being. This faith is absolutely necessary if the moral law is to keep its validity. Kant writes:

> We can [...] assume a righteous man (like Spinoza) who takes himself to be firmly convinced that there is no God [...]: how would he judge his own inner purposive determination by the moral law, which he actively honors? [...] The end [...], which this well-intentioned person had and should have had before his eyes in his conformity to the moral law, he would certainly have to give up as impossible; or, if he would remain attached to the appeal of his moral inner vocation and not weaken the respect, by which the moral law immediately influences him to obedience, by the nullity of the only idealistic final end that is adequate to its high demand

[…], then he must assume the existence of a moral author of the world, i.e. of God, from a practical point of view (*Kritik der Urtheilskraft,* 452–53; *Critique of the Power of Judgment,* 317–18).

Kant's thesis is that we have to believe in the idea of a final unification of nature and morality in the world if we intend to give energy to our good will: ethics gives to art, nature and history – through the aesthetic and teleological judgments – their end, i.e. a beautiful humanity. If ethics did not accept religion as its necessary help and supporter, the world would fall for us into chaos and the moral law would inspire no respect. But can ethics really lead to religion in this way? Or does the doctrine of virtue irreparably separate from the doctrine of hope precisely when God is supposed to be the creator of the world? As if the heroism of the good will only determined by the moral motive finally were beyond our human powers.

4 Kant's Religious Writings of the Nineties: Evil and Biblical Aesthetic Ideas

In the texts written in the nineties Kant deepens those two themes of evil and the "aesthetic idea" which he had introduced – as above remarked – in the *Critique of Judgment*.

In *On the Failure of All Philosophical Efforts in Theodicy* [*Über das Mißlingen aller philosophischen Versuche in der Theodicee*] (1791) he explains both why philosophy is not able to provide a justification of the evil in the world, while the Biblical book of Job gives us many interesting suggestions in this field. In fact, philosophy – when expressing a dogmatic metaphysics – identifies thinking and being, seeks to comprehend the All, almost to penetrate God's secrets, and so transforms evil into good with sophistic arguments. The book of Job, by contrast, gives the narrative of a man who, notwithstanding his sufferings and his protests against God, sincerely keeps his moral faith in God: this faith only allows him to find some sense in the world, although he cannot deny the reality of evil. The poetic expression gives philosophy many ideas and points of view in referring to a problem – the evil in human existence and history – which will always be insoluble for philosophy.

In *Religion within the Bounds of Bare Reason* [*Die Religion innerhalb der Grenzen der blossen Vernunft*] (1793) the question of the origin of evil is discussed together with the anthropological question of the good dispositions of man. Here too, as in the previous essay, Biblical narratives are used by Kant in order to throw light – as far as possible – on the topics that he presents. But here, unlike the previous essay, Kant also introduces prayers taken from the history of different religious faiths, theological concepts from their doctrines, symbols from their forms of worship. Therefore, the field of a reason giving an interpretation of religious traditions which helps the philosopher to broaden his reflection on religion, becomes more extended. This reason arrives at a faith which, like reflexive judgments, does not establish objects or gives a real truth, but points out subjective meanings: these meanings, in spite of their lack of certainty and objectivity, introduce a sense in human experience and – as they are grounded on practical reason – do not produce a mere appearance. Faith is here a *reflektierender Glaube*, a reflexive faith, which becomes an instrument to broaden reason when it is involved in pondering the problem of the connection between the moral law and the aim of this law against the evil in human life.

In this way a religion within the limits of bare reason introduces a final meaning into Being where theoretical and practical reason can neither affirm nor deny: we think that good will prevail over evil at the end of times because we believe with an enlarged rational faith that God helped us with His presence in history and will still help us in the future. But can a religion, which after all is a compromise between reason and religious traditions, keep a philosophical universal value? Can ethics really provide a basis for this complex and articulated religion when it is founded only on the pure moral law? Can an ethics, which puts aside the individuals in their concrete existence and peculiarities, really acquire vitality from a religion which is built on a subjective feeling of hope – a feeling of hope that as such has no moral value?

5 Beyond *Kant-Philologie*: Buber's New Approach to Kantian Religion

Kant's concept of religion, if reconstructed according to a philological reading of his main texts, is certainly original, suggestive, refined. But – as I tried to show – it also raises perplexities. Among those who questioned Kant's religious thought for its flaws, were Schleiermacher (*Über das höchste Gut*, 1789), Fichte (*Versuch einer Kritik aller Offenbarung*, 1793), Hegel (*Enzyklopädie der philosophischen Wissenschaften*, 1830), Nietzsche (*Zur Genealogie der Moral*, 1887), Georg Simmel (*Kant*, 1904), Hermann Cohen (*Kants Begründung der Ethik*, 1910), Ernst Cassirer (*Kants Leben und Lehre*, 1918).

I shall try to collect here their objections and to recall them briefly: a) If happiness is an element included in the *summum bonum* in order to take into account the natural inclinations in human beings, what about the respect [*Achtung*] for the moral law which is also a feeling, although produced only by a reason which affects sensibility? Is perhaps the respect ineffective in moving to actions in the concrete moral life, if compared with our search for happiness? b) If conformity of the subjective principle of action to the moral law, as the objective principle of practical reason, is sufficient to characterize the good will and make it active in the world, why is it necessary or at least advisable to also consider the end of action? In this last case, does not the correspondence between *Sollen* and *Sein*, ethics and the course of the world, become essential to ethics itself? c) If God is considered as the guarantor of bliss for the souls which acquire their perfection in a progress that indefinitely continues after death, is not God undermined, reduced to being a mere defender of human wishes? Moreover, if we think of God when we think of the last end of humanity in a reflexive judgment, does it mean that God is only an idea of ours? d) The relationship between the individual and universality is problematic in Kantian ethics: it seems that in Kant's ethics the individual appears only as a natural being. The universal moral law seems not to be able to particularize itself according to the will of the *homo noumenon* who really acts in the world. e) What is the relationship between faith, produced by our hope in a better future, and philosophy? Religion belongs to the field of the application of ethics: it seems to have only an educative and cultural role. On the other side, religion is necessary to philosophy and enters into philosophy, although it is only *innerhalb*, within, the limits of reason. Religion is not fully rational and therefore philosophy remains superior to it; however, philosophy without religion would be nothing but pure theory, an abstraction.

Now, what is remarkable in Buber's interpretation of Kant's concept of religion is the fact that it is not grounded as much on Kantian philology as on a very personal interest: Buber traces a new focus in Kantian thought which allows him – as we shall see – to liberate Kant's concept of religion of all these objections. Buber himself tells us how he came to Kant. In the work which collects the lectures he gave at the Hebrew University in Jerusalem in 1938, immediately after his arrival from Germany, entitled *The Problem of Man* [*Das Problem des Menschen*, 2017] he writes that the first book of Kant he read was the *Prolegomena* [*Prolegomena zu einer jeden küftigen Metaphysik, die als Wissenschaft wird auftreten können*] (1787), and that this book had an extraordinary effect on him. He had read the *Pensées* of Pascal and the idea of the infinite greatness of the universe and the mystery of the origin of the universe, which are there expounded, tormented him: he had then the perception of the nothingness on which human life is built and therefore of the nonsensicalness of existence. Nihilism was the consequence of his reading Pascal, who wrote his reflections on man after the Copernican revolution. Pascal reflects on man as a knowing being, and – in the face of the loss of the anthropocentrism that the Ptolemaic system maintained – becomes deeply aware of the difficulty of finding a new center for man. The *Prolegomena*, which the very young thinker read in this period, saved his life. So Buber describes this experience of his, which was much more than a purely intellectual experience:

> What torments and terrifies him [Pascal] is not the infinitude of space, recently discovered, contrasting with the finitude that common belief previously attributed to it. It is rather the fact that, in the face of the infinitude of space, any concept of space becomes troubling for him, both that of finite and of infinite space; since wanting to genuinely represent a finite space is as bold an undertaking as that of wanting to represent an infinite space. And this necessarily leads man to take stock of the fact that the cosmos is something that is beyond him. I myself, when I was about fourteen years old, experienced this to the extent that my whole life was influenced by it. An inexplicable inner need took hold of me then: I had to try repeatedly to represent a boundary to space or its lack of a boundary, or again, a time that begins and that ends, or a time without beginning and without end. The one was as impossible as the other, the one was as hopeless as the other. And yet the general view that there was no other choice than one or other of those absurdities. Driven by an irresistible compulsion I wavered from one to the other; at times the risk of going mad was such a close threat that I seriously thought of fleeing it with a timely suicide. A book led to the fifteen-year-old's redemption, Kant's *Prolegomena to Any Future Metaphysics*, which I had the temerity to read... (Buber 2017, 240; my tr.).

Reading this work by Kant, Buber realized that space and time are not characters of the Being but a priori forms of our faculty of knowledge, that – precisely through this new orientation given to the problem of knowledge – the antinomy between the finitude or the infinitude of the universe could find a solution in the rejection of both statements, and finally that the question of the relationship between the finite and the infinite should be shifted from theory to human life itself:

> From then on, I was no longer forced to torture myself seeking to represent something that could not be represented, any more than its opposite. I could think that Being itself is removed both from the finite and the infinite, whether spatial or temporal, as it could only appear in space and in time, without being itself resolved in its appearance. I then began to realize that there is the eternal, which is quite different from the infinite, just as it is totally different from the finite, and that, nevertheless, there can be a connection between me, man, and the eternal (*ibid.*, 241; my tr.).

Finitude and infinitude do not concern the being of the world because the world cannot be known as it is in itself but only according to the a priori forms of our reason. Instead, they concern the way in which we, finite beings with all our weaknesses and fragilities, nevertheless come into positive contact with the infinite or eternal. Buber thus points out how Kant maintains an ethico-religious dimension of human life as the center of his thought: this dimension is built on the dualism of man and God who are nevertheless in a dialogical relationship as I and Thou between each other. Hence the nearness-distance between the human and the divine: ethics and religion are inseparable. For Buber this means that in Kantian doctrine the deepest leitmotif is represented by the encounter of human beings with a God whom they conceive as a Subject who acts with goodness and justice in the world. Religion and ethics are necessarily connected as the individual and eternity are connected – eternity that is conceived not as a being, a *summum ens*, but as an infinite I. Religion precedes philosophy, it is the beginning of our reflection on man: without God as a person human beings could not orient themselves in the world; to respect the moral law means to receive a revelation from an eternal Thou.

6 Religion as Presence: Buber's Interpretation of Kant's Third Antinomy

In 1923 Buber published a book entitled *I and Thou* [*Ich und Du*, 2019]. It was only a small fragment of a large work, which he thought of as consisting of five volumes (never finished) and whose title was to be *Religion as Presence* [*Religion als Gegenwart*, 2017]: *I and Thou* was supposed to be the first volume (Kajon 2010, 63–64). Here we find an explicit reference to Kant in the pages where the author deals with the religious life. An analysis of this life shows how conflicting religion is; it is precisely this dramatic aspect that gives depth to religious life:

> Man's "religious" situation, existence in the presence, is marked by its essential and indissoluble antinomies. That these antinomies are indissoluble constitutes their very essence. [...] It is the sense of the situation that it is to be lived in all its antinomies – only lived – and lived ever again, ever anew, unpredictably, without any possibility of anticipation or prescription. A comparison of the religious and the philosophical antinomy will make this clearer. Kant can relativize the philosophical conflict of freedom and necessity by relegating the latter to the world of appearance and the former to that of being, so that the two positions no longer really oppose one another but rather get along with one another as well as do the two worlds in which each is valid. But when I mean freedom and necessity not in worlds that are thought of but in the actuality in which I stand before God; when I know, "I have been surrendered" and know at the same time, "It depends on me", then I may not try to escape from the paradox I have to live by relegating the irreconcilable propositions to two separate realms; neither may I seek the aid of some theological artifice to attain some conceptual reconciliation: I must take it upon myself to live both in one, and lived both are one (Buber 2019, 94–95; Buber 1970, 143–44).

The dialectic, which is inherent to religious life, unlike the philosophical dialectic opposing necessity and freedom, has no solution at all: a conceptual distinction between what concerns finitude and what concerns infinitude is impossible here because religion means precisely the duality-unity between man and God. Kant gives Buber the model of an antinomic condition that human beings experience when they become aware of their capacity to partially escape their natural or historical being in the name of an almost hidden eternity. This eternity becomes a "Presence" when we encounter the Thou's: God is the medium (*Mittlertum*) of all our relations (*Beziehungen*) in the world.

If one considers Kant's ethico-religious perspective as an important source of inspiration for the author of *I and Thou*, one can understand better the theses that this book defends about human being. The lexicon that Buber uses evokes Kant's language: every Thou [*Du*] forms the world of persons, while the world of It [*Es*] is the world of things, even when these things are animated beings; the first world, in spite of its existence in this world, is not spatial or temporal, while the second has space and time as its main characteristics; the first world is the world where the primary actions are to help [*Helfen*], to save [*Heilen*], to educate [*Erziehen*], to elevate [*Erheben*], to redeem [*Erlösen*], while the second is the world where the primary actions are to experiment [*Erfahren*] and to use [*Gebrauchen*]. When a human being lives in the field of Thou where death has no power, it is a *homo noumenon*, no more dominated by natural inclinations, circumstances, or its own egoism; while the *homo phenomenon* who deals with things depends on the Being which involves and determines its own being. The *Sollen* would be impossible without God as an infinite Thou: this Thou is the focus of all the connections which engage us with our entire being.

7 *Einen Gott glauben* vs. *An einen Gott glauben*: The Ethico-Religious Life in *Eclipse of God*

In *Eclipse of God* (translated as *Gottesfinsternis* in the German edition), which collects talks and lectures Buber gave in the United States in the early fifties, he quotes a Kantian work which was published only at the end of the nineteenth century, consisting of manuscripts, notes, simple reminders, the *Opus Postumum*. It is in this last work that an ethico-religious life is described which Buber considers prior to philosophy as centered on the "I think": God first of all is here mentioned as a Thou encountered by the individual when living its own ethical life. It is precisely in these texts, which were so spontaneous and intimate, according to Buber, that the line he followed in his Kantian interpretation clearly emerges.

In the chapter of *Eclipse of God* entitled "Religion and Reality" [*Religion und Wirklichkeit*] Buber makes a distinction between the ages where God first of all is a living reality, and the ages where God is only an idea of human reason:

> The relation between religion and reality prevailing in a given epoch is the most accurate index of its true character. In some periods, that which human beings "believe in" as something absolutely independent of themselves, is a reality, with which they are in a living relation, although they know well that they can produce only a most inadequate representation of it. In other periods, on the contrary, this reality is replaced by various representations that men "have" and therefore can handle, or by only a residue of the representation, a concept which bears only pale traces of the original image. Men who are still "religious" in such times usually fail to realize that the relation conceived of as religious no longer exists between them and a reality independent of them but has existence only within the *mind* – a mind which at the same time contains hypostatized images, hypostatized "ideas" (Buber 2017, 366; my tr.; Buber's italics).

If God is encountered as the eternal Thou, we are aware that we conceive this Person through anthropomorphisms – anthropomorphisms which represent God as an I who only has attributes of action, i.e. moral attributes. Without the encounter with God the ethical measures would be devoid of validity because it would be founded only on a reason which, being human, lives in history, with all its continuous changes and variations. Without a living God, whose ethical commandments individuals listen to, society would not have any common point of reference. With the loss of the consciousness of a true relation with God, i.e. religion, our age, according to Buber, has also lost ethics. In *Eclipse of God*, Buber maintains the idea that in Kant's very last writings the aim was the foundation of society on ethico-religious rules:

> The fact that […] only an Absolute can give the quality of absoluteness to an obligation, is the trace of Kant's restlessness. […] But do we not discover, in the depth of any true solitude, that even beyond all social existence – nay, precisely in this realm – there is a conflict between good and evil, between fulfilment and failure to fulfil the purpose embodied in us, precisely within the individual being? And yet I am constitutionally incapable of conceiving of myself as the ultimate source of moral approval or disapproval of myself, as the ultimate certainty for the absoluteness that I, to be sure, do not possess, but nevertheless imply with respect to this yes or no. The encounter with the primeval voice, the original source of yes or no, cannot be replaced by any self-encounter (Buber 2017, 369–70; my tr.).

In the chapter of *Eclipse of God* entitled "Love for God and the idea of God" [*Die Liebe zu Gott und die Idee Gottes*] Buber uses two different terms when he appeals to religion and to a philosophy that refers to God: the first expression is *"an einen Gott glauben"* [to believe in God], the second *"einen Gott glauben"* [to assume God]. In the first case God is an eternal Thou before the I, in the second the highest object of thought. In *Opus Postumum* we find both these expressions (Kajon 2018): Buber thinks that Kant finally considered the first expression the condition for the second. A real encounter with God – *absconditus, sed non ignotus* – should not be confused with our thinking God as an object.

*

Ligare means not only to connect, but – taking into consideration the term *legati* – also to entrust: human beings are charged to act in the world as if they were messengers of the Infinite. God is an infinite Thou who expresses ethical commandments: we stay in relation with God when acting in piety and justice. An unconditioned obligation requires the Unconditioned as its origin. To have a religious experience means to listen to ethical commandments coming from an eternal Thou. In this way Buber interpreting Kant gives a new meaning to the word "religion". It seems to me that this meaning could be accepted by non-secular people as well as secular people – by the former because they recognize in this religion the human reference to a divine which is beyond the human, by the latter because they perceive that a society could not survive without sticking to absolute values. Buber as a reader of Kant offers to our secular age a new perspective on religion.

Works Cited

Buber, Martin. *I and Thou*. Ed. W. Kaufmann. New York: Ch. Scribner's Sons, 1970.
Buber, Martin. *Religion als Gegenwart, Werkausgabe*. Ed. P. Mendes-Flohr, P. Schäfer, B. Witte und M. Urban, vol. 12: *Schriften zu Philosophie und Religion*. Ed. A. Noor und K. Schreck. Gütersloh: Gütersloher, 2017.
Buber, Martin. *Das Problem des Menschen, Werkausgabe*. Ed. P. Mendes-Flohr, P. Schäfer, B. Witte und M. Urban, vol. 12: *Schriften zu Philosophie und Religion*. Ed. A. Noor und K. Schreck. Gütersloh: Gütersloher, 2017.
Buber, Martin. *Gottesfinsternis, Werkausgabe*. Ed. P. Mendes-Flohr, P. Schäfer, B. Witte und M. Urban, vol. 12: *Schriften zu Philosophie und Religion*. Ed. A. Noor und K. Schreck. Gütersloh: Gütersloher, 2017.
Buber, Martin. *Ich und Du, Werkausgabe*. Ed. P. Mendes-Flohr, P. Schäfer, B. Witte und M. Urban, vol. 4: *Schriften über das dialogische Prinzip*. Ed. P. Mendes-Flohr, A. Losch und B. Witte. Gütersloh: Gütersloher, 2019.
Cassirer, Ernst. *Kants Leben und Lehre*. Berlin: Bruno Cassirer, 1918.
Cicero, Marcus Tullius. *De natura deorum*, with an Engl. transl. by H. Rakham. Cambridge (Mass.): Harvard UP, 1967.
Cohen, Hermann. *Kants Begründung der Ethik*. 2nd ed., Berlin: Bruno Cassirer, 1910.
Fichte, Johann Gottlieb. *Versuch einer Kritik aller Offenbarung*. 2nd ed., Königsberg: Hartungsche Buchhandlung, 1793.
Hegel, Georg Wilhem Friedrich. *Enzyklopädie der philosophischen Wissenschaften im Grundrisse*. 3rd ed., Heidelberg: Oβwald, 1830.
Kajon, Irene. *Contemporary Jewish Philosophy. An Introduction*. London: Routledge, 2010.
Kajon, Irene. "From *anthropologia transcendentalis* to the Question on Transcendental. Thinking of God in Kant's *Opus postumum*", in *Der Zyklop in der Wissenschaft. Kant und die* anthropologia transcendentalis. Ed. F. V. Tommasi. Hamburg: Meiner, 2018. 185–99.
Kant, Immanuel. *Critique of the Power of Judgment*. Cambridge: Cambridge UP, 2000.

Kant, Immanuel. *Die Religion innerhalb der Grenzen der blossen Vernunft*, Ges. Schriften. Akademie Ausgabe VI, Berlin 1907.
Kant, Immanuel. *Grundlegung zur Metaphysik der Sitten*, Ges. Schriften. Akademie Ausgabe IV, Berlin 1911.
Kant, Immanuel. *Kritik der praktischen Vernunft*, Ges. Schriften. Akademie-Ausgabe V, Berlin 1913.
Kant, Immanuel. *Kritik der Urtheilskraft*, Ges. Schriften. Akademie-Ausgabe V, Berlin 1913.
Kant, Immanuel. *Opus postumum*, Ges. Schriften. Akademie-Ausgabe XXI-XXII, Berlin 1936–1938.
Kant, Immanuel. *Prolegomena zu einer jeden künftigen Metaphysik, die als Wissenschaft wird auftreten können*, Ges. Schriften. Akademie Ausgabe IV, Berlin 1911.
Kant, Immanuel. *Über das Mißlingen aller philosophischen Versuche in der Theodicee*, Ges. Schriften. Akademie-Ausgabe VIII, Berlin 1923.
Lactantius. *Divinae institutiones. Corpus Scriptorum ecclesiasticorum latinorum*, vol. XIX. Vindobonae: Tempsky, 1890.
La querelle des Anciens et des Modernes, XVII-XVIII siècles, précédé de *'Les Abeilles et les Araignées'*, essai de M. Fumaroli, *Postface* de J.-R. Armogathe, éd. établie et annoté par A.-M. Lecoq. Paris: Gallimard, 2001.
Nietzsche, Friedrich. *Zur Genealogie der Moral. Eine Streitschrift*. Leipzig: Neumann, 1887.
Rosenzweig, Franz. *Der Stern der Erlösung*. Frankfurt a. M.: Kauffmann, 1921.
Schleiermacher, Friedrich Daniel Ernst. *Über das höchste Gut, Kritische Gesamtausgabe*, vol. I/1. Berlin: de Gruyter, 1983.
Simmel, Georg. *Kant: Sechzehn Vorlesungen Gehalten an der Berliner Universität*. Leipzig: Duncker und Humblot, 1904.

Sami Pihlström

(Secular) Theodicy, Antitheodicy, and the Critique of Meaning: Pragmatist Reflections

Abstract: This essay approaches the general theme of religion in the secular age by examining a classical question in theology and the philosophy of religion: the problem of evil and suffering. "Theodicist" and "antitheodicist" ways of dealing with this problem need to be distinguished. While the former postulate some meaning, purpose, or significance in suffering, the latter refuse to account for victims' experiences in terms of any such scheme of meaningfulness. In contrast, antitheodicism urges us to ethically acknowledge the victim's experiences of the meaninglessness of their suffering. The paper suggests that this opposition can be analyzed in terms of a pragmatic critique of meaning, inspired by classical American pragmatism (especially William James). The differences between theodicist and antitheodicist approaches can, furthermore, be highlighted by contrasting diverging reactions to the extreme suffering of the Holocaust regarding the issue of meaning(fulness). Pragmatist antitheodicism must, however, take seriously the potential problem of the "return" of theodicism, as it may be asked whether the critique of meaning is itself a problematic case of "meaning-making".

1 Introduction: Applying the Pragmatic Method

When considering with any ethical sensitivity – either religiously or secularly – the horrendous suffering that many human beings (and non-human beings, for that matter) have to go through in their lives, we should not overlook the tension between what may be called "meaning-making" (or meaning-construction), on the one hand, and the ethical need to acknowledge the meaninglessness of (at least some) suffering, on the other. While the concept of meaning-making is typically used by psychologists rather than philosophers or theologians, it can be (*mutatis mutandis*) applied to the *theodicy problem*. In brief, theodicies, while not denying the reality of evil and suffering, postulate a kind of meaning in suffering. Such meaning may not be known or even knowable by human beings, but according

---

Acknowledgements: I am grateful to Herta Nagl-Docekal, in particular, for the kind invitation to contribute this paper to the conference on "Religion in the Secular Age" at the Austrian Academy of Sciences in Vienna, and to the audience for many helpful comments and criticism. I more comprehensively develop the argument of this paper in my new book (Pihlström 2023), especially chapter 5.

https://doi.org/10.1515/9783111247878-004

to theodicies it is, in principle, available from an absolute "God's-Eye View". Theodicies, by attempting to "justify the ways of God to man" (to quote the famous phrase from Milton's *Paradise Lost*), thus seek to render suffering purposive, functional, or in some sense "meaningful" for the individual (or collective) victim of suffering.

While it is a natural and presumably unavoidable human need to impose a meaning-making pattern on one's life, the *theodicist* tendency to view suffering as (necessarily) meaningful in some deeper – religious, metaphysical, or secular – sense has been subjected to devastating *antitheodicist* critique.[1] According to such critique, theodicist "meaning-making" fails to adequately acknowledge the victim of suffering if victims cannot but view their suffering as meaningless. The debate is thus essentially about the ways in which the concepts of meaning, meaningfulness, and meaninglessness apply to human life (and the world generally),[2] and about the ethical constraints of our ways of applying such concepts.

This paper develops a critique of meaning and meaning-making by entangling pragmatism and antitheodicism with each other and emphasizing the irreducibly humanistic character of both. While I have explored antitheodicies and antitheodicism in some detail in my earlier work (see, e.g., Kivistö and Pihlström 2016; Pihlström 2020, 2021, 2023), there is a lot more to be said about the ways in which antitheodicism challenges the theodicist pursuit of meaning or meaningfulness, in particular. The critique of meaning(-making) relevant here must operate in (at least) two dimensions. First, there is, clearly, a need for a critique of too easy assumptions of *the cognitive or literal meaningfulness of religious language*, associated with theological or religious realism and cognitivism. Such views were challenged in early analytic philosophy of religion especially by logical empiricists defending non-cognitivism about religious language, but there is a tradition of challenging them in religious mysticism emphasizing the ineffability of religious thought and language, too. Secondly, and more importantly for the present inquiry, the antitheodicist critique of theodicies can be interpreted as a critique of *the pursuit of meaning(fulness) or significance* associated with theodicies – and religious worldviews postulating an ultimate meaning in the cosmos more generally, either a divine scheme of significance or some secular proxy thereof.

"Meaning-making" assumptions within the first dimension of this critique can be countered by questioning the referential and cognitive meaningfulness of reli-

---

[1] For excellent overviews, see, e.g., Trakakis 2013; Betenson 2016; see also Shearn 2013. I will specify the distinctions between (anti)theodicy and (anti)theodicism below.
[2] Susan Neiman's (2002) path-breaking study of the problem of evil in the context of the history of early modern philosophy emphasizes that the problem concerns the intelligibility of the world in general. (See also, e.g., Pihlström 2020.)

gious language along the lines of, for example, early analytic philosophers' debates on the falsifiability of religious statements. Within the second dimension, the critical arguments may focus on the absurdity and utter insignificance of suffering. A crucial observation here is that these two dimensions of the critique of meaning and meaning-making are deeply connected, as soon as we approach the matter from the standpoint of classical pragmatism. One way of investigating their entanglement emerges from the very idea of the pragmatic method, or "pragmatic maxim". Recall Charles S. Peirce's famous words from "How to Make Our Ideas Clear" (1878): "Consider what effects, that might conceivably have practical bearings, we conceive the object of our conception to have. Then, our conception of these effects is the whole of our conception of the object." (Peirce 1992 [1878], 132.) And recall William James's version (in *Pragmatism*, 1907, Lecture II) of this "principle of Peirce" as well: "To develop perfect clearness in our thoughts of an object, then, we need only consider what effects of a conceivable practical kind the object may involve – what sensations we are to expect from it and what reactions we must prepare."

There is no way of going into any detailed exegesis of the different versions of the pragmatic maxim and their historical development. However, as formulated by Peirce and James, the pragmatic method can be characterized with reference to a kind of ambivalence pertaining to our use of the concept of meaning. On the one hand, it is a method of tracing out the literal (linguistic, conceptual) meaning of our ideas, beliefs, concepts, and conceptions in terms of the conceivable practical effects of their objects. On the other hand, invoking practical effects here raises questions of "meaning" in a different sense, that is, the sense associated with the concept of *significance*. Our beliefs and concept(ion)s are literally meaningful (or meaningless) for us – within our human practices of conceptualization and inquiry, or of coping with the world generally – depending on their, or rather their objects', possibly or conceivably bearing some significance for us within those practices.

In short, an "idea" has (a) "meaning" if, and only if, it (or, rather, its object) is potentially significant (and in this sense also pragmatically "useful") in human life. Meaning and significance are as literally entangled with each other as beliefs are literally "habits of action" according to the classical pragmatists. This action-based account of meaningfulness ties conceptual thought and practice together as inextricably intertwined elements of our being-in-the-world. It is hardly surprising to suggest that this interpenetration of the conceptual and the practical is particularly relevant in religious, theological, and other worldview-related contexts. The significance that religious ideas, for example, may have in and for our lives is a crucial dimension of their "meaning" in the more literal or cognitive sense of the term.³ What pragmatism, as initially formulated by Peirce and James, shows us is that there is no (literal, linguistic) meaning without (practical, life-related) significance. While this is not a study on Wittgensteinian philosophy of religion, an analogy between these traditions is worth keeping in mind: famously, "meaning is use", according to Wittgenstein (1953, I, §23).

2 Antitheodicist Critique of Meaning-making

Keeping in mind this double meaning of "meaning", we may turn to a slightly more detailed discussion of how an antitheodicist critique of meaning may unfold. Just as theodicies (or their more moderate counterparts, "mere defenses")⁴ can be seen as particular arguments drawing attention to alleged justifications for suffering (e.g., the free will theodicy or the free will defense), antitheodicies can be regarded as arguments challenging or criticizing such, or any, theodicist claims. An antitheodicy could thus, for example, be an argument seeking to show that all, or perhaps any possible, theodicies are mistaken or problematic, and a moral antitheodicy would base such an argument on ethical reasons, that is, on the "moral offensiveness" of theodicies (cf. Franklin 2020).

However, the distinction between *theodicism* and *antitheodicism* operates on a meta-level, just as in the philosophy of religion the opposition between *evidentialism* and *fideism* functions on a normative meta-level in relation to the "first-order" debate between theism and atheism. Antitheodicism is a normative view according to which we *should not* approach the problem of evil and suffering by offering, or expecting others to offer, theodicies. We should, on the contrary, avoid such theodicist speculation (or expectations that others engage in it) as resolutely as possible. In contrast, theodicism, of course, is also a normative view that urges us to deliver a theodicy (at least if we are theists) and may proceed to argue (if we are atheists

---

3 One may also recall that Ludwig Wittgenstein uses the concept of "sense", in German *Sinn*, in an analogously double sense in his early work, *Tractatus Logico-Philosophicus* (1921), speaking about the sense of propositions and the sense of the world, or life.
4 This is an important distinction in the debate over theodicies, but I cannot dwell on it here. Very briefly, theodicies claim that some X *is*, or can justifiably be regarded as, God's (morally acceptable) reason for allowing apparently gratuitous evil and suffering, while mere defenses only suggest that X *might*, for all we know, be such a reason. Thus, while theodicies seek to excuse God directly, defenses merely try to shift the burden of proof to the atheist who claims that no such excuse is forthcoming. See, e.g., van Inwagen 2006; for a recent collection of articles on analytic debates on theodicy, in particular, see Wiertz 2021a.

or agnostics) against theism on the basis of this expectation, seeking to show that theodicies fail in this task. Antitheodicism maintains that there is something seriously wrong with this normative expectation itself, just as antievidentialism (or fideism) in the epistemic debates in the philosophy of religion questions the evidentialist premises on the basis of which mainstream disputes on theism and atheism take place.[5] Admittedly, it may often be difficult to clearly distinguish between general antitheodicism and specific criticisms of theodicies (Wiertz 2021b, 58), but in principle this distinction is important.

An examination of theodicism and antitheodicism from the perspective of a pragmatic critique of meaning may also serve the more general interest of critical methodological self-reflection in contemporary philosophy of religion, including analytic philosophy of religion in particular (as it is, indeed, analytic philosophy of religion that has actively kept the theodicist program on its agenda). This case study also gives us an opportunity to defend a conception of philosophy of religion, including the discourse on evil and suffering within it, as a thoroughly *humanistic* pursuit of understanding ever more deeply how we human beings think and speak, and how we ought to think and speak, about the world, including evil, suffering, and God. The emphasis on humanism in the antitheodicy discussion also motivates a serious consideration of *secular* theodicies and theodicism, that is, the ways in which we tend to render others' suffering in some sense "meaningful", functional, or purposive not only within religious or theological but also within entirely this-worldly, including political or economic, frameworks. Despite its critique of meaning, antitheodicism in its own way articulates a "concern over how to speak truthfully, meaningfully, and compassionately about human [...] suffering" (van der Lugt 2021, 3; cf. 12).

For those sharing the basic humanistic orientation of pragmatist philosophy of religion, in particular, it is easy to recognize that while the reality or unreality of God may certainly be among the topics debated within philosophy of religion, it is one of those metaphysical questions that cannot be resolved independently of ethical considerations – as pragmatists like James (1975 [1907]) have compellingly argued (cf. Pihlström 2013, 2020). In the theodicy debate, philosophers of religion go seriously wrong if they assume that we could responsibly speculate about the

---

5 Indeed, theodicism is typically closely connected with (albeit, I suppose, without entailment either way) evidentialism. (Antitheodicism, conversely, does not entail fideism.) It is also usually based on some version of metaphysical realism, primarily because it presupposes that it makes sense to ask questions about the explanation and justification of evil and suffering from an absolute "God's-Eye View", at a fundamental metaphysical level. In contrast, antitheodicism emphasizes the finitude of the human predicament and urges us to ethically respond to suffering without asking, or seeking to answer, such metaphysical questions. See Pihlström 2020, chapter 4.

moral situation God finds himself in when, for instance, considering whether to create this world or not[6] – in contrast to focusing on the moral situations *we* find ourselves in when looking at the evil and suffering around us. The very decision to engage in a discourse reaching out to an imagined divine standpoint overlooks the human predicament of radical metaphysical and ethical finitude, and is thus in a sense based on an illusory conception of the meanings available to us within that predicament. Pointing this out is a key to what I am calling pragmatic critique of meaning. Acknowledging our human limits, even when we are interested in the (legitimate) metaphysical question concerning the reality or unreality of God, is especially vital whenever we set out to consider the possible meaningfulness or meaninglessness of suffering. This helps us to see why theodicies can to a significant degree be considered (either intentional or unintentional) *failures* to acknowledge, or recognize, the meaninglessly, absurdly, suffering other.[7]

The intimate relationship between meaning and significance, which I regard as a core of the pragmatic method (as briefly sketched above), gives us a clue to what may be called the interpenetration of the theoretical and practical (that is, "intellectual" or epistemic and ethical or existential) aspects of the critique of meaning(-making). It may not only be epistemically problematic to associate cognitive meaningfulness to religious propositions (as the logical empiricists argued, on the grounds that such propositions cannot be reduced to any empirically verifiable content);[8] it may also be ethically problematic to do so, or even to attempt to do so, given the need to acknowledge the limits of any humanly possible meaning-making. It may, in particular, be a matter of *hubris* and self-righteousness to claim to possess a perspective of meaning-making on horrible suffering that escapes any reasonable articulation. At the same time, instead of succumbing to any unnecessary mystification, we should definitely continue to *try* to discuss – in language, engaging in meaning-making processes – whatever absurdities and ineffabilities (positive or negative) to which the world might introduce us. The limits of meaning can be critically shown, or reconsidered, only from within a sphere of meaningfulness which they constitute. Accordingly, philosophers of religion should take seriously what I have elsewhere (Pihlström 2021, chapter 6) called *pragmatic meaning agnosticism*, a critical warning against not simply taking for granted that our (e.g.,

---

[6] This is the way in which Franklin (2020), a recent critic of antitheodicism, phrases the discussion.

[7] See also Pihlström 2019 for a slightly different use of the concepts of recognition and acknowledgment in this context, arguing for the need to mutually recognize the relevance of theological and secular discourses on evil and suffering.

[8] See, however, Ramharter 2022 for interesting reconsiderations of the Vienna Circle thinkers' relations to religion.

religious) discourses are meaningful and truth-apt, especially when it comes to attributing meaningful structures to suffering. This meta-level agnosticism about our ability to make sense by using our religious, theological, or any other existentially loaded expressions must be explored in conjunction with recognizing the potential loss of (e. g., religious) significance due to the sheer meaninglessness of horrendous suffering.

This focus on meaning – and the loss of meaning – enables us to explore antitheodicist lines of thought not only in the philosophy of religion but also in literature and literary analysis. One literary genre within which these issues come up is, obviously, Holocaust literature. The history of the very concept of "meaning-making" has been associated with Austrian Holocaust survivor Viktor Frankl's famous book, *Man's Search for Meaning* (1946), even though the word was not explicitly used by Frankl.[9] We naturally seek meaning in our lives, and such a search could, as Frankl suggests, in many cases help victims survive through (even extreme) suffering, but the critical question asked by antitheodicists and pragmatist critics of meaning is whether our search for meaning, or our habit of meaning-making, is always appropriate. What is needed is a philosophical and ethical critique of the very project of meaning-making. In addition to being based on pragmatism, as I am proposing, such a critique can also take a Wittgensteinian shape by focusing on the metaphysical illusion of meaning – and thus, again, the link to early analytic philosophy of religion questioning too easy assumptions of cognitive meaningfulness (also made in later metaphysically realistic analytic philosophy of religion) is clear here.

A contrast within Holocaust literature itself can in fact be perceived between the Franklian emphasis on meaning(-making), on the one hand, and the kind of emphasis on meaninglessness that is exemplified by Primo Levi's writings, especially his seminal works, *If This Is a Man* (1958) and *The Drowned and the Saved* (1986). More generally, Holocaust studies faces the constant ethical question concerning the limits of meaning and understanding; some scholars may even find ethically problematic the very project of trying to understand what happened (cf. Patterson 2018). While this may be an exaggeration – we definitely have to try to understand, in order to deliver any ethical judgment – it is important to note that, according to Levi, the evil and suffering witnessed by Holocaust survivors (and, of course, non-survivors) may have exceeded any human boundaries of meaningfulness, destroying the conceptual machinery we are able to employ

---

9 This is how the Wikipedia entry on "meaning-making" puts the matter; see https://en.wikipedia.org/wiki/Meaning-making (accessed March 31st, 2023). See Frankl 1969 for his later reflections on the human "will to meaning" (to be returned to below).

in our meaning-making processes. Levi has therefore, in my view plausibly (cf. Pihlström 2020, chapter 6), been interpreted as an antitheodicist (though this is not his own term).

The general picture emerging from these conceptual distinctions is that one key way of approaching the debates on theodicy and antitheodicy in contemporary philosophy of religion (and related fields, such as the study of Holocaust literature) is to critically focus on the opposition between "meaning-making" and the ethical need to acknowledge the meaninglessness of suffering – an opposition epitomized by the figures of Frankl and Levi, respectively. While individual thinkers' positions may be complex here, it can be generally said that theodicies prioritize the former and antitheodicies the latter. This does not mean, of course, that antitheodicies would categorically deny the meaningfulness of all instances of suffering; everyone admits that in some, perhaps many, cases suffering *can* serve meaningful purposes. What antitheodicies firmly deny is that suffering *always* has *some* (at least hidden) meaningful function, and this seems to be something that at least most theodicies claim. In particular, antitheodicism remains suspicious of any attempt to justify the reality of suffering with reference to such meanings.[10] The issue, thus, primarily concerns the general habits of conceptualizing suffering as meaningful vs. meaningless, rather than assessments of individual cases such as, say, Frankl's or Levi's particular testimonies of Holocaust suffering. The issue of theodicy vs. antitheodicy can be cashed out in terms of these conflicting views on how we are generally able to, and how we ought to, construct meaning(fulness) in our lives. Clearly, this is a debate that can fruitfully be subjected to a pragmatist analysis and evaluation along the lines of the pragmatic method sketched in the introduction.

While pragmatism is my recommended avenue for launching this analysis, the critique of meaning and meaning-making can, furthermore, be developed along Kantian lines by taking seriously the idea that theodicies can be compared to the kind of *dialectical fallacies of reason* Kant analyzed in the Transcendental Dialectic of the *First Critique* (viz., paralogisms, antinomies, and theistic proofs). It can be suggested that the humanly natural habit of meaning-making is analogous to what Kant calls *transcendental illusion* – in Kant's case, our natural and unavoidable tendency to arrive at the transcendental ideas of soul, God, and freedom – and is in this sense, indeed, unavoidable. Yet, what is, according to antitheodicism, avoidable is the fallacious theodicist argumentation and theorization based

---

[10] For a resolute rejection of any temptation to theodicy in this sense, see Levinas 2006 [1986]. The ethical criticism of the justificatory tendencies of theodicism is central to the antitheodicist argument in Kivistö and Pihlström 2016.

upon this natural habit. It is avoidable analogously to the avoidability of the dialectical fallacies criticized by Kant. Insofar as we wish to utilize Kantian resources for a pragmatist articulation of these issues, it is also important to consider the *Third Critique*, in which Kant argues that it is unavoidable for us to think about nature (including organisms but also the world as a whole) teleologically; it is fallacious, again, to claim to know that such teleology really exists in nature.[11]

3 The Humanism (and Secularism) of Antitheodicism

The question raised in the theodicy vs. antitheodicy debate is, essentially, a question of how to "see the world rightly" (borrowing a phrase from the closing of Wittgenstein's *Tractatus*). The choice between seeking to discover – or construct – meaning in suffering, no matter how horrendous, on the one hand, and being able to (also) view the world and human lives in terms of meaninglessness, on the other, is a decisive existential choice that potentially changes everything in our world-viewing in general.[12] When rephrasing and further developing the issue along the lines of the critique of meaning and "meaning-making", as sketched above, we need to ask what is the ethically appropriate (or the least inappropriate) way of rendering our lives and the world we live in as "meaningful" or significant.

As already explained, I see antitheodicism, especially when pragmatically developed, as a thoroughly humanistic project; its critique is targeted not at a metaphysically postulated divinity but at human beings – us – whose attitudes to other human beings' sufferings can be argued to be ethically problematic if formulated within a theoretical theodicist discourse. In particular, such ethical critique should always primarily focus on *ourselves* – on our own theodicist tendencies of interpreting and justifying suffering on the basis of some alleged "good" it brings or might bring about, or instrumentalizing others' suffering in the service of such goods, including the meta-level "goods" related to our being able to see the

---

[11] While this is not a study on Kantian resources for antitheodicism, it is clear that my overall project of defending antitheodicism is crucially based on broadly Kantian premises (see Kivistö and Pihlström 2016), and I have more generally argued for an integration of pragmatism and Kantian critical philosophy in the philosophy of religion and more generally (see, e.g., Pihlström 2013, 2020, 2021, 2023). On transcendental illusions, pragmatically interpreted, see Pihlström 2022. (Note that teleology also plays a crucial role in typical theodicist justificatory arguments rendering suffering meaningful; see, again, Kivistö and Pihlström 2016.)
[12] To some extent indebted to Neiman (2002), I try to articulate this deep connection between the issue of (anti)theodicism and our finding the world in general intelligible in Pihlström 2020.

world and our lives in it as meaningful despite the suffering they involve. It is crucial to observe, then, that antitheodicist ethical critique is *not* directed at God and does not even have to take any stand whatsoever regarding the question concerning God's existence (*pace* Franklin 2020). It is for this reason that this consideration is, I believe, crucial for a study of "religion in the secular age". Whether or not God exists (and whether or not we believe God to exist), we human beings are responsible for the discourses through which we respond to evil and suffering around us.[13] Our belief or disbelief in God's existence may shape and color those responses, but the opposition between theodicism and antitheodicism as such remains neutral with regard to the question of theism and atheism. Just as there can be secular theodicies (i.e., secular proxies of theodicies postulating some morally justifiable reason for God to allow evil and suffering that could refer to, e.g., some teleological structure in history or economic purposiveness),[14] there may be theistic or religious forms of antitheodicism (along with secular ones, of course). A re-

---

[13] As briefly indicated above, antitheodicism goes well together with (without entailing) a generally *agnostic* view not only regarding God's existence but also – at a meta-level – regarding our ability to engage in a cognitively meaningful and truth-apt religious language-use. I develop this idea of meta-level meaning agnosticism (in a pragmatist context), with links to antitheodicism, in Pihlström 2021, chapter 6.

[14] While there is typically a teleological structure in religious theodicies, too (cf. Trakakis 2013, 365), the concept of a secular theodicy in particular needs further scrutiny. A more comprehensive discussion could explore the similarities and differences between quasi-theodicist ethical and political arguments we might be tempted to employ in various contexts, ranging from Covid-19 restrictions and prioritization issues in healthcare to, say, political or economic responses to the climate crisis, a variety of political decisions both causing and trying to prevent forms of "social suffering", as well as, at a certain extreme, considerations of "excusable casualties" in attempts to wage just war. Let me mention here a few specific cases which would deserve lengthy comments and discussion. First, for an illustrative political example, see Tony Judt's (1992) brilliant analysis of how a number of post-WWII French intellectuals (most famously Jean-Paul Sartre but many others as well) were unable to drop their faith in the historical meaningfulness of Communism despite the enormous suffering inflicted on innocent victims. The potential for further philosophical analysis of such cases of what Judt calls "intellectual irresponsibility" in terms of the (secularized) distinction between theodicism and antitheodicism is enormous. Secondly, see Mavelli 2016 for an original proposal to find a secular theodicy at work in what he calls the governance of uncertainty "in a secular age": a kind of rationalization of the processes of "securitization" and criminalization of entire groups of people takes place, he claims, through a Foucauldian "biopolitical logic" replacing traditional theodicies with a secular "theodicy of good fortune" (or "sociodicy") quasi-justifying the divisions between the fortunate and the suffering, also problematically flirting with the traditional theodicist project of rendering suffering meaningful, only now in the absence of any transcendence. (In my view, Mavelli goes rather far, however, in seeing this secularized theodicy as culminating in torture, because the very same modern processes of governance that he claims to yield quasi-theodicist torture also deal with torture as a war crime.)

ligious believer may very well resort to their own understanding of the divinity, and perhaps critically "rethink" that understanding,[15] in an attempt to develop a thoroughly antitheodicist account of evil and suffering with no divine or secular justification for suffering. This is because antitheodicism, as we have seen, does not simply amount to the rejection of theodicies but, rather, to a normative attempt to lead the entire discussion on evil and suffering away from the pursuit of theodicies, whether religious or secular. This "turn" itself can utilize any conceptual resources that are philosophically (or theologically) available, including the concept of God.

Even if we do use theological concepts in this context, this must be done in a humanistic way. If God were real, then God would, almost by definition, be entirely beyond any meaningful human moral critique. Job's revolt against God – his willingness to bring God to a kind of trial, charging God of colossal injustice, as an innocent man is made to suffer horribly and meaninglessly – itself verges on meaninglessness (or even blasphemy, according to some readers of the Book of Job) and in the end results in Job's silence, *not* because God would have given the kind of response Job had expected but on the contrary because of Job's realization that no such response is forthcoming.[16] The majesty of the creation that God portrays in his final speech renders Job speechless, as there is no moral order in the created universe. Now, a Biblical character like Job can challenge God with his antitheodicist argument, but a scholar in the 2000s can hardly do so. If God exists, then everything indeed is in his hands, and we human beings can only fall into a Joban silence in the face of the creation whose divine purposes remain utterly "other" to us. But as there is no way for us to know whether or not this is the case on the basis of any theoretical argument – indeed, my picture of our radically finite epistemic situation in relation to conceptions of the divinity is basically Kantian, and I have argued that pragmatism largely shares this Kantian predicament (cf. Pihlström 2013, 2020, 2021) – we can only consider our ways of relating to evil and suffering from the point of view of our inescapable human condition. Even if it were in some sense – in terms of some divine ethical logic – "acceptable" for God to use suffering as an instrument for some "good" purposes, for us humans such a logic is an impossibility, as the divine notion of moral acceptability simply is

---

15 For a discussion of Hans Jonas's famous "rethinking" of the concept of God after Auschwitz, see Pihlström 2014, 2021, chapter 6.
16 For a literary-cum-philosophical reading of the Book of Job and especially Kant's interpretation of that Biblical text in his Theodicy Essay (1791) criticizing all possible rationalizing theodicies, see Kivistö and Pihlström 2016, chapter 2.

not ours any more than there can be any moral dimension in, or reason for, Leviathan's existence from Job's point of view.[17]

From the perspective of a humanistic (either Kantian or pragmatist) antitheodicism, it is absurd to consider, for example, whether "God's moral situation" in creating the world resembles the "trolley problem" known from applied ethics (as the issue is conceptualized in Franklin 2020).[18] Antitheodicism, hence, should not be primarily viewed as a moral indignation against theodicies at the "first-order" level, so to speak, but as a challenge to the very ability of theodicism to contribute to the discourse on evil and suffering in an ethically serious manner in the first place. If this meta-level character of humanistic antitheodicism is insufficiently appreciated, the issue concerning the moral offensiveness of theodicies cannot be fully conceptualized. Franklin's (2020) reference to trolley problems is misleading at best and seriously distorting or even unethical (in this context) at worst, contributing to, rather than resolving, the mis- or non-acknowledgment of suffering characteristic of theodicism generally.

In exploring secular theodicies, in particular, we should, of course, keep in mind that they must not be conflated with the secular discourse on (both religious or theological and secular) theodicies and antitheodicies. Serious philosophy of religion must, qua humanistic, be secular, also when analyzing theodicies, including religiously phrased ones. This does not mean that it ought to be aggressively secularist or atheist, of course, but in a more general sense there is no serious alternative to a secular approach to these issues. It is only from the point of view of secular humanistic philosophy of religion that we can appreciate the, in my view,

---

17 Theodicies may postulate, weakly, only some *potential* meaning of suffering, unknown or unknowable to us humans lacking access to the "God's-Eye View". (This would come close to the strategy known as "mere defense" rather than theodicy proper.) However, even this reference to merely possible meaning could still be argued to be a morally reprehensible speculation about possibilities whose actuality would in worst cases turn God into a monster. Reference to mere possibility hardly helps the theodicist here.

18 More generally, I do not think that picturing moral problems in terms of such artificial analogies is really helpful at all – though this is a larger issue not to be settled here. The theodicism vs. antitheodicism discussion is better served by serious consideration of, for example, complex works of literature (and arts generally), as well as genuine historical examples, than by philosophical thought-experiments that may distract us due to their overly simplified form. Real cases of suffering, or carefully constructed literary depictions of fictional suffering, are often extremely complicated and surrounded by various contextual features that trolley-problem-like simplifications dramatically overlook. Moreover, reducing "God's moral standing" to something like a trolley problem (a scenario in which any action will lead to innocent victims) could also be seen as a crude form of anthropomorphism, which has been argued by many antitheodicists to be one of the sources of theodicist confusions (see Wiertz 2021b, 65–67). For a sustained (broadly Wittgensteinian) critique of anthropomorphism as a key problem of theodicies, see Schönbaumsfeld 2021.

ethically crucial idea that the opposition between theodicism and antitheodicism is more fundamental than the one between religious and secular (or theist and atheist) worldviews. However, a self-reflective issue arises here. If theodicism vs. antitheodicism really is, ethically, the most important distinction here (as argued, e.g., in Kivistö and Pihlström 2016; Pihlström 2020), this importance already presupposes secularism (on a meta-level, as our general approach). From a non-secular perspective (e.g., "Christian philosophy"), the order of importance would look very different. There are undoubtedly religious believers who would find it misguided to approach the theodicy issue at a secular level in the first place, arguing that only in a (say) Christian context does it ultimately make sense to even try to resolve this problem. From a philosophical perspective, there is little that can be said to continue *that* discussion. Is secularism in this debate, then, the fundamental starting point on the meta-level, after all? I would be tempted to reformulate this by suggesting that antitheodicism and (meta-level, non-militant, humanistic) secularism are mutually presupposing, reciprocally contained in each other – thus admitting that antitheodicism is not fully religiously neutral, after all. In particular, it must remain inescapably humanistic. But this does not entail that the antitheodicist (e.g., a pragmatist antitheodicist) could not arrive at a religious worldview from within the humanistic philosophical discourse s/he engages in. Religion would still be *available* in a secularized context.

Moreover, it is extremely important to avoid misunderstanding the humanism that I find inextricably entangled with antitheodicism as any crude form of anthropocentrism (let alone anthropomorphism). As William Dean Clement (2020) notes in his intriguing analysis of the figure of Behemoth in Milton's *Paradise Lost* – in comparison with the Book of Job, one of the most important pre-texts of Milton's epic poem – it is theodicy, at least in a sense, that seems to presuppose an anthropocentric worldview. When requiring (as Job initially does) a justification for suffering, we are presupposing that suffering ought to make sense, or to have some "meaning". This expectation is frustrated by God's speech to Job, culminating (according to Clement) in Behemoth as a monster destroying our confidence in any anthropocentric conception of the world having been created for human beings. Antitheodicy, then, is claimed to be anti-anthropocentric in the sense of admitting that there is no cosmic justice available; the world was *not* created for human beings but contains (among other things) Behemoth, a monster which, in its "esoteric otherness", "glorified in the Book of Job to humiliate and humble humanity, towers over mankind with disturbing and disinterested prominence" (ibid., 199) – only to be later "obscured for the sake of Milton's epic theodicy" in *Paradise Lost* (ibid., 201). While I see no reason to disagree with this way of locating a serious problem in Milton's theodicist reworking of the Book of Job, I find it important to emphasize the humanism (if not anthropocentrism) of Job's struggle: only humans (like Job) are able to ask for justice and pose the problem of theodicy – or argue for rephrasing it in an antitheodicist way. This is because meanings are only available, or missing or lost, for humans. A critique of meaning is only humanistically available.

There is, furthermore, no need for any crude anthropocentric presupposition of the world being "made for humans" in humanistic antitheodicism. Insofar as Job encounters a world without justice, with no morally acceptable divine scheme, but an amoral universe instead, he finds out, as a human being concerned with meaning and justice, that the world is devoid of ethics and value and that suffering is devoid of meaning; yet, this is a humanistic discovery all over again, because it also re-emphasizes the dependence of any value, normativity, or significance on human beings' "meaning-making" perspectives on the world (which, of course, themselves tend to take problematically theodicist forms precisely due to our attachment to the project of meaning-production). Accordingly, in brief, while the kind of antitheodicism I am proposing is humanistic, it is *not* anthropocentric in any problematic sense, and it can very well accommodate the criticism of excessive anthropocentrism we find vitally important in the age of the ever-worsening climate crisis, while remaining committed to the inescapable humanism of that criticism itself. Only the humanist can engage in a critique (antitheodicist or any other) of one's own anthropocentric assumptions.

4 Concluding Remarks: The Return of Theodicy?

If we regard Viktor Frankl's (1969) notion of the "will to meaning" (see above) as analogous to what William James (1979 [1897]) called the "will to believe", the question arises whether even James – who can be generally considered an antitheodicist – maintained at least traces of theodicism in his conception of our right to embrace a religious hypothesis if faced with a "genuine option" upon which our ability to experience our lives as meaningful, or worth living, depends.[19] Within American pragmatism, not only John Dewey, whose progressivism and relative lack of attention to the tragic in human lives and history could be argued to make him, at least potentially, a secular theodicist (though without any explicit teleology transcending our human "ends-in-view"), but even James, the resolute antitheodicist, would then have to be interpreted as remaining partly committed to theodicist ideas. While James, in *Pragmatism* (1907, especially Lectures I and VIII), rejects metaphysical theodicies because of their insufficient attention to

---

19 This question arises even though the Jamesian "will to believe" can also be employed to defend antitheodicism, as suggested in Pihlström 2021, chapter 6.

the perspective of the individual sufferer, typically reflecting the over-intellectualized rationalistic optimism of monistic idealism, he may not have been invulnerable to the theodicist tendency of meaning-making.[20]

This leads us, finally, to a more general self-critical question that not only theodicists but also antitheodicists need to pursue: is the antitheodicist critique of meaning-making itself a problematic form of meaning-making? Does antitheodicism naively presuppose that as soon as theodicies are rejected, the "true" meaning of suffering will be revealed (in its meaninglessness)?[21] My defense of (pragmatist) antitheodicism in this paper hopefully contributes to articulating a humanistic approach to the philosophy of religion (and, indeed, philosophy generally): the meanings available to us, in contexts of understanding and alleviating suffering, or in any other contexts for that matter, are inescapably human meanings, and our experiences of the *loss* of such meanings is a human loss. Thus, the theodicist pursuit of a "God's-Eye View" from which suffering could be rendered (actually or potentially) meaningful in a cosmic, metaphysical, or teleological sense is an illusion. In Kantian terms, it is, more specifically, a *transcendental* illusion violating the very conditions for the possibility of our being able to view the world "rightly" – ethically as well as epistemically. Yet, also in Kantian terms, this humanism itself invites reflexive self-criticism. We can never just rest content with our antitheodicist critique but must constantly inquire into the potential return of theodicist assumptions within such a critical project.

Such reflexivity can, I believe, be sufficiently elaborated on only via a pragmatic critique of meaning-making. In trying to make sense of our philosophical, theological, religious, and any other discourses on suffering, we should constantly seek to maintain a critical distance to this sense-making itself, being aware of the (presumably humanly natural) tendency of illusory "re-theodicization" (as we might call it), our habit of rendering suffering meaningful all over again, or our habit of postulating meaningfulness even where we ought to be able to see meaninglessness.

---

20 On the other hand, it is no surprise that there are essential tensions within the pragmatist tradition itself. This is so regarding the fundamental problem of realism vs. idealism, for instance, and there is no reason to believe that pragmatists would be immune to the tension between theodicism and antitheodicism. For an analysis of Josiah Royce's views on the problem of evil as a qualified theodicist position within the pragmatist framework, see Nagl 2021.

21 These reflexive issues are raised, for example, in Pihlström 2021, chapter 6, where I examine the worry about an almost inevitable return of a "theodicy by other means" in antitheodicist contexts.

Works Cited

Betenson, Toby. "Anti-theodicy". *Philosophy Compass* 11:2 (2016): 56–65.
Clement, William Dean. "'The Excess of Glory Obscured': Behemoth and Anti-Theodicy in *Paradise Lost*". *Milton Quarterly* 54 (2020): 191–204.
Frankl, Viktor E. *The Will to Meaning: Foundations and Applications of Logotherapy*. New York: Plume, 1988 [1969].
Franklin, James. "Antitheodicy and the Grading of Theodicies by Moral Offensiveness". *Sophia* 59 (2020): 563–576.
James, William. *Pragmatism: A New Name for Some Old Ways of Thinking*. Eds. Frederick H. Burkhardt, Fredson Bowers, and Ignas K. Skrupskelis. Cambridge, MA and London: Harvard UP, 1975 [1907].
James, William. *The Will to Believe and Other Essays in Popular Philosophy*. Eds. Frederick H. Burkhardt, Fredson Bowers, and Ignas K. Skrupskelis. Cambridge, MA and London: Harvard UP, 1979 [1897].
Judt, Tony. *Past Imperfect: French Intellectuals, 1944–1956*. Berkeley: U of California P, 1992.
Kant, Immanuel. *Kritik der reinen Vernunft*. Ed. Raymund Schmidt. Hamburg: Felix Meiner, 1990 [1781/1787].
Kivistö, Sari and Pihlström, Sami. *Kantian Antitheodicy: Philosophical and Literary Varieties*. Basingstoke: Palgrave Macmillan, 2016.
Levi, Primo. *The Drowned and the Saved*. Trans. Raymond Rosenthal. London: Michael Joseph, 1988 [1986].
Levi, Primo. *Survival in Auschwitz: The Nazi Assault on Humanity*. Trans. Stuart Woolf. New York: Touchstone Books, 1996 [1958]. (Also known with the title, *If This Is a Man*.)
Levinas, Emmanuel. "Useless Suffering". In Levinas, *Entre-nous: Thinking-of-the-other*. Trans. Michael B. Smith and Barbara Harshav. London and New York: Continuum, 2006 [1986], 78–87.
van der Lugt, Mara. *Dark Matters: Pessimism and the Problem of Suffering*. Princeton, NJ: Princeton UP, 2021.
Mavelli, Luca. "Governing Uncertainty in a Secular Age: Rationalities of Violence, Theodicy and Torture". *Security Dialogue* 47 (2016): 117–132.
Nagl, Ludwig. *Toward a Global Discourse on Religion in a Secular Age: Essays on Philosophical Pragmatism*. Berlin: LIT, 2021.
Neiman, Susan. *Evil in Modern Thought: An Alternative History of Philosophy*. Princeton, NJ: Princeton UP, 2002.
Patterson, David. *The Holocaust and the Nonrepresentable: Literary and Photographic Transcendence*. Albany: SUNY Press, 2018.
Peirce, Charles S. *The Essential Peirce*, vol. 1. Ed. Nathan Houser. Bloomington and Indianapolis: Indiana UP, 1992.
Pihlström, Sami. *Pragmatic Pluralism and the Problem of God*. New York: Fordham UP, 2013.
Pihlström, Sami. *Taking Evil Seriously*. Basingstoke: Palgrave Macmillan, 2014.
Pihlström, Sami. "A Pragmatist Approach to the Mutual Recognition between Ethico-Political and Theological Discourses on Evil and Suffering". *Political Theology* 20 (2019): 157–175.
Pihlström, Sami. *Pragmatic Realism, Religious Truth, and Antitheodicy: On Viewing the World by Acknowledging the Other*. Helsinki: Helsinki UP, 2020.
Pihlström, Sami. *Pragmatist Truth in the Post-Truth Age: Sincerity, Normativity, and Humanism*. Cambridge: Cambridge UP, 2021.

Pihlström, Sami. "On Natural and Transcendental Illusions in Kantian-Pragmatist Philosophical Anthropology". *Journal of Transcendental Philosophy*, 3 (2022): 193–212.

Pihlström, Sami. *Humanism, Antitheodicism, and the Critique of Meaning in Pragmatist Philosophy of Religion*. Lanham, MD: Lexington Books, 2023.

Ramharter, Esther, ed. *Vienna Circle and Religion*. Cham: Springer, 2022.

Schönbaumsfeld, Genia. "Was ist eigentlich eine Theodizee?" In Wiertz 2021a, 105–124.

Shearn, Samuel. "Moral Critique and Defence of Theodicy". *Religious Studies* 49 (2013): 439–458.

Trakakis, N.N. "Antitheodicy". In Justin P. McBrayer and Daniel Howard-Snyder (eds.), *The Blackwell Companion to the Problem of Evil*. Malden, MA and Oxford: Blackwell-Wiley, 2013, 363–376.

Wiertz, Oliver J. (ed.). *Logische Brillianz – Ruchlose Denkungsart? Möglichkeiten und Grenzen der Diskussion des Problems des Übels in der analytischen Religionsphilosophie*. Münster: Aschendorff, 2021 (a).

Wiertz, Oliver J. "Das Problem des Übels in der analytischen Religionsphilosophie: Geschichtliche Stationen und Kritik". In Wiertz 2021a, 29–104. (2021b)

Wittgenstein, Ludwig. *Tractatus Logico-Philosophicus*. Trans. Brian F. McGuinness and D. F. Pears. London: Routledge, 1974 [1921].

Wittgenstein, Ludwig. *Philosophical Investigations*. Trans. G.E.M. Anscombe. Oxford: Blackwell, 1953.

Ludwig Nagl
Beyond Dogmatic Scientism: Hilary Putnam on Religious Faith

Abstract: The *Introduction* points out, with reference to John Rawls and Charles Taylor, that modern states, unlike traditional ones, are decoupled from a (substantial) religious legitimation. Religious faith, in modern societies, has thus, as William James argues, the status of an "option". *Part two* of the paper shows how the Harvard logician Hilary Putnam – while fully affirming the important role of science – criticizes, with recourse to Wittgenstein and James, the self-sufficiency of a dogmatically closed "scientism", thus making room, in a Kant-informed, post-Kantian manner, for the "hypothesis" of religious belief. *Part three* analyzes Putnam's *Jewish Philosophy as a Guide to Life*, focusing on his religious position "between Dewey and Buber". *Part four* takes a brief look at the defense of religious pluralism in Putnam's essay "Let's Stop Using the Notion of 'Idolatry'".

1 Introduction: A Secular Age

In pre-modern societies, a dominant, socially accepted religion was the main source of political legitimation.[1] In modern constitutional democracies the relationship between politics and religion has changed substantially. Charles Taylor, in his seminal study *A Secular Age*, pointed out that "in 1500, in our Western societies it was virtually impossible not to believe in God, while in 2000 many of us find this not only easy, but even inescapable."[2] Contemporary constitutions are based on the discourse about "the just." As John Rawls asserts in his *Theory of Justice* "the concept of right is prior to that of the good."[3] The institutions of modern states have a secular character, while their constitutions *legally* make room for the broad variety of their citizens' "life plans" that are based on distinctive conceptions of "the good" – conceptions typically inspired by the "comprehensive doctrines"[4] they adhere to, which may be non-religious or religiously configured. In our secular age, Taylor writes, "the immanent frame" (a transcendence-excluding

---

[1] As, for instance, the expression "Bund von Thron und Altar" ("alliance between throne and altar") indicates.
[2] Taylor, *A Secular Age*, 25. See also Nagl, ed. "Symposium zu Charles Taylor, *A Secular Age*".
[3] Rawls, *A Theory of Justice*, 396.
[4] See Rawls, "The Priority of Right and Ideas of the Good", 450.

"picture of the natural, 'physical' world") is "common to us all":[5] "Our general understanding of the universe is the one defined by post-Galilean natural science: a universe governed by impersonal causal laws."[6] This science-based aspect of modernity is, however, not a full description of our contemporary situation, because the "immanent frame" which, as Taylor argues, we today all share, "permits closure, without demanding it."[7] "Some of us want to live it as open to something beyond, some live it as closed."[8] Thus, in our time, religious faith – as William James has shown, early on, in his essay *The Will to Believe* – attains the status of an "option."[9] "Issues of faith and non-faith are not settled lightly"[10], however, as Taylor, in accordance with James, asserts since they are related to the existential core of our self-understanding.

2 Approaching Religion "by Keeping the 'Immanent Frame' Open to What Lies Beyond the Observable": Hilary Putnam's Neopragmatic Critique of "Dogmatic Scientism" as a Prelude to his Interpretation of Religious Faith

In the 1990s, the Harvard philosopher Hilary Putnam – who, as a student of Hans Reichenbach, had gained prominence as an *analytic* philosopher in the early stages of his career – began to elaborate a non-reductive, neo-pragmatic approach to philosophy. He started to investigate, with an eye on Kant and with recourse to Wittgenstein, Dewey and James, the complex question whether our secularistically configured democratic culture inevitably leads us to a world-view that is *in toto* immanence-focused, or whether a careful (i.e., not "scientistically" narrowed down) reflection on the merits, as well as the limits of our sciences is able to sup-

---

5 Taylor, *A Secular Age*, 543.
6 Taylor, "Shapes of Faith Today", 270. See also Nagl, "Religion in einem 'säkularen Zeitalter'".
7 Taylor, *A Secular Age*, 543–44.
8 Taylor, *A Secular Age*, 544.
9 James, *The Will to Believe*, 2–4; see also Taylor, "Shapes of Faith Today", 269.
10 Taylor, "Shapes of Faith Today", 269.

port a non-relativistic, affirmative interpretation of religion[11] which at the same time is sensitive to pluralism.[12]

Mature Putnam asserts – in step one of his attempt to answer this question – that the functioning of modern democracies implies two modes of "knowledge": in his essay "Pragmatism and Nonscientific Knowledge"[13] he addresses what, he writes, "has been a focus for my philosophical interest for the past twenty years: the existence of and the importance of knowledge outside of the exact sciences ('nonscientific knowledge') [...], in particular the existence and importance of knowledge of values in the widest sense."[14] This focus, Putnam continues,

> has naturally led me to point out how 'paradigmatic' science (physics) itself depends on judgments which are 'nonscientific' [...], and it has led me to a close reading of the American pragmatists, who were my predecessors in the study of all these problems.[15]

"The idea that science (in the sense of exact science) exhausts rationality," Putnam asserts,

> is [...] a self-stultifying error. The very activity of arguing about the nature of rationality presupposes a notion of rationality wider than that of laboratory testability. [...] The horror of what cannot be 'methodized' is nothing but method fetishism. It is time we got over it. Getting

---

[11] The quote in the title of part 2 refers to the way in which Magnus Schlette appropriately characterizes (in recourse to Taylor) "Putnam's goal" (Schlette, "How you understand", 129–130).

[12] This option receives support, according to Putnam, from the arrival of a "third enlightenment" – a "pragmatist enlightenment" – (after the first *Aufklärung*, articulated in the work of Plato, and the second one, explored at the beginning of the modern age by Kant and his followers). [See Putnam, *Ethics without Ontology*, 96; as well as Hampe, *Die dritte Aufklärung*, 71.] Pragmatists like John Dewey and William James started to challenge that in today's globalized societies the notion of *Aufklärung* is often reduced to only one of its elements – to technological efficiency and "smartness". In contrast to this abstract approach pragmatists – as Putnam argues – "want to do justice to both the scientific forms of intelligibility associated with the rise of the natural sciences in the modern world, and the ideal-involving intelligibility associated with our various moral and religious images of the world." (Macarthur, "Introduction", 4.) The pragmatist's complex approach to natural as well as to social reality represents, as Putnam points out, a new stage of discourse – "a more enlightened enlightenment" that (in a Kant-inspired but post-Kantian manner) is able to overcome "apriorism, skepticism, and scientism." (Ibid.)

[13] Hilary Putnam, "Pragmatism and Nonscientific Knowledge", in: Putnam/Putnam, *Pragmatism as a Way of Life*, 55–70.

[14] Ibid., 55. Putnam explains this – praxis-related – "knowledge of values" in the following way: "What it is to know that something is *better* or *worse* than something else: a better way of life, or a better course of action, or a better theory (in science), or a better interpretation (of a text, etc.)" [ibid.]. See also Putnam, *The Collapse of the Fact-Value Dichotomy*.

[15] Putnam/Putnam, *Pragmatism as a Way of Life*, 55.

over it would reduce our intellectual *hubris*. We might even recover our sense of mystery; who knows?[16]

Putnam thus re-opens, in a post-analytic manner, the space for an (in part Kant-based, pragmatistic) exploration of "practical reason"[17] which avoids the problematic fact-value dichotomy that logical empiricists had hailed in early analytic philosophy.[18]

His critique of dogmatic "scientism" leads Putnam to step two of his investigation. Putnam's interest in a broader, non-restrictive conception of praxis-related reason terminates, ultimately, in a new exploration of the religious hope horizon of human action – an exploration that finds support, inter alia, in the writings of late Wittgenstein. "While religious discourse is commonly viewed (by atheists) as prescientific or 'primitive' discourse, Wittgenstein" – Putnam points out – "clearly believes no such thing,"[19] because the "religious language game" (i.e., the use of religious "pictures" which determine how we read the world[20]) is not theory-focused, but has its *locus*, as well as its proof, in the actions of the believer.[21]

---

[16] Ibid., 70. This is an allusion to Wittgenstein, *Tractatus Logicio-Philosophicus* 6.522: "There are indeed things that cannot be put into words. They make themselves manifest. They are what is mystical." (See in this context also Nagl, "Religion")

[17] For a general assessment of the influence of Kant on American Pragmatism (in particular on its philosophy of religion) see Nagl, "Transformationen der Kantischen Postulatenlehre", as well as Murphey, "Kant's children", and Carlson, "James and the Kantian Tradition".

[18] For an influential analytical text that advocated – along the lines of the fact-value dichotomy which Putnam rejects – a *scientistic closure* of the modern world view see Carnap/Hahn/Neurath "Wissenschaftliche Weltanschauung – Der Wiener Kreis", 87–89, where the authors argue: "Die wissenschaftliche Weltauffassung kennt keine unlösbaren Rätsel. Die Klärung der traditionellen philosophischen Probleme führt dazu, dass sie teils als Scheinprobleme entlarvt, teil in empirische Probleme umgewandelt werden. [...] Die Methode dieser Klärung ist die der logischen Analyse." [...] "Wenn jemand behauptet: ‚es gibt einen Gott', ‚der Urgrund der Welt ist das Unbewußte', ‚es gibt eine Entelechie als leitendes Prinzip der Lebewesen', so sagen wir ihm nicht: ‚was du sagst, ist falsch', sondern wir fragen ihn: ‚was meinst du mit deine[r] Aussage?' Und dann zeigt es sich, dass es eine scharfe Grenze gibt zwischen zwei Arten von Aussagen. Zu der einen gehören die Aussagen, wie sie in der empirischen Wissenschaft gemacht werden; ihr Sinn lässt sich feststellen durch logische Analyse, genauer: durch die Rückführung auf einfachste Aussagen über empirisch Gegebenes. Die anderen Aussagen, zu denen die vorhin genannte gehört, erweisen sich als völlig bedeutungsleer. [...] Die wissenschaftliche Weltauffassung kenne nur Erfahrungssätze über Gegenstände aller Art und die analytischen Sätze der Mathematik und Logik."

[19] Putnam, "Wittgenstein on Religious Belief", 143. For his interpretation of Wittgenstein see also Putnam, "Rules, attunement, and 'applying words to the world'".

[20] See Hilary Putnam, "The Religious Person 'Uses a Picture'" in: Putnam, "Wittgenstein on Religious Belief", 154–57.

Putnam's interest in a non-reductive exploration of all aspects of reason finds support not only in Wittgenstein's *Philosophical Investigations*, but – in substantial ways – also in the pragmatisms of John Dewey and of William James. Dewey's elucidations of the role that value-related discourses play in modern democracies, as well as William James's pragmatic analyses of the *locus* of religious belief in modern society[22] fascinate Putnam. Ultimately Dewey, however, as Putnam shows, turns out to be an ambivalent thinker *in at least two ways:* first, since he does not investigate, in-depth, our "limit experiences", i.e. the "existential choices" that we, as finite humans face; and secondly, since he accepts a "Feuerbachian" critique of religion which (as will be shown in part three of my paper) proves problematic.

Let us begin with a brief look at the first problem. In his essay "A Reconsideration of Deweyan Democracy" Putnam takes a nuanced approach toward Dewey's pragmatism. He begins by stressing that Dewey, in his social theory, convincingly shows that not rationality, analytically mis-read as "value free", but "practical reason" in its value-laden mode is the "precondition for the full application of intelligence to the solution of social problems."[23] A little later Putnam points out, however, that Dewey (in the context of his "experimentalist" re-reading of practical reason) does not *extensively explore* the fact that, as finite individuals, we are confronted, unavoidably, with *existential situations and questions* that occur under conditions which can be neither sufficiently elucidated, nor decided, by focusing on the socio-pragmatically dimensioned, "instrumentalist", ideal of Dewey's pragmatism: by the ideal, i.e., to "'maximize' the good."[24] Such existential questions

---

[21] See in this context also Schlette, "How you understand can only be shown by how you live", 136–37: "In the light of his understanding and adaptation of Wittgenstein, [Putnam] makes the point that the meaning of the word 'God' as much as its reference are entirely internal to the particular religious life-form that is substantiated and individualized by the texts, rituals, and practices of the according religion. The reality of this religion, so to speak, is the life-form that entails semantic and practical commitments, which decide over the question what it means to get it right or wrong to be in connection with God."

[22] William James (in his book *The Varieties of Religious Experience*, 500) rejects the scientism-induced "survival theory" of religion (i.e., the claim that in our science-informed age religion is a mere atavism) in a very strong manner: "I unhesitatingly repudiate the survival theory of religion, as being founded on an egregious mistake," he writes, attacking the abstract "objectivism" that forms its core: "The contention of the survival-theory that we ought to stick to non-personal elements exclusively" is seen by James as totally misleading: "I think that however particular questions connected with our individual destinies may be answered it is only by acknowledging them as genuine questions and living in the sphere of thought which they open up, that we become profound."

[23] Putnam, "A Reconsideration of Deweyan Democracy", 186.

[24] Ibid., 190.

were, however, as Putnam points out, carefully investigated by William James in his "famous essay 'The Will to Believe'"[25] – by a text that remains important for all attempts to philosophically explore the contemporary *locus* of religion.

There exists no theoretical (science-based or philosophical) 'confirmation' that a religious approach to the world is valid, James argues in his essay. The project to formulate stringent *theoretical* "proofs" for the "existence of God" has collapsed: "The bare fact that all idealists since Kant have felt entitled to scout or neglect [the theoretical arguments for God's existence] shows that they are not solid enough to serve as religion's all-sufficient foundation", James writes.[26] God cannot be theoretically 'demonstrated'. There exists, however, as Kant, in his *second Critique*, suggests, the possibility to relocate religion on the fringes of "practical reason": the idea of God can be re-conceived as a "postulate" which is tied to the "horizon" of our human praxis. James appropriates this shift in a pragmatically transformed manner: the theoretically non-confirmable, *risky* "option" of religious belief, he writes, rests on a "live hypothesis" – i.e., on a hypothesis which, though it cannot be empirically verified, "appeals as a real possibility to him to whom it is proposed."[27] "In all important transactions of life we have to take a leap in the dark," James continues. "If we decide to leave the riddles unanswered, that is a choice; if we waver in our answer, that, too, is a choice: but whatever choice we make, we make it at our peril."[28] Mature Putnam is willing to take this leap: he seeks to support his religious belief with philosophical arguments, however, thereby avoiding the peril of a mere 'fideistic' thought position.

---

25 In spite of the fact that James's essay "has received a great deal of hostile criticism," Putnam writes, "I believe that its logic is, in fact, precise and impeccable." (Ibid., 191–92) Complex practical situations of the "existential" kind have – as James points out – (at least) three characteristics: first, the choice that is faced is "forced" (i.e., the given options are the only options realistically available); secondly, the choice is "momentous" and not "trivial" (i.e., it matters deeply); and thirdly, it is not possible to decide what to do on intellectual grounds (see James, *The Will to Believe*, 3).
26 James, *The Varieties of Religious Experience*, 437.
27 James, *The Will to Believe*, 2.
28 Ibid., 3. See also Putnam, "Die anhaltende Aktualität von William James".

3 Jewish Philosophy as a Guide to Life: Rosenzweig, Buber, Levinas, Wittgenstein

Putnam's book with this title, published in 2008, contains his most elaborate reflections on religion.[29] Religious faith, Putnam writes, remains an abstract "object of description and control" as long as it has not become personal: "Religions are communal and have long histories, but religion is also a personal matter or it is nothing."[30] In consequence, he begins his investigations with an autobiographical introduction, in which he describes how for him and his wife – in preparation for the "bar mitzvah" that their elder son "wanted to have" – religious practices became an important part of their life: "That an adult Jew starts attending services when one of his children has a bar- or bat mitzvah is not at all unusual," Putnam notes. "But I am also a philosopher. What did I – what could I – make philosophically of the religious activities that I had undertaken to be a part of?"[31] This is a question "I am still struggling with," he continues, "and will very likely struggle with as long as I am alive."[32] "In a conversation I recently had with an old friend", Putnam notes, "I described my current religious standpoint as 'somewhere between John Dewey in *A Common Faith* and Martin Buber'."[33] What does Putnam mean by this "between"?[34]

3.1 Let us first consider the Deweyan component of Putnam's position. Putnam appreciates that Dewey keeps open the space for a philosophical discourse on value questions in society by avoiding the fact-value dichotomy prevalent in analytic philosophy. "Reality, as Dewey saw, *makes demands* on us," Putnam writes.[35] He praises Dewey as a sharp-sighted analyst of democracy, as well as a critic of (pre-Kantian) "ontotheology" and of institutionally frozen (mis-)readings of religion. Putnam doubts, however, (and this leads him to his reservation against Dew-

---

29 In the "Introduction" to his book Putnam briefly considers his religious thoughts "in personal terms" (Putnam, *Jewish Philosophy*, 1), thus avoiding Max Weber's 'neutral' position which Weber expressed in his famous claim to be "religiously unmusical" (a self-description which many contemporary theoreticians of religion repeat in order to strictly maintain distance to their "object" of research).
30 Putnam, *Jewish Philosophy*, 1.
31 Ibid., 2–3.
32 Ibid., 3.
33 Ibid.
34 For a more extensive analysis of Putnam's position "between Dewey and Buber" see Schlette, "How you understand can only be shown by how you live", 130–33 and 137–39; and Tumulty, "Hilary Putnam's Position between Dewey and Buber".
35 Putnam, *Jewish Philosophy*, 6.

ey's pragmatism) that Dewey, in his analyses of religious belief in *A Common Faith*, is able to provide a fully adequate reading of the core of religion. Dewey's mode of transforming the institutionalized "religions" into "the religious"[36] re-reads religion "adverbially": as a (quite vague) quality that is able to accompany all (serious) activities in politics, art and philosophy. Dewey thereby detaches this (adverbially re-configured) "religious" (along the line of Feuerbach's criticism of religion) from the belief in a divine being. In *A Common Faith* – Putnam writes – Dewey views God as a (wrongly substantialized) "human projection that embodies our highest ideals."[37] At the same time, Dewey, however, tries to avoid dogmatic atheism by tying the "adverbially" read "religious" to a "pious" naturalism.

3.2 These tensions in Dewey's reflections on religion lead Putnam to the second component of his "between", to his appreciative reference to the Jewish philosopher Martin Buber. While Putnam, on the one hand, fully agrees with Dewey that the predicates "just" and "good" (which, in religious discourse, are attributed *in perfectio* to God) are valid normative ideals for us humans too, Putnam defends – in contrast to Dewey – the idea that the "infinite" is "a person": "God is not an ideal of the same kind as Equality and Justice," Putnam writes. "The traditional believer – and this is something I share with the traditional believer [...] – visualizes God as a supremely wise, kind, just *person*."[38] Dewey's humanism, which seeks to avoid all reference to "transcendence", is thus seen by Putnam as problematic. In his lecture "Let's Stop Using the Notion of 'Idolatry'" Putnam said:

> The deification of humankind (which is always accompanied by the transformation of 'humanity' into a mere abstraction) is a frightening tendency – a tendency, however, which is attractive for many people who are basically good. My friend Benjamin Schwarz once said to me 'man is the worst God who exists' and this remark has made a deep impression on me.[39]

Putnam finds support in his search for a non-reductive conception of religion in Martin Buber's (in part Kant-inspired[40]) writings. According to Buber, the "I-You-relation" which characterizes the attitude of the religious believer toward God is a relation which excludes the possibility that one of the relata is "non personal" (as it is the case if this relation is read, in Dewey's manner, as a "religiously" con-

---

[36] "Indeed, organized religion is not something Dewey ever came to favor," Putnam rightly remarks (Putnam, *Jewish Philosophy*, 101).
[37] Ibid.
[38] Ibid., 102.
[39] Putnam, "Plädoyer für eine Verabschiedung des Begriffs ‚Idolatrie'", 50 (English translation Ludwig Nagl).
[40] See in this context the essay by Irene Kajon in this volume.

figured "piety" toward "the universe"). And Buber's reading of the "I-You-relation" also excludes the idea that there exists an insurmountable distance between the relata: between "us" and a "divine 'totally other'".[41]

It seems worth considering that the issues addressed here have been discussed (in a precarious, "ontotheological" setting, however, which Putnam seeks to avoid)[42] in the *analogia entis* discourse of the Middle Ages, where it was argued that the predicates used in human 'God speech' must neither be interpreted in a 'homologue' nor in a 'heterologue' manner but have to be read in an 'analogue' mode. (The core of this discourse is the thesis that the creator and the created are characterized by resemblances as well as by non-resemblances.) Elements of this *analogia entis thesis* which entails a twofold negation, are – it seems to me – reintroduced (in an indirect, ontology-distant and praxis-focused mode, however) by Putnam in his appreciative reception of Buber. In reference to God Putnam avoids, *on the one hand*, all linear, *homologue*, applications of human predicates (applications which characterize 'anthropomorph' references to God as well as – in a critical inversion – the Feuerbachian idea that God is nothing but the [illusionary] perfection of our own *human* ideals); and he sidesteps, *on the other*, the opposite, *heterologue*, thesis: the claim, i.e., that God is '*totaliter aliter*' and that his *complete* otherness implies that every relevant God speech has *in toto* to avoid any finite, human vocabulary.[43]

---

[41] This holds true, for instance, for the concept of God in Judaism as well as in Christianity, as Nicolas Wolterstorff has pointed out, criticizing postmodern theories inspired by negative theology: "The Hebrew bible/Old Testament tells us that we are created as icons of the Holy One; God is not *ganz anders*." (Wolterstorff, "The Religious Turn", 278).

[42] See Putnam's massive critique of "ontology" in: Putnam, *Ethics without Ontology*, Chapter "'Ontology' – An Orbituary", 71–85.

[43] Since Putnam defends the "first person perspective" of religious language use – the perspective of the "believer" – he affirms (albeit only inexplicitly and *in pragmatically transposed modes*) core motifs of the twofold negation contained in the classical *analogia entis* theory. To realize that Putnam's conception of "religious faith" is structured by a latent re-reading of (elements) of this theory can help to dissolve some of the (seeming) contradictions in his religious position. In an interview with Zackary Sholem Berger Putnam said: "In my spirituality, I visualize God as a person. It's not that I believe God is a person. I think what would an ideally wise, ideally good person [...] want me to do? That is the central spiritual experience. Okay, do you believe God has a mind? No, of course not" (Putnam, "Spiritual Encounters of a Philosopher of Science", 1). Putnam thus, quite unambiguously, removes from his *de-ontologized, neo-pragmatic version of God speech* all "homologue" predicate attributions to the idea of God: God is not a person *in the way humans are empirical persons*. (Or, as Wittgenstein once, quite similarly, argued: the valid religious image that "God's eye" is watching the world cannot be meaningfully interpreted in an *empiricist* mode which would allow question like whether God's eye does have eyebrows, etc.) And, in addition, Putnam also [as is argued in the *analogia entis* theorem] relativizes the *"heterologue" God (non-)image*

A theistically configured image of the Absolute is (with regard to its practical, motivating force) – for Putnam, as well as for Buber – on the whole more convincing than the alternative image of an 'infinite' which is identical with a physical, depersonalized 'force greater than us'. It is more plausible to think of God as "a supremely wise, kind, just person,"[44] Putnam writes. This must not be misunderstood in a 'homologue' way, however: "Although many intellectuals are afraid of this sort of 'anthropomorphism' because they are afraid [...] that it will be taken literally, I feel that it need not to be 'taken literally'", Putnam argues: to think of God in this manner is "still far more valuable than any metaphysical concept of an impersonal God, let alone a God who is 'totally other'."[45] Buber's reflections on the basic words I-You, which are focused on an "ultimate You"[46] are summarized by Putnam in the following two theses, which, while avoiding anthropomorphism, are at the same time person-related: Firstly, "it is impossible to describe God, or to theorize about him"; and secondly, "What one can do is speak *to* God, or rather to enter in an 'I-You' relation with God, a relation in which all the partial 'I-You' relations [...] are bound up and fulfilled without being obliterated."[47] Putnam, like Kant, Wittgenstein and Buber, thus argues that the complex images which organize religious belief are tied, in a structurally deep way, to practical reason. It is obvious therefore that a religious faith which – in a quasi-monastic mode of retreat – seeks to *abstractly isolate* the God-focused I-You-relation from all concrete, socio-ethical aspects of human praxis is a mere illusion: "The aim of a Buberian philosophy is to teach us that the experience of the divine is not an end in itself," Putnam writes[48]. This core idea is expressed by Sami Pihlström (in "Rorty versus Putnam", where he quotes *Jewish Philosophy*, 48) as follows: "The vertical dimension [...] means nothing without the horizontal dimension. It's not love of God if it doesn't lead to the commandment to love your neighbor."[49]

That religious belief (in Judaism, Christianity, and Islam) addresses a personal God is the focus not only of Putnam's neo-pragmatic re-reading of religion, it was an important concern already in many approaches to religious belief in classical American pragmatism. These earlier analyses investigate, on the one hand, some

---

of "negative theology". If this double-bind in Putnam's complex explorations is only imperfectly reconstructed, his religious position may seem to be quite problematic. (See in this context Pihlström, "Rorty versus Putnam", 89.)

44 Putnam, *Jewish Philosophy*, 102.
45 Ibid.
46 Ibid., 67.
47 Ibid., 65.
48 Ibid., 64.
49 Pihlström, "Rorty versus Putnam", 89.

of the questions that were briefly addressed here, but they explore, on the other, central problems also that Putnam does not extensively inquire: the problem of evil, for instance, which Josiah Royce in his philosophical reflections on the *Book of Job* carefully examines[50], as well as the question raised by Charles Sanders Peirce in his essay "A Neglected Argument for the Reality of God", whether (in the wake of Kant's *Critiques*) elements of a (semiotically re-dimensioned) "pragmaticist" metaphysics might contribute to a solidification of belief in our secular age.[51]

4 Pluralism, Tolerance, and "Respecting the Other": Putnam's Essay "Let's Stop Using the Notion of 'Idolatry'"

Putnam carefully analyzes one further problem, however, that we have not focused on as yet. In his appreciative re-reading of the core image of monotheistic religions, "God", he cautiously avoids the narrowness which often afflicts 'traditional' theologies.[52] In his lecture "Let's Stop Using the Notion of 'Idolatry'" – which Putnam presented in 1999 at the Jerusalem Center for Religious Pluralism (the German translation of which I had the honor to publish in the book *Religion nach der Religionskritik*[53]) – questions concerning pluralism-sensitivity and "respect for the other" take center stage in Putnam's analyses of religious forms of life. The idea "that in the history of world religions the appearance of monotheism marks the

---

50 See Nagl, "Facing the Finite Nature of Life" as well as Nagl, "Cornel West's Royce-inspired (Neopragmatic) Exploration of Religion". For substantial problems connected with philosophical attempts to 'justify' evil see Pihlström, "The Problem of Evil and the Limits of Philosophy".
51 See in this context Nagl, "Charles Sanders Peirce's 'A Neglected Argument for the Reality of God'". In his analysis of Putnam's philosophy of religion Philström ("Rorty versus Putnam", 89) rightly points out that a crucial aspect of Putnam's position is "that he wants to avoid metaphysics at all costs"; this intention, Pihlström argues, is problematic. It cannot be justified as a necessary result of the *pragmatist* approach to religion, if one interprets pragmatism as a (Kant-based) post-Kantian project.
52 Putnam's pluralism-sensitive approach is expressed in his "Introduction" to *Jewish Philosophy* (7–8) as follows: my book, he writes, "is simply a way of indicating how one person who is religious but averse to 'ontotheology' has found [the Jewish philosophers analyzed in it] helpful. But I believe that all of us, who feel attached to religion [...] but are unwilling to see that attachment as requiring us to turn our backs on modernity [...] can find spiritual inspiration in the different ways in which these writers [...] resolved the conflicts that go with this predicament." Putnam's book is thus written "for a general reader who is motivated and willing to struggle with difficult – spiritually difficult – ideas."
53 Putnam, "Plädoyer für die Verabschiedung des Begriffs ‚Idolatrie'", 49–59.

transition from darkness to light"[54] has to be abandoned, Putnam argues. Along the lines of William James (who in *The Varieties of Religious Experience* writes that a plurality of religions is preferable to the insistence on religious uniformity[55]), as well as in accordance with Wittgenstein (who in his "Remarks on Frazer's *Golden Bough*" claims that neither St. Augustine nor the "Buddhist holy man" were in error in their religious views, except when they "set forth a theory"[56]), Putnam contends that not only monotheistic, but also non-monotheistic religions are able to introduce valuable insights into the religious discourse of mankind[57] – into an open discourse, that is, which is still unfinished today. An impressive example of this, Putnam argues, is Buddhism:

> Buddhists have meditated for more than 2000 years about the importance of compassion, practicing a life form which has its center in these meditations, and developed concepts which support it. Thus, the idea that these believers during all these times were unable to get to know things about what it means to lead a compassionate life that Jews and Christians have not also seen, is arrogance, and – even worse – comes close to a form of blindness.[58]

This, however, does not mean – Putnam is quick to point out – that "all religions are equally good"[59]: "I once heard how Wilfred Cantwell Smith [Chairperson of the 'Committee on the Study of Religion'] has answered this question", Putnam writes: "His answer was: 'I do not say that all religions are equally good. I do not even believe that any of the existing religions is unambiguously good'."[60]. Putnam agrees

---

54 Ibid, 52 (English translation L.N.)
55 James, *The Varieties of Religious Experience*, 486–87.
56 Wittgenstein, "Remarks on Frazer's *Golden Bough*", 119.
57 As Jürgen Habermas points out in *Auch eine Geschichte der Philosophie* (Vol. I, 358) this "tolerance" is a rather recent product of history: "In order to tolerate foreign thinking modes and ethical perceptions that, in our own assessment, we reject as wrong, a basis of common convictions is necessary which makes this reciprocal acceptance in social intercourse possible. The ethics of mutual respect as the basis of a seriously tolerant dealing with cultural and world-view related differences [...] certainly starts to develop only with the secularly justified formation of the constitutional principles of liberal democracies." (English translation L. N. The German original runs as follows: "Um fremde Denkweisen und andere ethische Auffassungen zu tolerieren, die wir aus der jeweils eigenen Sicht als falsch ablehnen, ist eine Basis gemeinsamer Überzeugungen nötig, die eine reziproke Anerkennung im Umgang miteinander ermöglichen. Die Moral der gleichen Achtung aller als Basis für einen ernstlich toleranten Umgang mit kulturellen und weltanschaulichen Differenzen [...] bildet sich gewiss erst mit den säkular begründeten Verfassungsgrundsätzen liberaler Demokratien heraus.")
58 Putnam, "Pladoyer für eine Verabschiedung des Begriffs ‚Idolatrie'" (English translation L.N.), 58.
59 Ibid., 57.
60 Ibid.

with Cantwell Smith that in every religious tradition there exist "wonderful communities of faith, but also terrible ones, and many things in between."[61] William James expressed this ambivalence as follows: in their best form "the fruits of religion" are "the best things that history has to show"[62]; all religions are accompanied, however, "by religion's wicked intellectual partner, the spirit of dogmatic dominion."[63]

"No tradition has a monopoly with regard to religious values and religious virtues,"[64] Putnam continues: "Every great religion contains, in its best possible mode, forms of religious perception which are less developed in other religions. There does not exist a single religion, whose value – put in economic terms – 'dominates' all other religions."[65] Putnam thus agrees with William James's unambiguous affirmation of pluralism in his book *The Varieties of Religious Experience*, where James rhetorically asks: "Is the existence of so many religious types and sects and creeds regrettable?" To this question, "I answer 'No' emphatically", James continues: "The divine can mean no single quality, [and] different men may all find worthy missions. Each attitude being a syllable in human nature's total message, it takes the whole of us to spell the meaning out completely."[66]

Secular democracies are, thus, well advised to legally secure the social space for a free development of this unfinished learning process: a process which rests on the mutual respect of "the other" – of the plurality of religions, as well as the secular distance from them.

Works Cited

Carlson, Thomas. "James and the Kantian tradition." *The Cambridge Companion to William James*. Ed. Ruth Anna Putnam. Cambridge, UK: Cambridge UP, 1997. 363–83.

Carnap, Rudolf, Hans Hahn, and Otto Neurath. "Wissenschaftliche Weltanschauung – der Wiener Kreis." *Otto Neurath: Wissenschaftliche Weltauffassung, Sozialismus und Logischer Empirismus*. Ed. Rainer Hegselmann. Frankfurt/M.: Suhrkamp, 1979. 81–101.

Habermas, Jürgen. *Auch eine Geschichte der Philosophie. Band 1. Die okzidentale Konstellation von Glauben und Wissen*. Berlin: Suhrkamp, 2019.

Hampe, Michael. *Die dritte Aufklärung*. Berlin: Nicolai, 2019.

---

61 Ibid.
62 James, *The Varieties of Religious Experience*, 259.
63 Ibid., 337.
64 Putnam, "Plädoyer für eine Verabschiedung des Begriffs ‚Idolatrie'" (English translation L.N.), 58.
65 Ibid.
66 James, *The Varieties of Religious Experience*, 487.

James, William. *The Will to Believe and Other Essays in Popular Philosophy*. New York: Dover Publications, 1956.
James, William. *The Varieties of Religious Experience*. Harmondsworth, Middlesex, England: Penguin Books, 1986.
Macarthur David. "Introduction". Hilary Putnam and Ruth-Anna Putnam, *Pragmatism as a Way of Life. The Lasting Legacy of William James and John Dewey*. Ed. David Macarthur. Cambridge, MA, and London, UK: The Belknap Press of Harvard UP, 2017. 1–9.
Murphey, Murray G. "Kant's children, the Cambridge pragmatists". *Transactions of the Charles S. Peirce Society* 4.1 (Winter 1968): 3–33.
Nagl, Ludwig, Ed. "Symposium zu Charles Taylor, *A Secular Age*". *Deutsche Zeitschrift für Philosophie* 57.2 (January 2009): 288–327.
Nagl, Ludwig. "Transformationen der Kantischen Postulatenlehre im 'Cambridge Pragmatism' (Charles S. Peirce, William James, Josiah Royce)". *Kantian Journal* 40.4 (Winter 2021): 43–75. https://journals.kantiana.ru/upload/uf/585/Kant_2021_4.pdf . Accessed: 4 April 2022.
Nagl, Ludwig. "Facing the Finite Nature of Life. Royce on 'Negativity' and Religion, and his Reflections on the Immanentism of Feuerbach and Nietzsche." Ludwig Nagl, *Toward a Global Discourse on Religion in a Secular Age. Essays on Philosophical Pragmatism*. Vienna-Zurich: LIT, 2021. 229–48.
Nagl, Ludwig. "Cornel West's Royce-inspired (Neo-)Pragmatic Exploration of Religion." Ludwig Nagl, *Toward a Global Discourse on Religion in a Secular Age. Essays on Philosophical Pragmatism*. Vienna-Zurich: LIT, 2021. 221–27.
Nagl, Ludwig. "Charles Sanders Peirce's 'A Neglected Argument for the Reality of God'." Ludwig Nagl, *Toward a Global Discourse on Religion in a Secular Age. Essays on Philosophical Pragmatism*. Vienna-Zurich: LIT, 2021. 137–50.
Nagl, Ludwig. "Religion in einem 'säkularen Zeitalter': Glaube als 'Option' (Hans Joas) und 'Shapes of Faith Today' (Charles Taylor)". *Säkularismus, Postsäkularismus und die Zukunft der Religionen. Festschrift für Yvanka Raynova zum 60. Geburtstag*. Ed. Hans-Werner Ruckenbauer and Susanne Moser. Berlin: J.B. Metzler/Springer, 2022. 167–89.
Nagl, Ludwig. "Religion". *Wittgenstein-Handbuch*. Ed. Stefan Majetschak and Anja Weiberg. Berlin: J.B.Metzler/Springer, 2022. 362–66.
Pihlström, Sami. "Rorty versus Putnam." Sami Pihlström, *Pragmatic Pluralism and the Problem of God*. New York: Fordham UP, 2013. 73–97.
Pihlström, Sami. "The Problem of Evil and the Limits of Philosophy." Sami Philstrom, *Pragmatic Pluralism and the Problem of God*. New York: Fordham UP, 2013. 129–56.
Putnam, Hilary. "Wittgenstein on Religious Belief." Hilary Putnam, *Renewing Philosophy*. Cambridge, MA, and London, UK: Harvard UP, 1992. 134–57.
Putnam, Hilary. "A Reconsideration of Deweyan Democracy." Hilary Putnam, *Renewing Philosophy*. Cambridge, MA, and London, UK: Harvard UP, 1992. 180–200.
Putnam, Hilary. "Die anhaltende Aktualität von William James" ("The Permanence of William James," German translation Ludwig Nagl). *Deutsche Zeitschrift für Philosophie* 41.2 (Summer 1993). 189–99.
Putnam, Hilary. "Rules, attunement, and 'applying words to the world'. The struggle to understand Wittgenstein's vision of language." *The Legacy of Wittgenstein: Pragmatism or Deconstruction*. Ed. Ludwig Nagl and Chantal Mouffe. Frankfurt/M.: Peter Lang, 2001. 9–23.
Putnam, Hilary. *The Collapse of the Fact-Value Dichotomy*. Cambridge, MA, and London, UK: Harvard UP, 2002.

Putnam, Hilary. "Plädoyer für die Verabschiedung des Begriffs 'Idolatrie'" (German version of Putnam's lecture "Let's Stop Using the Notion of ‚Idolatry'"). *Religion nach der Religionskritik*. Ed. Ludwig Nagl. Vienna-Berlin: Oldenbourg: Akademie Verlag, 2003. 49–59.

Putnam, Hilary. *Ethics without Ontology*. Cambridge, MA: Harvard UP, 2004.

Putnam, Hilary. *Jewish Philosophy as a Guide to Life. Rosenzweig, Buber, Levinas, Wittgenstein*. Bloomington and Indianapolis: Indiana UP, 2008.

Putnam, Hilary. "Spiritual Encounters of a Philosopher of Science." Interview with Zackary Sholem Berger. *The Forward*, 4 September 2008, 1–4. https://forward.com/culture/14256/spiritual-encounter-of-a-philosopher-of-science/. . Accessed: 4 April 2022.

Putnam, Hilary, and Ruth Anna Putnam. *Pragmatism as a Way of Life. The Lasting Legacy of William James and John Dewey*. Ed. David Macarthur. Cambridge, MA, and London, UK: The Belknap Press of Harvard UP, 2017.

Rawls, John. *A Theory of Justice*. Cambridge, MA: The Belknap Press of Harvard UP, 1971.

Rawls, John. "The Priority of Right and Ideas of the Good". John Rawls. *Collected Papers*. Ed. Samuel Freeman. Cambridge, MA, and London, UK: Harvard UP, 1999. 449–72.

Schlette, Magnus. "'How you understand can only be shown by how you live.' Putnam's Reconsideration of Dewey's *A Common Faith*". *The Varieties of Transcendence. Pragmatism and the Theory of Religion*. Ed. Hermann Deuser, Hans Joas, Mathias Jung, and Magnus Schlette. New York: Fordham UP, 2016. 128–41.

Taylor, Charles. *A Secular Age*. Cambridge, MA, and London, UK: The Belknap Press of Harvard UP, 2007.

Taylor, Charles. "Shapes of Faith Today". *Renewing the Church in a Secular Age. Holistic Dialogue and Kenotic Vision*. Ed. Charles Taylor, José Casanova, George F. McLean and João J. Vila-Chã, The Council for Research in Values and Philosophy: Washington, D.C., 2016. 269–81.

Tumulty Peter J. "Hilary Putnam's Position between Dewey and Buber: A Pragmatist's Reconciling of Philosophy and Religious Faith." *The Pluralist* 14.2 (Summer 2019): 53–74. https://doi.org/10.5406/pluralist.14.2.0053. Accessed: 4 April 2022.

Wittgenstein, Ludwig. "Remarks on Frazer's *Golden Bough*." Ludwig Wittgenstein, *Philosophical Occasions*. Ed. James Klagge and Alfred Nordmann. Indianapolis and Cambridge: Hackett Publishing Company, 1993. 119–55.

Wolterstorff, Nicholas. "The Religious Turn in Philosophy and Art". *Religion nach der Religionskritik*. Ed. Ludwig Nagl. Vienna-Berlin: Oldenbourg-Akademie Verlag, 2003. 273–82.

Ruth Abbey
Angles and Angels: Charles Taylor and Steven Pinker on Moral Progress in History

> He was bursting with energy and optimism. "The world looks a dangerous place, but we're making progress. There are fewer and fewer wars [...]" he said, giving Blomkvist a book by Steven Pinker which was lying around somewhere, still unread.
> (Largerkrantz 126)

Abstract: This paper examines some of the areas of convergence between Steven Pinker's 2011 work *The Better Angels of our Nature: Why Violence has Declined* and some of Charles Taylor's most recent thinking on ethical growth across history. Part 1 provides an overview of Taylor's thoughts about this topic. Because the reduction of violence turns out to be central to Taylor's account of ethical growth in history, I move to Pinker's position on this topic in Part 2. In Part 3 I point out the ways in which it seems counter-intuitive to compare Taylor and Pinker based on some of Taylor's own remarks about Pinker. Part 4 takes up the fact that attitudes toward religion seem to be the key cleavage between them. I conclude by proposing that there is more overlap between Taylor and Pinker's work than Taylor's remarks permit, and that attending to their overlapping consensus is a more informed and more generous way of situating Pinker vis-à-vis Taylor.

This unnamed and unread book is probably *The Better Angels of our Nature: Why Violence has Declined.* Yet the key message that Johannes Forsell takes from Pinker's tome, that "we're making progress", is also a key point in some of Charles Taylor's most recent thinking. In late October 2021, Taylor presented his paper "History of Ethical Growth" to the Czech Christian Academy.[1] The paper was circulated at a conference in November 2021 on "Global History, Ethical Growth and Higher Time" sponsored by the Catholic University of America. Drawing upon these sources, and other writings by Taylor where relevant, I start by summarizing Taylor's thinking about ethical growth across history (Part 1). Because the reduction of violence turns out to be central to Taylor's account, I move to Pinker's thought on this topic (Part 2). I acknowledge the ways in which it seems counterintuitive to com-

---
[1] This document is divided into ten sections, so I cite the relevant section.

https://doi.org/10.1515/9783111247878-006

pare Taylor and Pinker based on some of Taylor's own remarks about Pinker (Part 3).[2] The status of religion seems to be an important sticking point in Taylor's response to Pinker, so Part 4 surveys Pinker's views about religion. I conclude by proposing that there is more connection between Taylor and Pinker than Taylor's remarks permit, and that attending to their overlapping consensus on modernity's moral progress is a more informed and more generous way of situating Pinker vis-à-vis Taylor.

1 Taylor on Ethical Growth

Taylor sees "human history" as "the site of a slow growth in ethical vision" ("History" 1) discerning "a drive to ethical ascent" ("History" 4) in it. He traces the arc of "mankind's ethical growth" ("History" 2) back to the Axial Age, as conceived by Karl Jaspers. Taylor defines this age as "the extraordinary period in the last millennium BCE when various "higher" forms of religion appeared seemingly independently in different civilizations, marked by founding figures such as Confucius, Gautama, Socrates, and the Hebrew prophets." ("Axial Revolution?" 34) Although he refers to religions here, some of his other references to the Axial Age speak of religions and philosophies. Part 3 of "History of Ethical Growth" refers to the "faiths or philosophies which descend from" this age, while Part 2 refers to them generically as "new doctrines". In *Retrieving Realism* Taylor likewise writes of "philosophy in the age of Plato and Aristotle" when describing the Axial Age (166).

Although these Axial Age traditions arose separately and in different places, Taylor detects two key features in this watershed in humanity's history of ethical growth. The first is that it "offered new ideals of the human which were genuinely universal, no longer simply dictated by the civilizational or social ethos" ("History" 2). The "great Axial revolutions [...] introduced the notion of the human being as such, or of universal humanity, an idea with strong normative consequences" ("Foreword" viii). Taylor signals his agreement with Jan Assman's claim about the "implied globality" of these ideals ("Axial Revolution?" 30 cf. "Fellow Travellers" 6). The second key feature is that no single tradition could capture the full gamut of this growth; instead, it can be seen, in retrospect at least, that a form of ecumenism was needed, with each tradition complementing the other. "We can see here the germ of what we now recognize as the ecumenical sources of ethical growth: this is not sustained and furthered alone by any one spiritual source." (Taylor "History" 2)

---

[2] I have not found any comments by Pinker about Taylor.

The first key feature, the universalism harbored in these traditions, was at odds with the actual practices of the societies from which they emanated. These values go against "the grain of the world" as Martin puts it ("Foreword" vii-ix), which throws up numerous obstacles to their realization. At its inception, each tradition existed at what Taylor, borrowing from David Martin, calls an "angle" of transcendence from that society ("Foreword" viii). That angle could be more or less acute but whatever its size, it meant that at first only a few atypical individuals – philosophers, prophets, sages, or small groups – could strive to live in accordance with these values ("Foreword" vii). But rather than being dismissed as appealing but utopian, the shared ideals of these traditions very slowly served to transform the societies they arose in and thus to reduce the angle of transcendence between them and ambient social practices. The vision was gradually disseminated to more and more people with the aim of bringing discordant social practices more fully into line with the vision.

The ideals of human equality and human rights provide one example of the moral growth to have emerged from the religions and philosophies of the Axial Age. These stretched from the French Revolution to the UN's Universal Declaration of Human Rights (Taylor "History" 3, 8). As a consequence of this view of human equality we have, along the way, seen the abolition of de jure slavery. Even if some individuals remain enslaved to others in the twenty-first century via forms of human trafficking and forced labor practices, in Taylor's estimation this still marks a qualitative advance on societies that institutionalized slavery. Insofar as anything analogous to slavery exists today, it is typically condemned. Or those who perpetuate it deny that they are doing so, and perhaps even redescribe these practices. Xi Jin-Ping is not, for example, enslaving China's Muslim Ouiguirs but re-educating them "to make them happy, lobotomized members of a socialist society with Chinese characteristics" ("History" 7, 8 cf. "Foreword" x).

The same applies to human rights. In an earlier expression of this point, Taylor uses a western example to illustrate his claim that human rights have become the expected standard. "Even when they are doing something terrible to other people's human rights, like going to war in Iraq, they find some justification precisely in the name of human rights: 'They [Saddam Hussein's government] are violating human rights! They're against peace!'" ("History, Critique" 4) Paradoxically perhaps, Taylor takes this fact that states or groups who violate the equality norm feel compelled to engage in hypocrisy to be an important strand of evidence for his claim about ethical growth ("History" 8). In making this point he could easily invoke La Rochefoucauld's maxim that 'hypocrisy is the tribute that vice pays to virtue'.

Taylor fully recognizes that this dissemination of Axial Age ideals and the transformation of societies to approximate them, although very gradual, has never been linear. The move toward realizing these values "is far from [an] assured and smoothly inevitable process" ("History" 1). It is "messy and chaotic" rather than "smooth and continuous" ("History" 2, cf. 1, 4, 6). He also concedes that some of the steps to realize Axial Age values can themselves breed violence, with the French Revolution and the Russian Revolution providing but two ready examples. Such violence challenges the ideal of equality advanced by both Revolutions ("History" 4). If, looking back on these developments, all Taylor saw was this sort of emancipatory action and violent reaction dynamic, it would be hard for him to maintain his belief in "ethical steps forward" ("History" 5). But in addition to the above point about hypocrisy, in these developments he sees the creation of genuinely new forms of political action and collective co-existence which suggests that humans are not mired in this sort of rigid binary movement between action and reaction.

Here Taylor attributes great weight to the rise of non-violent political action, non-violent struggles for recognition and emancipation. He associates this with Gandhi's anti-colonialism in the first instance but notes how this has been emulated across the globe by Martin Luther King in the US civil rights movement, the Philippine opposition to Ferdinand Marcos Senior, in uprisings in the former Communist eastern bloc countries, and of course in South Africa, culminating in the Truth and Reconciliation Commission. The "immense ethical advantage of such movements [...] is that they offer a hope of reducing the legitimacy, and also the frequency of acts of violence" ("History" 3). These developments reduce the angle of transcendence between their societies and Axial Age ideals and elevate "the repertory of effective historical action to new ethical heights" ("History" 8).

Yet in Taylor's estimation, such opportunities for peaceful resolution of a society's conflicts do even more than reduce the role of violence in human history. They point to a way of humans living together in diversity in more productive ways. In an earlier work Taylor had pointed to Poland's Adam Michnik and the Dalai Lama as figures whose attitudes toward violence presaged new ways for humans to live together ("Alchemy"). Another example he offers comes from the US civil rights activists Martin Luther King and John Lewis who argued that among its many benefits, lessening racism in US society would allow its white populations to relieve themselves of the burden of fear and hatred that goes with racism, however it manifests itself. This approach does not deny the many and significant harms that racism causes those on its receiving end, but at the same time it re-frames racism as a force that corrodes the well-being of those who harbor it and limits their capacity to lead a full and free life ("History" 8).

For Taylor this new possibility of human co-habitation and co-operation often has a religious underpinning, but it need not. It is, to quote a section he cites from the Papal encyclical *Fratelli Tutti* "a philosophical anthropology which sees us realizing more fully our humanity through contact and exchange with people and cultures beyond our original comfort zone." ("History" 9). Of course Taylor is asking for this view of fuller realization to be taken toward former enemies, who are more than just outside our comfort zone, but against whom there might be a long history of legitimate and well-founded grievances. But here he would no doubt point to South Africa's Truth and Reconciliation Commission as an example of this approach toward erstwhile oppressors.

As my reconstruction of his position shows, Taylor places violence reduction and delegitimation at the centre of his history of humanity's ethical growth. It is violence in multiple manifestations that the Axial Age values, and in particular Buddhism and later Christianity, militate against. As religions that call for the "total abandonment" of violence, they operate at especially acute angles to their societies and "regard political power, rivalry, dominance, as practices to be transcended." ("Foreword" ix) Taylor concedes that his argument about "the actual history of ethical growth" might "sound like a way-out, even crackpot thesis," but counters that "there are some interesting indications in history, which seem to lend it some support" ("Charles Taylor Responds" 813). As the following section demonstrates, Pinker agrees with the violence reduction and delegitimation part of Taylor's thesis. Indeed, Taylor's assertion that "we have in the modern world highly peaceful societies, where the level of everyday violence is quite low. Indeed, in some of these societies, the level is very much lower than in earlier epochs" ("Notes" 205) could have come straight out of *Better Angels*. For his part, Pinker also acknowledges that his own claims about violence reduction might seem counter-intuitive and hard for audiences to accept (Pinker xxii, 1).

2 Pinker on Violence

In contrast to Taylor's expansive view of humanity's moral growth in the two millennia since the beginning of the common era, *Better Angels* articulates and defends the more circumscribed thesis that western societies have grown less violent over the last five centuries. This might represent "the most important thing that has ever happened in human history" (Pinker xxi). Pinker engages in historical, cultural, sociological, political, and statistical analyses to defend his claim about violence reduction. He contends that "changes in our cultural and material milieu [...] have given our peaceable motives the upper hand" (Pinker xxiii), attributing declines in violence to "social, cultural and material conditions" (Pinker 671). His identification of six trends, nine psychological forces and five historical forces that have contributed to this outcome (Pinker xxiv-xxv) indicates the complexity of his approach. Because the ambition and scope of his work pose a challenge to summarizing it, my focus falls on those elements that dovetail most closely with Taylor's views of ethical growth.

As Ben Laws notes, Pinker nowhere provides a definition of violence. This lacuna frees him to range across multiple manifestations of violence – homicide, war, genocide, slavery, capital punishment, torture, domestic violence, sexual violence, violence based on sexual orientation, corporal punishment in families and schools, and animal cruelty. From this catalog, violence seems to be something that assaults and injures or kills the body. Indeed, toward the end of *Better Angels* Pinker lists the wide variety of violent phenomena to have declined and observes that "the only thing these superseded practices have in common is that they physically hurt a victim" (Pinker 672).

Yet as early as the second paragraph of the book's preface, we see that things are a bit more complicated than this as Pinker draws on, without naming, Thomas Hobbes in chapter XIII of *Leviathan*. "Daily existence is very different if you always have to worry about being abducted, raped, or killed and it's hard to develop sophisticated arts, learning or commerce if the institutions that support them are looted and burned as quickly as they are built." (Pinker xxi) This specter of chronic anxiety suggests that Pinker does recognize that fear of violence itself can be disruptive. While he might not equate fear of violence with violence, in such moments he tends toward a Hobbesian awareness about how corrosive worry, fear, and insecurity can be to quality of life.

This passage also intimates that the absence of violence might not be synonymous with the attainment of peace, contrary to Pinker's frequent implications. He claims, for example, that "today we may be living in the most peaceable era in our species' existence", enjoying "unprecedented levels of peaceful coexistence" (Pinker xxi). Chapter Five is entitled "The Long Peace" and chapter six "The New Peace". Yet since the work of Johan Galtung, many theorists have preferred a more positive conception of peace than simply the absence of violence. As Jeremy Waldron points out in his review of *Better Angels*, these "issues about Hobbesian fear" are very relevant given that the fear instilled in societies by the Cold War's pervasive threat of nuclear war could be construed as a form of violence. But because Pinker tends to take bodily damage as a measure of violence, this shows up as a non-violent phase of twentieth-century history (Waldron 2).

Pinker's Hobbesian moment early in the book's Preface might also go some way toward answering another of Waldron's questions about whether "the destruction of things […] like buildings and cities" (Waldron 2) is included in Pinker's concept of violence. Pinker's reference to looting and burning the institutions that support arts, education, and commerce would suggest so. There is, after all, no necessary reason why violence against bodies must damage property, although it can be hard to avoid during events like aerial bombing. Of course, destroying or damaging buildings and cities can be a means of harming bodies, but it is not synonymous with violence against them. So already we can detect that Pinker's claim that violence has reduced poses some very complicated questions, and in particular the philosophical one about what violence is and whether its absence is tantamount to peace.

Yet whatever violence encompasses for Pinker, cultural and structural changes in western societies play an important role in his narrative about its reduction over time. One seminal structural change has been the rise of the modern state. Pinker describes "the consolidation of a genuine Leviathan after centuries of anarchy in Europe's feudal patchwork of baronies and fiefs. Centralized monarchies gained in strength [and] brought the warring knights under control" (*Better Angels* 74). His emphasis on the consolidation of state power is one of the reasons why Jeremy Fortier imputes a Hobbesian liberalism to Pinker. As Fortier reads Pinker, "politics and political authority have an essential role to play in a peaceful world [... they] change the incentive structures that lead individuals to opt for immediate over aggregate benefits." (Fortier 469)

A key cultural change that complemented and furthered violence reduction is outlined in chapter 3, "The Civilizing Process" which signals Pinker's debt to the work of Norbert Elias. This civilizing process unfolded across six centuries, began with the upper echelons of European society but gradually trickled down to the middle classes, and focused on personal habits, practices, and etiquette (Pinker 72). It trained individuals to exhibit "refinement, self-control and consideration of others" (Pinker 70 cf. 592) and to experience shame should their conduct fall short of these new standards of appropriate behavior (Pinker 71).[3] Fortier proposes that a lot of what Pinker takes from Elias could also be found in Hobbes, who requires citizens to be sociable and self-controlled while recognizing that these virtues are not self-generated but need to be inculcated via education and continuing socialization (Fortier 464, 483). He advances a reading of Hobbes that he contrasts with the "well known accounts of liberal politics as a system of "atomistic individualism" (Fortier 464, cf. 483). He cites Taylor's "Atomism" essay as a way of reading Hobbes that Pinker would do well to avoid (Fortier 464 n18–19).

Yet this is a strange way to interpret Taylor's essay. "Atomism" is not about liberalism as such but about social contract theories that promote the primacy of individual rights or forms of utilitarianism that justify society in terms of the benefits it returns to individuals. Taylor is not, of course, implacably opposed to considering how society benefits individuals via rights or utilities, but the key la-

---

[3] Fortier suggests that Pinker has muted Elias' analysis of its critical tones and taken a more optimistic view of the civilizing process (469–70).

cuna of atomistic doctrines is their neglect of any corresponding attention to social belonging and the obligations it brings. Within this wider context, he mentions Hobbes as a thinker associated with "the seventeenth century revolution in the terms of normative discourse" ("Atomism" 187). But given the obvious difficulties of associating Hobbes too closely with the 'primacy of rights' thesis, Taylor advances Locke as a paradigm case of this approach, with Robert Nozick representing a twentieth-century legatee ("Atomism" 188). Hobbes is mentioned again in Taylor's essay as someone who recognizes the misery and poverty of life without society in the state of nature ("Atomism" 190). He makes his final appearance when Taylor illustrates his claim that primacy of rights approaches typically avoid rich theories of the human good, stripping this down instead to the satisfaction of desire ("Atomism" 201). Taylor's "Atomism" essay has been widely read and often misread but it is hard to follow Fortier in offering this as an interpretation of Hobbes' political theory as asocial. This also means that his implied contrast of Pinker and Taylor as readers of Hobbes misses its mark.

As is well known, Elias also plays a key role in Taylor's analysis of secularity. Taylor focuses on what Elias teaches us about the gradual disciplining of the body and behavior and connects it with changing conceptions of intimacy, the rise of the buffered self, and the larger process of religious reform and what Taylor calls excarnation (*Secular* 137–43). Taylor does, however, touch in passing on what Pinker derives from Elias which is the delegitimation of violence. In a passage that would be right at home in *Better Angels*, Taylor reports that

> Elias shows that the "civilizing process" involved our taking this distance from a whole range of powerful emotions: rage and the fascination with violence, sexual desire, and our fascination with bodily processes [...] Our ancestors permitted themselves accesses of rage, they more frankly glorified in violence, they flocked to scenes of cruel punishment, inflicted on humans and animals; all things that tend to horrify us today [...] We allow ourselves to enjoy violence only when it is derealized, in fiction, or television presentations which have the same feel as fiction. (*Secular* 141)

As Fortier recognizes, Pinker's account of violence reduction in western history "eventually does move beyond Hobbes, because he is not satisfied with the absolutist political solution" (Fortier 471). Pinker does acknowledge that the state itself can inflict violence on its citizens and claims consequently that "once raiding and feuding have been brought under control in a society, the greatest opportunity for reducing violence is reducing *government* violence" (Pinker 159, emphasis original). He adds the importance of the state being democratic to continue its contribution to violence reduction. Democracy "would turn out to be one of the greatest violence reduction technologies since the appearance of government itself" (Pinker 161 cf. 278–9, 341).

Pinker also lays out how the state's power over its citizens has increasingly been constrained by the Humanitarian Revolution which brought about a change not just in private sensibilities, per the Civilizing Process, but also brought less tolerance for violence in public capacities. "Superstitious killing, cruel punishments, frivolous executions, and chattel slavery may not have been obliterated from the face of the earth, but they have certainly been pushed to the margins" (Pinker 188). In these ways, the modern state became less and less Leviathan-like towards its citizens. This development was further compounded by what Pinker calls in chapter seven "The Rights Revolutions":

> Though people have lost none of their taste for consuming simulated and voluntary violence [...] Western culture has been extending its distaste for violence farther and farther down the magnitude scale. The post war revulsion against [...] war and genocide has spread to forms that kill by the hundreds, tens, and single digits, such as rioting, lynching and hate crimes. It has extended from killing to other forms of harm such as rape, assault, battering and intimidation. It has spread to vulnerable classes of victims ... such as racial minorities, women, children, homosexuals, and animals. (Pinker 379–80)

Another similarity between Pinker and Taylor's approaches appears as Pinker concedes that the reduction in violence he traces "has not been smooth, [and] it has not brought violence down to zero" (Pinker xxi). He recognizes, for example, the counter-Enlightenment's rejection of the Enlightenment assumption "that violence was a problem to be solved" (Pinker 187, cf. 239–42). Just as Taylor points to setbacks in the progress of non-violence, such as the violent reactions to the French and Russian revolutions, so Pinker acknowledges that decivilizing processes have undone some of the cultural and psychological work of the civilizing process. He sees the 1960s as one such phase of decivilization (Pinker 106–16) where, despite high levels of economic growth, low levels of unemployment, relatively high levels of economic equality, a growth in social programs, and progress in racial equality, homicide rates in the US increased. Other forms of violent crime such as rape, assault, robbery and theft rose too (Pinker 107–8).[4] He explains this by reference to "a change in cultural norms" (Pinker 108 cf. 109–110) where the emphasis shifted away from self-restraint to self-expression and personal liberation. However, the 1990s saw, according to Pinker, a recivilizing process that undid some of these effects (Pinker 116–28).

And just as the road to violence reduction has not been straight or narrow, so it "is not guaranteed to continue" (Pinker xxi). Pinker counsels against complacen-

---

4 His inclusion of robbery and theft again suggests that, as noted above, he sometimes includes damage to property rather than just to persons in his conception of violence.

cy: "we enjoy the peace we find today because people in past generations were appalled by the violence in their time and worked to reduce it, and so we should work to reduce the violence that remains in our time." (Pinker xxvi) But "[o]nly preachers and pop singers profess" that violence could be expunged from social life entirely (Pinker 646). Pinker's best hope is that excess and unnecessary violence will continue to diminish while "a measured degree of violence, even if only held in reserve" remains "necessary in the form of police forces and armies to deter predation or to incapacitate those who cannot be deterred" (Pinker 646). Of course one major difference between Pinker and Taylor is that Pinker sources these outcomes to Enlightenment Humanism (Pinker 180, 183, 188, 696) rather than the Axial Age. To discern what might be at stake in this difference, Taylor's treatment of Pinker, and then Pinker's treatment of religion are explored in the following sections.

3 Taylor on Pinker

In *The Language Animal: The Full Shape of the Human Linguistic Capacity*, Taylor engages with Pinker as a theorist of language. His first reference appears quite positive, as Taylor seems to agree about language's transformative role in facilitating co-operation (70). In a later work, however, Taylor elaborates on and criticizes Pinker's emphasis on language as a mechanism for co-ordination in his 1994 work *The Language Instinct*. Pinker is said to give "a short scientific sermon" ("Language not mysterious?" 14n12) on the fact that having language to afford such cooperation does not make humans markedly different from animals. Taylor is dubious about whether such a "reductive theory of language entirely focused on the factual-practical" ("Language not mysterious?" 14n12) is viable. He accuses Pinker of misconstruing the debate about the role of language by insisting that the understanding of humans should not be separated from their biology. Taylor describes this misrepresentation as "typical of his approach" ("Language not mysterious?" 14n12) without providing further examples of Pinkerian misrepresentation. Towards the conclusion of *The Language Animal*, Pinker is paired with Noam Chomsky as Taylor claims that we do not fully understand the role of language in encoding information. The Chomsky-Pinker version of how this works has its problems but it is not something we fully understand yet (*Language Animal* 332). Of the other three references to Pinker in this work, one is made in passing (*Language Animal* 86n3), while two mention his views about the relationship between color vocabularies and color discriminations (*Language Animal* 324n11; 328n21).

Taylor has been more overtly critical of Pinker on other topics, pairing him with Richard Dawkins as a thinker he disagrees with. Pinker "feels at home in an Immanent Frame and thinks that the world is getting better, i.e. less violent, by itself as part of our evolution" ("Democracy" 245 cf. 246). Yet if Taylor is imputing to Pinker the view that the forms of violence reduction he lays out have an evolutionary basis, that would be a misreading. In chapter 9 Pinker entertains but rejects the hypothesis that humans have evolved away from violence, saying that "while recent biological evolution may, in theory, have tweaked our inclinations toward violence and nonviolence, we have no good evidence that it actually has." Instead, we "have good evidence for changes that could not possibly be genetic, because they unfolded on time scales that are too rapid to be explained by natural selection" (Pinker 621). As we have seen, Pinker takes a multifaceted, non-reductive approach to the move away from violence in modernity and much of his explanation draws from political and cultural changes. His explanation privileges "transformations that are strictly environmental: changes in historical circumstances that engage a fixed human nature in different ways" (Pinker xxv). And to compound this non-evolutionary interpretation, we have seen Pinker's belief that the future of violence reduction is not guaranteed.

While Taylor errs in imputing an evolutionary approach to Pinker, he might be more accurate in suggesting that "[f]or Steven Pinker, we already have all we need to know or decide what to do, what is bad, what is good, within this … purely immanent, perspective." ("Democracy" 245) Preserving and reproducing a less violent society is, for Pinker, a matter of correct understanding and political will. However, the type of knowledge needed is not about evolutionary trends but about cultural attitudes and practices and political structures. Pinker is coupled again with Dawkins as Taylor reflects on the concept of postsecularity. For Taylor this term signals a future in which people occupy the Immanent Frame in different ways – some immanently, others transcendentally – and all respect this diversity. Living within the Immanent Frame does not negate the need for and experience of transcendence. But we are not yet at the point of postsecularity because "people like Dawkins and Pinker [...] think that everybody who does not agree with them is stupid, evil, unsophisticated, or whatever" ("Democracy" 246).

It seems then that what really divides Taylor and Pinker is the status of religious belief in modernity. Pinker self-defines as a Jewish atheist (Pinker 374), and in Taylor's terms, he is an exclusive humanist who accepts "no final goals beyond human flourishing; nor any allegiance to anything else beyond this flourishing" (*Secular* 18 cf. 245). In addition to this, Pinker qualifies as one who is content to live the immanent frame in a closed way, not feeling any lack or shortcoming in the absence of personal religious belief (*Secular* 548–50, 555–57, 579, 595, 774). As a religious believer, Taylor strives to persuade that the immanent frame can be lived in an open way that is amenable to the experience of transcendence (*Secular* 291, 544–45, 548–49, 556–57, 565). But, per Taylor, Pinker goes beyond these two features of personal religious belief or lack thereof and experience of this as satisfying or not by espousing that his is the superior way to live, free of religious belief. As we have seen, Taylor's hope is that those within the immanent frame can recognize and respect the different ways in which that frame can be lived. Pinker (and Dawkins) are not there yet according to Taylor.

4 Pinker on Religion

Some of Pinker's critics accuse him of taking a one-sided approach to the Enlightenment and modernity by seeing only their positive features (Mitzen 527, Gray, Waldron 5). This one-sidedness seems, initially at least, to be mirrored in his attitude toward religion. *Better Angels* launches a broadside against the Hebrew Bible (6–12), finding in it "one long celebration of violence" (6 cf. 146) while the New Testament and early Christianity are seen as "sanctifying cruelty" (Pinker 15). It is helpful to recall that Pinker is using these cultural sources to illustrate how much more normalized violence was when they were created compared to today (Pinker 11–12). Contemporary religious believers "respect modern norms of nonviolence and toleration" (Pinker 17) but turn reverently to sources that convey very different attitudes toward violence. His characterization of this as "benevolent hypocrisy" (Pinker 17) reminds us of Taylor's point about those who violate contemporary norms of equality and rights being unwilling to admit that they do so. But this is an exaggeration when applied to Pinker's believers because they are not doing one thing while saying another. If they adopt "discreet neglect of the bloodthirsty passages of the Old Testament" (Pinker 678) they nonetheless practice what they preach – i.e. nonviolence. It is just that Pinker deems their practice to be discordant with their religious sources.

Yet religious believers do not seem to be unique in being oddly positioned toward their sources. Pinker chooses an image from Abraham Lincoln to capture his psychology of violence reduction, saying that "the better angels of our nature ... incline us toward cooperation and peace" (Pinker xxiii). Yet he nowhere reflects on the biblical source or religious resonances of this titular imagery, nor on the fact that Lincoln was addressing a largely religious audience when closing his first inaugural address as President-elect in 1861. Pinker thus appropriates a religious image as a title for what seems to be his argument against religion playing any productive role in violence reduction.

Yet *Better Angels* does modify this one-sided picture of religion, citing Isaiah on converting swords to ploughshares, Jesus on turning the other cheek, and Christianity's beginnings as "a pacifist movement" (162). However, Pinker laments what little difference these attitudes made to the "nearly constant state of warfare" (Pinker 162) in the ensuing centuries. But in a major concession, he proposes that "the foundation of morality" can be observed in "the many versions of the Golden Rule that have been discovered by the world's major religions" (Pinker 182). Morality's foundation is the possibility of co-operation and reciprocity facilitated by "the interchangeability of perspectives and the opportunity the world provides for positive-sum games" (Pinker 182).

Pinker also contends that the Enlightenment Humanism that bequeathed so many of the attitudes and practices against violence was "not necessarily atheistic" (183), being compatible with a form of Deism, for example. But his key point is that its arguments against violence were proposed in secular terms. Enlightenment Humanism "makes no use of scripture, Jesus, ritual, religious law, divine purpose, immortal souls, an afterlife, a messianic age, or a God who responds to individual people" (Pinker 183). As such it could potentially appeal to a wide cross section of people, no matter what their religious convictions. Although the book does not mention John Rawls, Pinker is portraying Enlightenment Humanism as offering a form of public reason. And as Pinker is quick to acknowledge, Enlightenment Humanism must sweep aside any secular sources of value as well that are incompatible with the project of violence reduction (Pinker 183).

The book's final chapter provides a balance sheet of how Pinker sees religion. He reiterates his earlier view that "the scriptures" – by which he seems to mean the Old Testament – "present a God who delights in genocide, rape, slavery and the execution of nonconformists" (Pinker 676). For centuries these texts were used to justify violence toward infidels, women, children, heretics, homosexuals, and animals. The European Wars of Religion were "the second-bloodiest period in modern Western history" (Pinker 677 cf. 234). When the Enlightenment strove to curb some of these practices, institutionalized religion resisted. Any "theory that religion is a force for peace [...] does not fit the facts of history" (Pinker 677).

Yet contrary to these appearances Pinker does not, pace Christopher Hitchens, maintain that religion poisons everything (Pinker 678). For one thing, Pinker recognizes that religion is not one thing. He is cognizant that *"particular* religious movements at particular times [...] *have* worked against violence" (Pinker 677 emphasis original). His examples include the abolitionism and pacifism of Quakerism, the role of African American churches in the civil rights movement, and individuals such as Martin Luther King Jr, and the late Bishop Desmond Tutu. Hence his conclusion that "[r]eligion plays no single role in the history of violence" (Pinker 678). Nothing in this more balanced appraisal suggests to me that Pinker thinks that religious people are "stupid, evil, [or] unsophisticated" (Taylor "Democracy" 246). Instead, Pinker's admissions – that Judaism and Christianity can endorse peace; that their followers could support the principles of Enlightenment Humanism because they were not based on atheistic premises; and that religion should not be essentialized – indicate that he is less hostile toward religion than he might appear. They also signal that he might be more amenable to Taylor's narrative, which locates the beginnings of violence reduction in the Axial Age, than the reading of him as taking a one-sided, antagonistic approach to permits.

Taylor, conversely, does not shy away from the fact that "most historical religion has been deeply intricated with violence, from human sacrifice down to inter-communal massacres" (*Secular* 639, 688–89). He has also written about "categorical violence" directed against whole groups of people ("Notes on Sources" 188). And he is cognizant of the role that religions have traditionally played in fomenting such violence (*Secular* 688). While occupying quite different underlying positions toward religion, Pinker and Taylor might be able to attain an overlapping consensus when it comes to violence reduction, agreeing on its manifestations and values and even on some of the historical narrative.

Borrowing it from Rawls, this ideal of an overlapping consensus appears a number of times in different contexts within Taylor's work. He employs it initially as a device for thinking about the attainment of a genuine, international agreement on human rights ("Conditions Unforced Consensus"). He returns it to its original Rawlsian domestic context in *Secularism and Freedom of Conscience* where he and Jocelyn Maclure accept, as their point of departure, Rawls' depiction of the conditions of modern pluralism, including such ideas as the burdens of judgment and the need for an overlapping consensus on the principles of political co-operation (10–12, 15–18, 20–21, 107–08). The ideal recurs toward the end of *Retrieving Realism* when Taylor says that, "[a]t its strongest" an overlapping consensus "would never amount to unanimity in religious ethical outlook but rather to a convergence, from out of very different outlooks, and for different reasons, on a certain table of norms" (164). Taylor's way of putting this in the 2021 video is to say that "we are in a world in which there is some convergence on the ethical – but continued nonconvergence, continued difference on the spiritual" ("History" at minute 74).

5 Conclusion

Pinker's *Enlightenment Now: The Case for Reason, Science, Humanism, and Progress* followed *Better Angels* while reprising some of its themes. Indeed, Fortier calls this later work a sequel to *Better Angels* (484n111). Commentators have once again drawn attention to Pinker's hostile attitude toward religion. A sympathetic reviewer, Christian Alejandro Gonzalez, observes that "Pinker displays nothing less than contempt for faith; he never fails to take cheap shots at God, and after a while the relentless jabs start to feel rather gratuitous." Gary Gutting places Pinker "in the camp of the New Atheists" and links him with Richard Dawkins just as we have seen Taylor do. Gutting holds that "many of Pinker's claims about religion are open to serious philosophical challenge" and faults him for not engaging with opposing views on these topics. Gutting nominates Taylor as a philosopher who represents a different view from Pinker on whether religion's legitimate ethical tenets can be wholly transposed into secular terms. Instead of responding responsibly to these challenges, Pinker remains mired in "New Atheist polemics". Deeming Pinker to be "an excellent scientist and engaging popular writer", Gutting laments this missed opportunity for someone with Pinker's credentials to write in a philosophically more responsible manner about the important issues he treats.

I suggest that the converse also applies. Because of Pinker's credentials, including his commitment to inquiring into the place of violence over time, it would be a missed opportunity not to engage with him in a serious and philosophically responsible manner. There are a number of ways in which Taylor's developing ideas about moral growth in history could profit from an encounter with Pinker's work. Taylor needs, for example, to address the question that Pinker does of whether violence can ever be wholly eliminated. According to Taylor "[t]he omega point of this growth is this universal living up to the demands of this space [...] this is the tough demand, which we have never succeeded in living up to" ("History" 1). Elsewhere he observes that "the central values or norms that we find preached and acted out in the Gospels [...] could never be realised at the level of whole societies" ("Foreword" vii). He lists a number of ways in which pacifism would be counter-productive, such as when the use of force serves an injustice, in the face of external conquest and so on ("Foreword" vii). He concludes that "[t]here are restrictions built into our politico-moral predicament that set limits to our living the Gospel fully at the level of the collectivity, let alone the globe" ("Foreword" viii). Although Taylor writes this as part of his summary of Martin's position, there is nothing to suggest that he demurs in any way from this view. But if so, it will be helpful as he moves forward in this project to specify when and how the use of violence is acceptable, even if only in the sort of general way that Pinker does.

Insofar as Taylor's thinking about violence is a development of some of his thoughts in *A Secular Age*, an engagement with Pinker would be fruitful. Part of that work's purpose is to reduce the perceived distance between those who are and those who are not religious. In Part V in particular, Taylor strives to reveal that the supposed antagonists in the debate have more in common than either side realizes, and to expose a more fertile, complex, uncertain middle ground (*Secular* 674–75). Identifying these dilemmas not only deconstructs the supposed binary oppositions of belief and non-belief but also creates a space for beginning to articulate the experience of many people who recognize themselves in neither of these opposing positions (*Secular* 431, 627). One of the dilemmas each side shares is how to make sense of violence (*Secular* 639, 668, 688–89).

Nor is there any reason why Taylor's belief that when it comes to understanding fullness, we need "a conversation between a host of different positions, religious, nonreligious, anti-religious ... and so on in which we eschew mutual caricature" ("Afterword" 318) should not also apply to violence. Engaging with Pinker would also exemplify and extend the ecumenism that, as we saw in Section 1, Taylor identifies and values about the Axial Age. Although an exclusive humanist position was not present at that watershed period, including such an outlook in Taylor's project and pointing to areas of common concern with religious views could be immensely beneficial. It is also strongly consonant with what Taylor calls "the ecumenism of friendship" which recognizes that "although you are very different from me, I have a sense that I can *learn* something from you [...] we can accompany each other, encourage each other in our paths, even though we are on quite different paths" ("Fellow Travellers" 7 emphasis original).

Works Cited

Bohman, Ulf and Dario Montero. "History, Critique, Social Change and Democracy: An Interview with Charles Taylor." *Constellations*, 21.4 (2014): 3–15.

Costa, Paolo. "'Democracy is always going to be hard': An Interview with Charles Taylor." *The Review of Politics*, 84.2 (2022): 238–51.

Dreyfus, Hubert and Charles Taylor. *Retrieving Realism*. Cambridge, Mass.: Harvard University Press, 2015.

Fortier, Jeremy. "On Steven Pinker's Hobbesian Liberalism." *Polity*, 50. 3 (2018): 460–84.

Gonzalez, Christian Alejandro "Steven Pinker's *Enlightenment Now* Is Mostly Right." *National Review*, July 14, 2018. https://www.nationalreview.com/2018/07/book-review-steven-pinker-enlightenment-now-mostly-correct/. Accessed July 2, 2022.

Gray, John. "Delusions of Peace." *Prospect Magazine*, September. 21, 2011. https://www.prospectmagazine.co.uk/magazine/john-gray-steven-pinker-violence-review. Accessed July 2, 2022.

Gutting, Gary. "Is Ours the Best World Ever? Steven Pinker's Enlightenment", *Commonweal*, March 26, 2018. https://www.commonwealmagazine.org/ours-best-world-ever. Accessed July 2, 2022.

Largerkrantz, David. *The Girl Who Lived Twice*. Trans. George Goulding. London: Machlehose Press, 2019.

Laws, Ben. "Against Pinker's violence." *CT Theory*, March 21, 2012. https://journals.uvic.ca/index.php/ctheory/article/view/14949. Accessed July 2, 2022.

Maclure, Jocelyn and Charles Taylor. *Secularism and Freedom of Conscience*, Cambridge. Mass.: Harvard University Press, 2011.

Meijer, Michiel. "Fellow Travellers on Different Paths: A Conversation with Charles Taylor." *Philosophy and Social Criticism*, 46.8 (2020): 895–1002.

Mitzen, Jennifer. "The Irony of Pinkerism." *Perspectives on Politics*, 11.3 (2013): 525–28.
Pinker, Steven. *The Better Angels of our Nature: Why Violence has Declined*. New York: Viking, 2011.
Taylor, Charles. *A Secular Age*, Cambridge Mass.: Harvard University Press, 2007.
Taylor, Charles. "Afterword: Apologia pro Libro suo." *Varieties of Secularism in A Secular Age*. Eds. Michael Warner, Jonathan Vantantwerpen and Craig Calhoun. Cambridge Mass..: Harvard University Press, 2013. 300–324.
Taylor, Charles. "Atomism." *Philosophy and the Human Sciences: Philosophical Papers 2*. Cambridge: Cambridge University Press, 1985. 187–210.
Taylor, Charles. "Charles Taylor Responds." *International Journal of Philosophical Studies*, 29.5 (2021): 809–23.
Taylor, Charles. "Conditions of an Unforced Consensus on Human Rights." *Dilemmas and Connections: Selected Essays*. Cambridge, Mass.: Harvard University Press, 2011. 105–123.
Taylor, Charles. "Foreword." *Ruin and Restoration: On Violence, Liturgy and Reconciliation*. Ed. David Martin. Abingdon: Routledge, 2016. vii-xii.
Taylor, Charles. "History of Ethical Growth." https://www.youtube.com/watch?v=LV8zlm_7Kn8 and https://charlestaylor.net/Docs/Global_History_Conf/History%20of%20ethical%20growth.pdf. Accessed July 2, 2022.
Taylor, Charles. "Language not mysterious?" *Analysis: Claves de Pensamiento Contemporáneo*, 21.7 (2018): 1–25. https://hal.archives-ouvertes.fr/hal-02163085/document. Accessed July 2, 2022.
Taylor, Charles. "Notes on the Sources of Violence: Perennial and Modern." *Dilemmas and Connections: Selected Essays*. Cambridge, Mass.: Harvard University Press, 2011. 188–213.
Taylor, Charles. "The Alchemy of Violence." *Project Syndicate*, July 18, 2001. https://www.project-syndicate.org/commentary/the-alchemy-of-violence. Accessed July 2, 2022.
Taylor, Charles. *The Language Animal: The Full Shape of the Human Linguistic Capacity*. Cambridge Mass.: Harvard University Press, 2016.
Taylor, Charles "What's Wrong with Negative Liberty." *Philosophy and the Human Sciences: Philosophical Papers 2*. Cambridge: Cambridge University Press, 1985. 211–229.
Taylor, Charles. "What was the Axial Revolution?" *The Axial Age and its Consequences*. Eds. Robert N. Bellah and Hans Joas. Cambridge, Mass.: Harvard University Press, 2012. 30–46.
Waldron, Jeremy. "A Cheerful View of Mass Violence." *The New York Review of Books*, January 12, 2012. https://www.nybooks.com/articles/2012/01/12/cheerful-view-mass-violence/. Accessed July 2, 2022.

Part II Religion in Critical Theory and Deconstruction

Brendan Moran
Benjamin's Time of Healing: The Messianic as Remembrance, Happiness, and Justice

Abstract: According to Walter Benjamin, the idea of a classless society shows that Karl Marx "secularizes the notion of messianic time." Messianic time is secular by healing with the justice that rebuffs ascription of fate to life-conditions. Messianic time renders transient any ascribed fate. Time is confined to no space and is controlled by no space. In this freedom from fate, time has a claim upon us; we can only dishonestly ignore it. Whereas some argue against Benjamin that past injustice is complete (over and done with, so to speak), messianic time redeems the past by showing victories to be somehow incomplete – that is, illusory in their completeness. Benjamin draws upon the motif of the Last Judgement to attest to the time that heals with the justice of release from imposed fate. Messianic time is the cosmos, the ineradicable experience, that convalesces with the happiness, which is also the justice, recognizing no fate.

For Walter Benjamin, messianic time heals with the justice that rebuffs ascription of fate to any life-conditions. Messianic time renders transient an ascribed fate no matter how strongly certain powers might seem to dominate history. This justice of messianic time heals with the time over which there is no complete control. Time is confined to no space and is controlled by no space. Precisely in this freedom from any specific space, time has a claim upon us. We can only dishonestly ignore it.

Whereas some argue against Benjamin that past injustice is complete (over and done with, so to speak), messianic time redeems the past by showing victories to be incomplete – that is, illusory in their completeness. Even the utterly hopeless can be recalled in a hope they did not or could not allow themselves. Benjamin draws upon the motif of the Last Judgement insofar as this motif attests to the time that heals with the justice of release from imposed fate.

Messianic time is the cosmos, the ineradicable experience, that convalesces with the happiness, which is also the justice, recognizing no fate. Happiness requires the temporality, the transience, in which lives are not fates to be treated as veritably divine burdens. Happiness and justice converge in the hope that finds healing as the breaking of an ostensible fate.

Time heals with the justice in which no meaning is so inviolable that it can be considered God's meaning. The motif of the Last Judgement concerns not retribution but the time releasing everyone from those deeds that otherwise incur guilt.

The sole irrevocable significance of notions of God, and of God's remembrance, is that there is always something beyond the meaning ascribed by humans.

Remembering Messianic Time

In 1940, Benjamin writes that, with "the conception [*Vorstellung*] of classless society," Karl Marx "secularized [*hat ... säkularisiert*] the conception of messianic time" (*SW*4, 401/ *GS*I:3, 1231/ *WuN*19, 152).[1] It might seem a contradiction for Benjamin to associate secularization with an expressly messianic conception of time. An anticipation of this development seems to exist, nonetheless, in Hermann Cohen's *Religion of Reason out of the Sources of Judaism* (first published in 1919). Cohen refers to "the overcoming of the person of the Messiah" and "the dissolution of the personal image [*Sinnbilds*] in the pure notion of time."[2] Notwithstanding his divergences from Cohen, Benjamin too conceives of the messianic as time.[3]

The messianic is not, moreover, time as consolation. It is not the "opiate" religiosity that Benjamin expressly sidesteps in his Surrealism-essay of 1929, where he envisions the "true creative overcoming of religious illumination [*Erleuchtung*]" (*SW*2, 209/ *GS*II:1, 297). In his writings on Franz Kafka, Benjamin suggests that Kafka could not found a religion, for religions entail the pretence of creating the atmosphere of a consolatory village (*SW*2, 805/ *GS*II:2, 424; *GS*II:3, 1231). Benjamin is never far, moreover, from Kafka's thought that there could be a condition utterly devoid of consolation.[4]

Yet Benjamin *does* propose that messianic time can heal, albeit with a healing that can also be enormously challenging for some: for instance, in revisiting a past that had previously been understood to be necessary, a *fate* to be accepted. In "On the Concept of History" (1940), Benjamin depicts messianic time as brushing history against the grain (*SW*4, 392/ *WuN*19, 73; also: *WuN*19, 34, 64, 86, 97) so that the "angel of history" can show "catastrophe" where there would normally just be oc-

---

[1] Abbreviations for works by Benjamin: *AP* = *Arcades Project*; *EW* = *Early Writings*; *GB* = Benjamin, *Gesammelte Briefe*; *GS* = *Gesammelte Schriften*, Vols. I–VII; *SW* = *Selected Writings*, volumes 1–4; *TCV* = *Toward the Critique of Violence*; *WuN*8 = *Einbahnstraße*; *WuN*19 = *Über den Begriff der Geschichte*. If a translation has been modified, the pagination for the original German is italicized (*SW*4, 407/ *WuN*19, *137*).
[2] Cohen, *Religion of Reason*, 249/ *Religion der Vernunft*, 291.
[3] There is vast research on Benjamin and Cohen. See, for instance, Deuber Mankowsky, Tagliacozza, and Ng and Tobias.
[4] Kafka, *Nachgelassene Schriften und Fragmente* II, 31. Kafka's relevant sentences form a leitmotif of Luc Dardenne's *Sur l'affaire humaine*, 15.

currences (*SW*4, 392/ *WuN*19, 74; also: 20, 35, 64, 87, 98) or the consolation of putative progress (*SW*4, 392, 393/ *WuN*19, 74, 76; also: 19, 21; 35, 37; 64; 88, 89; 98, 99–100).

"*Das messianische Reich*" has a regal denotation and is often translated into English as "the messianic kingdom" and into French as "*le royaume messianique.*" The English "realm" for "*Reich*" could seem to pertain to something less kingly, although "realm" does have an early etymological association with "kingdom."[5] There is, in any case, a continuous effort on Benjamin's part to associate "*das messianische Reich,*" "the messianic realm," with unautocratic and secular priorities of healing. As early as 1914–15, he relates "the idea of the French revolution" to "the messianic realm" (*SW*1, 37/ *EW*, 197/ *GS*II:1, 75).[6] In "On the Concept of History," he suggests the ultimate impetus of the French revolution was "now-time [*Jetztzeit*]," the "open air of history" (*SW*4, 394–95/*WuN*19, 78–79; see too: *WuN*19: 24, 40, 102). Now-time is ineradicably open. In its perpetuity, now-time is the ongoing basis for hope that history could be healthier, less stricken with *fates* that are only illusorily necessary.

There is, of course, the constant risk that a self-acclaimed messianism will licence domination, bullying, or killing. Benjamin himself sometimes incurs this risk. In "Toward the Critique of Violence" (1921), Benjamin is critical of those who would always – perhaps on the basis of the commandment not to kill or on the basis of some other view that all human life is sacred – disallow "the dreadful [*ungeheuren*] cases" in which, despite a guideline to the contrary, there may emerge the "responsibility" of killing or there may emerge "in an extreme case" "the revolutionary killing of the oppressors" (*SW*1, 250–51/ *TCV*, 58/ II:1, *201*). In a letter of 1920, Benjamin mentions that he is writing on violence, rejecting state violence "but more or less apologetic with respect to its revolutionary kind" (*GB*II, 101 cited in Fenves). In times of war, moreover, it might seem necessary to draw (however reluctantly) conclusions that justify killing. The killing might seem the only possibility of averting a murderous aggressor. Yet there is also Benjamin's claim that "divine violence," in contrast with "mythic violence," can be recognized in a "true war" or in the "divine judgement of the multitude upon a criminal" (*SW*1, 252/ *TCV*, 60/ *GS*II:1, 203).[7] The latter comments in particular seem to place Benjamin among those who might too readily ascribe divine value to conditions

---

5 Onions ed., *Oxford Dictionary of English Etymology*, 743.
6 For this passage "*das messianische Reich*" has been translated as "the messianic realm" (*EW*, 197) and as "the messianic domain" (*SW*1, 37). Maurice de Gandillac and Rainer Rochlitz translate it as "*le royaume messianique*" (Benjamin, *Œuvres*, vol. 1, 126).
7 A cryptic addendum to the comment about killing a criminal is made in *One-Way Street:* "The killing of a criminal can be ethical [*sittlich*] – but never its legitimation" (*SW*1, 481/ *GS*IV:1, 138/ *WuN*8, 67).

that themselves could require less eagerness to assume divine legitimacy. I can endorse a war against an army or aggressor and consider the situation one of those dreadful cases in which killing is required. To ascribe divine value to my judgement could, however, be a questionable oversimplification given the very compromising and imbricated conditions in which war takes place.

Benjamin is usually more careful in his relevant formulations, as should become evident in remarks below. These formulations indicate a concern with healing that largely avoids putatively divine prerogatives of killing and even prerogatives of hierarchy; hence, the aforementioned classlessness in messianic time. In some sense, everyone is entitled to this time that they always already experience (even though they might not be aware of experiencing it).

Theology in Benjamin's work involves heeding the messianic time that is hidden in the disregarded, the oppressed, or the suppressed. The relationship of *heil* (healed) and *heilig* (sacred) is noted in etymological dictionaries as well as elsewhere,[8] although the history of the very early interaction of these terms is not always clear.[9] The relevant theological element in Benjamin's work has, however, been criticized as unserviceable for historical materialism. A *theological* tendency supposedly made it impossible for Benjamin "to make the messianic theory of experience serviceable [*dienstbar*] for historical materialism."[10] This objection is accompanied by the claim that Benjamin's redemptive critique is "conservative,"[11] a "conservative revolutionary hermeneutic."[12] More receptive obviously is Jacob Taubes's summation that "Benjamin's programme" was "to tear away" certain "motifs from the reactionaries."[13] Theology as redemptive critique could be something other than conservative and it could be salutary for Marxism.

Theology is conceived by Benjamin as integral to historical materialism. Without messianism, the legacy of hope for healing is more likely to be diminished in scientistic and brutal versions of Marxism. The latter versions of Marxism tend to legitimize the purported necessity for certain sufferings and deaths. In messianic time, as described in "On the Concept of History," we are – in contrast – the hope

---

[8] See Jacob and Wilhelm Grimm, *Deutsches Wörterbuch*, some of the entries for "heil" as adjective as well as for "Heil" as noun. Peter E. Gordon notes the relationship of "healing" and "the Holy" in this context; he especially refers to "heilen" and "das Heilige" (*Critical Theory and the Question of Secularization*, 75).

[9] *Das Herkunftswörterbuch* (Duden), 330–31: entries for *heil* and *heilig*.

[10] Habermas, "Walter Benjamin: Consciousness-Raising or Rescuing Critique" (1972), 152/ "Bewußtmachende oder rettende Kritik," 364–65. See too 155/ 368.

[11] Habermas, 138/ 346.

[12] Habermas, 161/ 376.

[13] Taubes, *The Political Theology of Paul*, 83–84/ *Die politische Theologie des Paulus*, 116.

of past generations, whose sufferings and subjugation can concern us in a way that might barely have been possible when they happened.

> The past carries with it a secret index by which it is referred to redemption [*Erlösung*]. ... [T]here exists a secret agreement [*Verabredung*] between past generations [*Geschlechtern*] and ours. ... [L]ike every generation that preceded us, we have been endowed with a *weak messianic force* [*Kraft*] to which the past has a claim. That claim cannot be settled cheaply. The historical materialist knows that (*SW*4, 390/ *GS*I:2, 694/ *WuN*19, 70; see too: *WuN*19, 16–17, 31, 60, 83, 94).

Our agreement, our bond, with the past is secret, for its pressure exceeds any attempt to respond to it. Our expressions are not adequate to its pressure. The claim of the past is thus secret, somehow inexplicable, even though it might feel utterly compelling. Minimally, it requires concern about what preceded us, and this concern – as concern – cannot be fraudulent or superficial. At least once, Benjamin's "On the Concept of History" refers to "temporal index" instead of "secret index": "The past carries with it a temporal index by which it is referred to redemption [*Erlösung*]" (*WuN*19, 94). Time registers itself as that with which we can have a redemptive rapport. Notwithstanding this "hope," the messianic force is weak, for the powers discouraging consideration of the past are overwhelming. This enemy, which is also thereby the "enemy" of the dead, "has not ceased to be victorious" (*SW*4, 391/ *GS*I:2, 695/ *WuN*19, 72; see too *WuN*19, 18–19, 33, 62, 85, 96). In trying to grapple with Benjamin's notion of inheriting a weak messianic force, Jacques Derrida reformulates "claim" (*Anspruch*) as "injunction" (*injonction*): the past interpellates us – practically questions us – with this injunction to consider it in ways we might not otherwise.[14] These ways of consideration are not easy to exercise or to maintain with even a modicum of sincere vigilance. There is much enmity towards the past, not only in reluctance to engage the past but also in the view that the past is simply lost.

For historical materialism, says Benjamin in his essay on Eduard Fuchs (1937), "the work of the past is not completed [*nicht abgeschlossen*]" (*SW*3, 267/ *GS*II:2, 477). Although Max Horkheimer's later views were openly influenced by theology, it is in objection that Horkheimer in 1937 writes to Benjamin: "Past injustice [*Unrecht*] has occurred and is completed [*abgeschlossen*]. The slain are really slain. ... If one takes the lack of closure [*die Unabgeschlossenheit*] seriously, one must believe in the Last Judgement [*das Jüngste Gericht*]."[15] Benjamin does *not* say that he *believes*

---

14 Derrida, *Specters of Marx*, 181 n181/ *Spectres de Marx*, 96 n1.
15 Horkheimer, *Briefwechsel 1937–1940. Gesammelte Schriften*, vol. 16, 83. For later reflections on religion, see for instance: Horkheimer, "Theism and Atheism," *Critique of Instrumental Reason*, 34–

in the Last Judgement. He can be critical of belief, as is evident in his criticism of certain politicians' "belief in progress" (*Fortschrittsglaube*) (*SW*4, 393/ *WuN*19, 75; see too *WuN*19, 88, 99). The Last Judgement is a motif he variously uses, however, at least partly to accentuate the incompleteness of judgement. As he puts it in 1940: "[e]very moment is a moment of judgement [*des Gerichts*] concerning certain moments that precede it" (*SW*4, 407/ *GS*I:3, 1245/ *WuN*19, 135). Past judgements can always be revisited; the conception of Last Judgement could remind us of this. Apparently with regard to the relationship of Marxist historiography and the notion of Last Judgement, Benjamin wonders if "critique and prophecy" converge "in the 'saving [*Rettung*]' of the past" (*SW*4, 407/ *WuN*19, *137*). In prophesying the possibility of a judgement more responsive than any prevailing judgement to the subjugated, critique might help save history from the self-satisfaction of many of its agents.

In notes on Horkheimer's aforementioned letter, Benjamin writes: "What science has 'established,' remembrance can modify." A past suffering can be modified from something ostensibly complete (*das Abgeschlossene*) to something incomplete (*einem Unabgeschlossenen*). There is undoubtedly suffering that will happen unnoticed. Even, however, a long past suffering, if we have only the slightest awareness of it, can be revisited so that prevailing conceptions of it can be questioned. This revisiting is the indispensable work of "theology" "in remembrance" (*im Eingedenken*); theology can aid in regarding history as incomplete (*AP*, 471/ *GSV*:1, *589*). In this sense of incompletion, what manifests itself can be considered in hitherto dismissed or disregarded ways. Something shunted to the background can be reconsidered. The sense of incompletion is also an acknowledgement that history does not manifest all that *could* be relevant to it.

Part of human suffering is, for instance, phantom; this suffering is quite profoundly effective and yet not as readily discernible as other kinds of suffering. This is the case as one is haunted by aspects of one's own past that are no longer, or never were, entirely clear. It is also the case with transgenerational suffering, the effects of which we might feel without being thoroughly conscious of them. In this way (as well as innumerable other ways), we could somehow be experiencing those preceding us. For Benjamin, the historical materialist *knows* there is such suffering and is prepared to make incomplete any presumed completeness regarding the suffering – any celebrated victory over, or other effective dismissal of, the suffering. The historical materialist is prepared to revisit the past so that disregard can be opposed.

50/ "Theismus – Atheismus," *Gesammelte Schriften*, vol. 7, 173–86; Horkheimer, "Bemerkungen zur Liberalisierung der Religion," *Gesammelte Schriften*, vol. 7, 233–39.

This historiographic practice runs counter, therefore, to the assessment that the dead, who are no longer capable of discursively establishing norms with us, are thereby simply in the "irreversibility" of their "unatoned" suffering.[16] Such emphasis on the primacy of discursive normativity has included the argument that the slain, and the denigrated, of the past, can – in ethical respects – only occasion *Mitleid* (pity or compassion) that will be a limit concept of discourse ethics: "[c]ompassion for the violation of moral or bodily integrity ... is a limit concept of the discourse ethic, just as 'nature-in-itself' is a limit concept of the transcendental-pragmatic theory of knowledge."[17] This preoccupation with setting limits to ethics has included reference to "Horkheimer's justified skepticism towards Benjamin's effusive [*überschwängliche*] hope for the reparative [*wiedergutmachende*] force of humane remembrance."[18] For Benjamin, historical materialism *knows* precisely what is treated here as a beyond, but historical materialism does not know it as complete reparation. Historical materialism knows *this beyond* requires rather that revisited past suffering be considered always somehow incomplete. This is the knub of Benjamin's difference with Horkheimer. The past is incomplete no matter how much history treats it as *over and done with* – finished, concluded, irreversible.

Mitleid is not, moreover, part of Benjamin's vocabulary with regard to the messianic time that impels revisiting the past. Perhaps he shares Nietzsche's view that *Mitleid* can easily involve aggrandizement of the donor and belittlement of the recipient.[19] Such belittlement is something Benjamin tries to avoid. It has been argued that Benjamin imagines we could now let "dead victims" assume "anew the form of animated beings [*erneut die Gestalt von beseelten Wesen*]"; the argument is that Benjamin thinks "personal integrity" could or should be "restored retroactively" by admitting these victims into the "moral community" of humankind.[20] It is mistaken, however, to suggest Benjamin thinks there is a *current moral being* who is to bring about a "communicative disclosure of the past" for the sake of "a symbolic restitution of the victims' moral integrity."[21] It is not

---

[16] This is from a passage in which Habermas cites with a little more sympathy than usual Benjamin's disagreement with Horkheimer's view of past injustices as solely that – past. See Habermas, *Auch eine Geschichte der Philosophie*, vol. 1, 72, although here too there is reference to "the irreversibility of the unatoned suffering of innocent victims."
[17] Habermas, "A Reply to my Critics," 246–47/ *Vorstudien und Ergänzung zur Theorie des kommunikativen Handelns*, 516–17.
[18] Habermas, *Glauben und Wissen*, 25.
[19] For instance see Nietzsche, "Von den Mitleidigen," *Also Sprach Zarathustra*, 109–12.
[20] Axel Honneth, "A Communicative Disclosure of the Past," 92/ "Kommunikative Erschließung der Vergangenheit, 109–10.
[21] Honneth, 94/ 113

quite correct to think one is criticizing Benjamin with the comment that it is "still unclear to what extent it would be meaningful [*sinnvoll*] to speak of a communicative relationship to people or even groups of people who belong to the realm of the dead."[22] In contrast, nonetheless, with a certain complacency in this view of the dead, Benjamin does treat the relationship with the dead as an acute problem. *Angelus Novus*, the angel of history, cannot "awaken the dead, and put together what has been smashed" (*SW*4, 392/ *WuN*19, 75; *WuN*19, 20, 36, 87, 98). Hence, Benjamin's "disempowerment [*Entmachtung*] of the arrogant present."[23] The relevant remembrance does not entail that a past "injustice can at least be virtually reconciled."[24]

Benjamin does not imagine that we could now let dead victims assume anew the form of animated beings, although of course historiography (along with some historically oriented literature, film, or other arts) might do so to some extent. Benjamin is not really claiming that *personal integrity* could be restored retrospectively by admitting the dead into the current moral community of humankind. There is no current moral being or community who is to bring about *a communicative disclosure of the past* for the sake of *a symbolic restitution of the victims' moral integrity.* Those in a redemptive rapport with the past are not presenting themselves as a discursively established pinnacle so self-satisfied that they think they bestow moral value.

None of us is a bestower of messianic time. For Benjamin, messianic time is known, or can be known, as that which thrusts the past upon us and thereby disturbs complacency now and in the future. A more recent theologian notes that to insist on discourse as the sole medium of reason is to assert "a privilege of contemporaneity [*Gleichzeitigkeitsvorbehalt*]." In an "anamestically constituted ... reason," in "remembrance" (*Eingedenken*), there is however a countermeasure to the presupposition "that what is past is past."[25] With a privileging of contemporary discursivity, it has also been noted, the dead are in some way made dead once more.[26] For Benjamin, exceptions to discursive normativity are not simply exceptions corroborating the rule from which they deviate. Engagement with the dead could, in a

---

22 Honneth, 94/ 113.
23 Jeanne Marie Gagnebin, "'Über den Begriff der Geschichte,'" 287.
24 Cf. Habermas, *The Philosophical Discourse of Modernity*, 15/ *Der philosophische Diskurs der Moderne*, 26.
25 Johann Baptist Metz, "Anamnestic Reason," 191/ "Anamnestische Vernunft," 735–36.
26 Düttmann, 302–06, especially 306.

Benjaminian context, emphasize the unduly limited and limiting reach, indeed the failure, of an ethics of discursive answerability.²⁷

Messianic time is not something over which the contemporary, or the discursively empowered in the contemporary, has a monopoly. To subordinate human history to the contemporaneity of some variation of discursively established normativity would be to create *an ethical fate*, a subordination to the implied or purported temporal and ethical superiority of a specific form of contemporaneity. Messianic time is without fate and is thus time to which we, those in the past, and those in the future all belong. All are in this inconclusive time. In 1940, Benjamin writes: "The messianic world is the world of all-round and integral actuality [*Aktualität*]. Only in this world is there a universal history" (*WuN*19, 109). In messianic time, complacency – including complacency about any supposed ethical prerogative of the contemporary – is always challenged.

Another note of 1940 by Benjamin cites the Torah's emphasis on "remembrance" over "inquiry into the future." This remembrance, this perpetual revisiting of the past, was to disrupt assurances about the past and precisely thereby change the future. The future was also "disenchanted [*entzaubert*]," for the future was in no way "homogenous, empty time"; "every second was the small gateway in time through which the Messiah might enter" (*SW*4, 397/ *WuN*19, 106). Such references to *the messiah* might seem anthropomorphic. Benjamin seems, however, to move beyond any personal image of the messianic. This is worth repeating, not least given concerns that notions of "weak responsibility for the collective fate of one's neighbors and of distant peoples … sometimes misleads obstinate or fanatical individuals who fail to recognize their own fallibility."²⁸ Messianic time is the intrusion of fallibility where fallibility might not be acknowledged. With a messianic awareness of time, the "historical materialist seizes [*erfaßt*]" a conjuncture of the current "epoch" with "a very specific earlier one." Regarding the temporality involved in this "constellation," Benjamin says the "present [*Gegenwart*]" becomes "the 'now-time' [*Jetztzeit*]" sprinkled with "splinters of messianic time" (*SW*4, 397/ *WuN*19, 105). Now-time could be characterized as time without fate; it is antithetical to hubris of the present over the past. As time without fate, now-time includes the capacity to revisit history in a way that could utterly change peoples' regard on the past, so much so that the change is also of the present and the future. The explicit critique of fate plays a smaller role in Benjamin's later writings than in his

---

27 For more such remarks, see Moran, *Politics of Benjamin's Kafka*, 307–08 and, more generally, Rrenban, "Community of the Dead," *Wild, Unforgettable Philosophy*, 199–291.
28 Habermas, "The Boundary between Faith and Knowledge," 241/ "Die Grenze zwischen Glauben und Wissen," 250. For some reflections on behalf of philosophical stubbornness, see "Ir(r)enstrasse" in Rrenban.

earlier ones.[29] Even for Benjamin's later writings, nonetheless, the closures to which people of the past were subjected can be broken, and this breaking can have an unsettling effect on our relationship with all closures that we and our descendants might propagate. For notes towards "On the Concept of History," messianism is a perpetually interruptive force: "the messiah does not emerge at the end of an evolution"; "[t]he messiah interrupts history [*bricht die Geschichte ab*]" (*WuN*19, 131/ *GS*I:3, 1243).

Hope can intrude. Benjamin is usually careful, of course, not to insult the hopeless with insistence that they should be hopeful. In a very early text (1913), he refers to an idealessness in contemporary youth that attests to their honesty (*EW*, 103, 132–33/ *GS*II:1, 44, 47). In his 1934 essay on Kafka and in related notes, he cites Kafka's alleged statement that there is "'plenty of hope, an infinite amount of hope – but not for us'" (*SW*2, 798/ *GS*II:2, 413–14; also: *GS*II:3, 1218, 1246, 1262).[30] Hope is infinite in its capacity to return; there are, nonetheless, those who quite credibly lose hope. Yet the latter, the hopeless, can be recalled in a hope that they did not or could not effectively allow themselves. In "On the Concept of History," Benjamin proposes a historian who has the "gift" of "fanning the spark of hope in the past" (*SW*4, 391/ *WuN*19, 72; see too *WuN*19, 18, 33, 62, 85, 98). This hope includes the hope "for the sake of the hopeless" mentioned in the last sentence of Benjamin's essay on Goethe's *Elective Affinities* (1921–22) (*SW*1, 356/ *GS*I:1, *201*). Hope tells the "'catastrophe'" that in other respects is or was simply lived (354–56/199–201). Hence, the hopefulness underlying the perception – in "On the Concept of History" – of history as "catastrophe" (*SW*4, 392/ *WuN*19, 74; also: *WuN*19, 20, 35, 64, 87, 98). This hope cannot be appeased by superficially engaging, or simply disregarding, the past. Such superficiality or disregard would indeed be a *conservative* option; in this respect, and contrary to what is sometimes alleged, Benjamin is not conservative. The past is instead the pressure of time that we – like the aforementioned "historical materialist" – can know is not subordinate to any closures imposed then, currently, or in the future. In that sense, messianic time may be formulated as perpetual, inextinguishable freedom from fate.

---

29 Eiland, "Benjamin's Concept of Fate."
30 Benjamin is citing from Brod, "Der Dichter Franz Kafka," 1213.

Insubordinate Time as Convalescence, Happines, and Justice

Messianic time convalesces in its universally *insubordinate* relationship with fate or any such closure. This insubordination allies with transience, for in transience there cannot be fate. This non-fated condition makes transience not only a convalescing force but also coevally a force of happiness and justice.

Insubordinate time is a cosmic experience, Benjamin suggests in *One-Way Street* (from the mid-1920s). For this experience to convalesce, technological developments might be helpful precisely insofar as they project temporally beyond dominant social orders. A "*physis* is being organized" whereby humankind's "contact with the cosmos" "forms itself anew and differently than in nations and families." With this technology, we can feel ourselves move into time that is not subordinate to nations and families. There can be "the experience of velocities" in which humankind prepares "to embark on incalculable journeys into the interior of time." The relevant temporality involves "rhythms from which the sick shall draw strength as they did earlier on high mountains or on the shores of southern seas." Physical experience of this time can heal in going beyond family, nation, or indeed hitherto dominant understandings of nature. The "frisson [*Schauer*] of genuine cosmic experience is not tied to that tiny fragment of nature that we are accustomed to call 'Nature.'" This less constrained – *cosmic* – experience can strengthen, even somewhat heal, those debilitated in human organization. Hence, Benjamin's correlation of the proletariat's "power [*Macht*]" with "its convalescence [*Gesundung*]" (*SW*1, 487/ *GS*IV:1, 147–48/ *WuN*,8, 76). In 1938, he critically remarks that the nineteenth century was "incapable of responding to the new technological possibilities with a new societal order" (*SW*4, 94/ *GS*I:3, *1154*). A new societal order would entail convalescence by virtue of receptivity to time that surpasses any fatefulness associated with a specific form of human organization. In the words of "Fate and Character" (1919), "character" manifests itself in the release from "fate" (*SW*1, 202/ *GS*II:1, 173).

In its innermost, time is antithetical to notions of a lot in life. This is at least implied in Benjamin's characterization of capitalism as a questionable "cult" of guilt ("Capitalism as Religion" [1921], *SW*1, 288–91/ *TCV*, 90–92/ *GS*VI, 100–103).[31] In "Fate and Character" and in his essay on Goethe's *Elective Affinities*, Benjamin says: "Fate is the guilt-context of the living" (*SW*1, 204/ *GS*II:1, 175; *SW*1, 307/ *GS*I:1, 138). A cult of guilt, such as capitalism, suggests that there is no escape from this

---

31 See too Dirk Baecker ed. *Kapitalismus als Religion*.

implicitly divine "human fate" ("Capitalism as Religion," *SW*1, 288–89/ *TCV*, 90–91/ *GS*VI, 100–1). Messianic time subjects fate to transience; it is perpetual escape from guilt. Even the most egregious violation does not make the perpetrator equivalent to guilt. No one is reducible to their guilt.

A judge might see "fate" but "every punishment" proclaimed by the judge entails that the judge "must blindly dictate [*mitdiktieren*] fate. It is never the human but only the mere life [*das bloße Leben*] in the human that it strikes – the part involved in natural guilt and misfortune by virtue of semblance [*des Scheins*]" (*SW*1, 204/ *GS*II:1, *175*). The "natural guilt" in this statement from "Fate and Character" is the nature that instils acquiescence to semblance; the natural guilt is not the messianic nature that treats misfortune as something other than necessary, as not equivalent to time itself.[32] Messianic time, cosmic time, heals by recognizing no fate.

Benjamin's so-called theological-political fragment (dated variously at 1920–21, 1922–23, or 1937–38)[33] proposes that happiness is reliant on transience. In this sense, "all that is earthly seeks its downfall [*Untergang*]" (*SW*3, 305/ *GS*II:1, *204*). On the one hand, "[t]he profane" is "no category of the messianic realm." In other words, the profane is not the messianic realized.[34] On the other hand, however, the profane "is … a category – indeed the most pertinent one" – of the "quietist approach" of the messianic. The messianic is quiet in its constancy; it is always there – in misfortune and in release from misfortune. Neither the misfortune nor the release from misfortune is irrevocably necessary, but precisely the transience underlying these experiences binds the profane with happiness. The profane as downfall brings the "unhappiness" of "suffering" and yet it also brings "happiness" as release. With regard to suffering, Benjamin remarks: "the immediate messianic intensity of the heart, of the particular human being, passes through misfortune [*Unglück*] as suffering." This intense experience of unhappiness is messianic in its recognition that the suffering does not have to be. "[J]ust as a force can, through its way, promote another going in the opposite direction, so the order of the profane, through being profane, can promote the coming of the messianic realm." Profanation as profanation bears the promise of release from ostensibly necessary suffering. Regardless of what happens in life, there is this capacity to think suffering is unnecessary.

---

32 On these two distinct natures, see Moran, "Nature, Decision, and Muteness."
33 See Werner Hamacher, "Das theologische-politische Fragment," 175.
34 Perhaps Benjamin is alluding to this in his speculation that "the profoundest contrast to 'world' is not 'time' but rather 'the coming world'" ("World and Time" [1919–20], *SW*1, 226/ *TCV*, 83/ *GS*VI, *99*).

In Benjamin's words, a "spiritual *restitutio in integrum* ... introduces immortality." Immortality is a *restitutio in integrum* in the literal sense that it pertains to the possibility of restoration to an uninjured condition – the possibility that is twofold: the suffering is not necessary; we thereby recognize time's independence from closure. To the "spiritual *restitutio in integrum*," moreover, there "corresponds a worldly" *restitutio in integrum* "that leads to the eternity of a downfall." In other words, "the rhythm of this eternally transient worldly condition [*Weltlichen*]" is "transient in its totality, in its spatial and temporal totality." The eternally transient worldly condition is "the rhythm of messianic nature."

As messianic nature, the eternally transient worldly condition is "happiness." Happiness is possible by virtue of spatio-temporal transience; happiness is possible because space and time are never entirely locked, never entirely closed. First, "nature is messianic by reason of its eternal and total passing away"; second, there is a correlation of transience and happiness (305–6/ *204*).

A striving for "transience" (*Vergängnis*) is so fundamental that Benjamin's theological-political fragment associates the striving with "the task of world politics, whose method is to be called nihilism" (306/ *204*). This nihilism is simply the recognition that time passes, and that even nature itself might pass away in the human. "To strive for this passing away," this "transience [*Vergängnis*]," "even the passing away of those stages of the human that are nature," is the nihilistic task of world politics (306/ *204*). There might be anthropocentrism in Benjamin's conception of nature that itself passes away in the human, as though the human is the culmination and the overcoming of nature. This does not entirely annul, however, the importance of his association of world politics with the happiness immanent in transience. In *world-political* nihilism, transience and its prospective happiness pertain to questions of justice.

In this world-political emphasis, happiness converges with justice.[35] Happiness requires the temporality, the rhythm, the transience, in which lives are *not* fates that are treated as a veritably divine burden and guilt. Benjamin's "Fate and Character" cites a lament heard by Goethe's Wilhelm Meister: "'You let the poor person become guilty'" (*SW*1, 204/ *GS*II:1, 175).[36] It is characteristic of capitalism, for instance, to ascribe to oppressive life something resembling a divinely justified hue (*SW*1, 288–91/ TCV, 90–92/ *GS*VI, 100–103). In an outline of his 1934 essay on Kafka, Benjamin correlatively refers to the "full weight of justice ... that so de-

---

35 See Antonia Birnbaum, *Bonheur Justice*.
36 Citing Goethe, *Wilhelm Meisters Lehrjahre*, 136: "Ihr laßt den Armen schuldig werden."

grades everything divine" (*GS*II:3, 1220).³⁷ Messianic time disenchants, and could thus recall a statement made by Salomo Friedlaender in a work Benjamin admires: "God is an atheist."³⁸ God repels claims upon God. In a text of 1916, Benjamin remarks that justice is "no order of possession" and "in the final analysis can only be as a condition of the world or as a condition of God."³⁹ God can be the world-condition, the cosmos, that transforms ostensible fates into something transient and thereby proffers justice. In a text written while discussing with Benjamin in 1918–19, Gershom Scholem concludes: "Justice eliminates fate [*Die Gerechtigkeit eliminiert das Schicksal*]."⁴⁰

In the justice that eliminates fate, transience is convalescent temporality. With Benjaminian influences, Derrida says for the messianic, which he considers indispensable, a loan can be made from "God" to convey "absolute hospitality."⁴¹ Elsewhere Derrida refers to "disenchantment as the *very resource of the religious.*"⁴² In Benjamin's words, disenchantment of fate is possible by virtue of messianic transience. With regard to Kafka's theatre of Oklahoma, Benjamin says this "nature theatre" is juxtaposed with the "damnation" (*Verdammnis*) of the "world theatre," the theatre in which the characters of Kafka's novel, *Der Verschollene* (*The Missing Person*), otherwise live. In the theatre of Oklahoma, the world theatre is disenchanted; imperatives specific to the world theatre become somewhat less compelling (*GS*II:3, 1262; see too *SW*2, 801/ *GS*II:2, 418 and *GS*II:3, 1227).⁴³ Although it cannot guarantee us a theatre of Oklahoma, messianic time convalesces with the justice

---

37 Benjamin refers to a text by his friend Werner Kraft. For Kraft's later reworking, see Kraft, "Geld und Güte. Der Kübelreiter," *Franz Kafka*, 32. This seems to be a reworking of a text not previously published.
38 Salomo Friedlaender/ Mynona, *Schöpferische Indifferenz*, 314. For brief comparisons of Friedlaender and Benjamin, see Moran, "Politics of Creative Indifference" and Thiel, *Maßnahmen des Erscheinens*, chapter IV.
39 Benjamin, "From a Notebook Walter Benjamin Lent to Me [Gershom Scholem]: 'Notes Toward a Work on the Category of Justice,'" *TCV*, 65/ "Aus dem mir geliehenen Notizbuche Walter Benjamins. 'Notizen zu einer Arbeit über die Kategorie der Gerechtigkeit,'" 401.
40 Gershom Scholem, "Zwölf Thesen über die Ordnung der Gerechtigkeit," *Tagebücher nebst Aufsätzen und Entwürfen*, 534. See too: Gershom Scholem, "Über Jona und Begriff der Gerechtigkeit" (1919), *Tagebücher nebst Aufsätzen und Entwürfen*, 529 (here the sentence is specially emphasized); also *Tagebücher nebst Aufsätzen und Entwürfen*, 359.
41 Derrida realizes this is a very "inhospitable" notion of hospitality for many (Derrida, *Spectres*, 168/ 267).
42 Derrida, "Faith and Knowledge,'" 65/ Derrida, *Acts of Religion*, 99/ "Foi et savoir," 85.
43 The phrase "Nature Theater of Oklahoma" is Max Brod's interpolation, but Benjamin did not know this (see Moran, *Politics of Benjamin's Kafka*, 57). For a reading that claims Kafka is much more critically rendering the theatre of Oklahoma, see Marie José Mondzain, *K comme Kolonie*, 54, 155–64, 166–67, 178, 235–36.

that renders transient the imperatives of the world theatre. For Benjamin like Scholem, justice maintains the hope for healing that would break an ostensible fate, an ostensible damnation.

Epilogue: Just Time beyond Retribution and Meaning

In messianic time, no one is damned. Benjamin's note titled "The Significance [*Bedeutung*] of Time in the Moral World" (1921) accordingly opposes attempts to conceive of the Last Judgement as a time of conclusive "retribution" (*Vergeltung*). The "immeasurable significance [*unermeßliche Bedeutung*]" of the Last Judgement is the "constantly postponed day" that "flees so relentlessly into the future" after the commission of "every misdeed." The immeasurable significance concerns, therefore, time in its elusion of judgements that are made concerning misdeeds. This significance does not emerge in law, "where retribution rules," but "only in the moral world" where there is "forgiveness" that "finds its powerful ally in time" (*SW*1, 286/ *GS*VI, *98*). Time "not only extinguishes the traces of the misdeed but also – by virtue of its duration, beyond all remembering or forgetting – helps, in ways that are wholly mysterious, towards forgiveness even though never to reconciliation [*Versöhnung*]" (287/ *98*). Around when this note on time is written, Benjamin distinguishes mythic reconciliation from "true" reconciliation (*SW*1, 342–43/ *GS*I:1, 184). Messianic time rejects reconciliation that involves sheer surrender to a presumed occupation of time. Messianic time also does not even equate self-acclaimed occupants of time with the misdeed of their occupation. They are not themselves the illusions of domination that they propagate. To recognize this would require of them that they accept the justice rejecting their illusions.

Justice is possible by virtue of freedom from fate, a freedom from closure, a freedom that is the now-time of everyone. We can pretend to ignore now-time. All of us, or almost all of us, customarily do so. Yet we do so in utter disregard of others and ourselves. In that respect, Benjamin is not far from one of Scholem's many accounts of *tikkun* – mending. In Scholem's account, messianic time is not a "person," a personified deity executing "*tikkun*" – that is, someone divine entrusted with "redemption" (*Erlösung*). *Tikkun* pertains rather to "your deed and mine" as possible "guarantor" of the "restitution of all things [*Restitution aller Dinge*]."[44] In Benjamin's terms, the restitution can be to transience, the temporality that

---

44 Scholem, "Kabbalah and Myth," *On the Kabbalah and its Symbolism*, 117/ "Kabbala und Mythos," *Zur Kabbala und ihrer Symbolik*, 157.

heals by suspending all ascribed fates, including all impositions of meaning. After all, no one will be able to cite the past entirely; that could happen only, as Benjamin puts it in a French version of "On the Concept of History," to "*une humanité restituée et sauve*" (*WuN*19, 61).

In justice, there is simply healing from meaning as semantic content. Benjamin's 1916 essay on language notes that language is inherently insubordinate, indomitable by any communication (*SW*1, 65/ *GS*II:1, 144). In the essay of 1921 on translation, he refers to a linguistic indomitability that is unforgettable, somehow presupposed, regardless of how much we seem to forget it. As ineradicable release from meaning, it is "God's remembrance" (*ein Gedenken Gottes*) (*SW*1, 254/ *GS*IV:1, 10). This remembrance concerns language beyond where "meaning" [*Sinn*] is "the watershed of language" (262/ 21). Messianic time heals in the justice of necessarily rebuffing semantic contents. As what Benjamin sometimes calls "community" (*SW*1, 67, 67/ *GS*II:1, 147, 150; *C*, 52/ *GB*1, 164), messianic time is the community in which time convalesces with the justice of giving no rest to meaning, no more rest than is given by the cosmos. This unrest is the justice, and the sole irrevocable significance, of time. In an essay of 1931 on Karl Kraus, Benjamin considers it an inheritance from Judaism that Kraus has "justice and language remain founded in each other" (*SW*2, 443–444/ *GS*II:1, 349). The justice involves "a humanity that proves itself by destruction" (456/ 367). This is simply the destruction that will not indulge or submit to hypostasis. Any correlative health and happiness are bound to the justice with which the "new angel" frees humans by taking from them – rather than providing – any happiness that is in denial of time (456/ 367), any happiness that assumes it itself is fated.

Works Cited

Baecker, Dirk ed. *Kapitalismus als Religion*. Berlin: Kadmos, 2003.
Benjamin, Walter. *Arcades Project*. Ed. Rolf Tiedemann. Trans. Howard Eiland and Kevin McLaughlin. Cambridge MA: Harvard UP, 1999.
Benjamin, Walter. *Early Writings 1910–1917*. Trans. Howard Eiland and others. Cambridge MA: Harvard UP, 2011.
Benjamin, Walter. *Einbahnstraße, Werke und Nachlaß, Kritische Gesamtausgabe*, vol. 8. Ed. Detlev Schöttker with Steffen Haug. Frankfurt am Main: Suhrkamp, 2009.
Benjamin, Walter. "From a Notebook Walter Benjamin Lent to Me [Gershom Scholem]: 'Notes Toward a Work on the Category of Justice,'" In Benjamin, *Toward the Critique of Violence*, 65–66/ "Aus dem mir geliehenen Notizbuche Walter Benjamins. 'Notizen zu einer Arbeit über die Kategorie der Gerechtigkeit,'" in Gershom Scholem, *Tagebücher nebst Aufsätze und Entwurfen bis 1923. 1. Halbband 1913–1917*, eds. Karlfried Gründer and Friedrich Niewöhner with Herbert Kopp-Oberstebrink. Frankfurt am Main: Jüdischer Verlag, 1995, 401–2.

Benjamin, Walter. *Gesammelte Briefe*, vols I-VI. Eds. Christoph Gödde and Henry Lonitz. Frankfurt am Main: Suhrkamp, 1995–2000.
Benjamin, Walter. *Gesammelte Schriften*, Vols. I–VII. Eds. Rolf Tiedemann, Hermann Schweppenhauser, and others. Frankfurt am Main: Suhrkamp, 1974–89.
Benjamin, Walter. *Œuvres*, 3 vols. Ed. Rainer Rochlitz. Trans. Maurice de Gandillac, Rainer Rochlitz, and Pierre Rusch. Paris: Gallimard, 2000.
Benjamin, Walter. *Selected Writings*. 4 vols. Eds. Michael Jennings and others. Cambridge MA: Harvard UP, 1996, 1999, 2002, 2003.
Benjamin, Walter. *Toward the Critique of Violence. A Critical Edition*. Eds. Peter Fenves and Julia Ng. Stanford: Stanford UP, 2021.
Benjamin, Walter. *Über den Begriff der Geschichte, Werke und Nachlaß, Kritische Gesamtausgabe*, vol 19. Ed. Gérard Raulet. Berlin: Suhrkamp, 2010.
Birnbaum, Antonia. *Bonheur Justice. Walter Benjamin. Le détour grec*. Paris: Éditions Payot & Rivages, 2008.
Brod, Max. "Der Dichter Franz Kafka." *Die neue Rundschau*. Vol. 32, No. 1 (November 1921), 1210–16.
Cohen, Hermann. *Religion of Reason. Out of the Sources of Judaism*. Trans. Simon Kaplan. Atlanta, GA: 1995/ *Religion der Vernunft aus den Quellen des Judentums*. Wiesbaden: Fourier Verlag, 1988 (second edition).
Dardenne, Luc. *Sur l'affaire humaine*. Paris: Seuil, 2012.
Deuber-Mankowsky, Astrid. *Der frühe Walter Benjamin und Hermann Cohen. Jüdische Werte, Kritische Philosophie, vergängliche Erfahrung*. Berlin: Vorwerk 8, 2000.
Derrida, Jacques. "Faith and Knowledge: the Two Sources of 'Religion' at the Limits of Reason Alone." Trans. Samuel Weber. In Jacques Derrida and Gianni Vattimo eds. *Religion*. Stanford: Stanford UP, 1998, 1–78/ "Foi et savoir: les deux sources de la 'religion' aux limites de la simple raison." In Jacques Derrida and Gianni Vattimo, eds. *La Religion*. Paris: Éditions du Seuil, 1996, 9–86.
Derrida, Jacques. *Acts of Religion*, ed. Gil Anidjar. New York: Routledge, 2002.
Derrida, Jacques. *Specters of Marx: The State of the Debt, the Work of Mourning, and the New International*, trans. Peggy Kamuf. London: Routledge, 1994/ *Spectres de Marx. L'État de la dette, le travail du deuil et la nouvelle Internationale*. Paris: Galilée, 1993.
Düttmann, Alexander García. *Das Gedächtnis des Denkens*. Frankfurt am Main: Suhrkamp, 1991.
Eiland, Howard. "Benjamin's Concept of Fate." In Brendan Moran and Paula Schwebel eds. *Benjamin and Political Theology*. London: Bloomsbury, forthcoming.
Fenves, Peter. "Introduction." In Benjamin, *Toward the Critique of Violence*, 1–37.
Friedlaender, Salomo/ Mynona. *Schöpferische Indifferenz, Gesammelte Schriften*, vol. 10. eds. Hartmut Geerken and Detlef Thiel with the Kant-Forschungstelle der Universität Trier Herrsching: WAITAWHILE, 2009.
Gagneben, Jeanne Marie. "Über den Begriff der Geschichte." Trans. Marion Schotsch. In Burkhardt Lindner with Thomas Küpper and Timo Skrandies eds. *Benjamin-Handbuch: Leben – Werk – Wirkung*. Stuttgart: Verlag J.B. Metzler, 2006, 284–300.
Goethe, Johann von. *Wilhelm Meisters Lehrjahre. Werke* (Hamburger Ausgabe). Vol. 7. Munich: Deutscher Taschenbuch Verlag, 1998.
Gordon, Peter E. *Migrants in the Profane. Critical Theory and the Question of Secularization*. New Haven, CT: Yale UP, 2020.

Grimm, Jacob and Wilhelm (and the Berlin-Brandenburgische Akademie der Wissenschaft). *Deutsches Wörterbuch*. Leipzig: Verlag von. S. Hirzel, https://woerterbuchnetz.de, Accessed March 31st, 2023.

Habermas, Jürgen. *Auch eine Geschichte der Philosophie*, vol. 1. Berlin: Suhrkamp, 2019.

Habermas, Jürgen. "The Boundary between Faith and Knowledge: on the Reception and contemporary Importance of Kant's Philosophy of Religion," *Between Naturalism and Religion. Philosophical Essays*. Trans. Ciaran Cronin. Cambridge, UK: Polity, 2008, 208–47/ "Die Grenze zwischen Glauben und Wissen. Zur Wirkungsgeschichte und aktuellen Bedeutung von Kants Religionsphilosophie," *Zwischen Naturalismus und Religion. Philosophische Aufsätze*. Frankfurt am Main: Suhrkamp, 2005. 216–57.

Habermas, Jürgen. *Glauben und Wissen. Friedenspreis des Deutschen Buchhandels 2001*. Frankfurt am Main: Suhrkamp, 2001.

Habermas, Jürgen. *The Philosophical Discourse of Modernity. Twelve Lectures*. Cambridge, MA: MIT Press, 1990/ *Der philosophische Diskurs der Moderne. Zwölf Vorlesungen*. Frankfurt am Main: Suhrkamp, 1985.

Habermas, Jürgen. "A Reply to my Critics," in John B. Thompson and David Held eds. *Habermas. Critical Debates*. Cambridge, MA: MIT Press, 1982, 219–83/ "Replik auf Einwände,"*Vorstudien und Ergänzung zur Theorie des kommunikativen Handelns*. Frankfurt am Main: Suhrkamp, 1984, 475–570.

Habermas, Jürgen. "Walter Benjamin: Consciousness-Raising or Rescuing Critique." *Philosophical-Political Profiles*. Trans. Frederick G. Lawrence. Cambridge MA: The MIT Press, 1972, 131–65/ "Bewußtmachende oder rettende Kritik." *Philosophisch-politische Profile*. Frankfurt am Main: Suhrkamp, 336–76.

Hamacher, Werner. "Das Theologische-politische Fragment." In Burkhardt Lindner with Thomas Küpper and Timo Skrandies eds. *Benjamin-Handbuch: Leben – Werk – Wirkung*. Stuttgart: Verlag J.B. Metzler, 2006, 175–92.

Das Herkunftswörterbuch. Etymologie der deutschen Sprache. Mannheim: Dudenverlag, 2001.

Honneth, Axel. "A Communicative Disclosure of the Past: On the Relation between Anthropology and Philosophy of History in Walter Benjamin." Trans. J. Farrell. *New Formations*, no. 20 (Summer 1993), 81–94/ "Kommunikative Erschießung der Vergangenheit. Zum Zusammenhang von Anthropologie und Geschichtsphilosophie bei Walter Benjamin," *Die zerrissene Welt des Sozialen. Sozialphilosophische Aufsätze* Frankfurt am Main: Suhrkamp, 1999 (expanded edition), 93–113.

Horkheimer, Max. *Briefwechsel 1937–1940. Gesammelte Schriften*, vol. 16. Frankfurt am Main: Fischer, 1995.

Horkheimer, Max. *Critique of Instrumental Reason*. Trans. Matthew J. O'Connell and others. New York: Continuum, 1974.

Horkheimer, Max. *Gesammelte Schriften*, vol. 7: *Vorträge und Aufzeichnungen 1949–1973*. Ed. Gunzelin Schmid-Noerr. Frankfurt am Main: Fischer, 1985.

Kafka, Franz. *Amerika: The Missing Person*. Trans. Mark Harman. New York: Schocken Books, 2008/ *Der Verschollene*. Ed. Jost Schillemeit. *Schriften, Tagebücher, Kritische Ausgabe*. Eds. Jürgen Born, Gerhard Neumann, Malcolm Pasley, and Jost Schillemeit. Frankfurt am Main: Fischer, 2002.

Kafka, Franz. *Nachgelassene Schriften und Fragmente* II. Ed. Jost Schillemeit. *Schriften, Tagebücher, Kritische Ausgabe*. Frankfurt am Main: Fischer, 2002.

Kraft, Werner. "Geld und Güte. Der Kübelreiter," *Franz Kafka. Durchdringung und Geheimnis*. Frankfurt am Main: Suhrkamp, 1968, 30–35.

Metz, Johann Baptist. "Anamnestic Reason: A Theologian's Remarks on the Crisis in the *Geisteswissenschaften.*" Trans. Barbara Fultner. In *Cultural-Political Interventions in the Unfinished Project of Enlightenment*, eds. Axel Honneth, Thomas McCarthy, Claus Offe, and Albrecht Wellmer. Cambridge, MA: The MIT Press, 1992, 189–194/ "Anamnetische Vernunft. Anmerkungen eines Theoloen zur Krise der Geisteswissenschaften." In *Zwischenbetrachtungen. Im Prozeß der Aufklärung. Jürgen Habermas zum 60. Geburtstag.* Eds. Axel Honneth, Thomas McCarthy, Claus Offe, and Albrecht Wellmer. Frankfurt am Main: 1989, 733–38.

Mondzain, Marie José. *K. comme Kolonie. Kafka et la décolonisation de l'imaginaire.* Paris: La fabrique éditions, 2020.

Moran, Brendan. "Nature, Decision and Muteness." In Brendan Moran and Carlo Salzani, eds. *Towards the Critique of Violence. Walter Benjamin and Giorgio Agamben.* London: Bloomsbury, 2015, 73–90.

Moran, Brendan. *Politics of Benjamin's Kafka. Philosophy as Renegade.* London: Palgrave Macmillan, 2018.

Moran, Brendan. "Politics of Creative Indifference." *Philosophy Today.* Vol. 55, No. 3 (Fall 2011), 321–36.

Ng, Julia and Rochelle Tobias, eds. *Walter Benjamin, Gershom Scholem, and the Marburg School. Modern Language Notes.* Vol. 127 (3), 2012.

Nietzsche, Friedrich. *Werke. Kritische Gesamtausgabe.* Vol. VI:1. Eds. Giorgio Colli and Mazzimo Montinari. Berlin: Walter de Gruyter, 1968.

Onions, C.T. ed. with G.W.S. Friedrichsen and R.W. Burchfield. *Oxford Dictionary of English Etymology.* Oxford: Oxford UP, 1966.

Rrenban, Monad. *Wild, Unforgettable Philosophy in Early Works by Walter Benjamin.* Lanham, MD: Lexington Books, 2005.

Scholem, Gershom. *On the Kabbalah and its Symbolism.* Trans. Ralph Mannheim. New York: Schocken Books, 1969/ *Zur Kabbala und ihrer Symbolik.* Frankfurt am Main: Suhrkamp, 1989.

Scholem, Gershom. *Tagebücher nebst Aufsätzen und Entwürfen bis 1923 2. Halbband 1917–1923.* Eds. Karlfried Gründer, Herbert Kopp-Oberstebrink, and Fridrich Niewöhner with Karl E. Grözinger. Frankfurt am Main: Jüdischer Verlag, 2000.

Tagliacozzo, Tamara. *Experience and Infinite Task. Knowledge, Language and Messianism in the Philosophy of Walter Benjamin.* London: Rowman and Littlefield International, 2018.

Taubes, Jacob. *The Political Theology of Paul*, trans. Dana Hollander. Stanford, CA: Stanford UP, 2004/ *Die politische Theologie des Paulus*, eds. Aleida and Jan Assmann with Horst Folkers, Wolf-Daniel Harwich, and Christoph Schulte. Munich: Wilhelm Fink Verlag, 2003.

Thiel, Detlef. *Maßnahmen des Erscheinens. Friedlaender/ Mynona im Gespräch mit Schelling, Husserl, Benjamin und Derrida.* Nordhausen: Verlag Traugott Bautz, 2012.

Herta Nagl-Docekal
Re-considering the Distinction between Atheists and Believers, or: Max Horkheimer's Reading of Kant

Abstract: *Part I* introduces Max Horkheimer's thesis that all human beings share "the desire for the totally other". Even atheists, he argues, feel a longing "that the murderer must not triumph over the innocent victim". *Part II* examines this thesis in the light of Immanuel Kant's claim that there is a "need" for moral reason to assume "the existence of God and a future life", and highlights Kant's distinction between "the purely moral religion" and the teachings of the diverse historical churches. *Part III* discusses different arguments employed in theories of the shared hope for transcending human finiteness, focusing not only on concepts of justice and morality but also on experiences of love and grief, as explored by G.W.F. Hegel. *Part IV* raises the question whether, under the contemporary economic and technological conditions, humans may eventually lose their intuition for a better understanding of life, ending up in the "suffocation of the spirit" that Charles Taylor addresses.

1 "The Desire for the Totally Other"

When Max Horkheimer, in a conversation on the occasion of his seventy-fifth birthday that was published in *Der Spiegel* in January 1970[1], advocated a "theology of hope" (Horkheimer 1970, 61), a storm of indignation broke out. Numerous critics blamed him for betraying the key principles of the Frankfurt School. This heated reaction failed, however, to notice that Horkheimer, as well as Adorno, had expressed thoughts on religion that were not in line with mainstream Marxist positions as early as the 1930s.[2] Furthermore, it is worth noting that Horkheimer's habilitation thesis, submitted in 1925, as well as his previous doctoral thesis, focused on Immanuel Kant's *Critique of Judgment* (Horkheimer 1925).

---

[1] Cf. *Der Spiegel* 1970. For a slightly modified version of that conversation, see: Horkheimer 1970. The passages cited from the *Spiegel* conversation as well as from Horkheimer 1970 have been translated by Herta Nagl-Docekal.
[2] For instance, Lutz-Bachmann, based on a chronological investigation, argues that "Horkheimer's understanding of religion has been consistent all along." Lutz-Bachmann 1986, 108 (transl. H.N.-D.)

What stands out in the *Spiegel* interview, is the thesis that a "desire for the totally other" (Horkheimer 1970, 62) is known even to atheists. With reference to the heinous crimes committed under the totalitarian regimes of the twentieth century, Horkheimer claims that, facing the tremendous pain that has been inflicted on innocent people, we find ourselves unable to accept the idea that there might be no ultimate "sense". Just like "every thinking human being" (*Der Spiegel*, 1970, 81), atheists would dismiss this idea – albeit without reflecting – as they feel a longing "that the murderer must not triumph over the innocent victim." (Horkheimer 1970, 62) This longing indicates, he argues, a rudimentary "theology of hope," which is based on the claim "that the injustice which characterizes our world [...] may not represent the final verdict." (Horkheimer 1970, 61) It is important to consider, however, Horkheimer adds, that this basic hope does not represent a transition into an explicit religious conviction. "The consciousness of our forlornness, our finiteness, is no proof for the existence of God; it can only generate the hope that there might be a positive absolute." (Horkheimer 1970, 56) Yet even this vague kind of hope can be of relevance for our practice: "We cannot appeal to God. We can only act with the internal feeling that a God does exist." (Horkheimer 1970, 72)

Two implications of these reflections need to be considered: firstly, that human beings will never be able to overcome fully the pains of their finiteness, even if they were eventually to succeed in cooperatively establishing just socio-economic conditions; secondly, that Horkheimer links the internal hope to morality: "Anything related to morality is ultimately based on theology, certainly not on secular reasons" (*Der Spiegel* 1970, 80), he argues. Significantly, both claims correspond with key concepts elaborated by Kant; let us therefore turn to Kant's in-depth philosophical exploration of the basis of religion.

2 The "Purely Moral Religion"

In contrast to a widely shared opinion, we need to note that the prime focus of Kant's philosophy of religion is not on historical creeds or churches; he rather explores what religion is all about – that is to say, why people in all past eras and cultures across the globe have developed religious teachings and practices, albeit in very different forms. He maintains that religion is anchored in our experience of the unavoidable limits of moral life. Pondering over the earliest humans, Kant notes: "As soon as human beings began to reflect on right and wrong [...], the judgment must inevitably have occurred to them that it could not in the end make no difference if a person has conducted himself rightly or falsely, fairly or violently, even if to the end of his life he has found at least no visible reward for his virtues or punishment for his crimes. It is as if they heard an inner voice that things must come out differently" (Kant 2000, 322–323; 5:458).³

In systematic philosophical terms, Kant explains that, as the human being is an "animal capable of reason (*animal rationabile*)," we find ourselves unavoidably caught up in the tension between virtue and bliss. As living creatures, we strive for our well-being: "To be happy is necessarily the desire of every rational but finite being, and thus it is an unavoidable determinant of its faculty of desire" (Kant 1996b, 159; 5:25); our (practical) reason, however, confronts us with the moral law that demands that we make respect for the dignity of every human being (including ourselves) the highest maxim of our actions, rather than our desire for happiness. This demand constitutes the core of Kant's concept of the "categorical imperative" (Kant 1996a, 67–89; 4:413–40). Clearly, the moral imperative does not suggest a form of action that might preserve us from experiencing the tension that characterizes the human condition. As we all know, to abide by the moral law often requires putting aside our personal well-being, in some cases even risking grave repercussions.

Hence Kant focuses on the question: can we expect, eventually, to achieve the degree of happiness that we assume "being worthy of" (Kant 1998, 680; A:810/B: 838)? At first sight, he notes, there is no good reason for such an expectation – obviously, humans are incapable of bringing about a congruence of virtue and bliss by their own efforts. Rather, we find ourselves trapped in an absurd position: while our practical reason demands that we persistently act in a way that makes the harmony of virtue and bliss possible, and while this harmony represents "the highest good" (Kant 1996b, 255; 5:144) of human beings, we face the unlikeliness of this concurrence under real life conditions. Resignation and despair seem to be the obvious response. However, Kant argues, it is only from an empirical, that is to say, immanent perspective that the human condition appears absurd. (We might recall folk wisdom here, which holds that "the sun shines alike on the good and the evil.") Our practical reason challenges the impression of absurdity, including the resignation and despair provoked by it, as it opens up the hope that virtue and bliss will ultimately be reconciled by God.⁴ Kant maintains that religion, in the fundamental form that he calls "natural religion," (Kant 1996d, 177; 6:154) constitutes a crucial implication of our practical reason.

---

3 The citation 5: 458 refers to the German edition of Kant's works published by the Berlin-Brandenburgische Academy of Sciences (Kant AA), specifying volume and page. All the following quotations from Kant will be cited in this manner.
4 The way in which "hope" proves to be a key concept of Kant's philosophy of religion is explained in: Nagl-Docekal 2020a.

Kant summarizes the logic of his argument in this manner: "It is a duty to realize the highest good as far as it lies within our power to do so; therefore, it must be possible to do so. Consequently, it is unavoidable for every rational being in the world to assume whatever is necessary to its objective possibility." (Kant 1996b, 255; 5:144) Thus, it is "*a need* of pure practical reason" (Kant 1996b, 254; 5:142) to presuppose the existence of a "supreme intelligence" (Kant 1996b, 241; 5:126), that is to say, "it is morally necessary to assume the existence of God" (Kant 1996b, 241; 5:125). This need of pure practical reason constitutes the "certainty" of my "belief in the existence of God and of a future life" (Kant 1998, 689; A 828/B 857)[5]. In order to emphasize the practical character of this "certainty", Kant introduces the concept of the "postulates of pure practical reason": "These postulates are not theoretical dogmas but presuppositions having a necessarily practical reference" (Kant 1996b, 246; 5:132)[6].

We need to consider what Kant is seeking to achieve here: he addresses the distinct character of faith, as we perceive it in the context of ordinary language. Typically, we understand the term "religious belief" as referring neither to the sphere of theoretical knowledge (we do not normally view non-believers as displaying a lack of logical thinking), nor to the sphere of mere "opinion" (that would refer to individual conceptions). Specifying the kind of "certainty" that he addresses here, Kant explains that

> conviction is not *logical* but *moral* certainty and, since it depends on subjective grounds (of moral disposition), I must not even say '*It is* morally certain that there is a God,' but rather '*I am* morally certain', etc. That is, the belief in a God and another world is so interwoven with my moral disposition that I am in as little danger of ever surrendering the former as I am worried that the latter can ever be torn away from me" (Kant 1998, 689; A 829/B 857). [7]

In systematic terms, Kant argues that it is only through the postulates of our practical reason that the world can be conceived as one consistent whole. Unless we suppose one "highest intelligence", we face an unavoidable breach: while the laws of nature cover everything that is empirically given, human moral action would represent an insurmountable fissure undermining the very idea of *one* cosmos.

It is important to note how Kant defines the role of philosophy here: his claim that "the grounds of proof" he proposes "can be grasped universally and are suf-

---

[5] See also: Kant 2004, 125.
[6] Kant further elucidates this thought in: Kant 1996b, 238–247; 5:122–133. An in-depth examination of Kant's concept of the postulates is provided in: Byrne 2007, 84–93.
[7] For a re-construction of Kant's thoughts on the intrinsic relation between our moral disposition and the belief in God see: Nagl-Docekal 2010.

ficient from a moral standpoint" (Kant 1998, 118; B XXXIII) is not based on the idea of a philosophy that suggests adopting certain religious convictions. Rather, Kant maintains that this "proof" is furnished by the pure practical reason that we all share, while the task of philosophy is only to spell out what each of us has already performed, albeit in an inexplicit manner. He argues: "This moral proof is not any newly invented argument, but at most only a newly articulated one." (Kant 2000, 322; 5:458) Accordingly, Kant emphasizes that the "moral proof" is not only intelligible to learned people. Rather, he states, "the pure religious faith [...] is a plain rational faith which can be convincingly communicated to everyone" (Kant 1996d, 136–137; 6:102–03). Kant finds himself in agreement with 1 Corinthians 1:26 and 27 here, as he notes that "it is reasonable to assume that not just the 'wise after the flesh,' the learned or skilled in ratiocination, are called to this enlightenment [...] – for the whole human race should be capable of this faith – but rather 'the foolish things of the world,' even the ignorant and those most limited conceptually, must be able to lay claim to such instruction and inner conviction." (Kant 1996d, 175; 6:181)[8]

Thus, Kant's most important claim is that religion is originally rooted in every human being. As "natural religion" – which is characterized as "a purely moral religion" (Kant 1996d, 137; 6: 103) – contains the very essence of religion, it provides the foundation for all the different creeds that have been developed in the course of history. Kant maintains: "All religion is based on *Theismus moralis*." (Kant AA 28: 1141). Accordingly, he argues: "There is only one (true) *religion*; but there can be several kinds of *faith*." (Kant 1996d, 140; 6:107–08) Kant regards the various forms of "historical (ecclesiastical) faith" (Kant 1996d, 147; 6:116) as important "vehicles" (Kant 1996d, 149; 6:118) for the progress of education that have allowed humans, within the framework of their respective socio-economic conditions, to become ever more clearly aware of the moral essence of their faith. This thesis is of relevance with regard to current conflicts with religious connotations: Kant's prime focus is not on addressing the disparities – or similarities – of religious confessions on the surface level, as it were, but on considering their shared moral basis. From this perspective every creed, since humanity's earliest religious ideas, has had intrinsic value, and the task is to examine which contribution each of them has made to enhancing humanity's understanding of moral duty.

On this basis, Kant undermines the distinction between believers and non-believers. He explicitly defends the concept of "pure religious faith" with regard to

---

[8] See: "For ye see your calling, brethren, how that not many wise men after the flesh, not many mighty, not many noble, are called." (1 Corinthians 1:26) And: "But God hath chosen the foolish things of the word to confound the wise; and God hath chosen the weak things of the world to confound the things which are mighty." (1 Corinthians 1:27)

persons who claim to be atheists, emphasizing the difference between theory and practice: "Atheism can be in pure speculation, but in *praxi* such a person can be a theist or can venerate God; his error concerns theology rather than religion."[9] In other words, Kant's distinction between the one moral religion and the many forms of historical faith suggests that people who claim to be non-believers do, in fact, specifically reject any form of ecclesiastical faith. By contrast, his conception of "pure religious faith" allows him to state poignantly: "Religion is that what is of interest to everybody."[10] It is obviously this claim that Horkheimer sought to render convincing to his contemporaries of Marxist conviction (as reported above).[11]

3 Hoping for Love to Transcend Finiteness

While Horkheimer as well as Kant seek to underpin the "theology of hope" with reference to our perception of justice and morality, one may wonder whether yet another path of argumentation might be proposed. As we consider on which occasions people – including persons who identify themselves as non-believers – are most likely to express confidence in a future life, we typically encounter situations of utmost grief over the death of a beloved person. Evidently, many people share the hope for a happy reunion with lost loved ones in another world.

Thus we need to examine what the intimate bond between persons who love each other – be it the bond between spouses, or parents and children, or close

---

9 "Der Atheismus kann in der puren Speculation sein, aber in der praxi kann ein solcher [Mensch] ein Theist oder ein Verehrer Gottes seyn; dessen Irrtum erstreckt sich auf die Theologie und nicht auf die Religion" (Kant 2004, 125. Transl. H. N.-D.). Allen Wood re-constructs a complex line of thought in Kant: "What moral arguments show is that morally disposed people are involved in a kind of practical irrationality unless they believe in a future life and a providential and gracious Deity." (Wood 1992, 404) He goes on to note: "Occasionally Kant weakens his conclusion [...]. The 'minimum of theology,' he says, is not that God exists but only that God is possible. [...] Devoted pursuit of one's final moral end might be better served by a confidence that the highest good will at last be attained, but the bare minimum reason requires is belief that it is possible of attainment. Hence Kant thinks that morality is compatible with a hopeful agnosticism about God's existence, even though something stronger than this would be preferable." (Wood 1992, 405) Wood further states: "only the minimum cognition (it is possible that there is a God) has to be subjectively sufficient [...]. I can have religion in this sense even if I am an agnostic". (Wood 1992, 406) Wood refers here to: Kant 1998, 153.
10 "Religion ist das, was jeden interessiert." (Kant AA 28: 1323, transl. H. N.-D.) For a systematic examination of Kant's concept of shared hope see: McCammon 2006.
11 A comprehensive exploration of the ways in which Horkheimer adopted key elements of Kant's philosophy of religion is provided in: Nagl-Docekal 2020b.

friends – is all about. In this regard, it is worth re-reading Hegel's most elaborate theory of genuine love that is based on his key concept "Spirit". As Hegel explains, in a loving relationship we give up our particularistic attitude, as we mutually heed and support the uniqueness of the other. Precisely because – as Spirit – we share the same mode of being, our uniqueness does deserve equal attention. To love someone, he notes, means "to relate to this person's singularity" (Hegel 1970c, 283), that is to the "whole subjective personality – with all that it is and contains" (Hegel 2014, vol. II, 562). (For further elucidation of this point one might refer to Hannah Arendt's considerations maintaining that "only love is fully receptive to *who* somebody is" (Arendt 1998, 242–243).[12]) In order to illustrate the importance of individual distinction, Hegel refers to Shakespeare: "Compare Juliet in *Romeo and Juliet:* 'the more I give to thee, the more I have'. This wealth of life love acquires in the exchange of every thought, every variety of inner experience, for it seeks out differences and devises unifications ad infinitum; it turns to the whole manifold of nature in order to drink love out of every life." (Hegel 1975, 307) This mode of full involvement entails that love liberates our "opposite of all foreign character […]. In love the separate does still remain, but no longer *as* separate, rather as something united." (Hegel 1975, 305)[13]

Neither individual, however, simply brings his or her specific identity into the relationship – as something external, as it were – rather, lovers are also being shaped by their relationship. It is only through their love "that they acquire their subjectivity […] which constitutes their personality" (Hegel 1970b, 233). Thus Hegel argues: "Love is the distinction of two who are, at the same time, absolutely indistinct for one another. The feeling and consciousness of this identity is what constitutes love, this being beside myself: I have my self-consciousness not in myself but in the other, yet this other, in whom alone I am satisfied […], as he is equally being beside himself, has his consciousness only in me, both of us being nothing but the consciousness of this being beside oneself. To perceive, to feel, to know this unity – this is what constitutes love." (Hegel 1970c, 222) As they have developed, in this manner, a shared identity, lovers typically speak in terms of 'we,' by which they mean as one single person. Hegel chooses a poignant mode of expression: "The I is 'we' [a plurality], and the 'we' is a single I." (Hegel 1967, 227) Obviously, love in the sense of such a comprehensive bondage does have an exclusive character: "The human beings whom one is able to love and towards whom love is real, are only a few special ones." (Hegel 1971, 283)

---

[12] The importance of individuality for the loving relationship is also analyzed in: Nussbaum 1998 and Nussbaum 2000.
[13] The English translation was slightly altered here by H. N.-D., according to the German original.

These reflections also bring to light the specific temporality of love: The 'exchange of every thought' and the overcoming of 'all foreign character' can be aimed at only in a continuous process. Moreover, individuality always remains open to change – as long as we live, it does never reach a point of completion. Therefore, love unavoidably has an aspect of futurity. Hegel maintains that this close relation involves subjectivity "as this individual, as I was, am, and will be" (Hegel 2014, vol. II, 562). From this perspective, he emphasizes the importance of forgiveness, arguing in the following way: When one of the partners has offended the other, they both fall back into separateness; yet, while it is evidently impossible to undo an offensive act, love is able to bring about full reconciliation – "only love is capable of forgiving" (Hegel 1991, 393). It is worth noting here that Hegel's Jesus, "the prophet of universal love", represents primarily the attitude of "loving forgiveness" (Harris 1993, 30).

The competence which allows us to develop such a personal attachment is "feeling," but "not a single feeling [among other single feelings]" (Hegel 1975, 304). As Hegel emphasizes, we need to consider the difference between love and a fragmented Eros. The latter, typically, is guided by a "single feeling" and therefore bound to move on continuously: "A single feeling is only a part and not the whole of life; the life present in a single feeling dissolves its barriers and drives on till it disperses itself in the manifold of feelings with a view to finding itself in the entirety of this manifold." (Hegel 1975, 305) This aim can never be achieved, however, since dispersion can only result in a series of "many particular and isolated feelings" (Hegel 1975, 305), Hegel maintains. In contrast to such an idea, he emphasizes that in love the "whole life is not contained [...] in the same way as it is in this sum of many particular and isolated feelings" (Hegel 1975, 305)[14]. It is a feeling of a different kind where love is located in Hegel's view – a feeling that lies beyond the sphere of momentous attraction and alienation, and also of momentous "happiness and unhappiness" (Hegel 1970a, 312)[15]. Hegel describes this feeling as "the deep feeling of the spirit" (Hegel 2014, vol. II, 539) [16] that "has the form of feeling, concentrated into itself," which, "instead of revealing its content [...], rather draws directly together into the simple depth of the heart that content's extent and boundlessness" (Hegel 2014, vol. II, 540).

Underscoring the comprehensive character of love, Hegel contends: "In the lovers there is no matter; they are a living whole." (Hegel 1975, 305) Consequently, it would seem totally inappropriate to view love as being grounded in a desire fo-

---

14 The English translation was slightly altered here by H. N.-D., according to the German original.
15 This passage is not contained in the English translation used here.
16 The German expression Hegel uses here is "Innigkeit des Geistes" (Hegel, 1970b, 154).

cusing on bodily features or on the social status of a person. In Hegel's terms, such a form of fixation would mean "that something dead here forms one term of the love relationship, [that] love is girt by matter alone" (Hegel 1975, 303). Similarly, any attempt to "captivate" someone by means of physical attractiveness would disclose an attitude which attributes "intrinsic worth" to the "mortal body" (Hegel 1975, 306). In this context, he also addresses the scandal of sexual abuse: as he points out, the "hostility in a loveless assault does injury to the loving heart itself" (Hegel 1975, 306).

One crucial element of the intimate bondage of love is, as Hegel emphasizes, our grief over the death of a beloved person. The passing of this precious, unique individual, he notes, causes "infinite pain" (Hegel 2005, 211). Yet, true love also opens up a perspective that transcends our finiteness; our grief carries with it a sense that death does not have the final word. Since love represents a relation between Spirit and Spirit, "this pain implies necessarily that [...] the natural, obviously, is not identical with the spiritual" (Hegel 2005, 160). In his lectures on art, Hegel interprets the medieval paintings of "Mary at the Cross" as the most subtle rendering of this insight. What is "expressed in this absolute pain of the soul, that is love itself" (Hegel 2005, 211): "The heart of this mother is broken, but her pain does not petrify her like Niobe"; the expression of her face rather reveals "that Spirit is blissful elsewhere" (Hegel 2005, 211).

It seems that Kant's reflections on love – that operate with the dyad of "pathological love," defined by sensual inclination, and "practical love," based on moral duty (Kant 1996a, 55; 4:399) – fail to fully capture the distinctly personal relation portrayed by Hegel.[17] Therefore it might be appropriate to introduce Hegel's thoughts into the framework of Kant's "moral proof". Thus we may find that, in love, we are gifted with a concurrence of morality and happiness that allows us to know, in this world already – albeit merely in a manner marked by finiteness – what represents our highest good. Significantly, Hegel defines love as the "worldly religion of the heart" (Hegel 1970b, 186)[18]. In Kantian terms, we may conclude that, as the loss of a beloved individual represents the utmost bereavement, we respond with the postulate that death must not have the final word.

---

[17] This failure characterizes not only Kant's reflections. We also find it in traditional naturalistic conceptions of love that, typically, move from Eros (with the perspective of procreation) to the universal love of our neighbors, failing to address the specific character of intimate bonds. For a further discussion of this problem see: Nagl-Docekal, 2015.
[18] A detailed examination of Hegel's reflections on love is provided in: Nagl-Docekal 2013 and Nagl-Docekal 2014, 129–47.

4 Is the Stifling of the Spirit Imminent?

Under the present conditions, however, people seem to be losing their shared fundamental hope. In view of the fact that the logic of capitalism has permeated all spheres of life on a global scale, Horkheimer warns that the "powers of technology and ruthless competition" will result in a specific form of totalitarianism. Humanity is bound to end up in "the totally administered world," he claims, where "people will adopt the rationalistic rules, eventually observing them instinctively and acting in an automatic manner" (Horkheimer 1970, 83–4). In his earlier book *Critical Theory* he had noted: "it is as if thinking itself is about to be reduced to the level of industrial processes [...], in short, to be incorporated as a regular component of production" (Horkheimer 1968, vol. II, 234)[19].

Horkheimer anticipates that this development will affect believers and non-believers alike: "[T]he greater the progress achieved, the more endangered will be not only belief but also the true longing for the better. For this reason, any form of non-positivist thinking and feeling will increasingly be considered a phenomenon of humanity's childhood" (Horkheimer 1970, 75–6). When "the theological is abolished," he notes, "what we call 'meaning' will vanish from the world. [...] And one day philosophy, too, will be considered a matter of humanity's childhood" (Horkheimer 1970, 88–9). In accordance with his diagnosis of the "eclipse of reason," as formulated in 1947[20], Horkheimer observes "a brutalization of personal as well as public life" that will cause "spiritual misery" (Horkheimer 1970, 70). He claims in particular that "the cultivation of conscience is being endangered" (Horkheimer 1970, 79). Significantly, both Horkheimer and Adorno share Kant's view that the loss of hope is bound to have a serious effect on our moral motivation. Kant writes in this regard: Were I to give up the reason-based hope that my life may, ultimately, make sense, the consequence would be that "my moral principles themselves [...] would thereby be subverted" (Kant 1998, 689; A828/B856).

Horkheimer and Adorno put forward an example of the devastating consequences of the loss of hope that marks our time. In *Dialectic of Enlightenment*, they address "the panic which nowadays is ready to break out at every moment: men [people] expect that the world, which has no exit, will be set on fire by a totality which they themselves are and over which they have no control" (Adorno

---

[19] In his "Brief an den S. Fischer Verlag", dated 3 June 1965, Horkheimer articulated a similar perception, noting that his previously "auf Analyse der Gesellschaft bauender Glaube an fortschrittliche Aktivität schlägt in Angst vor neuem Unheil, vor der Herrschaft allumfassender Verwaltungen um." (Horkheimer 1968, vol. I, IX). Horkheimer's "pessimism" is discussed in: Rosen 1995, 135.
[20] See Horkheimer 1947.

and Horkheimer 2016, 29). Taking a look at the products of cultural industry that are currently highly esteemed across the globe, we find, I think, that this diagnosis is even more appropriate today than when it was first conceived.

About twenty years after Horkheimer's *Spiegel* conversation, and from a different philosophical point of view, Charles Taylor, in his book *The Sources of the Self*, reaches a similar verdict on the rationalized life in what he calls Western modernity[21]. Examining the widely adopted "prosaic worldly attitude that lacks any religious dimension," he claims that this attitude amounts to a "stifling," as it "involves stifling the response in us to some of the deepest and most powerful spiritual aspirations that humans have conceived" (Taylor 1989, 520). Taylor notes that "we tend in our culture to stifle the spirit," and he adds that, since the rejected goods "are our goods, human goods, *we* are stifling" (Taylor 1989, 520). In search for a way out of that malaise, he pleads for a "retrieval" of the immense variety of "suppressed goods" (Taylor 1989, 504), advocating a broad process of education that includes the reception of works of art.[22] As he explains, "humanity's highest spiritual ideals and aspirations" (Taylor 1989, 519) have been mediated through "languages which resonate within him or her" (Taylor 1996, 880). (In order to illustrate this claim, he frequently refers to Dostoyevsky.[23])

One key concept in this context is "resonance"[24]; Taylor typically contends that, today, "we need new languages of personal resonance to make crucial human goods alive for us again" (Taylor 1989, 513). Evidently, he attributes to human beings a shared original predisposition that makes our internal resonance to languages that express our "moral sources" (Taylor 1989, 512) possible. Taylor does not provide an in-depth examination of that predisposition, however; he prefers not to confront the loss of meaning felt in the present time with a deep-seated desire in every human being ultimately to transcend the misery that characterizes our finiteness. The fact that he leaves this fundamental question unanswered does eventually affect his view on the relation between believers and non-believers – an issue that Taylor discusses more extensively in *A Secular Age*. We find a significant ambivalence in this regard.

On the one hand, Taylor deems these two groups of people "brothers under the skin" (Taylor 2007, 675), as he claims that all human beings are inspired by conceptions of meaning that provide the guidelines "by which we moderns live, even

---

21 Cf. Taylor 1991.
22 Taylor deplores that the widely shared prosaic attitude is "not only closed to any theistic perspective," but cannot even find a place for what "has been an important part of modernist art, be it in Rilke, Proust, Mann, Eliot or Kafka" (Taylor 1989, 506).
23 See, for instance, Taylor 1989, 451–5, 516–17.
24 Cf. Goldstein 2018.

those who believe they deny them" (Taylor 1989, 511). Analyzing the "exclusive humanism" (Taylor 2007, 18, 245) that motivates non-believers, he introduces the notion of "fullness," arguing that "there is no escaping some version of [...] 'fullness'" (Taylor 2007, 600). While our ways of understanding human life may differ widely, we all "have the powerful intuition of what fullness would be" (Taylor 2007, 5). Commenting on that thought, Ruth Abbey notes that Taylor, in fact, "offers his idea of fullness as a heuristic device in the current debate about and between religious and non-religious positions" (Abbey 2016, 226), suggesting that we "try to understand what 'fullness' means for the other" (Taylor 2013, 318). On the other hand, Taylor clearly keeps the two sides apart by emphasizing that the aspirations of "exclusive humanism" are bound to remain on a purely immanent level, while religious convictions provide what may be called a "vertical" perspective, that is to say, a "view of human existence that is open to transcendence" (Abbey 2016, 229). As Abbey points out, Taylor in *A Secular Age* even "associates exclusive humanism with forces of darkness" (Abbey 2016, 230)[25].

Confronted with this ambivalence in Taylor, we need to take a nuanced stance. In addition to appreciating his concept of "resonance," there are good reasons for turning to theories which claim that a perspective of transcendence is anchored in every human being. Thus, it seems worth reconsidering Horkheimer's idea of a "theology of hope" and Kant's conception of the "need" of moral reason. Furthermore, it is important to note that both authors assign a crucial task to philosophy. Horkheimer, for instance, calls for a critical theory that, by insisting on the "unavoidable finiteness of humans," is able to "warn society away from a stupid optimism, i. e., from puffing up its limited knowledge into a new religion" (Horkheimer 1970, 54).

Works Cited

Abbey, Ruth. "Siblings Under the Skin. Charles Taylor on religious believers and non-believers in a Secular Age." *Religion and Atheism: Beyond the Divide*. Ed. Anthony Carroll and Richard Norman. Oxford, UK: Routledge, 2016. 221–31.
Adorno, Theodor W. *Negative Dialektik*. Frankfurt a. M.: Suhrkamp, 1970.
Adorno, Theodor W. and Max Horkheimer. *Dialectic of Enlightenment*. London: Verso, 2016.
Arendt, Hannah. *The Human Condition*. Second edition, Chicago and London: The University of Chicago Press, 1998.
Brandt, Reinhard. *Die Bestimmung des Menschen bei Kant*., Hamburg: Felix Meiner, 2007.
Byrne, Peter. *Kant on God*. Aldershot, UK – Burlington, VT: Ashgate, 2007.

---

25 Abbey cites here: Taylor 2007, 376.

Goldstein, Jürgen. "Resonance – A key concept in the philosophy of Charles Taylor." *Philosophy and Social Criticism* 44 (7) 2018: 781–83.
Harris, H.S. "Hegel's intellectual development to 1807." *The Cambridge Companion to Hegel*. Ed. Frederick Beiser. Cambridge, UK: Cambridge UP, 1993.
Hegel, Georg Wilhelm Friedrich. *The Phenomenology of Mind*. Trans. J. B. Baillie. New York and Evanston: Harper Torchbooks, 1967.
Hegel, Georg Wilhelm Friedrich. *Grundlinien der Philosophie des Rechts*. Hegel, *Werke in zwanzig Bänden*, vol. 7, Frankfurt a. M.: Suhrkamp, 1970 a.
Hegel, Georg Wilhelm Friedrich. *Vorlesungen über die Ästhetik II*. Hegel, *Werke in zwanzig Bänden*, vol. 14, Frankfurt a. M.: Suhrkamp, 1970b.
Hegel, Georg Wilhelm Friedrich. *Vorlesungen über die Philosophie der Religion II*. Hegel, *Werke in zwanzig Bänden*, vol. 17. Frankfurt a. M.: Suhrkamp, 1970c.
Hegel, Georg Wilhelm Friedrich. *Early Theological Writings*. Trans. T.M. Knox. Philadelphia: U of Pennsylvania P, 1975.
Hegel, Georg Wilhelm Friedrich. *Hegels Theologische Jugendschriften*. Ed. Hermann Nohl. Frankfurt a. M.: Suhrkamp, 1991.
Hegel, Georg Wilhelm Friedrich. *Philosophie der Kunst. Vorlesung von 1826*. Frankfurt a. M.: Suhrkamp, 2005.
Hegel, Georg Wilhelm Friedrich. *Aesthetics. Lectures on Fine Art*. Trans. T. M. Knox. Oxford, UK: Oxford UP, 2014.
Horkheimer, Max. *Kants Kritik der Urteilskraft als Bindeglied zwischen theoretischer und praktischer Vernunft* (Habilitationsschrift). Frankfurt a. M., 1925.
Horkheimer, Max. *Eclipse of Reason*. New York: Oxford UP, 1947. Reprint: London: Bloomsbury, 2013. German translation: "Die Verdüsterung der Vernunft." Horkheimer 1974. 11–174.
Horkheimer, Max. *Kritische Theorie. Eine Dokumentation*. Ed. Alfred Schmidt. 2 vol., Frankfurt a. M.: Suhrkamp, 1968.
Horkheimer, Max. *Die Sehnsucht nach dem ganz Anderen*. Ein Interview mit Kommentar von Helmut Gumnior. Hamburg: Furche-Verlag, 1970.
Horkheimer, Max. *Zur Kritik der instrumentellen Vernunft*. Frankfurt a. M.: Suhrkamp, 1974.
Kant, Immanuel. *Kants gesammelte Schriften*. Ed. Berlin-Brandenburgische Akademie der Wissenschaften 1900 ff. Berlin: de Gruyter. Sigle: AA.
Kant, Immanuel. *Groundwork of the Metaphysic of Morals*. Immanuel Kant, *Practical Philosophy*. Trans. Mary J. Gregor. Cambridge: Cambridge UP, 1996a. 37–108.
Kant, Immanuel. *Critique of Practical Reason*. Immanuel Kant, *Practical Philosophy*. Trans. Mary J. Gregor. Cambridge: Cambridge UP, 1996b. 133–271.
Kant, Immanuel. *The Metaphysics of Morals*. Immanuel Kant, *Practical Philosophy*. Trans. Mary J. Gregor. Cambridge: Cambridge UP, 1996c. 353–603.
Kant, Immanuel. *Religion Within the Boundaries of Mere Reason*. Immanuel Kant, *Religion and Rational Theology*. Trans. Allen W. Wood and George di Giovanni. Cambridge: Cambridge UP, 1996d. 39–215.
Kant, Immanuel. *The Critique of Pure Reason*. Trans. Paul Guyer and Allen W. Wood. Cambridge: Cambridge UP, 1998. Sigle: A/B.
Kant, Immanuel. *Critique of the Power of Judgment*. Trans. Paul Guyer and Eric Matthews. Cambridge: Cambridge UP, 2000.
Kant, Immanuel. *Vorlesung zur Moralphilosophie*. Ed. Werner Stark. Berlin: de Gruyter, 2004.

Lutz-Bachmann, Matthias. "Humanität und Religion. Zu Max Horkheimers Deutung des Christentums." *Max Horkheimer heute: Werk und Wirkung*. Eds. Alfred Schmidt and Norbert Altwicker. Frankfurt a. M.: Suhkamp, 1986. 108–28.

McCammon, Christopher. "Overcoming Deism: Hope Incarnate in Kant's Rational Religion." *Kant and the New Philosophy of Religion*. Eds. Chris L. Firestone and Stephen R. Palmquist. Bloomington and Indianapolis: Indiana UP, 2006. 79–89.

Nagl-Docekal, Herta. "Ist die Konzeption des ‚Herzenskündigers' obsolet geworden?" *Philosophisches Jahrbuch im Auftrag der Goerres-Gesllschaft*. Ed. Thomas Buchheim et al. 2. Halbband, 2010: 319–38.

Nagl-Docekal, Herta. "Liebe ‚in unserer' Zeit. Unabgegoltene Elemente der Hegelschen Ästhetik." *Hegels Ästhetik als Theorie der Moderne*. Eds. Annemarie Gethmann-Siefert, Herta Nagl-Docekal, Erzsébeth Rózsa and Elisabeth Weisser-Lohmann. Berlin: Akademie, 2013. 197–220

Nagl-Docekal, Herta. *Innere Freiheit. Grenzen der nachmetaphysischen Moralkonzeptionen*. Berlin: de Gruyter, 2014.

Nagl-Docekal, Herta. "Geschlechtergerechtigkeit: Wie könnte eine philosophische Perspektive für die theologische Debatte von Relevanz sein?" *Theologische Quartalschrift Tübingen* 195 (2015): 75–94.

Nagl-Docekal, Herta. "Immanuel Kant's Concept of Reasonable Hope." *Hope. Where does our Hope Lie?* Ed. Miloš Lichner. Vienna: LIT, 2020a. 177–92.

Nagl-Docekal, Herta. "Nach einer erneuten Lektüre: Max Horkheimer, Die Sehnsucht nach dem ganz Anderen." *Deutsche Zeitschrift für Philosophie*, 5(68)2020b. 659–88.

Nussbaum, Martha C. "Love." *Routledge Encyclopedia of Philosophy*. London-New York: Routledge, 1998, 842–846.

Nussbaum, Martha C. "'Beatrice's Dante': Wie liebt man das Individuum?" *Analytische Philosophie der Liebe*. Ed. Dieter Thomä. Paderborn: Mentis, 2000, 45–64.

Rosen, Zwi. *Max Horkheimer*. Munich: Beck (Beck'sche Reihe Denker), 1995.

Der Spiegel. "Was wir ‚Sinn' nennen, wird verschwinden. Spiegel-Gespräch mit Max Horkheimer." *Der Spiegel*, 5 January 1970. 79–84.

Taylor, Charles. *The Malaise of Modernity*. Concord: Ontario, 1991. Reprinted as *The Ethics of Authenticity*. Cambridge, MA: Harvard UP, 1992.

Taylor, Charles. *Sources of the Self: The Making of the Modern Identity*. Cambridge, MA: Harvard UP, 1989.

Taylor, Charles. *A Secular Age*. Cambridge, MA: Belknapp Press of Harvard UP, 2007.

Taylor, Charles. "Afterword: *Apologia pro libro suo*." *Varieties of Secularism in a Secular Age*. Eds. Michael Warner, Jonathan VanAntwerpen and Craig Clahoun. Cambridge, MA: Harvard UP, 2013. 300–24.

Wood, Allan W. "Rational Theology, Moral Faith, and Religion." *The Cambridge Companion to Kant*. Ed. Paul Guyer. Cambridge, UK- New York: Cambridge UP, 1992. 394–416.

Maureen Junker-Kenny
Defining What is "Extraterritorial": Religion and Utopia in Habermas and Ricœur

Abstract: The role given to the "extraterritorial" in two conceptions of reason and culture are compared in three steps. 1. In *Auch eine Geschichte der Philosophie* (2019), Habermas reconstructs the course towards postmetaphysical thought as enabled by the encounter of Greek philosophy with biblical monotheism, yet concludes with confirming religion as "extraterritorial" and autonomous reason as "secular". It is from its foundation in ritual that religion is deemed capable of offering heuristic resources that renew the dwindling motivation for solidarity. 2. Ricoeur draws on a similarly external location when he assumes the genre of "utopia" to be able to contest the ideological character of the established social order. Unlike Habermas, he has defended the link between religion and hope established in Kant's doctrine of postulates. 3. I conclude with the theological proposal to redefine the "extraterritorial" as what is beyond necessitation by reason, such as the free action of God or the human other.

The conference title, "Religion in the Secular Age", seems to perfectly capture the result of Habermas's new major work, *Auch eine Geschichte der Philosophie* (2019). Its two volumes contain in-depth discussions of the momentous encounters of religion and reason in European thinking, followed up to the contemporary stage where "reason" prevails as a "secular" power on its own. Yet "religion" remains a reservoir for secular self-resourcement exactly through its distinct status with a separate basis in an internally regulated ritual system. The theory decisions involved in this argumentation will be examined in Section One.

Regarding the development of Ricœur's thinking on religion, a recent study has claimed that it shows a process of "laicization".[1] In contrast to Habermas, whose new, seminal analysis includes chapters on major turning points in Christian theology that have shaped European thinking, the French philosopher treats "religion" mainly as it appears in the foundational scriptures of religious traditions, with a special focus on Hebrew and Christian biblical texts. The real "raw" material for philosophy is not theology which counts as a second order, conceptual reflection on the message of the Bible. The new dimension its genres open up is accessed under the rubric of the "poetic", thus, as sharing in the capacity of

---

[1] Frey, *La Religion dans la philosophie de Paul Ricœur*, 29–51.

"proposing [...] a world we might inhabit", exemplifying "modalities of our relation to the world that are not exhausted in the description of objects".² Unlike the "otherness" of ritual in Habermas's division of the field, religious scriptures are part of the symbolic mediations through which humans access reality. For the hermeneutical philosopher, no introspective short-cut is available that could avoid taking on board the self-conceptions of agents which are marked by such cultural-historical mediations. Ricoeur uses the term "ideology" already for this first level of integration into existing social imaginaries and proceeds to its negative assessment as a manipulated, oppressing construct only as a second step. Ideology critique is presented as applying to this subsequent level which is distinct from the basic integrative function. What makes critiques possible is the imaginative power of "utopia" which serves as the counter-pole to established conceptions of social and political life. They are challenged by the second pole's design of the "possible", which at present is "extraterritorial" to the existing social order.³ While utopias envisage what is radically new to their current context, they are seen at the same time as drawing on symbolic resources projecting a fulfilling life, and on memories of the hopes of past struggles which did not come to pass. In this respect, utopia is not completely "other" but avails of a continuity with previous quests for flourishing and liberation, such as "the Exodus and the Resurrection."⁴ Ricoeur's hermeneutical enquiry will be analysed in Section Two, concluding with a comparison of the two approaches.

1 Habermas's Conception of Religion as "Extraterritorial"

The designation of religion as "not simply 'irrational',", yet "extraterritorial," "opaque" and "profoundly alien to discursive thought" is a long-standing part of the third phase of the Frankfurt philosopher's view of religion.⁵ In his recent detailed reconstruction of the historical development of philosophical thinking towards a definitively postmetaphysical shape in late modernity, he explains the factors and steps in a trajectory that ends up placing "reason" as the realm opposite to "religion". Three aspects will be treated: Habermas's explanation of the major shift exerted by biblical monotheism on the Greek cosmological framework (1.1);

---

2 Ricœur, *Figuring the Sacred*, 222–223.
3 Cf., e.g., Ricœur, "Ideology and Utopia," 320.
4 Ricœur, *Hermeneutics and the Human Sciences*, 99.
5 Cf. Habermas, *Between Naturalism and Religion*, 112. 130. 142. 143.

his ongoing dismissal of possible bridges between "knowledge" and "faith," as outlined, for example, in Kant's *Critique of Practical Reason* (1.2); and the sociological lens on religion from its ritual practices as the single phenomenon that distinguishes it from reason-generated processes (1.3).

1.1 Jerusalem's Enriching Role for Athens in the Genealogy of Postmetaphysical Reason

Even at the second, "abstemious" stage in which Habermas depicted religion and reason as two parallel understandings which at least currently co-exist, since religion has not after all disappeared into a completely secular outlook, did he highlight the impact of biblical monotheism on Greek philosophy. Against Johann Baptist Metz's political theological support for a critique of the "hellenization" of the biblical message, the discourse theorist reminded theology and his own discipline of the decisive role of theology's insistence on history as the place of salvation and on the individualizing effect of the believer's calling by a personal God.[6] Since his exchanges with Metz and with other theological interlocutors supporting the idea of "communicative reason" like Helmut Peukert, Francis Fiorenza and David Tracy",[7] a third phase has begun with his remarkable Peace Prize speech in 2001 some weeks after the attacks of 9/11. Since then, he has called for mutual translations between secular and religious fellow citizens, based on a reflective appreciation of the sensitivity of religions for questions of an unfailed life and of human suffering.

The new work of 2019 not only devotes a most instructive chapter to the world religions as one of the two streams of the "axial age" change in human consciousness; it also offers in-depth analyses of key works of Christian theologians, such as Augustine, Thomas Aquinas, Duns Scotus, and Luther. It designates as the key turning point to modernity the late medieval critique of Aristotelianism in the new approach to divine and human freedom elaborated by Duns Scotus.[8]

Yet despite the knowledgeable and intriguing analyses of these authors' differing positions on the relationship between faith and human reason, the evaluation remains the same and is stated in an even more principled way: contemporary reason is secular, and religion offers its insights from an area external to commu-

---

6 Habermas, *The Liberating Power of Symbols*, 78–89.
7 Cf. their contributions in *Habermas, Modernity, and Public Theology*.
8 Habermas, *Auch eine Geschichte der Philosophie*, Vol. 1, 765–804. I have discussed his portrayal of Western Christianity as "Pauline" and his reconstruction of theologies from the Patristic to the medieval eras in chapters 1–6 of Junker-Kenny, *"The Bold Arcs of Salvation History,"* 5–156.

nicative rationality, namely ritual.[9] How does Habermas argue for this long-term position on the grounds of his own discipline? Philosophy has absorbed intuitions from religion that have led to seminal change in self and world orientation, but their source is fenced off from the realm of reason. Here, his assessment of Kant's differentiated considerations of the role of religion in relation to autonomous ethics is crucial.

1.2 Confirming his Rejection of the Bridge Between "Knowledge" and "Faith" in Kant's Autonomous Ethics

The reasons for Habermas's sustained rejection of Kant's highlighting of the limits of agency in his analysis of the antinomy of practical reason have been the subject of long-standing questioning by theologians and philosophers.[10] One of these angles is his departure from the support found in the first generation of the Frankfurt School – especially Benjamin, Adorno and Horkheimer – for reason (*Vernunft*) as the ongoing quest for meaningful agency, the hope for salvation and restitution above all in view of the evil committed by humans in history. The Frankfurt philosopher's reason for dismissing Kant's analysis of an antinomy faced by practical reason and its solution through the postulate of the existence of God is that it "overextends" the power of the human agent.[11] The objection that a less principled account of morality would avoid the necessity of this conclusion has been uncovered as reconfirming a Hegelian view of Kant's ethics as promoting an "empty ought:"[12] an extreme positioning of morality in its unconditioned outreach which overlooks the existing ethos (*Sittlichkeit*) within family, bourgeois society and state. For Habermas, Kant's argumentation for the postulate of God as the solution of the antinomy is circular, a *petitio principii*.[13] Yet the question remains whether reducing "hope" to what is predictable and feasible, rather than overtax persons in their ethical life, is able to capture also the everyday understanding of "morality:" it is accepted as denoting a different category than mutually reciprocal, that is, ultimately transactional, conduct. In her analysis of Kant's counter-position to the merely legal level of external conformity to mutual expectations of rule-keeping, Herta Nagl-Docekal points to the substitution of the inner experience of

---

[9] Habermas, *Auch eine Geschichte der Philosophie*, Vol. 1, 182–272; "Postskriptum," Vol. 2, 767–807.
[10] Cf., e. g., Langthaler and Nagl-Docekal, eds. *Glauben und Wissen. Ein Symposium mit Jürgen Habermas* (2007).
[11] Cf., e. g., Habermas, *Auch eine Geschichte der Philosophie*, Vol. 2, 356–357.
[12] Cf. Nagl-Docekal, *Innere Freiheit*, 167.
[13] Habermas, *Auch eine Geschichte der Philosophie*, Vol. 2, 355–356.

the moral ought by a discursive consensus on the principles to be followed in actual cases of conflict. This shift of moral judgement to an intersubjective agreement on other persons' compliance with laws loses Kant's distinction between legal conduct as a citizen, and the internal capability for morality which directs scrutiny of motives to oneself.[14] Only if this insight is maintained, does the meaning of the antinomy of practical reason constituted by the gap between morality and justified desire for happiness become clear. If the exigency of the moral law is toned down, as Habermas proposes to, effectively in line with Hegel – while admitting that the "embedding of morality in ethical life robs it of its critical edge (*Stachel*)" –,[15] a lighter, more limited and accurately balanced version of the demands for individual and social life is the result. The antinomy may then be replaced by a graduated commitment to support progress. More insistent questions are put off, as Habermas's interpretation of the "ethical community" envisaged by Kant alongside the legal constitution of the state will now show.

When Habermas refers to the "ethical community" (*ethisches Gemeinwesen*) as a "collective variant of the highest good",[16] it should be specified that for Kant, this interpretation solely spells out the side of morality which gains empirical support by the presence of equally well-intentioned fellow humans. Yet the question of happiness has not been broached; it is not absorbed by "virtue" which figures as the precondition of "worthiness" for happiness.[17] Kant demonstrates that the "synthesis" of the two components of the "highest good" is not achievable by human effort, the success of which remains an open question even in positive interactions, and much more so when encountering strategic, instrumentalizing counterparts. The "hope" that inspires agency will be returned to in Section Two

---

14 The "procedural transformation" of the categorical imperative proposed by John Rawls and Habermas misses its key dimension, its ongoing validity even if it is not reciprocated, as Nagl-Docekal clarifies: "Kant stresses that our moral duty cannot be defined in contractual terms: rather than being based upon the principle of reciprocity, the moral law demands that we treat others as persons even when we have good reasons to doubt that they would behave towards us likewise" ("Why Kant's 'Ethical State'", 164). The "procedural" turn is also in danger of falling into "heteronomy" if the agent's own moral judgement is replaced by the result of a discourse to which consent is given (Nagl-Docekal, *Innere Freiheit*, 84–85). It is true that Habermas opposes a more demanding concept of "citizen" to the negative freedom espoused in Rawls's liberal view, as I have tried to show in *Religion and Public Reason*, 136–137. Yet the benchmark of reciprocity obscures the asymmetric or "unilateral" (180) character of the moral demand: "the main focus of the moral law – which Kant specifies in his conception of the 'categorical imperative' – is on how *I treat* human beings rather than on how others treat me" (Nagl-Docekal, "Why Kant's 'Ethical State'", 164).
15 Habermas, *Auch eine Geschichte der Philosophie*, Vol. II, 348.
16 Habermas, "Versuch einer Replik," 251.
17 Kant, *Critique of Practical Reason*, A 199.

as one of the Kantian elements elaborated by Ricoeur. Habermas attaches the term "hope" directly to Kant's doctrine of virtue which is said to serve "the justification of a scope of hope (*Hoffnungsspielraums*) which points beyond (*hinausweisenden*) the doctrine of morality."[18]

Thus, it seems that the "ethical community" can achieve a "collective highest good" without any antinomy. Its meaning, however, has been altered to signify the highest good in terms of globally agreed laws. Having noted the tendency of "post-metaphysical" approaches to limit morality to the conditioned reciprocity of legal relations, Nagl-Docekal uncovers a further discrepancy from Kant's argumentation: the "encouragement" Habermas wishes to draw from the achievements of an "ethical community" ignores the incompleteness and ongoing "fallibility" of these efforts[19] which give Kant reason for caution, while appreciating "signs of history" in the direction of autonomous, non-instrumentalizing freedom. In other words: there is a difference between not even trying to do the best that is possible under the circumstances, and putting forward a misleading goal, namely that of adding up historical achievements as if these could respond to the individual's hope for his or her action to be met with success. The step taken by Rawls and Habermas to base their trust in the future on expectations of gradual progress may be commendable in their resistance to a culturally accelerating "defeatism of reason".[20] Yet in taking the individual agent's perspective seriously, Kant's analysis is more radical. It also allows to identify a problem in the choice of categories that aggravates the pathological conditions which civic engagement seeks to counteract: the loss of solidarity observed by the critical theorist may in fact be enhanced by reducing morality to external legality. A self-understanding of citizens "as isolated, self-interested monads who use their individual liberties exclusively against one another like weapons"[21] may equally be promoted by empirical conceptions of autonomy merely in the sense of "independence" when its core, "self-legislation," is threatened with becoming "obsolete."[22]

Habermas perceptively identifies how "system imperatives" encroach on all aspects of the shared lifeworld and on individual self-conceptions to the point of self-objectification and "self-instrumentalization" – for example, by treating one's body as well as one's children as assets due to be commercially enhanced.[23]

---

[18] Habermas, "Versuch einer Replik," 252. Cf. 247.
[19] Nagl-Docekal, "Why Kant's 'Ethical State'," 170.
[20] Habermas, *Auch eine Geschichte der Philosophie*, Vol. II, 805.
[21] Habermas, *Between Naturalism and Religion*, 107, quoted by Nagl-Docekal, "Why Kant's 'Ethical State'," 174.
[22] Cf. Nagl-Docekal, "Why Kant's 'Ethical State', 158.
[23] Habermas, *The Future of Human Nature*, 66.

Yet the question about the reduction implicit in an exclusively secular remit of reason remains. What is the role left for religion if its correspondence especially with practical reason is dismissed as transporting an exaggerated view of the moral ought?

1.3 No Space Shared with Reason: Ritual as Religion's Ground of Its Own

On the one hand, Habermas's insistence that in ritual, religion occupies a ground unrivalled by reason allocates a distinct, irreducible place to religious traditions. As long as they are functioning as communities of ritual celebration, they must be reckoned with as still vibrant contenders in the public realm. While for theology, the argument must go beyond such external visibility, it does supply a location that caters for a distinct origin. This source cannot be reduced to reason, even if it is able to respond to its unconditioned outreach. On the other hand, exegetical and systematic studies show a wide variety in the interpretation and practice of the "solidarity" renewed in ritual, whether merely internal or also external – that is, including the insistence on universal justice –, and of the connection between the rites and the founding events of each particular faith tradition. In his chapter on world religions, he spells out their distinctive basic intuitions. Yet what would be needed to account for the variety in the internal development of their core concepts, emerging from the *noyau créateur* which Ricœur sees at work in religions as "poetic" traditions? Which conceptions of the divine give rise to their reflections on human life in its thrust and finitude, its flourishing and suffering? Habermas relates his meticulous examination in Volume I of new and contested translations to different thought forms in the history of Christian thinking to new eras of social and political self-organisation. But how do these changes affect the internal understanding of the core rituals? Rather than taking publicly visible practices at communal gatherings as the key difference from reason, should they not be analysed as the locus of remembering a specific experience of the divine in history, which itself is to be accredited as the searched-for "Other" of reason? "Exterritorial" in the sense of not originating from human action would then capture the religious community's understanding of God's revelation as encountered in history, and not produced by human powers of constructive thinking.

By envisaging "extraterritoriality" on the model of "two countries,"[24] the independent origin of religion is protected, yet at the price of a complete separation.

---

24 Harrington, "Habermas's Theological Turn?", 59.

Does Habermas account for the quest for the unconditioned which the systematic theologian Saskia Wendel terms "religiosity",[25] or is his opposition between religion and reason owed to the Barthian premise of revelation as the "totally Other"? It is instructive to compare the presence of utopian thinking in his critical theory, with "utopia" representing the literal meaning of being outside the landscape shared as common ground. It offers an urgently needed counterbalance to instrumental rationality: "When the utopian oases dry out, a desert of banality and perplexity spreads."[26] The capacity of offering concrete counter-models to an unthinking, utilitarian conduct of life oblivious of the great questions posed by human agency, fallibility and finitude, extends to utopian as well as to religious extraterritoriality. In his comparison with Ricoeur, Michaël Foessel highlights the "constant thesis" of the German philosopher: "only communicative reason is capable of concrete utopias. In contrast to Paul Ricoeur, Habermas does not delegate to the social imaginary the power of indicating the possibility of a rupture with the present."[27]

As we shall see, the difference of Ricoeur's approach is his hermeneutical perception of the symbolic sources of self-understandings as present in a culture or religion. They provide guiding images for the social imaginary that can be drawn on in response to a society's specific challenges. Before differences in the anthropological premises of the two theorists are explored, however, an important distinction between religion and utopia arising from Kant's philosophy of religion should be noted. The discrepancy to Kant regarding the effect for moral motivation that Habermas accords to religion is pointed out by Rudolf Langthaler:

> Thus, not a functional instrumentality [*Zweckdienlichkeit*] as a remedy for such 'motivational weakness' is the determining perspective; rational faith [*Vernunftglaube*] is not an adequate means (*probates Instrument*) to lend wings to moral motivation. This is not at all the primary intention of hope but at best a desirable side effect (as indeed serving the moral incentive) [*Triebfeder*]. Religion does not compensate for a missing moral motivation.[28]

This point will be followed up in comparison with Ricoeur's approach to human agency, ethics and religion. To sum up, on the one hand, as Nagl-Docekal has pointed out, for contemporary authors of the Frankfurt School including Habermas, the "moral" is at risk of becoming identified with reciprocity which in turn is prone to

---

25 Wendel, "Die religiöse Selbst- und Weltdeutung," esp. 242–261.
26 Habermas, *Die neue Unübersichtlichkeit*, 161, quoted by Langthaler, *Führt Moral unumgänglich zur Religion?*, 410, Fn. 398.
27 Foessel, "Une ambition philosophique par gros temps," 10.
28 Langthaler, *Führt Moral unumgänglich zur Religion?*, 332.

a descent into a merely contractual basis of social relations.[29] The stringency of Kant's conception of morality as the opposite of a self-serving intention is undermined by this tendency, which for Habermas is based on the reciprocity of roles in speech acts. On the other hand, the goal of a true, not just a factual consensus aimed for in discourse as the alternative to violence has been marked as one of the "utopian" elements in Habermas's theory project, together with the ideas of an "unfailed life" and of reciprocal recognition.[30] While sharing in the function of providing critique and inspiring visions, they are not "extraterritorial" in the same sense as religion. There is a continuity between the human capacity for linguistic communication and the optimal forms of fulfilling them. They do not constitute rituals set apart from the processes of communicative reason. Similarly, Ricoeur's enterprise is to outline "utopia" as belonging to the matrix of poetic imagination as a foundational human faculty; yet in contrast to the Frankfurt thinker, so does religion.

2 Human Agency, Utopia and Religion in Ricoeur's Hermeneutical Philosophy

Ricoeur's framework will be outlined in three sections, before assessing the differences to Habermas's position with its rejection of a connection between religion and reason (2.4): First, his hermeneutical perspective on the sources of self-understanding as the lynchpin of agency and the design of his ethics will be explored (2.1), followed by elucidating the social imaginary positioned between the two poles of "ideology" and "utopia" (2.2). Thirdly, an analysis of the role of "hope" for agency and its link to religion will be pursued (2.3).

2.1 Ricoeur's Theory of Agency and Tripartite Ethics

From an anthropological starting point that considers human existence as *"effort pour exister, désir pour être"* and as disclosing itself in "works which testify to this effort and this desire",[31] it is not surprising that the entry level of ethics is taken in

---

[29] Nagl-Docekal, "Why Kant's 'Ethical State'," 156. 161. 164.
[30] Roman, "Consensus et utopie," 78.
[31] Ricœur, "The hermeneutics of symbols and philosophical reflection II," 328–29. Identifying as roots "both the Platonic idea that the source of knowledge is itself *eros*, desire, or love, and the Spinozistic idea that it is *conatus*, effort" (329), he specifies the new direction given to reflexivity:

"striving" (*visée*). Already at this stage, the desire for one's own life to flourish extends to promoting the same for others, within supportive, equitable structures. In a much-quoted formula, it is summed up as aiming (*visée*) "to live well, with and for others, in just institutions".[32]

When Ricœur calls himself a "post-Hegelian Kantian,"[33] a complex and critical intellectual heritage is indicated. What he esteems in Hegel's "philosophy of the will" is the "diversity of problems it traverses and resolves: union of desire and culture, of psychology and politics, of the subjective and the universal [...] an inexhaustible reservoir of descriptions and mediations [...] I abandon the ethics of duty to the Hegelian critique with no regrets."[34] Some decades later, an acknowledgement of Kant's concept of morality as universalization is combined with repeating the reason for his reserve:

> Kantian moral philosophy can be taken [...] for an exact account of our common moral experience, one which holds that the only thing that can be taken as obligatory are maxims of action that can satisfy a test of universalization. Still, for all that, it is not necessary to take duty as the enemy of desire.[35]

This statement follows the development of a model of ethics in 1990 which includes morality as its second step. He explains the shift to the deontological type of ethical reflection from the need to protect the other as a limit to one's own striving:

> the transition from the wish to the imperative, from desire to interdiction appears to be inevitable. Why? For the fundamental reason that action implies [...] *power over* others" which "offers the permanent occasion for violence in all its forms: from the lie, where only the instrument of language seems to be misused, to the imposition of suffering, culminating in the

---

"I maintain, along with Fichte and his French successor Jean Nabert, that reflection is less a justification of science and duty than it is an appropriation of our effort to exist [...] We must recover the sense of existential activity, the positing of the self within all the density of its works" (328).
32 Ricœur, *Oneself as Another*, 172.
33 Ricœur, "Freedom in the Light of Hope," 412: "But the Kantianism that I wish to develop now is, paradoxically, more to be constructed than repeated; it would be something like a post-Hegelian Kantianism, to borrow an expression from Eric Weil [...] we are as radically post-Hegelian as we are post-Kantian [...] the task is to think them always better by thinking them together – one against the other, and one by means of the other."
34 Ricœur, "Freedom in the Light of Hope," 414. 413.
35 Ricœur, *Reflections on the Just*, 46–47. In view of Ricœur's endorsement of imperative, obligation and prohibition as necessary components of ethics, it seems useful to examine Kant's texts on morality and distinguish his core thesis on autonomy as the self-legislation of an agent equipped with "good will" from passages that may be read as anchoring the conflict between duty and inclination in a pessimistic anthropology.

imposition of a violent death and in the horrible practice of torture [...] it is owing to the wrong that one person inflicts on another that the moral judgment [...] has to add the predicate of the obligatory to that of the good, usually under the negative figure of what is prohibited.[36]

The deontological step is concretized by "practical wisdom", a third stage of judgement in respect of the singularity of all involved. By representing the moral ought by the term "rule" and the image of a "sieve"[37] that separates good from selfish intentions, the Kantian evidence of the moral calling may still appear to be subordinated to external "norms". Yet the hermeneutical philosopher distinguishes "imputability" from the other human capabilities – speaking, acting and narrating – as rising to a different level,[38] presupposing therefore an internal capability for morality.

Since the agency rooted in the originary striving for existence manifests itself in "works", "expressions", "signs, symbols and texts,"[39] which are "appropriated" in a person's self-understanding, the concrete, historical material provided by cultures in their diversity is included from the start. Their reservoir of symbolic forms and practices is seen as organized around a "creative nucleus on the basis of which we interpret life", containing a "fundamental conception of time, space and interhuman relations",[40] thus providing a plurality of reason-led approaches to reality.

2.2 The Two Poles of the Social Imaginary: Ideology and Utopia

Among the positions discussed in outlining his own conception of the social imaginary are Karl Mannheim, Karl Marx, Max Weber, Clifford Geertz and Jürgen Habermas. Sébastien Roman analyses the way in which the French philosopher examines the problem whether Habermas's political theory may in fact include the existence of a symbolic dimension, even if he does not call it a "social imaginary."[41] Ricoeur identifies this aspect in the critical theorist's acknowledgement of the role

---

[36] Ricœur, *The Just*, Preface, xvi – xvii.
[37] Ricœur, *Oneself as Another*, 215.
[38] Cf. Ricœur, *Reflections on the Just*, 82–83.
[39] In *From Text to Action*, 15, Ricœur summarizes: "there is no self-understanding that is not *mediated* by signs, symbols and texts; in the last resort, understanding coincides with the interpretation given to these mediating terms."
[40] Ricœur, *History and Truth*, 276. 279.
[41] Cf. Roman, "Consensus et utopie," 69–79.

cultures play in the specific legitimation of governance.[42] Yet he finds a crucial step missing: the transition from the legitimating to the integrating function of ideology. Only if this level is taken into account, is the necessity of "ideology" in a basic, neutral sense acknowledged, a symbolic layer that holds society together. For him, the "integration of the common world by means of symbolic systems immanent in action"[43] is the most elementary and inescapable level of ideology. The dimension of a collective self-understanding of a society itself cannot be discarded, even if the symbolic means of the social imaginary may of course be used in the negative sense of "ideology" which is the only one Habermas avails of. It is here that "utopia" announces its alternative to current interpretations, thus offering a different view of the origins and of the current orientations of a polity. While Habermas, too, regards utopia as the antidote to ideology, the difference is that Ricoeur sees both as operating at the level of the social imaginary without which there is no "society" in the sense of a shared space. Habermas's ideal of engaging in the universalising procedure of finding a consensus based on arguments as the decisive bond that holds a democracy together is critiqued as offering a rationalising concept of the political. Ricoeur's model highlights the enduring conflict within discourse as well as the inevitability of "ideology" as a primary symbolic mediation through which subjects appropriate their de facto belonging to a social context that existed prior to them.

Thus, even if both authors link "utopia" to an idea of the "possible" beyond what is currently given, their understandings differ. Ricoeur credits language with the ability to open up worlds, to connect the subjects to their space of agency through imagination. In the genre of utopia, this decisive mediation acquires the edge of a practical transformation, expressed in a close connection between wish and "imperative".[44]

For Habermas, the role of language for intersubjective understanding is more central than its innovative capacity. In his theory, the question of relating to the world (which Ricoeur highlights as an originary task of the imagination where symbolic mediation is at work) risks being absorbed into the issue of interaction.[45] For the hermeneutical philosopher, in contrast, the presuppositions of understanding and acting in a world include a social imaginary constituted by historical, cul-

---

42 Cf. Roman, "Consensus et utopie," 51, Fn. 26, with reference to Habermas, *Knowledge and Human Interests*.
43 Ricœur, *Memory, History, Forgetting*, 82.
44 In his "Introduction", 13, Roman points out that "the optative of utopia is not a 'vain dreaming' but indissoluble from the register of the imperative" before summarizing Olivier Mongin's contribution as relating the "imperative" register of utopia to its "power to allow to live together" (25).
45 Cf. Langthaler, *Postmetaphysisches Denken?*, 324.

tural and religious factors that are both resonant and contested in their meaning for the future. The arc from historical sources to new projects provides a timeline in which persons can forge their practical self-understandings and engage in motivated action.

The two theorists classify and concretize terms like utopia and critique, governance and legitimation, recognition and conflict differently, with a basic aspect dividing them: the significance of symbolic mediation. For Ricoeur, its unavoidability rules out a complete rupture between motifs from culture and from religion, in this case biblical monotheism. Both utopian and biblical texts achieve similar openings by projecting alternative worlds with different social relations. In each case, utopian and religious visions of a new world take up the founding hopes and promises of a community's history. In relation to the Enlightenment's call for emancipation, Ricoeur highlights the precedent expectations raised by the biblical messages of the "Exodus and the Resurrection".[46] Such anchorage in earlier symbols in the history of a culture leads Jean-Luc Amalric to characterize his position as proposing a "memory of utopia".[47] If religions share in the "poetic" function of the imagination with its power of configuring a world to inhabit, where does Ricoeur locate their specificity?

2.3 Religions in their Particularity and in their Correspondence to Practical Reason

On the one hand, the particularity of each tradition contained in its "noyau créateur" goes back to its founding event, a new departure in history that cannot be deduced from reason. On the other hand, religions connect with practical reason on irrefutable questions that are decisive for agency: the meaning of the moral effort when it collides with the justified quest for happiness and meaning, and the problem of culpability for the agent in her need to be able to begin anew after becoming guilty. Both of these problems, if they are to be resolved, require the step from ethics to philosophy of religion. This is the reason for Ricoeur to return to Kant's approach:

> And yet, Kant remains [...] he surpasses Hegel from a certain point of view [...] which is precisely essential for our present dialogue between a theology of hope and a philosophy of rea-

---

46 Ricœur, *Hermeneutics and the Human Sciences*, 99.
47 Amalric, "Le statut de l'utopie," esp. 49–55.

son. The Hegel I reject is the philosopher of retrospection, the one who [...] reabsorbs all rationality in the already happened meaning.[48]

To carry out this stance, the Hegelian perspective needs to mediatize suffering as part of a dialectic. In contrast, morality and the fulfillment of the quest for meaning cannot be assumed as being reconciled for Kant: "No one as much as Kant has had a sense for the transcendent character of this connection, and this against the whole of Greek philosophy to which he is directly opposed, rejecting Epicurean and Stoic equally: happiness is not our accomplishment: it is achieved by superaddition, by surplus." The synthesis is one that an agent can only hope for, not belonging to what can be "produced by his will".[49]

In *Religion Within the Boundaries of Mere Reason*, this "surplus" of religion is related to its ability to distinguish the person from the morally evil act she has committed, reopening access to her good will as an active source "regenerated".[50] Ricoeur states clearly that these are problems which arise from the ground of autonomous morality: "the first origin of the question, 'What may I hope for?' [...] is situated again at the heart of moral philosophy, itself engendered by the question, 'What should I do?' Moral philosophy engenders the philosophy of religion when the hope of fulfilment is added to the consciousness of obligation."[51]

While the completion of the "highest good" as *"bonum supremum"* is achievable by human forces, as *"bonum consummatum"* that includes happiness it is dependent on a moral creator of the world. Without this, as Kant states in a radical readiness to put the validity of his own analysis in question, the human sense of ought founders since the moral law risks being "fantastic, directed to empty, imaginary ends, and consequently inherently false."[52]. The postulate of a God who can achieve the synthesis arises at the point where human moral agency reaches its limit: "if we act as well as lies in our power, what is not in our power will come to our aid from another source, whether we know in what way or not."[53] Ricoeur asserts: "Kant explicitly brings religion to the question 'What can I hope for?' I do

---

48 Ricœur, "Freedom in the Light of Hope," 414.
49 Ricœur, "Freedom in the Light of Hope," 417.
50 Cf. Ricœur, "Freedom in the Light of Hope," 422. In "Hope and the Structure of Philosophical Systems" (1970), 211, he judges: "the notion of radical evil leads to that of regeneration, which is another name of hope", and states why he returns to Kant's "critique" from Hegel's "system": "Hope is not a theme that comes after other themes, an idea that closes the system, but an impulse that opens the system [...] it is a way of reopening what was unduly closed."
51 Ricœur, "Freedom in the Light of Hope," 421.
52 Kant, *Critique of Practical Reason*, A 205–06. Trans. L. W. Beck, 118.
53 Kant, *Critique of Practical Reason*, A 230, Anm., quoted by Ricœur, "Freedom in the Light of Hope," 421, with reference to L. W. Beck's translation, 132, n. 2.

not know any other philosopher who has defined religion exclusively with that question."[54]

Which conceptions of human reason, action and sociability stand behind the differences between the two post-Kantian thinkers?

2.4 Taking Stock: Differences between Ricoeur and Habermas

For both theorists, the "extraterritorial" is a source of questioning, reorienting and renewing current late modern conditions marked by threats such as defeatism and self-objectivization through a scientistic empiricist worldview and commercializing colonizations.[55] For Ricoeur, they limit human agency by restricting imagination through their focus on predictability and control. For both, all historical traditions, religious or secular, count as living if they can reinterpret or "translate" their core to the current age.

Yet in comparison with the French hermeneutical philosopher, Habermas's procedural understandings of discourse and democracy seem to underrate the role of prior self-understandings, social imaginaries, and a cohesion-forging basic "ideology" which captures the "symbolic dimension of social relations".[56] As Roman begins his comparison of the two approaches, instead of "discursive rationality," the starting point for "understanding political rationality is the larger concept of the social imaginary, in order to clarify its meaning [*signification*] or its conflictual exercise by the imaginative practices of ideology and utopia."[57] For Ricoeur, Habermas is of interest because his position is "exemplary of the modern social imaginary,"[58] especially his "procedural understanding of democracy".[59] Ricoeur's alternative is to see the civic sphere as constituted by traditions which are competing with each other and with their own original core intuitions that admit the fulfilment of their promise to be still outstanding, as betrayed and as in need of further attempts of realization.[60] These groups are thus internally motivated to re-engage in critiques and new initiatives from their traditions' utopias. These form part of the social imaginary which extends between the poles of ideol-

---

54 Ricœur, "Freedom in the Light of Hope," 417–18.
55 Roman, "Consensus et utopie," 71: "Utopia is an extraterritoriality […] which allows contesting the established order by an opening towards new possibilities [*de nouveaux possibles*]."
56 Roman, "Consensus et utopie," 69.
57 Roman, "Consensus et utopie," 69.
58 Roman, "Consensus et utopie," 70.
59 Roman, "Introduction," 9.
60 E.g., Ricœur, *Reflections on the Just*, 164.

ogy as basic integration, as manipulation and distortion, and utopia, which risks perfectionism and disconnection but as the pole of innovation harbours inspiration from the historical roots of its vision.

A crucial second difference appears in their conceptions of reason. For Ricoeur, the scope of reason clearly encompasses an outreach towards the unconditioned. Here, he follows Kant more closely than Habermas does. The theorist of communicative action quotes Kant on the "signs of history" that allow for hope in achieving new standards in realising autonomous freedom.[61] Yet it is unclear whether history is actually considered as a possible place of the radically new which may include a space for the action of a God who can at least be "thought", although not "known" in the epistemological sense of objects of the world. Ricoeur refers to this distinction of Kant's which keeps a space within reason for a transcendence which cannot be proven but assumed without verging into the irrational. The final question to Habermas's insistence on religion being "extraterritorial" in having no shared ground with reason undermines the territorial image by pointing out the existing real heterogeneity of the freedom of the other encountered by the self. No one can be forced to relate, and the choice of giving attention to another human subject remains a gift, or, in Ricoeur's terms, marks a "superabundance" and a "surplus". "Extraterritorial", in the sense of not being able to be necessitated by reason, is already the freedom of the other, and a fortiori the freedom of God: "Why should there only be potential for reason in what is completely out of its reach (instead of what is not at its disposal because of its freedom)?"[62] It is what rituals can at best point to, as commemorations of turns and breakthroughs in history by a God whom reason cannot exclude as their possible author.

Works Cited

Amalric, Jean-Luc. "Le statut de l'utopie dans la philosophie de l'imagination de Ricoeur." In: Sébastien Roman (ed.), *Penser l'utopie aujourd'hui avec Paul Ricoeur.* Paris: Presses Universitaires de Vincennes, 2021. 37–55.

Fiorenza, Francis Schüssler. "The Church as a Community of Interpretation: Political Theology between Discourse Ethics and Hermeneutical Reconstruction." *Habermas, Modernity, and Public Theology.* Ed. Don Browning and Francis Schüssler Fiorenza. New York: Crossroad, 1992. 66–91.

Foessel, Michaël. "Habermas, le dernier philosophe. Une ambition philosophique par gros temps." *Esprit* 417 (August-September 2015): 6–11.

Frey, Daniel. *La Religion dans la philosophie de Paul Ricoeur.* Paris: Hermann, 2021.

---

[61] Cf. Habermas, *Auch eine Geschichte der Philosophie*, Vol. II, 790–92 ("Postskriptum").
[62] Pröpper, *Theologische Anthropologie*, Vol. II, 765, Fn. 127.

Habermas, Jürgen. *Auch eine Geschichte der Philosophie*. Vol.1: *Die okzidentale Konstellation von Glauben und Wissen*. Vol. 2: *Vernünftige Freiheit. Spuren des Diskurses über Glauben und Wissen*. Berlin: Suhrkamp, 2019.

Habermas, Jürgen. *Between Naturalism and Religion*. Trans. Ciaran Cronin. Cambridge: Polity Press, 2008.

Habermas, Jürgen. *Die neue Unübersichtlichkeit. Kleine politische Schriften V.* Frankfurt: Suhrkamp, 1985.

Habermas, Jürgen. "Israel or Athens: Where Does Anamnestic Reason Belong? Johann Baptist Metz on Unity amidst Multicultural Plurality." *The Liberating Power of Symbols: Philosophical Essays*. Trans. Peter Dews. Cambridge: Polity, 2001. 78–89.

Habermas, Jürgen. *Knowledge and Human Interests*. Trans. J. J. Shapiro. Boston: Beacon Press, 1971.

Habermas, Jürgen. *The Future of Human Nature*. Trans. William Rehg, Max Pensky and Hella Beister. Cambridge: Polity Press, 2003.

Habermas, Jürgen. "Versuch einer Replik." *Wissen und Glauben*. Theologische Reaktionen auf das Werk von Jürgen Habermas *Auch eine Geschichte der Philosophie*. Ed. Franz Gruber and Markus Knapp. Freiburg: Herder, 2021. 224–252.

Harrington, Austin. "Habermas's Theological Turn?" *Journal for the Theory of Social Behaviour* 37 (2007): 45–61.

Junker-Kenny, Maureen. *Habermas and Theology*. London/New York: T & T Clark International, 2011.

Junker-Kenny, Maureen. *Religion and Public Reason: A Comparison of the Positions of John Rawls, Jürgen Habermas and Paul Ricoeur*. Berlin/Boston: De Gruyter, 2014.

Junker-Kenny, Maureen. *"The Bold Arcs of Salvation History". Faith and Reason in Jürgen Habermas's Reconstruction of the Roots of European Thinking*. Berlin/Boston: De Gruyter, 2022.

Kant, Immanuel. *Critique of Practical Reason*. Trans. Lewis White Beck. New York: Liberal Arts Press, 1956.

Kant, Immanuel. *Religion Within the Boundaries of Mere Reason And Other Writings*, edited by Allen Wood and George di Giovanni. Intro. Robert M. Adams. Cambridge: Cambridge UP, 1998.

Langthaler, Rudolf. *Postmetaphysisches Denken? Kritische Anfragen an Jürgen Habermas*. Berlin: Duncker & Humblot, 1997.

Langthaler, Rudolf. *Führt Moral unumgänglich zur Religion?, Zur Kritik der Kantischen Religionsphilosophie bei Jürgen Habermas – eine Entgegnung*. Freiburg/München: Karl Alber, 2021.

Langthaler, Rudolf, and Herta Nagl-Docekal, eds. *Glauben und Wissen. Ein Symposium mit Jürgen Habermas*. Wien: Oldenbourg Verlag/Akademie Verlag, 2007.

Nagl-Docekal, Herta. *Innere Freiheit. Grenzen der nachmetaphysischen Moralkonzeptionen*. Berlin/Boston: De Gruyter, 2014.

Nagl-Docekal, Herta. "Why Kant's 'Ethical State' Might Prove Instrumental in Challenging Current Social Pathologies." *Kantian Journal* 40/4 (2021): 156–186.

Peukert, Helmut. "Enlightenment and Theology as Unfinished Projects." Trans. Peter Kenny. *Habermas, Modernity, and Public Theology*. Ed. Don Browning and Francis Schüssler Fiorenza. New York: Crossroad. 1992. 43–65.

Pröpper, Thomas. *Theologische Anthropologie*, 2 vols. Freiburg: Herder, 2011.

Ricœur, Paul. *Figuring the Sacred, Religion, Narrative and Imagination*. Trans. David Pellauer. Ed. Mark Walker. Minneapolis: Augsburg Fortress, 1995.

Ricœur, Paul. "Freedom in the Light of Hope." Trans. Robert Sweeney. *The Conflict of Interpretations Essays in Hermeneutics*. Ed. Don Ihde. Evanston: Northwestern U P, 1966. 402–424.

Ricœur, Paul. "Hope and the Structure of Philosophical Systems." *Figuring the Sacred, Religion, Narrative and Imagination.* Trans. David Pellauer. Ed. Mark Walker. Minneapolis: Augsburg Fortress, 1995. 203–216.

Ricœur, Paul. "Ideology and Utopia." (1983). *From Text to Action. Essays in Hermeneutics II.* Trans. Kathleen Blamey and John B. Thompson. Evanston: Northwestern UP, 1991. 308–324.

Ricœur, Paul. *Lectures on Ideology and Utopia.* Ed. George H. Taylor. New York: Columbia Press, 1986.

Ricœur, Paul. *Memory, History, Forgetting.* Trans. Kathleen Blamey and David Pellauer. Chicago: U of Chicago P, 2004.

Ricœur, Paul. "Naming God." *Figuring the Sacred, Religion, Narrative and Imagination.* Trans. David Pellauer. Ed. Mark Walker. Minneapolis: Augsburg Fortress, 1995. 217–235.

Ricœur, Paul. "On Interpretation." Trans. Kathleen Blamey. *From Text to Action. Essays in Hermeneutics II.* Evanston: Northwestern UP, 1991.1–20.

Ricœur, Paul. *Oneself as Another.* Trans. Kathleen Blamey. Chicago: U of Chicago P, 1992.

Ricœur, Paul. *Reflections on the Just.* Trans. David Pellauer. Chicago: U of Chicago P, 2007.

Ricœur, Paul. "The Hermeneutics of Symbols and Philosophical Reflection II." Trans. Charles Freilich. *The Conflict of Interpretations Essays in Hermeneutics.* Ed. Don Ihde. Evanston: Northwestern UP, 1966. 315–334.

Ricœur, Paul. *The Just.* Trans. David Pellauer. Chicago: U of Chicago P, 2000.

Ricœur, Paul. *The Symbolism of Evil.* Translated by Emerson Buchanan. New York: Harper & Row, 1967.

Ricœur, Paul. "Universal Civilization and National Cultures." *History and Truth.* Trans. and intro. Charles Kelbley. Evanston: Northwestern UP, 1965. 271–284.

Roman, Sébastien. "Consensus et utopie: Lecture de Habermas par Paul Ricœur." *Esprit* 417 (8/9) (August-September 2015): 69–79.

Roman, Sébastien, ed.. *Penser l'utopie aujourd'hui avec Paul Ricœur.* Paris: Presses Universitaires de Vincennes, 2021.

Roman, Sébastien. "Introduction." *Penser l'utopie aujourd'hui avec Paul Ricœur.* 5–33.

Tracy, David. "Theology, Critical Social Theory, and the Public Realm." *Habermas, Modernity, and Public Theology.* Ed. Don Browning and Francis Schüssler Fiorenza. New York: Crossroad, 1992. 19–42.

Wendel, Saskia. "Die religiöse Selbst- und Weltdeutung des bewussten Daseins und ihre Bedeutung für eine 'moderne Religion'. Was der 'Postmetaphysiker' Habermas über Religion nicht zu denken wagt." *Moderne Religion? Theologische und religionsphilosophische Reaktionen auf Jürgen Habermas.* Ed. Thomas Schmidt and Knut Wenzel. Freiburg: Herder, 2009. 225–265.

John D. Caputo
Secularizing Both Religion and Reason: Upending the Secular/Religious Distinction

Abstract: The divide between the religious and the secular in modernity results from taking both categories in overstated terms- as supernatural revelation, inaccessible to reason, on the one hand, and transcendental rationality, on the other hand. This opposition obscures the unique quality of religion and the theological discourse. I propose a two-fold "suspension" (Husserl), first of the "supernatural attitude," which treats religious phenomena as having an origin in an order of being beyond space and time, and second of the "rationalistic attitude," which claims overarching ahistorical authority. Once we have disabled the categories of supernaturalism and transcendental rationality, each of which is an illusion spawned by the denial of the facticity of human existence, then religious and theological beliefs and practices come into view in their distinctive particularity, protected from both superstition and rationalist dismissal. Secular culture can be seen to be animated with religious motifs and religion can be seen to be an intrinsically cultural form of life. Religion can be found anywhere in the culture, and every culture stirs with religious life.

The Whistle-Blowers. Theology underwent a deep mutation in the mid-twentieth century. The German Lutheran theologian Dietrich Bonhoeffer described the possibility of a "religionless Christianity." In modernity, he said, we have come to realize that "everything gets along fine without God." "The world has come of age," and humankind has attained its "adulthood," which was, in a word, also Kant's definition of Enlightenment.[1] As humankind becomes more and more, God becomes less and less, like the "last fading smile of the Cheshire cat" (Julian Huxley).[2] If religion means "God is the answer," then Bonhoeffer prefers Christianity religionless. "Religion" tries to return humankind to its pre-modern adolescence, to a state of dependence where it can shamelessly exploit human weakness. Against this, Bonhoeffer's counsel is, "Before God and with him we live without God." That paradoxical formulation meant that, in a world come of age, we are required to assume

---
[1] Dietrich Bonhoeffer, *Letters and Papers from Prison*, ed. Eberhard Bethge (London: SCM, 1971), 325–27, 360–61.
[2] Julian Huxley, *Religion without Revelation*, 2nd ed. (New York: Mentor Books, New American Library, 1957), 49–64 ("Science and God").

responsibility for our own lives and not expect God to do the heavy lifting, which also means rethinking what we mean by God.

While Bonhoeffer spoke of a "religionless" Christianity, Bultmann proposed "demythologizing" it. That did not mean to mock it for being superstitious, but to realize that the background understanding of the world in the New Testament, the cosmology – heaven above, hell down below, spirits good and evil doing battle over the fate of us humans in the middle – is obsolete, and that the "message" it contains must be discerned, ferreted out from these creatures of a pre-modern imagination. Paul Tillich, in turn, criticized the "supernaturalism" of religion, its belief in a power that supervenes upon the natural order, a Supreme being whose existence is up for debate. Instead of this transcendent God, which he considered "half-blasphemous and mythological,"[3] Tillich thought of God as the ground on which we stand, located right here in the *depths* of *culture*, where we articulate what matters most to us. Every theology is a theology of culture, or else it just sits idly on a seminary library shelf. To these three German Lutheran theologians I would add the work of the French Roman Catholic theologian Yves Congar who argued for a more genuine *laïcité*. Over and above its standard meaning, keeping the state safe from the church, Congar intended it as a way to keep the *world* safe from *God*, to protect the world from being swallowed up by God, emptied of all significance, thereby allowing us to treasure the world *for itself*.[4]

Religionless, demythologized, desupernaturalized, laicized – these are so many "secularizing" forces *inside* theology, like whistle-blowers alerting us that something is out of joint in the corporation, mid-twentieth century theologians enjoining us to rethink religion, theology and God in terms of the *saeculum*, of the age, of the world. Later on, we would hear the expression "secular theology" as opposed to an other-worldly one. They sought to close the gap between the religious and the secular *from theology's standpoint*, advancing a *new* theological frame of mind, one which realized that the *prophetic* critique of the world, calling out the injustices of the world, which cannot compromise itself with the greed of the world, should not be confused with an *ontological* denunciation of the being of the world, demeaning its reality and worth, since the world is, after all, what there is.

But these theologians were *theo*logians; they had not given up on God. They were looking for a new way to think of God, calling for a new species of theologians, who would make sense in a world that had come of age. What they were experiencing, each in their own way, is that God is not a discrete agent who

---

[3] Paul Tillich, *Theology of Culture*, ed. Robert C. Kimball (New York: Oxford University Press, 1959), 25.

[4] Yves Congar, *Lay People in the Church*, trans. Donald Attwater, 2nd rev. ed. (London: Geoffrey Chapman Ltd., 1965).

does things (however discreetly), like stepping in and acting on our behalf, no more than God can serve as the answer to our questions in science. We in the United States are tired of saying to the families of the victims of gun violence that "our prayers are with you" because we know that does not change anything; worse, with right-wing politicians in the pockets of the gun lobby, "our prayers" is actually a cover for doing nothing. So the theologians want to find a way to think and speak of God, to frame a discourse proper to God, one which neither mystifies nor dismisses God. They want to close the gap between religion and the world without giving up on God. Bonhoeffer speaks of living "before God with God" – so he does not give up on God – but "without God," so he does give up on God, on *that* God. Tillich, for his part, said we should not stop thinking about God but we should stop thinking of God heteronomously, as a power *over* the world, ruling from without, and start thinking "theonomously," as a ground or power *of* the world, an inner wellspring which gives us power from *within*, which he called the courage to be. For Bultmann, we must discern what the scriptures are proclaiming.

For these theologians religion is a mode of being-in-the-world (Heidegger), a *Lebenswelt*, to cite Edmund Husserl's famous "Vienna Lecture" (1935).[5] God's existence or being is *realized* in the *world*, in the *secular* order, as a "form of life," to cite Ludwig Wittgenstein, another son of Vienna. Where *else* could it have its being? In some other world? After death? That is precisely the old species of theologians, the old theological paradigm from which they were distancing themselves. They were one step away from saying God does not exist, which is, I think, what they should have said. That does not mean we are done with God. Atheism about the transcendent God of classical theology is not the end of theology; it is the beginning of another and radical post-theistic theology. To say God does not exist, is to say God insists, God calls – and it is up to us to respond, to lend God the existence that God lacks, putting the burden of the response, the responsibility for God, on us, and we may or may not respond. It is not a question of what God can do for us, but of what we can do for God.

The Suspension of the Supernatural Attitude. At this point I admit to following these theologians where they did not intend to lead, which is to claim that the secular life of religion is not some additional quality which we should also bear in mind, but essential, that religion is translated *without remainder* into the world, and that the discourse formerly and normally called theology is better understood

---

5 Edmund Husserl, "Philosophy and the Crisis of European Humanity" in *The Crisis of European Sciences and Transcendental Phenomenology*, trans. David Carr (Evanston: Northwestern University Press, 1970), Appendix A, 269–99.

as *theopoetics*, where the *logos* of theology is weakened into a *poetics*. The condition under which theopoetics is possible is, to slightly adapt Husserl, an *epochē*, which I call here the "suspension of the supernatural attitude." This cuts off in advance the belief that the phenomena of religion – its beliefs and practices, its "revelation" and "inspiration" – enjoy a heavenly provenance and divine authority. By suspending supernaturalism, we release these phenomena from the mystification of their origins; we allow these images and narratives to speak for themselves and from themselves, to stand on their own feet and enjoy their *own* authority. *Zu den Sachen selbst.* We release the power proper to these figures, which is neither magical or supernatural nor some kind of pathological illusion but strictly, rigorously poetic, *theo*-poetic. A poetics exerts the powerless power of a story or saying that cuts through prosaic life and leaves us shaken, disturbed, solicited, having "revealed" – as poets "reveal" a world to us – an alternate, head-turning vision of life.

Notice that the distinction between religious and secular now looks more like the distinction between poetry and prose. Religion is the poetry, specifically, the *theo*-poetry of the world; it is a depository of what we are dreaming of, of a faith beyond beliefs, of a hope against hope, of a love that surpasses understanding. The poetry is directed at the point of *excess*, of what exceeds the present limits of the world. It is dreaming of living and being otherwise, not otherwise than the world, but of a world otherwise than the present. If we want to call this "transcendence" then it is a transcendence that does not leave the plane of immanence but keeps it ecstatically open to the future. Relieved of the misunderstanding, deprived of the magic, their supernatural credentials revoked, their theo*logical* backup weakened, the economy of promises and threats put out of play, these images are forced back upon their own inherent theo-poetic force, the powerless power they have to persuade. They are reduced to speaking on their own behalf – where the weak forces of mercy and forgiveness, of hospitality and neighbor-love, speak for themselves. They play no part in a soteriology of rewards and punishments, a cosmology of natural and supernatural forces, an epistemology of faith and reason, all of which have been put out of action.

Instead of distinguishing between the Jesus of history and the Christ of faith, we distinguish instead the Jesus who belongs to the prose of history from the Jesus elevated into theopoetic space, where, over and above the body of flesh and blood who walked the dusty roads of ancient Galilee and lived in calendar time, he became an *iconic* body. There they killed him, but he would not stay dead. They could kill the man but not the poem. There, a lifeless body on the cross lives on in and as the "dangerous memory" of unjust suffering, which condemns the injustice of the world, a theopoetic figure of what the world *would look like*, in the poetic subjunctive, if the Kingdom of God came true, which for Bonhoeffer meant "being for others." For this the work of rigorous historical-critical investigation into the Jesus of history is of the utmost importance. It is a necessary step in the demythologization of Jesus and in correcting the mistakes of literalism and supernaturalism. It makes a mockery of the foolish disjunction that Jesus was either a liar, a madman or God. He was none of these things. He was a poem, a theo-poem, providing an insight into what is going on in the name of God. But if historical-critical work is the first word, it is not the last; if it is necessary, it is not sufficient. Once we see that the narratives of the New Testament enjoy a theopoetic status, we have not seen through them, as if they were fraudulent, as if they do not have anything to say. What matters about Jesus is the iconic force of his name, the weak force of the poem that he became, and the non-coercive power of that poem to galvanize a form of life.

The Suspension of the Transcendental Attitude. Of course, there is another way to reach the conclusion that God does not exist and religion is poetry, which is the path of secular rationality. The tendency of this discourse is not supernaturalistic but naturalistic, not mystifying but dismissive, where religion is not turned into magic but exposed as illusion. This is the discourse of reductionism, of saying that the religious imagination is "nothing more than X" – an opiate, a projection, a pathology, resentment, fantasy, delusion, primitive superstition. This is as ham-fisted and dogmatic in a rationalist way as religion is in a supernaturalist way. That is why we need a second *epoché*, which I call the "suspension of the transcendental attitude," an alternate attitudinal shift directed at the notion that has gotten into our head in modernity of Pure Reason (in ironic caps), transcendental rationality. The pretense of Pure Reason is to propose a set of overarching ahistorical categories meant to hold for all times and places, sitting like a court of final appeal before which everything else is brought to stand. So Pure Reason suffers from illusions of its own, no less blasphemous and mythological, that it has immunized itself, kept itself pure of empirical contact and gained access to transcendental resources. Kant entertained the illusion that the historically contingent, highly datable and locatable, white-male, western-German and Newtonian categories of the "pure understanding" he deduced enjoyed "transcendental" status, valid for everyone and everywhere for all time! Exactly twelve, he said, not eleven or thirteen! This he thought exposed everything in religion that is not ethics, pure rational ethics, that is, as superstition.

Transcendentalism (masquerading as "reason") and supernaturalism (masquerading as "faith") share the common illusion that we can transcend or supersede our "factical" situation. That is the word that Schelling and Heidegger use to say that as soon as we awake in the world, we find ourselves in a world that is already up and running, in a body, a place, a time, a culture, a language, all of which has us before we have it, and which is constantly running in the background without our knowledge or consent. Transcendentalism and supernaturalism share a *common other-worldliness*, a common degradation or distortion of the *saeculum*. So the second *epochē* asks of Pure Reason what the first asks of the theologians, to agree to come down to earth and to live in the *world* – in the *saeculum* – down here with the rest of us. I am trying to deprive religion of its transcendence and reason of its transcendentalism. In that sense, I am trying to "secularize" both *religion and reason*, trying to protect the world from being swallowed up by God (Congar) and to sharpen our sense of the depths of the world (Tillich). I am trying to embody religion in the world and to animate the world with a religious pulse. I am trying to close the gap between the religious and the secular by taking religion down a notch and raising the world up a notch, by depreciating religion's celestial illusions and appreciating culture's terrestrial depths.

When seen thus, deprived of transcendental status, "reason" means having "good reasons," the most persuasive interpretation available in the present state of the evidence, which does not mean it is immutable or even that it is right, but it is the best we can do at the moment. It is what Thomas Kuhn meant by saying we work within contingent paradigms until they do not work anymore and then we have to get inventive, and what Wittgenstein meant by a "language game" where having an intuition of an ideal essence meant, as Richard Rorty said, knowing how to play a language game – and all this takes place down here on earth, in the *saeculum*. That is what continental European philosophers call "hermeneutics," making the best judgment in a singular circumstance while making no promises about the future, which is wise counsel in both life and science.[6] It is what Schelling – the great nemesis of Hegel, who inspired Kierkegaard's philosophy of existence – called "ecstatic" reason,[7] not a closed system but an open-ended one, open to what he called, pace Hegel, the "unprethinkable." It is what Derrida liked to call "the coming of what we cannot see coming," or the "possibility of the impossible." By *the* impossible Derrida did not mean a square circle but a heightened sense of the contingency of our present horizon of expectation, a readiness to be overtaken by something wholly unforeseen. So, on this scenario, reason does not descend into madness and chaos, but it becomes more pliable and plastic, more open-ended, upended, decentered, prepared to be taken by surprise. Post-transcendental reason assumes the relative instability of our constructions which tend to sediment and are in need of de-sedimentation in order to keep the future open and to keep memory alive. The work of de-sedimentation, of exploiting the instability in this relative stability, is called deconstruction, and the ex-

---

[6] See my account of the state of hermeneutics today in *Hermeneutics: Facts and Interpretation in the Age of Information* (London: Penguin/Pelican, 2018).
[7] F.W.J. Schelling, *The Grounding of Positive Philosophy: The Berlin Lectures*, trans. Bruce Matthews (Albany: State University of New York Press, 2008), 203.

planatory theory behind this discourse is *différance*. *Différance* is not a transcendental subject as in Kant or Husserl, but an anonymous field, a quasi-transcendental condition of possibility, the "quasi" meaning it produces unstable effects, unlike a Kantian transcendental which pretends to produce fixed effects, or an Husserlian transcendental, which pretends to produce ideal objects, both of which are too strong.

In *post*modern theory, both post-transcendental and post-theistic, we do not destroy the categories of modernity; we weaken them, destabilize them, make them plastic, porous and open-ended. We avoid taking categories like religious and secular, faith and reason, in inflated terms – as *supernatural revelation*, transcending purely natural reason, on the one hand, and *transcendental rationality*, which extinguishes every phenomenon which does not stand up to rational legitimation, on the other hand. Postmodern theory deflates both metaphysical transcendence and epistemological transcendentalism, depriving both of their illusions, thereby weakening the divide between the religious and the secular that has been widened in modernity, where it has become toxic, a menace to the public weal. Postmodern theorists are not attacking reason just as the progressive theologians were not attacking religion. They were together rendering the opposition or dichotomization of the religious and the secular porous, by suspending both beliefs, both attitudes, supernaturalism and transcendentalism, as hermeneutic misunderstandings. Both attitudes represent a failure to know how to read religious texts and to understand theological discourse, the one by *believing* them, the other by *disbelieving* them, the one by being innocent and uncritical, the other by treating them with cynical critical disdain, the *odium theologiae*.

Once both are disabled, once both the belief and the disbelief are suspended, then the so-called secular culture can be seen to be permeated with religious motifs and religion can be seen to be an intrinsically cultural form of life. This twofold suspension opens the door to revised conceptions of phenomena like faith, hope and even prayer, which stripped of supernaturalism and relieved of reductionism, cut across a previously uncrossable divide. Is our passion for the promise of justice or of democracy – the "democracy to-come," the "justice to-come" – free of a certain religious impulse? Is our faith and hope in them free of a certain prayer? Religious depths can be found anywhere in the culture, and every culture requires them, otherwise it is not a culture at all, just a place on the map. Just so, every religion requires a culture, otherwise it is a free-floating abstraction mainly confined to academic seminars. The two are co-dependent, interdependent, interwoven, inseparable, entangled, each saturated by the other.

Behaving like Adults, A New Enlightenment. Bonhoeffer brought the religious and the secular together by advising the faithful that God expects us to behave like adults, which was his definition of a religionless Christianity and a new monasticism, and Kant's definition of the *old* eighteenth-century (modern) Enlightenment, whose motto was "dare to think." We are all for thinking, the more, the better. What I am asking for is to dare to think *radically*, which would represent a *new* (postmodern) Enlightenment, a posthuman age, and an even more mature adulthood, one which is enlightened about the old Enlightenment, which exacerbated this divide. If we do so dare, we will upend the dichotomy of religious and secular by exposing the one to the other. *Theological* thinking eventually hits *radical* ground. The problem for theology here is its supernaturalism, which discourages thinking that challenges its dogmas. Second, radical *thinking* eventually hits *theological* ground, which encounters the prejudices of the *old* Enlightenment, the old *odium theologiae*, which I think is every bit as thoughtless as is bible-thumping is dogmatic.

The challenge for secular culture, which is to get over its *odium theologiae*, is steep. The challenge for religion is even steeper. Religion has fallen into the wrong hands, and it is making itself increasingly unbelievable, the shelter of the uncultured, undereducated, and reactionary in a multicultural, hyper-informational, global, postmodern and increasingly posthuman world. The question is whether religion has a future, or even deserves to have a future. Maybe the adult thing to do for religion would be to admit that it is *time to move on* and look for other ways to address the mystery of our lives, to give word and image to what matters most to us, a task which, hitherto the task of religion, has today more and more fallen to the work of art. If I were to conjecture, I would say that is where things are headed, to a new coalition of art and science that will squeeze religion out, and the three great categories of the "absolute spirit" described by Hegel – art, religion, and philosophy (knowledge) – will be reduced to two.

My hypothesis is that something will take the place of religion, something will take over the work that was getting done by religion, which is to expose our lives to the mystery of who we are and of what our place is in the universe. The future calls for a new species of theologians, of theologians to come, who will arrive bearing other names. I imagine a future in which the opposition of religion and secularity will be consigned to a by-gone dark age, displaced by an entirely different framework in which we will experience a new sense of mystery, where what was called "religion" and what religion called "God" will also bear new names. God is unconditional, Schelling said, but the unconditional is not God. The name of God is but a finger pointing at the moon, a pre-Copernican image which can be updated, aided by the Webb telescope, as a finger pointing at the edges of the universe, off at an unfathomable distance and the beginning of cosmic time, back at an unprethinkable beginning. The mystery has always been the mystery of what is described in the New Testament as "that in which we live and move and have our being" (Acts 17:28), which, fittingly, tellingly, is actually a case of the New Testament citing an unnamed Greek poet. This supports the hypothesis that while the calculable problems of our lives are expounded in prose, the incalculable mystery of the things is sheltered in the poetry of the world, its theopoetry, in which the tension between the religious and the secular will have become the "last fading smile of the Cheshire cat."

Works Cited

Bonhoeffer, Dietrich. *Letters and Papers from Prison.* Ed. Eberhard Bethge. London: SCM, 1971.
Caputo, John D. *Hermeneutics: Facts and Interpretation in the Age of Information.* London: Penguin/Pelican, 2018.
Congar, Yves. *Lay People in the Church.* Trans. Donald Attwater. 2nd rev. ed. London: Geoffrey Chapman Ltd., 1965.
Husserl, Edmund. "Philosophy and the Crisis of European Humanity" in *The Crisis of European Sciences and Transcendental Phenomenology.* Trans. David Carr. Evanston: Northwestern University Press, 1970, Appendix A, 269–99.
Huxley, Julian. *Religion without Revelation.* 2nd ed. New York: Mentor Books, New American Library, 1957, 49–64 ("Science and God").
Schelling, F.W.J. *The Grounding of Positive Philosophy: The Berlin Lectures.* Trans. Bruce Matthews. Albany: State University of New York Press, 2008.
Tillich, Paul. *Theology of Culture.* Ed. Robert C. Kimball. New York: Oxford University Press, 1959.

Getrude Postl
This Incredible Need to Believe: Julia Kristeva's Reinvention of Secular Humanism at the Crossroad of Religion, Psychoanalysis, and Politics

Abstract: Focusing on Julia Kristeva's text *This Incredible Need to Believe*, this paper aims in a first step to explore Kristeva's account of secular humanism. On the basis of affinities between key configurations of monotheistic religions and the psychoanalytic process, she locates the problems of contemporary secularized societies in the failure to recognize a prelinguistic "need to believe" – understood as the foundation for the speaking being itself and indicative of the human condition as such. In a second step this subjective belief of the early stages of subject formation will be related to Kristeva's concept of "intimate revolt" and its intersection of inner psychic life, art/literature, and religion. It will be argued that Kristeva's work on religion and her proposed "radical reformation of humanism" also has a political dimension.

Introduction

In her text *This Incredible Need to Believe* (2009), Julia Kristeva mentions the famous 2004 debate between Jürgen Habermas and Josef Ratzinger, referring in particular to Habermas' "Pre-political Foundations of the Democratic Constitutional State" (later published in *The Dialectics of Secularization: On Reason and Religion*). The two thinkers, Kristeva claims, argue for a *"return to faith"* as "the last chance" for countering "the perils of liberty" and for "creating some sort of moral stability" (Kristeva *This Incredible Need*, 26). Although herself more than discontent with the conditions of contemporary Western cultures (e.g. the society of the spectacle, religious fundamentalism, political violence, nihilism, the *New Maladies of the Soul*), she outright rejects the position allegedly held by Habermas and Ratzinger: "As a counterpoint to this hypothesis, I would like to suggest that we are already confronted [...] with experiences that render null and void any call for a 'normative conscience' and the reason/revelation duo" (Ibid.). She is opposed to any kind of unifying normative bond as well as the opposition between faith and reason, or, put differently, the questionable alternative between "a narrowly rationalist humanism" and "a romantic spirituality" (Ibid. 27). As Amy Hollywood observes,

"Kristeva refuses any clearly drawn distinction between religion and secularism" (Hollywood 314). What she suggests instead is a turn to the unconscious and – related – to language, literature, and art. In her view, Enlightenment humanism fails to account for the underside of and the precondition for an idealized rationality and, therefore, needs to be reformed – what she calls "new forms of humanism" (Kristeva *This Incredible Need*, 28). If there is any unifying bond at all, a "'unifying bond' that secularized political rationality lacks," it has to come from "the Freudian discovery of the unconscious" (Ibid. 26) and the literary experience.

The problem of secularized societies, according to Kristeva, is not the absence of religion but rather the failure to recognize and acknowledge a necessary, yet paradoxical 'need to believe.' Countering the ills of contemporary Western societies cannot be done by reviving religion, by expecting it to provide unifying moral standards to tame the dangers of contemporary individualism, but rather, by looking at the unacknowledged undercurrents of secular cultures as a key for assigning faith its deserved place. This paradoxical 'need to believe,' according to Kristeva, has always been with us; it is built into the psychic development of early subject formation; it becomes the foundation for the speaking being itself, a "prepolitical and prereligious need" (Ibid. xvi), indicative of the human condition as such. Traces of this 'need to believe' may be encountered in two related areas: psychoanalysis and the psychoanalytic process on the one hand, language, literature, and art on the other. Thus, the two parts of the present paper.

"This Incredible Need to Believe" – Religion and Psychoanalysis

Kristeva describes 'this incredible need to be believe' in terms of "an unshakable certainty, sensory plentitude, and ultimate truth" (Ibid. 7), as some archaic, prelinguistic assurance that is related to a desire to know: "when I say 'I believe,' I mean 'I hold as true'" (Ibid. 3). She locates this incredible but also paradoxical 'need to believe' in the early stages of psychic development, before any structured language or rational justification. It is a 'prepolitical and prereligious need' since no ideological commitments have yet been formed. But most importantly, "the 'need to believe' [...] is the foundation of our capacity to be [...] *speaking beings*" (Ibid. vii). It becomes a precondition for the acquisition of language and, thus, for signification in general. "Faith holds the key to the act of speech itself [...]. Because I believe, I speak: I would not speak if I didn't believe" (Ibid. x). Without some archaic sense of certainty, linguistic meaning would be impossible.

But according to Kristeva, "'the need to believe' [...] constitutes [...] only one of the elements in this complex experience of faith" (Ibid. xvi). Since she locates this form of belief at the threshold of language, it has to be discussed as part of what she famously termed the semiotic[1] – a prelinguistic, not yet symbolic organizing structure of bodily rhythms and excitations in their interplay with the body of the mother. Given the crucial role of the mother body for the transition from the body to structured language, Kristeva associates the semiotic with the feminine. It is this connection which lends further support to the importance of a religious dimension for signification. Women, for Kristeva, are connected to the sacred. Contrary to a sacrificial sacred which is based on a form of metaphysical universalism, she introduces "a second type of sacred, [...] signifying 'overflowing life' and 'growth' [...] that refers to fertility and force of spirit" – an inscription of sexual difference into the universal (Kristeva *Hatred and Forgiveness*, 52). Placing women at the intersection of sensory intimacy and a concern for the species, between nature and culture, Kristeva claims that "the sense of the divine and the sacred arises at the very point of the emergence of language" (Ibid. 12).

Thus, the human being's entry into language, the transition from the semiotic to the symbolic (from the mother body to the symbolic law of the father) is conceived by Kristeva in religious terms. The beginning of the capacity to speak depends on the 'need to believe,' on the divine and the sacred – all of which to be understood in an anti-metaphysical sense. "My preoccupation with the sacred is [...] anti-metaphysical" (Ibid.). There is no separation of physis and meaning, of affects and language, accordingly no opposition between faith and reason since within Kristeva's framework of thought, metaphysical dichotomies do not exist. Without recurrence to faith or what she calls the divine, expressions of reason would be lacking the unconscious grounding of these expressions, the semiotic foundation for meaning. The divine is not in opposition to the mortal, the sacred not in opposition to the profane. Rather, the forms of signification that emerge at that point of individual human history (what will later become the symbolic) are always already the result of an interplay between the body and the psyche, between physiological and mental processes, between belief and truth. Kristeva talks about "the very borderline between biology and sense on which our languages and our discourses depend" (Kristeva *This Incredible Need*, 28). Linguistic meaning rests on bodily materiality; the body always also speaks. Belief and the divine are conditions for meaning, lastly for reason, not its opposites. "By understanding the 'semiotic' as

---

[1] For a detailed explanation of Kristeva's concepts of the Semiotic and the Symbolic, see the first section of Kristeva, *Revolution in Poetic Language*, trans. Margaret Waller. New York: Columbia UP, 1984. 19–106.

the 'emergence of meaning' we can overcome the dichotomies of metaphysics (soul/body, physical/psychical)" (Kristeva *Hatred and Forgiveness*, 12), including the dichotomy of faith and reason.

These prelinguistic developments that establish the emergence of meaning as grounded in belief and the sacred can be encountered within the context of the psychoanalytic process. The analyst in his/her capacity as interpreter consciously attends to the remnants or traces of these early transitions as they present themselves in a particular case scenario. In this context, it is important to note that Kristeva views the psychoanalytic process as a translation of purely subjective expressions (manifesting itself through the 'I believe' and a desire to know) into objective statements. Claims based on belief but offered as truth are part of the everyday experience of the analyst. The psychoanalytic process, comparable to art and literature (to be discussed later), takes the 'need to believe' seriously in that it allows the transformation of mere subjective certainties (stories, fictions, personal narratives) into meaning, making them objectively accessible through the interpretative intervention of the analyst (comparable to the critic as interpreter of a work of literature or art). A prelinguistic and also pre-epistemological desire to believe and to know are part of the psycho-sexual dynamics of individual human development and as such encountered in the psychoanalytic process:

> [...] the analyst begins by 'believing' in the psychic reality of his analysands: it doesn't matter if the analysand himself entrusts me with inept phantasms, I begin by believing in these beliefs [...]. I integrate the tales, myths, and theories of the analysands in my interpretation, which, from the subjective, purifies itself into something objective [...], I return them to the fields of knowledge and of therapy (Kristeva *This Incredible Need*, 4–5).

The analyst transforms instances of subjective beliefs into epistemologically valid claims that might eventually contribute to the therapeutic effects which render the analysand a proper member of the (moral) community. The analyst's interpretative activity, in due application of psychoanalytic theory, is in itself an overcoming of metaphysical dichotomies in that any meaningful interpretation of the words of the analysand presupposes signification as grounded in bodily drives (the semiotic). In particular, it is through the processes of transference and countertransference that the analyst recovers traces of the analysand's early 'need to believe' in order to put those into language. In the words of Amy Hollywood: "The analyst [...] plays the role of the 'Father of individual prehistory,' the loving father who brings the subject into language" (Hollywood 315).

This is in reference to Kristeva's appropriation of what Freud – in *The Ego and the Id* – called the 'father of individual prehistory.' She invents a pre-oedipal, loving father, an imaginary father, actually a "father-mother conglomerate" (Kristeva *Tales of Love,* 40) who has the "'attributes of both parents'" (Kristeva *This Incred-*

ible Need, 10) and who 'softens' the trauma of the child's necessary separation from the mother body. "A *third party* henceforth infiltrates the archeology of the need to believe: this is an oblative paternity, endowed with a subliminatory capacity" (Ibid.). This imaginary loving third, Freud's 'father of individual prehistory,' assists the child in transitioning from the body to language, from the semiotic to the symbolic. And, according to Kristeva, this imaginary father has resemblances with the loving Christian father-God who is willing to sacrifice his son. Without this father's loving authority "I would not be able to achieve any norm, accept any frustration, obey any prohibition, take upon myself any law or moral code" (Ibid.). Language as well as the moral code are not the result of the threat of punishment or castration, they are not brought about by a vengeful Biblical God or an Oedipal father. Rather, they are learned through love and trust, through acceptance of one's beliefs, and thus through a smooth transition from a prelinguistic (or incomprehensible, for the analysand) stage to signification and meaning. The child as well as the analysand rely on love and on a relationship of reciprocal trust that takes their beliefs seriously. A loving acceptance and interpretation of the 'need to believe' and the desire to know is indispensable not only for the formation of structured language and meaning but also for the development of the Ego – this applies to the healthy development of the child as much as the therapeutic success of the analysand.

Kristeva has been exploring the "similarities/dissimilarities between psychoanalysis and faith" (Ibid. 5) for several decades,[2] starting with selective texts in her essay collection *Tales of Love* (1987, French 1983) and *In the Beginning was Love: Psychoanalysis and Faith* (1987, French 1985). Contrary to the common reading of Freud as atheist who famously claimed religion to be an illusion, Kristeva views psychoanalysis as offering new perspectives on religious phenomena: "When approaching the immense continent of religious experience from a psychoanalytic point of view, my thoughts are directed to Sigmund Freud [… who] opened up a new way of thinking religious experience" (Kristeva "The Need to Believe and the Desire to Know, Today", 75). The points of affinity between psychoanalysis and faith, in particular in the case of monotheistic religions, are numerous and range from the belief in an ideal father (God the father, role of the father in individual psycho-sexual history, e.g. the Oedipus conflict), the importance of love and forgiveness, the prohibition of desires, the connection between sacrifice and sublimation, all the way to the proximity between word and flesh. But in particular, given

---

2 Kristeva is a declared atheist. However, given her extensive work on religious issues, she was invited to the Interfaith Peace Summit in Assisi, 2011, called by Pope Benedict, to celebrate the 25th anniversary of the first interfaith meeting called by Pope Jean-Paul II in 1986. There, she presented her "Ten Principles for Twenty-First-Century Humanism" (see Kristeva *Passions of Our Time*, 279–83).

Kristeva's interest in issues of language and representation, she searches for traces in Freud's texts that confirm her own approach of connecting belief with the onset of signification. "Freud's texts showed me that *Homo sapiens* is *Homo religiosus*. From *Totem and Taboo* to *Moses and Monotheism*, including *The Future of an Illusion*, he considers religion to be coextensive with humans' capacity to create meaning" (Mock).

For Kristeva, religion is not something that disappeared with the onset of Enlightenment humanism and now has to be brought back again. Rather, religion is part of the human condition. One could say, she is interested in the spiritual grounding of the human ability to create meaning. "Human beings' apperception of their complex aptitude for representation and symbolization is at the basis of what has been imagined, since the dawn of the hominid, as a 'beyond,' 'spirituality,' or a 'divinity'" (Kristeva *Hatred and Forgiveness*, 209–210). And since, in Kristeva's account, it is psychoanalysis which explores the unconscious foundation of this 'complex aptitude for representation and symbolization,' it should not be surprising that she sees an affinity between (Christian) faith and psychoanalytic theory. "Religions, in short, seem to be a recognition of what Freud calls *das höhere Wesen im Menschen*, 'the higher side of man' in which the subject's freedom is inscribed" (Ibid. 211). And this freedom, for Kristeva, has to do with the capacity to signify and to create representations.

The Scared Source of Art and Literature – Intimate Revolt

According to Kristeva, it is exactly this "höhere Wesen im Menschen" and "the subject's freedom" which are in danger at the moment. In her view, we live in a society of the spectacle (borrowing Guy Debord's famous phrase), a culture dominated by media images, commodity exchange, and the superficiality of entertainment. Art and literature have lost their meaning; immediate satisfaction is the goal. People are guided by the pleasure principle and do not realize that they suffer from the *New Maladies of the Soul:* "[...] today's men and women – who are stress-ridden and eager to achieve, to spend money, have fun, and die – dispense with the representation of their experience that we call psychic life... Modern man is losing his soul, but he does not know it [...]" (Kristeva *New Maladies of the Soul*, 7–8). Soulless and empty, a far cry from representing the higher side of man, "man has become [...] a person barely free enough to use a remote control to choose his channel" (Kristeva *Intimate Revolt*, 4). Revolt against these nihilistic trends, especially political resistance, seems impossible since a disappearance of recognizable political authority and a dissemination of power have created a power vacuum that renders any form of revolt meaningless: "(W)ho can revolt, and against what?" (Kristeva *The Sense and Non-Sense of Revolt*, 8) Kristeva asks. The only revolt possible at this moment in history is a turn towards one's inner psychic life, a revolt on the individual level or an 'intimate revolt.' And this concept of intimate revolt is a plea for finding an inner space as defense against the society of the spectacle and the overall lack of meaning. In times when the pleasure principle reigns, and people are caught up in finding satisfaction in the superficiality of the show, the turn towards some subjective inner experience or psychic life constitutes a form of revolt: "[...] the intimate is what is most profound and most singular in the human experience" (Kristeva *Intimate Revolt*, 44).

In Kristeva's view, it is not simply a turn to religion in its previously established forms that would counteract the problems of contemporary secular societies but a turn towards one's inner subjective experience. Kristeva's work on religion and her revolt project are connected – it is within the inner psychic life that the 'need to believe' is first found and expressed. And, as has been explained already, for the individual psycho-sexual development, this inner realm serves as the foundation for any creation of meaning or representation in general, thus, lastly for the manifestations of meaning in writing, literature, and art. This is to say, Kristeva's interest in religion, just like Habermas' position, has a political dimension. Her concept of intimate revolt is intrinsically intertwined with what she calls a reformed humanism – the search for a subjective inner realm that involves art and literature as bulwarks against the perils and pitfalls of contemporary Western societies. "People today are eager for introspection and prayer: art and culture respond to this need [...]" (Kristeva *The Sense and Non-Sense of Revolt*, 9).

This importance of art and literature for any possible forms of revolt is further elaborated with an eye on modernism: "Our modern world has reached a point [...] where a certain type of culture and art, if not all culture and all art, is threatened, indeed impossible [...] specifically the art and culture of revolt" (Ibid. 8). In Kristeva's view, the art and literature of modernism – "a crucial moment in the history of thought" (Kristeva *This Incredible Need*, 29) and in a sense the last remnant of Enlightenment Humanism – did establish a revolt culture that depended on a kind of subjective inner commitment to questioning and a critical re-evaluation of established cultural signs. Literary and artistic creations, just like the narratives shared in the psychoanalytic process, come from an archaic, unconscious, prelinguistic space that assures the certainty of belief. With the help of the analyst, writer, critic, this subjective, drive-driven dimension of belief (part of the semiotic) enters the already existing linguistic or formal codes of the symbolic order – subjective belief is turned into culturally mediated forms of expression. "[...] in our civilization [...] psychoanalysis, on the one hand, and a certain literature, on the other, perhaps constitute possible instances of revolt culture" (*The Sense and Non-Sense of Revolt*, 29). And this revolt is possible only if some psychic inner life, including the 'need to believe,' is explored and assured rather than repressed and forgotten. The religious dimension enters the political realm.

Intimate revolt is a response to the failure of secularized Enlightenment humanism, which focused too strongly on a disembodied form of reason and dismissed not only the 'need to believe' but also the sacred dimension that informs all creation of meaning: "[...] art and literature are in fact a continuation of the sacred by other means [...]" (Ibid. 13). Kristeva argues for a "radical reformation of humanism" (Kristeva *This Incredible Need*, 28) which, in her view, means a humanism freed not only from metaphysical dichotomies but also from its seeming rejection of religion. According to Kristeva, Enlightenment humanism contains a Christian legacy ("certain fundaments essential to modern humanism, such as notions of 'freedom' or 'personal dignity,' go back to theology," Kristeva *Hatred and Forgiveness*, 211). But this legacy was never sufficiently acknowledged and the repression of the religious roots of Western secular culture led to a continuation of metaphysical dichotomies as manifestation of a form of rationalism that, in Kristeva's view, is partly responsible for the disastrous situation we find ourselves in today. Letting oneself be numbed by the images of the spectacle is the by-product of a way of thinking that relegates anything drive-related or any form of desire to the irrational. And it is a form of thinking that excludes or wants to overcome the necessarily subjective roots of the speaking being. In Kristeva's view, literature and art are on the forefront when it comes to escaping this narrow form of rationalism and they are therefor assigned a central role in her view of revolt and of a reformed humanism. "[...] literature and art [together with psychoanalysis, GP] [...] offer themselves as laboratories of new forms of humanism" which allow us "to confront the new barbarities of automation [...]" (Kristeva *This Incredible Need*, 28).

Due to its rootedness in the semiotic and its connection to the feminine, the sacred origin of art and literature gains special relevance in our contemporary age: "I am convinced that this new twenty-first century, which seems to be in such need for religion, is actually in need of the sacred. I understand the sacred as the desire of human beings to think, not in the sense of calculation, but rather in the sense of a need for fundamental questioning" with language or meaning itself emerging out of a "sense of the divine and the sacred" (Kristeva *Hatred and Forgiveness*, 12). In Kristeva's account, we have a need for the sacred because we have a need for meaning – "because I believe, I speak" (Kristeva *This Incredible Need*, x). But it is exactly this need for meaning and the desire to think and to question which are endangered in a culture of the market and of the show. The media-generated specular inhabitants of the society of the spectacle, unable to even use their remote control, are disconnected from their 'need to believe' and not very likely to develop 'a need for fundamental questioning.' To revolt, for Kristeva, entails to return, to bring back, to revive what has been lost. And what has been lost is not religion per se, but the sacred grounding of signification – of speaking, writing, the creation of art. In a sense, Kristeva's concept of intimate revolt connects the religious with the political dimension – revolt is possible only if we acknowledge the sacred origin of language itself.

In addition to serving as a condition for the human capacity to create meaning, religion also provides some of the 'material' that then gets transformed into works of literature or art. "Religions [...] have accumulated vast stores of knowledge on the human soul and its relationship to the world and to others, notably and especially in the form of fables, illusions, or imaginary constructions" (Kristeva *Hatred and Forgiveness*, 210). Comparable to the analyst who responds to the tales and myths of the analysand, artists and writers make use of these 'vast stores of knowledge' in their creative process so as to create new fables, illusions, imaginary constructions. The artworks and texts that make up the so-called European cultural tradition are not objectively proven scientific facts but products of the imagination. They are intertextually connected phantasms, the results of individual as well as cultural processes of sublimation. And they can – in one way or the other – be traced back to a subjective inner realm. It is for those reasons that Kristeva's project of an intimate revolt can be related to 'this incredible need to believe.' Contrary to "the culture of entertainment, the culture of performance, the culture of the show" (Kristeva *The Sense and Non-Sense of Revolt* , 6), intimate revolt is an active engagement with an individual psychic life that eventually translates into culturally coded forms of expression. "[...] it is not exclusively in the world of action that this revolt is realized but in that of psychical life and its social manifestations (writing, thought, art) [...]" (Kristeva *Intimate Revolt*, 11). This revolt entails taking seriously the fables, stories, myths, phantasms that inform the rich historical tradition of European humanism by unearthing a kind of knowledge, facets of meaning that are rooted in a purely subjective, intimate realm.

And this process requires interpretation. "Interpretation, as I understand it, is itself a revolt" (Kristeva *The Sense and Non-Sense of Revolt*, 2). Interpretation is a revolt because it is a form of questioning that actively engages with other texts, other artworks, other speech acts, rather than passively consuming them. It is meaning enacted rather than commodified (as is the case with culture in the society of the spectacle). Comparable to the psychoanalyst, it falls upon writers, critics and artists to revolt against a culture of the spectacle and of commercialization by giving meaning to the sublimated manifestations of a prelinguistic, individual 'need to believe' and a desire to know. "[...] it is our responsibility to be interpreters, givers of meaning" (Ibid. 8). 'Meaning' here is not opposed to the body since any form of signification, for Kristeva, is rooted in the drives. The semiotic haunts the symbolic order, it disrupts and undermines it – the subjective genesis of meaning construction cannot be erased through the grammatical and semantic rules of the symbolic order. It is, thus, the role of the interpreter to trace back the social manifestations of psychic life (cultural expressions that are currently in danger of being either commodified or forgotten) to this bodily realm or to reconnect language, writing, literature, and art with the sacred and divine space of their origin.

> [...] literature and writing work out a risky kind of knowledge, singular and sharable, concerning the desire for sense rooted in the sexual body. In doing so, literature – writing – shake up the metaphysical duo *reason versus faith* [...] They invite us to shape an interpretive, critical, and theoretical discourse that [...] involve[s] the interpreter's own subjectivity (Kristeva *This Incredible Need*, 27–28).

Transforming the 'need to believe' into 'a risky kind of knowledge' locates the writer, artist, or interpreter at the threshold between body and language, drives and signs, the semiotic and the symbolic. This transition from the singular to the sharable, from the subjective to the objective, from belief to knowledge involves imagination and sublimation. And it certainly is very similar to Kristeva's account of the analytic process – the analyst, like the writer or artist, is an interpreter who attempts to give meaning to expressions of mere belief.

Summary and Conclusion

From Kristeva's perspective, it makes little sense to talk about a return of religion or to aim at bringing established forms of religion back into secularized societies. Instead, she conceives the mostly unconscious beginnings of the human subject formation itself in religious terms. The sacred, the divine, a 'need to believe' describe the human transition from a prelinguistic state to the realm of signification: "[...] not to eradicate the sacred but to rediscover it in the very depth of language [...]" (Kristeva *Hatred and Forgiveness*, 25). The goal is, therefore, to acknowledge the existence of this unconscious underpinning of the social order that grew out of enlightenment rationalism. Only if we recognize the 'incredible need to believe' as a condition for the speaking being and the divine source of literature and art can we embark on an intimate revolt – the only revolt, in Kristeva's view, that might successfully respond to the inherent dangers and drawbacks of the society of the spectacle and the contemporary maladies of the soul. Circumventing the opposition between faith and reason, this prelinguistic belief is much more than an idiosyncratic subjective aberration. Rather, it brings about stories, fables, imaginary constructions, similar to those found in our religious heritage but also in the psychoanalytic process. Being interpreted by the analyst, writer, artist, or critic, 'this incredible need to believe' is a creative force – radically subjective but sharable – which might become the springboard for a form of revolt against the society of the spectacle, a form of revolt that is as much secular as it is religious.

Works Cited

Habermas, Jürgen. "Pre-political Foundations of the Democratic Constitutional State?" Jürgen Habermas and Josef Ratzinger. *The Dialectics of Secularization: On Reason and Religion.* San Francisco: Ignatius Press, 2007. 19–52.
Hollywood, Amy (2010), Review of Julia Kristeva, *This Incredible Need to Believe*, in: *Spiritus: A Journal of Christian Spirituality*, Vol.10, No 2 (2010): 314–18.
Kristeva, Julia. *Revolution in Poetic Language*, trans. Margaret Waller. New York: Columbia UP, 1984.
Kristeva, Julia. *In the Beginning was Love: Psychoanalysis and Faith*, trans. Arthur Goldhammer. New York: Columbia UP, 1987.
Kristeva, Julia. *Tales of Love*, trans. Leon S. Roudiez. New York: Columbia UP, 1987.
Kristeva, Julia. *New Maladies of the Soul*, trans. Ross Guberman. New York: Columbia UP, 1995.
Kristeva, Julia. *The Sense and Non-Sense of Revolt. The Powers and Limits of Psychoanalysis.* Volume 1, trans. Jeanine Herman. New York: Columbia UP, 2000.
Kristeva, Julia. *Intimate Revolt. The Powers and Limits of Psychoanalysis.* Volume 2, trans. Jeanine Herman. New York: Columbia UP, 2002.
Kristeva, Julia. *This Incredible Need to Believe*, trans. Beverly Bie Brahic. New York: Columbia UP, 2009.
Kristeva, Julia. *Hatred and Forgiveness*, trans. Jeanine Herman. New York: Columbia UP, 2010.
Kristeva, Julia. "The Need to Believe and the Desire to Know, Today." *Psychoanalysis, Monotheism and Morality. The Sigmund Freud Museum Symposia 2009–2011.* Ed. Wolfgang Müller-Funk, Ingrid Scholz-Strasser and Herman Westerink. Leuven: Leuven UP, 2013. 75–91.
Kristeva, Julia. *Passions of Our Time*, ed. Lawrence Kritzman, trans. Constance Borde and Sheila Malovany-Chevallier. New York: Columbia UP, 2018.
Mock, Keren. "The Need to Believe and the Archive: Interview with Julia Kristeva," *Dibur. Literary Journal*, Issue 3 (Fall 2016). https://arcade.stanford.edu/dibur/need-believe-and-archive-interview-julia-kristeva, Accessed March 31st, 2023.

Part III **Religion in U.S. Literature and Politics in a Global Context**

Waldemar Zacharasiewicz
Critical Perspectives on Self-Sufficing Humanism in Southern Fiction

Abstract: The essay focuses on the philosophical reflections and the fiction of the novelist Walker Percy, whose ideas and novels are discussed against the background of the American South, where the collective experience of defeat in the American Civil War dampened the optimism of the American Dream (Fl. O'Connor). The greater role given to religion there, not only among African Americans, is demonstrated in the firm belief of the memorable figure of Dilsey in W. Faulkner's novel *The Sound and the Fury*. Having been forced to give up his career as a physician, Percy devoted himself to an intensive reading of twentieth century existentialist philosophers, of the early semiotician Ch. S. Peirce, and especially S. Kierkegaard. The latter's harsh warning against a complacent and hedonistic life style is echoed and dramatized in Percy's two dystopias set in the late 20th-century South. In these novels Percy exposes the shortcomings of behaviorists, who try to shape society in tune with their self-sufficing humanism (Ch. Taylor). The crimes of Nazi physicians also implicate the aesthetic products of the Viennese musical tradition, which were sources of their sophisticated pastimes.

The essay by Ch. R. Wilson in this volume succinctly describes prominent features of the social role and political function of religion in the American South in the form of a regional civil religion roundabout 1900 and the different application of religious thought in the 1950s and 60s, and thus exempts me from the need to elaborate on the great importance of religion and the spread of fundamentalist beliefs in the region.

The news of an emotional religiosity linked to fundamentalist beliefs rampant in the American Heartland, including parts of the American South, which was named the Bible Belt, have reached many Europeans.[1] The advocacy of such religious beliefs by televangelists, who in the South have a reach far exceeding that of their counterparts in other regions, may also be familiar to attentive European readers of newspapers or consumers of TV news. And a sense of the very wide variety of religious denominations, their important social function and role, and the

---

[1] See esp. the opening volume 1 on religion of *The New Encyclopedia of Southern Culture*. Ed. Charles Reagan Wilson. Chapel Hill: U of North Carolina P, 2014, 929–1000.

existence of sometimes clearly irrational practices in this section of the USA has also been filtered through the media to Europeans.

It is therefore not surprising that the numerous fiction writers rooted in this region have also dealt with the significant role of religion in the lives of the characters they include in their stories and novels. And in these texts religious themes seem to be more prominently addressed than in the fictional fruits of other regions of the USA, especially the urban northeast of the country or the Far West. One might ask oneself, as R.P. Warren did, whether the collective experience of defeat in the region in the 19th century and the aftermath of the disaster of the Civil War may have lessened the secular optimism, which at times has characterized the world-view and the resulting fiction ostensibly reflecting the American Dream.[2] This idea has been expressed in essays by prominent modern writers from the American South, such as Flannery O'Connor and Walker Percy, and seems to have been echoed in fictional representations of such modes of coping by other authors from the region as well.[3] This collective memory may have supported the search for alternative ways of coping with the precarious human condition, in particular by embracing religion.

Readers of classic modernist fiction from the American South, e.g. by Nobel Prize laureate William Faulkner, will recall the description of the impact of the Easter Sunday sermon by the physically insignificant preacher Rev. Shegog in the final, fourth part of Faulkner's first major achievement *The Sound and the Fury*. The magic of Rev. Shegog's voice, when addressing the congregation with his sonorous voice in their African American idiom as "brethren and sistuhn," captures the imagination of the congregation in the weathered church of the black community in Jefferson. He mesmerizes them with the evocation of stages of Christ's mission and passion, and deeply moves Dilsey Gibson, who weeps without restraint over the images evoked of Calvary and the resurrection. They give her hope and her simple belief, which is fed by the visualization of these events, strengthens her resolve and makes her carry on as the only reliable prop of the

---

[2] Cf. Robert Penn Warren's ostensibly pessimistic presentation of a corrupt and hollow modern America in his fiction. In his poem "Homage to Emerson, On a Night Flight to New York," he, by implication, blames Emerson for facile optimism, implying that Americans drew from him the optimism and self-confidence which had adversely shaped American society, while Warren himself gives expression to a resigned awareness of man's fallen nature.

[3] O'Connor expressed this in a talk and essay under the title "The Regional Writer" and refers expressly to Walker Percy, who ascribes the existence of so many good southern writers to the fact that "we lost the war." What he had in mind was the salutary effect of an awareness of man's limitations as a result of the South's collective experience of defeat. O'Connor's essay is included in *Mystery and Manners*, 51–59, reprinted in *Flannery O'Connor: Collected Works*. Ed. Sally Fitzgerald. New York: The Library of America, 1988, qtd. from p. 847.

declining Compson family. She cares loyally for the idiot Benjy in her acceptance of human suffering.[4]

The limitations of space, however, require the selection for consideration of the two southern authors mentioned before in whose fiction the struggle with the challenges in human life is intricately linked to an engaged and protracted intellectual effort to consolidate their trust in religious views. They adopted a very critical perspective on what Charles Taylor has described as "self-sufficing humanism,"[5] the exclusion of the transcendent dimension by relying only on a scientific analysis of the "objective empirical" as one of the two, Walker Percy, termed this philosophical stance. Both attempted to perceive the acute problems of the modern world through the lens of religious beliefs which they strengthened through an intense study of philosophers and theologians.

It is perhaps not coincidental that Walker Percy, who embraced normative Christian concepts, belonged to a fairly large group of intellectual converts to Catholicism,[6] while the other, Flannery O'Connor, represented the originally small minority of Catholics in the Deep South (if we except Louisiana, where they were much more numerous since the colonial period under French and Spanish domination). Both authors, born in 1916 and in 1925 respectively, emerged on the literary scene after World War II.

While O'Connor, after composing two novels and preparing two collections of stories, which were widely admired and prompted a spate of critical analyzes in dozens of books and articles, fell victim to an inherited disease as early as 1964, Percy gained wider attention only in 1961 with *The Moviegoer*. Both authors offered very explicit statements about their critical perception of modern society and also about their goals when writing fiction.

O'Connor's first novel *Wise Blood* (1952) attracted attention but it was her short stories, first collected in the volume *A Good Man is Hard to Find* in 1955, which appealed to a very large readership and prompted a very wide range of criticism.[7] In her lectures and essays O'Connor deplored the lack of insight, and ex-

---

[4] See *The Sound and the Fury*. Ed. David Minter. A Norton Critical Edition. 2nd ed. New York: Norton, 1994, 183–185. On the complex religious references in Faulkner's *A Fable*, see Butterworth.
[5] See Charles Taylor, *A Secular Age*. Cambridge, Mass.: Harvard UP, 2007. Taylor, in the introduction to this book, p. 16, coins this term. An alternative he uses is "exclusive humanism" (p.19).
[6] On the group of Catholic writers including Thomas Merton, later to become a Trappist monk, and Dorothy Day, see Paul Elie, *The Life You Save May Be Your Own: An American Pilgrimage*. New York: Farrar, Straus and Giroux, 2003.
[7] O'Connor, with her second collection of stories, which appeared posthumously in 1965, entitled *Everything That Rises Must Converge*, achieved the status of a canonical writer when she was included in the Library of America in 1988.

plained that as a fiction writer with her perspective had to deal with a hostile, often complacent audience, she had to use radical techniques, "you have to make your vision apparent by shock – to the hard of hearing you shout, and for the almost-blind you draw large and startling figures" ("The Fiction Writer and His Country", *Mystery and Manners*, p. 34).

In the case of Fl. O'Connor this strategy has resulted in the evolution of contrasted camps of readers, a polarization between enthusiastic admirers and radical opponents, the latter summarily questioning the plausibility of her fictional methods, and the values implicitly upheld in her stories.[8]

The publication of O'Connor's lively and witty correspondence with many friends, among them quite a few agnostics, in *The Habit of Being* (1979) made it difficult for some decades, however, to ascribe to her (a) narrow-mindedness, and her wide reading of contemporary thinkers has shown her broad interests and intellectual energy.[9]

But nobody who has read "Good Country People"[10] can forget the painful discomfiture of the arrogant and skeptical Hulga, who has a Ph.D. in philosophy but cannot use her degree because of her being an invalid with a weak heart and a prosthesis. She is compelled to live on the family farm with her garrulous mother and complacent talkative farmhands. Her intended seduction of a seemingly simple-minded Bible salesman ends in disaster, as the evil figure dupes her and wanders off with the prosthesis of her leg, leaving her helpless in the barn after their tête-à-tête, thus humbling her and exposing the shallowness of her ostensible agnosticism.

The rigidity in the harsh judgment on often arrogant freethinkers, who experience complete defeat through the actions of irrational religious figures, sometimes with more than a trace of fundamentalist fanaticism, which seems to shape the plots of several stories in O'Connor's first collection of stories, is later softened. While critics have sensed a touch of dehumanization in the earlier stories through figurative language, the Manichean tendency in the gallery of charac-

---

[8] On the division and polarization among her readers, see my early study in *Die Erzählkunst des amerikanischen Südens*. Darmstadt: Wissenschaftliche Buchgesellschaft, 1980, 173–89, and on her reception in Europe in comparison with that of Carson McCullers, see "Antecedents and Trajectories of Two Twentieth-Century Writers from Georgia in Europe" in *Transatlantic Exchanges: The American South in Europe – Europe in the American South*. Ed. Richard Gray and Waldemar Zacharasiewicz. Vienna: Verlag der ÖAW, 2007, 115–34.

[9] Flannery O'Connor. *The Habit of Being: Letters Edited and With an Introduction by Sally Fitzgerald*. New York: Farrar, Straus and Giroux, 1979.

[10] See its inclusion in *Flannery O'Connor: The Complete Stories*. New York: Farrar, Straus and Giroux, 1971, 271–91. Reprinted in *Collected Works*. Ed. Sally Fitzgerald, 1988, 263–83.

ters is later replaced, as it were, by O'Connor's adoption of more positive concepts, potentially due to her reading of Teilhard de Chardin.[11]

The thorough analysis of O'Connor's work and lively debate during the last fifty years in scores of books and many essays exempts me from the need to show in detail her affirmation of the religious dimension. Her stories, in particular, provide literary representations of the major challenge to mundane characters and hint at the irrepressible assertion of the power of religion even in the secular age.[12]

Restrictions of space compel me only to consider in detail how Walker Percy, whose life and perspective show intriguing parallels with that of O'Connor,[13] adopted a philosophical stance which was shaped by his intense reading of European fiction writers, existentialist philosophers – thus evidence of a true transatlantic impact – and philosophers of language. It manifests itself in the six novels published during his lifetime.[14] They offer a sardonic criticism of contemporary society in severe and scathing satires of the rampant evils and shortcomings in the secular modern world, exposing the insufficiency of a "self-sufficing" / "exclusive humanism", but they also lambast superficial religious practices and dubious trends in organized Christian religion.

Walker Percy was the scion of a fairly prominent family in the Deep South who grew up in the home of his older cousin William Alexander Percy, who adopted both Walker Percy and his two brothers, who were orphaned after the suicide of their father and the death in an accident of their mother.

William Alexander Percy, who resided in Greenville, MS, was the son of a US senator and vehement opponent of vulgar racists in his state. He was a poet and writer with a stoic world view as reflected in his autobiography *Lanters on the Levee* (1941). After his formative experience in the household of this accomplished

---

11 Cf. Frederick Asals, *Flannery O'Connor: The Imagination of Extremity.* Athens: U of Georgia P, 1982.
12 Recently the accessibility of her private notes – after the death of her mother, whose opposition and longevity prevented the projected authoritative biography by Sally Fitzgerald, has been grist to the mill of harsh critics of her fiction, who stress her conformity with the racism of her native state and her environment. For a very recent collection of essays on Flannery O'Connor by Marshall Bruce Gentry, who teaches at O'Connor's former college in Milledgeville and is editor of *The Flannery O'Connor Review,* see his *Better to See You With: Perspectives on Flannery O'Connor, Selected and New.* Macon, GA: Mercer UP, 2022.
13 Biographies of the author have been provided by Jay Tolson, *Pilgrim in the Ruins: A Life of Walker Percy.* New York: Simon & Schuster, 1992, and Patrick Samway, *Walker Percy: A Life,* New York: Farrar, Straus & Giroux, 1997.
14 After the success of his novel *The Moviegoer* (1961), Percy published *The Last Gentleman* (1966), *Love in the Ruins* (1971), *The Second Coming* (1980), and *The Thanatos Syndrome* (1987).

and cultivated relative, Walker Percy himself attended school at UNC Chapel Hill and then prepared himself for the medical profession. But he had to completely abandon his career of a physician after having first infected himself with TB during his internship in New York, and finally after a recurrence of the illness after years in a sanatorium. His personal search for meaning in his life in the 1940s – when he was in his thirties – prompted his extensive reading of European novelists (Dostoevsky, Tolstoy) and then French philosophers, of Jean Paul Sartre and Albert Camus, but especially the "Catholic" Gabriel Marcel, as well as Martin Heidegger and Karl Jaspers. As his numerous interviews given after he had achieved recognition with his novel *The Moviegoer*, which won the National Book Award in 1961, and after he had found a growing readership with the following novels,[15] show that his analyses of the conditio humana mirrored in the crises his characters experience are both rooted in the specific demographic reality of the South, with its rampant racism and the sharp economic divisions in society, and shaped by his awareness of and response to the philosophical world view of Sören Kierkegaard. Percy grappled with Kierkegaard's demanding reflections over the years as several interviews, especially the annotated interview with Bradley R. Dewey (1974), illustrate.[16]

The inclusion of other regions of the USA, e.g. New York in his second published novel, *The Last Gentleman* (1966) and the exposure of the – in the eyes of the protagonist Will Barrett – unhelpful / dubious role of psychoanalysis – show that his critical examination of typical phenomena of contemporary culture is certainly not restricted to his home region.]

What makes Percy however particularly relevant in the context of this thematic volume is the fact that apart from his six novels published during his lifetime – among them two dystopias – he was also the author of many essays and treatises on philosophical issues and on semiotics. They are contained in three volumes of essays and other non-fiction.[17] Several of these essays contain explicit statements of his realization that the scientific methods appropriately used lead to insights and discoveries but do not solve the existential question which elude the most successful medical / scientific researcher. Repeatedly speaking from the position of a trained physician diagnosing the insufficiency of scientific results, which are cer-

---

[15] Two volumes of his interviews were published by Lewis A. Lawson and Victor A. Kramer: *Conversations with Walker Percy*, Jackson: UP of Mississippi, 1985, and *More Conversations with Walker Percy*, Jackson: UP of Mississippi, 1993.
[16] *Conversations with Walker Percy*, 101–128.
[17] *The Message in the Bottle*, NY: Farrar, Straus and Giroux, 1975, *Lost in the Cosmos: The Last Self-Help Book*, NY: Farrar, Straus and Giroux, 1983, and *Signposts in a Strange Land*, ed. Patrick Samway, NY: Farrar, Straus and Giroux, 1987.

tainly in themselves valuable and relevant for the human species as such, but do not resolve the dilemma of the individual, he referred, for instance, to a narrative by Anton Chekhov. "A Dreary Story" shows that the protagonist, an eminently successful and greatly honored physician, does not enjoy his professional accomplishments, and eventually even fails to see any meaning in life.[18]

And in a thinly veiled autobiographical essay entitled "Physician as Novelist" (*Signposts* 191 ff.) Percy relates how a "devotee of science" discovers that other ways of knowing are called for, which are probably "of more critical significance in one's personal life". Percy's reflections in his protracted personal crisis had led him to adopt a sense of the (hu)man as a "homo viator," a wayfarer like an old-fashioned pilgrim on a serious quest, a concept borrowed from Gabriel Marcel.[19] His essential question "what it means to be a man living in the world who must die"[20] had not been answered by the progress in the sciences, which he naturally did not deny.

His thoughts about man's nature as "Homo symbolificus" – man as "the symbol-mongerer" (contained in his long essay entitled "Is a Theory of Man Possible?", in *Signposts* 111–129, p.120) are inspired by his interest in the work of no other than Charles Sanders Peirce, whose influence on early twentieth-century pragmatism, especially on Josiah Royce and William James, has been investigated and demonstrated by contributors to this conference such as Ludwig Nagl.[21] Peirce's full recognition of the function of religion in the dispute with advocates of scientism, who had dismissed religion as an obsolete phenomenon, clearly appealed to Percy. In several essays and interviews he referred to Peirce as a trailblazer of semiotics, e.g. in this long essay just quoted "Is a Theory of Man Possible?" (*Signposts* 111–129), and in his rejection of behaviorists in language studies, such as, e.g. Leonard Bloomfield, *Language* 1933, he stressed the exceptional and unique human gift of language acquisition and use acknowledged by a new group of semioticians. His

---

18 See "Diagnosing the Modern Malaise", in *Signposts in a Strange Land*, 205.
19 Cf. the first studies of Percy's philosophical worldview by Robert H. Brinkmeyer, *Three Catholic Writers of the Modern South*, Jackson: U of Mississippi P, 1985, and esp. William Rodney Allen, *Walker Percy: A Southern Wayfarer*, Jackson: UP of Mississippi, 1986.
20 This quotation is from the essay "From Fact to Fiction" first published in *Writer* 80 (Oct. 1967) and reprinted in *Signposts* (188). It is also cited in Brinkmeyer's chapter on Percy (123).
21 Cf. esp. his essay "Charles Sanders Peirce's 'A Neglected Argument for the Reality of God': its Structure, its Limits, and its Merits" and his essay "Josiah Royce's Kant- and Hegel-Inspired Interpretation of Religion and his Interest in Asian Thought". In: Ludwig Nagl, *Toward a Global Discourse on Religion in a Secular Age: Essays on Philosophical Pragmatism*. Vienna: LIT, 2021, 137–50, and 165–99, esp. 170.

essays also provide more explicit comments on human dilemmas demonstrated in his novels.[22]

The complete lack of awareness of complacent modern individuals ignorant of their malaise shown in a number of characters in his novels is reflected upon in memorable essays such as "The Man on the Train"[23], in which the alienation of a commuter riding in a train (and staking everything on the objective-empirical) is thrown into relief.

Percy also published several essays accompanying and indirectly accounting for his approach to the art of fiction, describing his perspective on his own mission as a novelist with a religious orientation. "Novel-Writing in an Apocalyptic Time" (*Signposts*, 153–67) and "How to Be an American Novelist in Spite of Being Southern and Catholic" (*Signposts* 168–85), and earlier, "Notes for a Novel about the End of the World" (*The Message in the Bottle*, 101–18) offer his very critical assessment of the current state of American literature, his sense of "man by his very nature an exile and wanderer rather than an organism in an environment" (*The Message in the Bottle*, 111), and his perception of the phoniness of many contemporary fictional texts.

And in these essays and in numerous interviews Percy quite openly discussed the inspiration he received from his close reading of many philosophers, especially through his painstaking study of and reflection on Sören Kierkegaard, to which we referred earlier.[24]

His application of various concepts introduced by the Danish thinker, such as "rotation" and "repetition" – which he employs in his essay "The Man on the Train" to illustrate the ultimate futility of such practices, and on which he sheds light in his instructive conversation on his novels with the Hungarian scholar Zoltan Abády-Nagy (*Conversations*, 72–86) – reveal his incisive inquiry into human attempts to cope with the trials and the plight of the conditio humana – "the recovery of the real through ordeal" (*Conversations* 81).

That Percy's sophisticated rendition of the modern world and man's precarious role in it in its complexity appealed also to an international readership is apparent in the fact that no other than Peter Handke devoted much time and energy

---

22 What is implicit in *The Moviegoer* in the fictional interrogation of the stoicism prevalent among upper-class Southerners, such as Aunt Emily in that novel, a fictional variation on William Alexander Percy, is thus illuminated in Percy's essays.
23 In: *The Message in the Bottle*, 83–100.
24 See esp. Note 16, reference to Bradley R. Dewey's annotated interview with the author.

to translating Percy's first novel *The Moviegoer* [*Der Kinogeher*], as well as his second novel, *The Last Gentleman,* [*Der Idiot des Südens*].[25]

Percy's rejection of an "exclusive humanism" is explicit in the gallery of characters populating his two dystopian novels, *Love in the Ruins* (1971) and in *The Thanatos Syndrome* (1987), in which the author extrapolates future developments from contemporary trends. A brief discussion of the plots and themes of these novels seems particularly apposite, as ostensible patterns of behavior associated with Vienna and Central Europe are subjected to Percy's critical analysis, which draws on ideas inspired by Percy's interest in Kierkegaard, and the Danish philosopher's reflection on the "three stages of existence: the aesthetic, the ethical, the religious" (*Conversations*, p.75).

In both novels Percy includes significant references to the ostensible life style associated with this city of Vienna and its musical culture. The events in these two dystopias are rendered from the perspective of a distant descendant of Thomas Morus, the originator of the utopian genre, whose name is also Tom More. He is a practicing psychiatrist originally with huge ambitions as an inventor and definitely gifted with diagnostic skills, but burdened with the memory of a failed marriage and the loss of a dear child, and with a dangerous inclination to whiskey. Through the first-person perspective Percy renders a satirical picture of the hedonism and the blunt irresponsibility in the secular society of the near future, set in 1983 in *Love in the Ruins*, and in the mid-to late 1990s in *The Thanatos Syndrome*.

Two parallel episodes in these novels illustrate the connection established between the frivolous conduct and irresponsible Epicureanism associated with and allegedly practiced in Vienna,[26] and adopted by several characters in More's environment and medical profession. This occurs first in *Love in the Ruins* in the lighter satirical exposure of More's inability to choose between three nubile young ladies, as he gives in to amorous temptations in the face of the concrete threat of a rebellion by African Americans and the eruption of violence in the parish in Louisiana. A longish conversation with Dr. George Rhoades, the father of one of Tom's loves, the beautiful Lola, in Rhodes's new electric car, in which the hedonistic proctologist makes Tom a very advantageous material proposal, is accompanied by Viennese Waltz Favorites, with the music in the car suggesting "drifting along in a Jules Verne gondola over happy old Austria" (pb 74–87, quote 77). Sensuous

---

[25] It must be admitted, however, that Handke was perhaps not sufficiently familiar with Percy's precisely rendered social and cultural reality in the South of the USA (as a fairly negative review of the translation in *Der Spiegel* revealed).

[26] On the traditional association of the city as a place where the people are given to light-hearted amusement see my essay "Mask, Minstrels and Melancholy" in my collection of essays with the title *Imagology Revisited*, Amsterdam: Rodopi, 2010.

music is also associated with the intervention of the Mephistophelian figure of Art Immelmann, who is eager to lay his hands on Tom's own utopian project, the lapsometer – the "Qualitative Quantitative Ontological Lapsometer" – with which Tom tried to combine diagnostic and therapeutic measures to heal all the woes of the world by massaging certain areas of the brains of his patients.[27] The failure of this project which is finally recognized by Tom, who eventually chooses the most reliable of his three loves as his mate, provides evidence of the miscarriage of merely immanent attempts to cure the ills in society which behaviorists would rely on.

The problematical role of the unconditional enjoyment of music associated with Vienna is also evoked in the much darker mood expressed in the dystopia *The Thanatos Syndrome*, published three years before Percy's death. This dystopia employs strategies of crime fiction, and successfully creates suspense as the narrative traces the discovery by Tom More and his associates that behaviorists are manipulating the humans in his parish in Louisiana. They manage to do so through the secret addition of isotopes of chemicals. A fictional heavy isotope of sodium is put into the drinking water of the district, with the aim of reducing the inclination to violence and redirecting the human drives. One of the directors of this dubious and illegitimate project, Bob Comeaux, a chief physician in the "Qualitarian Center," which manages both euthanasia of the old and the termination of unwanted pregnancies, turns on the music in his splendid Mercedes car while he makes Tom, whose license has been temporarily made invalid, a very attractive professional offer. "...the Mercedes is filled with Strauss waltzes coming from all directions" and music from "Artist's Life," "Wiener Blut," and "Tales from the Vienna Woods" envelops them (188 ff, esp. 190, 193, 194). Comeaux cannot, however, remove Tom's objections to the elimination of the free will through the application of the drug as part of the secret "Blue Bird" project. Tom is also opposed to the general practice of terminating the lives of old patients and unhealthy babies, regular usage in this dystopian community – in which the sacredness of human life Walker Percy commented upon in several interviews is ignored.

The complete discomfiture of the radical behaviorists and the termination of their project is, however, brought about by the indirect link between the ideology of euthanasia and the abuse of minors by ostensible educators in the boarding school Belle Âme under the aegis of the unscrupulous "Renaissance Man" Dr. Van Dorn. His features are not coincidentally closely associated with German mili-

---

[27] There are references especially to the effectiveness of massaging the Brodmann areas 18, 24, and 28.

tary from World War Two.[28] This disconcerting connection between the darkest phases of Central European history and late 20th century Louisiana is perceived through the lens of Kierkegaard's judgment on the pitfalls of a purely aesthetic existence – he rejects the desire enticing humans to enjoy a maximum of hedonistic pleasure.

In *The Thanatos Syndrome* Percy introduces a narrative in two parts offered by Father Rinaldo Smith, who is a physically and mentally weak character, but nevertheless manages a hospice for terminally sick people. He highlights the dangers of the attitude of mere aestheticism by retelling his experiences gained during a visit to distant relatives in Nazi Germany who were sophisticated music lovers. Percy employs the eccentric Father Smith to describe the eventual transformation of these originally highly sensitive figures, physicians of the Weimar Republic, into perpetrators of inhuman actions. In "Father Smith's Confession" (239–51) and the later "Footnote" (251–55) to this confession Percy reveals his own experience gained during a visit to Germany as a young student at UNC Chapel Hill in the company of his German teacher, and admits the appeal to himself as a young Southerner of the ostensible ideals of the National Socialists shown in the radical dedication of a young German to be inducted into the SS. A visit immediately after the war to a hospital outside Munich where mentally challenged children had been gassed by those sophisticated physicians exposed him, Rinaldo Smith, to the horrifying consequences of the denial of what Percy elsewhere described as the recognition of "the sacredness of human life". A list in this "Footnote" (255) refers to some of the prominent Weimar physicians involved in such actions,[29] and includes also a "charming Austrian", a truly provocative indictment of "a self-sufficing humanism", which radicalizes Kierkegaard's warning and leads to a culmination of Percy's critical perspective on self-sufficing humanism.

It was probably no coincidence that after deciding on the topic of my contribution to this volume and drafting its outline I discovered that Charles Taylor, whose trailblazing study of the complexities of *The Secular Age* largely inspired this conference, chose to include both southern authors in the penultimate chapter of his *Secular Age* on "Conversions" (728–72, esp. 731–2). They serve among other writers as representatives of intellectuals who through epiphanies or through coping with the burden of an irreligious climate of opinion embraced religion and in

---

28 I have examined Walker Percy's extensive references and use of heterostereotypes of Germans in this novel as well as his other works of fiction in an essay presented at a conference on Walker Percy in Denmark titled "Stereotypes in Walker Percy's Fiction", first published in *REAL* 8 (1991/2), and included in *Imagology Revisited* (321–37).
29 For the pertinent information Percy drew on Frederic Wertham's *A Sign for Cain: An Exploration of Human Violence*. NY: MacMillan, 1966.

their literary work bore witness to the relevance of religion in their individual lives.[30] And it seems significant that the title of one of Flannery O'Connor's most memorable stories "The Life You Save May Be Your Own", which Paul Elie chose for the title of his study, is also cited by Taylor in this context.

Works Cited

Allen, William Rodney. *Walker Percy: A Southern Wayfarer.* Jackson: UP of Mississippi, 1986.
Asals, Frederick. *Flannery O'Connor: The Imagination of Extremity.* Athens: U of Georgia P, 1982.
Butterworth, Keen. *A Critical and Textual Study of Faulkner's* A Fable. Ann Arbor: UMI Research Press, 1983.
Brinkmeyer, Robert H. *Three Catholic Writers of the Modern South.* Jackson: U of Mississippi P, 1985.
Elie, Paul. *The Life You Save May Be Your Own: An American Pilgrimage.* New York: Farrar, Straus and Giroux, 2003.
Faulkner, William. *The Sound and the Fury.* Ed. David Minter. A Norton Critical Edition. 2nd ed. New York: Norton, 1994, 183–185.
Gentry, Marshall Bruce. *Better to See You With: Perspectives on Flannery O'Connor, Selected and New.* Macon, GA: Mercer UP, 2022.
Lawson, Lewis A., and Victor A. Kramer, eds.: *Conversations with Walker Percy.* Jackson: UP of Mississippi, 1985.
Lawson, Lewis A., and Victor A. Kramer, eds.: *More Conversations with Walker Percy.* Jackson: UP of Mississippi, 1993.
Nagl, Ludwig. *Toward a Global Discourse on Religion in a Secular Age: Essays on Philosophical Pragmatism.* Vienna: LIT, 2021.
O'Connor, Flannery. *Everything That Rises Must Converge.* New York: Farrar, Straus and Giroux, 1965.
O'Connor, Flannery. "The Fiction Writer and His Country." *Mystery and Manners: Occasional Prose.* New York: Farrar, Straus and Giroux, 1969, 25–35.
O'Connor, Flannery. "Good Country People." *Flannery O'Connor: The Complete Stories.* New York: Farrar, Straus and Giroux, 1971, 271–91. Reprinted in *Collected Works.* Ed. Sally Fitzgerald, 1988, 263–83.
O'Connor, Flannery. *The Habit of Being: Letters Edited and With an Introduction by Sally Fitzgerald.* New York: Farrar, Straus and Giroux, 1979.
O'Connor, Flannery. "The Regional Writer." *Flannery O'Connor: Collected Works.* Ed. Sally Fitzgerald. New York: The Library of America, 1988, 847–52.
Percy, Walker. *The Last Gentleman.* New York: Farrar, Straus and Giroux, 1966.
Percy, Walker. *Lost in the Cosmos: The Last Self-Help Book.* New York: Farrar, Straus and Giroux, 1983.
Percy, Walker. *Love in the Ruins.* New York: Farrar, Straus and Giroux, 1971.

---

30 Charles Taylor in *A Secular Age* refers to Flannery O'Connor's awareness of coming to insights "from out of the immanent order," and to her sense of the artist's role in taking readers "past psychology and sociology 'towards the limits of mystery'." And he considers Walker Percy's conversion as having been "based in part on a shift in anthropology." Both writers have thus influenced the thoughts of the thinker whose ideas have provided a frame for this talk.

Percy, Walker. *The Message in the Bottle*. New York: Farrar, Straus and Giroux, 1975.
Percy, Walker. *The Moviegoer*. New York: Knopf, 1961.
Percy, Walker. *The Second Coming*. New York: Farrar, Straus and Giroux, 1980.
Percy, Walker. *Signposts in a Strange Land*. Ed. Patrick Samway. New York: Farrar, Straus and Giroux, 1991.
Percy, Walker. *The Thanatos Syndrome*. New York: Farrar, Straus and Giroux, 1987.
Percy, William Alexander. *Lanterns on The Levee: Recollections of a Planter's Son*. New York: Alfred A. Knopf, 1941.
Samway, Patrick. *Walker Percy: A Life*, New York: Farrar, Straus and Giroux, 1997.
Taylor, Charles. *A Secular Age*. Cambridge, Mass.: Harvard UP, 2007.
Tolson, Jay. *Pilgrim in the Ruins: A Life of Walker Percy*. New York: Simon & Schuster, 1992.
Warren, Robert Penn. "Homage to Emerson, On a Night Flight to New York." *The Collected Poems of Robert Penn Warren*. Ed. John Burt. Baton Rouge, Lousiana State UP, 1998, 194.
Wertham, Frederic. *A Sign for Cain: An Exploration of Human Violence*. New York: MacMillan, 1966.
Wilson, Charles Reagan, ed. *The New Encyclopedia of Southern Culture, Vol.1*. Chapel Hill: U of North Carolina P, 2014.
Zacharasiewicz, Waldemar. "Antecedents and Trajectories of Two Twentieth-Century Writers from Georgia in Europe." *Transatlantic Exchanges: The American South in Europe – Europe in the American South*. Ed. Richard Gray and Waldemar Zacharasiewicz. Vienna: Verlag der ÖAW, 2007, 115–34.
Zacharasiewicz, Waldemar. *Die Erzählkunst des amerikanischen Südens*. Darmstadt: Wissenschaftliche Buchgesellschaft, 1990, 173–89.
Zacharasiewicz, Waldemar. "Masks, Minstrels and Melancholy: From Waltzing in the German Paris to Descending into Dreams of Decadence." *Imagology Revisited*. Amsterdam: Rodopi, 2010, 345–7.
Zacharasiewicz, Waldemar. "Stereotypes in Walker Percy's Fiction." *Imagology Revisited*, 321–337.

Charles Reagan Wilson
The Southern Civil Religion: The Intermingling of the Sacred and the Secular in the American South

Abstract: The southern civil religion was an ideological construct that saw providential meaning in the American South. It rested alongside the evangelical Protestant tradition that most white and black southerners embraced in organized religion. The southern civil religion rested as well alongside, and intertwined with, secularism. Southerners invested religious meanings into secular spaces and events. The religion of the lost cause, a social and cultural movement in the late nineteenth and twentieth century, sacralized the memory of the Confederate States of America after its defeat in the Civil War. A close look at that movement reveals specific ways in which the sacred and the secular intertwined in the South. The civil rights movement showed how the southern civil religion could be reimagined into a new view of providential meanings in the southern historical experience.

Lester Flatt and Earl Scruggs were one of bluegrass music's most popular duos, and their post-World War II song, "Preachin', Prayin', Singin'," provides a beginning point for thinking of religion's role in the public life of the American South. The narrator is an outsider in a community, one who, the lyric says, is "intent upon [my] way," but he notices a crowd that proves to be a religious meeting near a courthouse. He hears "a welcome voice," which in good evangelical Protestant style is "pleading me to come and share the preachin', prayin', singin' down on the public square." The narrator observes that "all of God's children were together there," as the group shouted God's "love and care." He is "so much at home amid the nameless throng" that he can "lay the burdens down." The narrator urges everyone to continue to "leave the doorbell on, down on the public square."[1]

Religion in the American South has been distinguished by the long dominance of evangelical Protestants, and the Flatt and Scruggs song was a classic statement of its expectation to be at ease not only in the region's churches but also on its public squares. Evangelical Protestants—a category that includes Baptists, Methodists, low-church Presbyterians, and Pentecostals—have been closely connected to dominant southern cultural styles and traditions, at the center of a regional context

---

[1] Flatt and Scruggs, "Preachin', Prayin', Singin'."

that defined parameters for private selves and public identities. They have represented a peculiar establishment because of close connections between a particular religious tradition, that of evangelical Protestantism, and the political and legal worlds, represented by the courthouse on the public square. It was not a political or legal establishment, but a cultural one. Beginning in the early nineteenth century, evangelical groups rose to cultural dominance in the American South, and then after the Civil War they became numerically dominant. Close to ninety percent of people who joined churches in the region joined evangelical churches, making the South the most cohesive religious region in the United States. They provided the "symbols, style of self-control, and rules of social decorum" that became dominant in the social system. It is an individualistic faith, focusing on the need for conversion, but also on the need to build moral communities after conversion.[2]

The Flatt and Scruggs song comes, however, from the secular world of entertainment that is a central part of the modern South. Although it sounds like it could be an ancient tradition, it is not. Bill Monroe invented this style of fast-paced, banjo- and fiddle-driven rhythms in the 1940s. To be sure, its lyrics and instrumentation come out of mountain and hill country places of the South, but the song that speaks of preaching and praying on the public square represents a secular infusion of religious sentiment onto that square. Moreover, the song and its meaning should be seen in connection to the South being a racially segregated society at the time. The lyrics say that "all of God's children" were on the square, but in fact, African Americans would have likely been on the margins of the crowd. Their religious traditions were similar to those of the white people around them (they were all mostly evangelicals). But those African Americans had their own denominations separate from those of white people and with a theology, style, and history that made for a distinct religious group. Still, most of the South's people would have been familiar with the intermingling of sacred and secular on the public square.[3]

In addition to representing the South's evangelical Protestant tradition, the song illuminates the southern civil religion. The concept of a civil religion goes back perhaps to the Romans, but Jean-Jacques Rousseau coined the term in his book *The Social Contract* in 1762. He saw it as a generalized religiosity, a part of an emerging modern world that would contribute to social cohesion by giving national polities a sacred grounding beyond particular sectarian groups. It took on new meanings as a result of the American Revolution. Preachers and politicians evoked a civil religion when they saw the new nation's destiny as embodying

---

2 Heyrman, *Southern Cross*; Mathews, *Religion in the Old South*, 83.
3 Kalra, "Bluegrass," 2–31; Raboteau, "Religion, Black," 131–34.

and spreading democracy and the republican form of government. The origins of that outlook trace back to the New England Puritans in the colonial period. A sermon by Puritan minister John Winthrop drew from biblical typologies in seeing that Puritan New England would be a "city upon a hill," a New World extension of the Protestant Reformation onto a new stage. In the mid-nineteenth century, American expansion came out of the idea of "Manifest Destiny," that it was God's destiny for the United States to expand into the West and possibly elsewhere to spread democracy—again an example of an American civil religion. The Civil War was the greatest challenge to this sense of providential destiny, and Abraham Lincoln saw the bloody war as God's judgement on the North and the South for tolerating slavery.[4]

A shorthand definition of civil religion, then, is religious nationalism, or in the case of the South, religious regionalism. By that, I mean many people invested providential meanings in the American South itself. The southern civil religion has been a religious system parallel to southern churches, with beliefs, ethics, and rituals relevant to the political state. It had its own theology and liturgies. Southern civil religious rhetoric began with the defense of slavery before the Civil War and with the investment of religious meaning in a slave society. Baptist minister Leonidas Spratt, for example, wrote in 1853 of "a great destiny" awaiting slave owners, whom he called "the chosen people of the South." Another white southerner, William Holcombe, predicted early in the Civil War that "future ages will appreciate the grandeur and glory of our mission." The sense of providential mission that white southerners had once applied to the nation, now was adapted to strengthen the belief that emerging southern nationalism was divinely ordained.[5]

Southern ministers said the Confederate States of America was engaging in a holy war against a disordered northern society, but defeat in the Civil War caused spiritual turbulence after the war for white southerners. But it did not last long as their ministers assured them after a while that God had simply chastised them with defeat. They had been purged, purified in wartime fires, to face future struggles for such conservative values as social hierarchy, individual freedom, patriarchalism, paternalism, and white supremacy that they now saw as being at the heart of the Confederate crusade. The evangelical faith prioritized individual conversion and disdained interest in social injustices as a secular concern that was not part of true religion. White ministers used the term "the spirituality of the church"

---

4 Bellah, "Civil Religion in America," 21–44; Albanese, *Civil Religion of the American Revolution*, 1–10.
5 McCardell, *The Idea of a Southern Nation*, 135; Holcombe, "The Alternative," 84.

to describe this attitude that distanced churches from most social reforms that white southerners would have seen as part of the secular world.[6]

Secularism was important, though, in the formation of moral communities based around race and the memory of the Confederacy. Secularism in the South "located ancillary sites and sights of social power, which residents used alongside their principally religious site or sight—the congregation—for the ritual performance and observation of moral community. Secular sites might include the factory, bank, street, retail store, city hall, neighborhood, hospital, railroad, or automobile. And courthouse. People believed those places were secular, they were not formally religious, by a commonsense determination that religion was what happened in the congregation when believers cultivated the interior spirituality associated with evangelical Protestantism. Anything away from that congregational space was a secular occurrence, it was "of the world," as evangelicals would put it. But religious felling was moveable. The faithful could take it with them into the world and onto its secular sites. The southern roadside, for example, both rural and urban, is marked by religious signs appropriate to the faith—"Get Right with God," "Jesus Saves," "Prepare to Meet Thy God." Secularism sanitized those places, enabling southern evangelicals to enter and exit secular spaces, leaving visible signs of formal religious presence. White southerners saw religious and secular spaces as separate, as set apart from each other. But they were part of the same system, part of the same social body. White southerners used ritual to smooth over striated places. They did so in abridging the "logical contradictions between spiritual equality and racial segregation, secular universality and religious particularity." To them, movements that intertwined those contradictions were "fluid and harmonious." Democracy was not the striving for equality, but "the protection of divinely sanctioned difference."[7]

The religion of the Lost Cause represented the white memory of the sacred qualities of the Confederate wartime experience after the war ended. It became the main expression of the southern civil religion, as the sacred objects, rituals, and monuments of the civil religion came to center on the saints in gray. The Lost Cause was the memory of the Confederacy that became enshrined in southern legend and ideology after Appomattox. Mourning for the Confederate dead immediately after the war gave way to a spirit of celebration of the Confederate war effort by the 1890s. Although the pro-slavery argument and the Confederate secession ordinances made clear that slavery was the cause of sectional conflict and the Confederate war effort, the Lost Cause ideology after the war insisted on the

---

6 Wilson, *Baptized in Blood*, 7, 57, 77.
7 Seales, *The Secular Spectacle*, 12–13, 15; Butler, "Civil Religion," 45–53.

legality of secession and the centrality of constitutional issues to secession. Still, many white commentators admitted the centrality of race. Just after the war, Virginia editor Edward Pollard first used the term "Lost Cause" to describe the failed Confederacy's efforts, and he insisted that "the supremacy of the white race, and along with it the preservation of the political traditions of the country," had been the real issue of the war. The Lost Cause ideology launched a movement that solidified in the 1890s at the same time as southern states codified racial discrimination through disfranchisement, Jim Crow segregation laws, racial violence, and economic marginalization of African Americans. They were all part of the same world view that sought to normalize southern civilization as a white-dominated world rooted in the supposed virtues of white Confederates.[8]

The Civil War experience had led white southerners to see their historical experience in transcendent, cosmic terms, and the ideology of the Lost Cause became the key expression of a southern civil religion by the turn of the twentieth century. The Lost Cause had icons, including pervasive images of Robert E. Lee, Jefferson Davis, and Stonewall Jackson—the Lost Cause Trinity. Presbyterian theologian Robert Lewis Dabney claimed the South needed "a book of 'Acts and Monuments of Confederate Martyrs.'" White southerners indeed portrayed the Confederate heroes as saints, prophets, and martyrs. From the 1890s into the 1930s, white southerners celebrated regional rituals such as Confederate Memorial Day, the dedication of Confederate monuments, the funerals of Confederate veterans, and the reunions of still-living Confederate veterans. The Confederate battle flag became the southern civil religion's most sacred object. It was, of course, on display at the rituals commemorating the war effort, but by the early twentieth century that flag waved over political rallies, at social events, and was the school symbol for countless athletic programs—all secular occasions. Religions need a hymnody, which the southern civil religion provided in the song "Dixie" that became a triumphal regional tribal anthem. Most importantly, remembering the Lost Cause promoted a continuing southern white consciousness that the region would always have a providential mission.[9]

The southern civil religion showed the intermingling of the sacred and the secular. Images of saintly Confederate heroes could appear as stained-glass windows in churches, but also on the material, commercial items that became a part of an emerging southern commercial world in the late nineteenth century. Lee's image, for example, adorned a bag of flour, as the bakery that made it hoped consumers

---

8 Carlson, "Edward Pollard."
9 Wilson, "Religion of the Lost Cause," 219–38; Jones, *White too Long,* 89–92; Dabney, *The New South,* 15–16.

would trust the spirit of Lee as they made their morning biscuits. The song "Dixie" evoked sacred memories of the Confederacy and its mission to witness for the values of a conservative society, but it would in the twentieth century become the sporting fight song for endless southern public and private schools and colleges and universities that reflected the religion of the Lost Cause in secular settings. What was important was that combining religious sentiments with secular expressions gave a moral authority to the segregated society that helped to normalize the racial customs and laws that undergirded that society.[10]

The development and cultural triumph of the religion of the Lost Cause came in the late nineteenth and early twentieth centuries at a time when the region was changing as secular forces came increasingly into the region as modernization reached a new stage there. Before that happened, though, Reconstruction was the name for various efforts by the federal government to remake southern society and prepare for southern states reentry into the Union. During the fifteen years or so after the war, Reconstruction witnessed a ferocious contest for control of the South's public spaces and the memory of the southern past, with sacred and secular forces intermingling. Confederate widows honored wartime southern heroes in graveside rituals that would develop into large commemorations by the end of the century. However, African Americans and some northern whites in the South staged hundreds of commemorative celebrations during Reconstruction, a sign of their new rights of citizenship and voting power. African Americans paraded on southern city and town squares, displayed banners, waved American flags, said an "amen" to prayers of thanksgiving for their emancipation as slaves, and applauded speeches at biracial occasions. Black churches and civic organizations became important sites for black people in a new southern public culture that showcased African American achievements, blessing them with prayers to the divine sometimes in such secular settings as male social clubs and female uplift societies. White people at their public events waved the Confederate battle flag and sang "Dixie," while black southerners waved the U.S. flag and sang spirituals that told of freedom. The Lost Cause rhetoric spoke of the tragedy of Confederate defeat, while Emancipation Day commemorations spoke of the blessedness of freedom that came as a result of the war. Both black southerners and white southerners used secular public spaces but invested competing civil religious meanings into those spaces.[11]

The triumph of the religion of the Lost Cause by the 1890s reflected the end of the contest for control of southern public spaces as white southerners had re-

---

10 Wilson, "The Modernization of the Lost Cause," 102–4.
11 Blair, *Cities of the Dead*, 1–10.

gained dominance of society at the expense of African American aspirations. One could see this change especially in terms of a changing public landscape through the erection of hundreds of Confederate monuments in virtually every city and town in the region. The dedication of monuments to Confederate heroes showed the southern civil religion at its high point. By 1914 over a thousand monuments existed in the South. Preachers converted the innumerable statues dotting the southern countryside into religious objects, almost idols, that quite intentionally taught Christian religion and moral lessons in secular spaces. "Our cause is with God" and "In hope of a joyful resurrection" were among the most typical inscriptions on the monuments. El Dorado, Arkansas, erected a marble drinking fountain to the Confederacy. Its publicity statement said—in a phrase culled from countless hymns and sermons on the sacrificial Jesus—that the water in the fountain symbolized "the loving stream of blood" shed by southern soldiers. Drinkers from the fount were thus symbolically baptized in Confederate blood.[12]

All this preaching, visual display, and ritual activity focused on the Confederate heroes represented moral lessons for white southerners. The ministers used the Confederate Man of Sorrows as a moral lesson on suffering, humiliation, defeat, and death, but the religion of the Lost Cause could also stoke grievance against northerners and black southerners. Many white southerners continued after the war to fear what they saw as the materialistic, ethnically diverse, disordered northern society, and they continued to see the Yankee as a monster symbolizing the moral evil of secularism.[13]

Richmond, Virginia, had been the capital of the Confederate States of America, and it hosted one of the first large post-war gatherings to honor Confederates in October 1875. It showed the intertwining of the sacred and the secular. The ceremony honored Confederate General Thomas "Stonewall" Jackson. He was killed in battle and southern white ministers saw him as a martyr hero. They were there on this dedication day and their prayers and presence made it a religious occasion. The procession included representatives from religious colleges and denominational societies. Methodist Bishop D.S. Doggett gave the opening prayer that beseeched God that "the monument erected on this spot, to the honor of thy servant, may ever stand as a permanent memorial to thy praise, and a perpetual incentive to a high and holy consecration to thy service, in all the avocations of life. May it silently and effectually inculcate noble ideas and inspire lofty sentiments in all spectators for all time to come. Above all, may it teach the youth of the land, the solemn lesson of thy word, that the foundation of true greatness is fidelity to thee." The Grand Arch

---

12 Cox, *No Common Ground*, 118–13, 21–23; Wilson, *Baptized in Blood*, 29.
13 Bledsoe, "Chivalrous Southrons," 109, 117.

in downtown Richmond celebrated Jackson with the large letters: "Warrior, Christian, Patriot." Just above the arch was a painting that represented a stonewall upon which rested a bare sabre, a Bible, and a Confederate cap, with the angel of peace ascending, pointing heavenward; and on the pinnacle of the arch was a pennant bearing the cross, as the emblem of Christianity.[14]

The ceremony, like the emerging southern civil religion at that point, proclaimed not a generalized religiosity such as would be seen in ceremonies of the American civil religion that fostered a nondenominational, Protestant, Catholic, and Jewish cultural outlook on the public square. The southern civil religion was an explicitly evangelical Protestant outlook. But the dedication of the monument was not on church grounds but in a secular setting in a large southern city. In 1907, Richmond would host another monument dedication, the largest one in history, with 200,000 people gathering to honor Confederate president Jefferson Davis. At such occasions, the sacred intertwined with commercial secular activities, as vendors sold flags, buttons, banners, and other items. Racial segregation had been put into practice by then, and the intertwining of secular and sacred within the segregated urban society made it seem natural and normal, a part of everyday life and not to be questioned.[15]

The religion of the Lost Cause solidified at the same time in the late nineteenth and early twentieth centuries that modernization advanced in the region, as a carrier of secular influences. The New South movement represented and promoted economic and social changes that brought secular influences more to the front. Southerners had been overwhelmingly rural people, but by the 1880s, more of them were moving to the crossroads market towns now key to marketing the region's main economic resource, cotton. Those towns introduced a new town culture, and southerners, white and black, adjusted to a different way of life. Shopkeepers, lawyers, physicians, small businessmen, and other professional people became increasingly influential, as a new middle class shared the outlook of those in growing cities. The vast expansion of railroad mileage became a new symbol of modern ways blanketing the South. The rise of industry in a region that had been agricultural was symbolized by new mill villages that also promoted modern ways. Along with new commercial outlooks came secular values as never before. Champions of the sacred often dismissed the idea of a secular New South that they believed threatened a southern identity based in religious outlooks. Charles C. Jones Jr., for example, was a prominent Presbyterian minister who preached against the materialistic values that would threaten the South's religiosity. He

---

14 John Esten Cooke, *Stonewall Jackson*, 533–7, 57–77; Wilson, *Baptized in Blood*, 18.
15 Foster, *Ghosts of the Confederacy*, 80.

said he wanted to place "the glories of the Old South and our struggle for constitutional right . . . in noble contrast to all the modern bosh about a New South." He wanted a New South purged of all modern commercial methods, and he insisted that the values of the Lost Cause were the best protection against the baleful effects of commercialization. To Jones and other unreconstructed white southerners, the sacred and the secular were a fundamental binary with no intermingling in order to protect the purity of the sacred. New South advocates nonetheless embraced a more materialistic outlook while clinging to the religion of the Lost Cause. Atlanta newspaper editor Henry Grady said, "the new South is simply the old South under new conditions." He promised that the new order would always honor the Confederate dead and cherish "the memory of the old regime, its tradition and its history."[16]

One might argue that the Lost Cause, the memory of the Confederacy, was born modern, although surely with a nineteenth-century twist. By the last decade of that century, the Lost Cause had become a well-organized social movement, institutionalized in organizations like the United Confederate Veterans, the United Daughters of the Confederacy, the Sons of Confederate Veterans, and the Children of the Confederacy. These were patriotic groups that operated in secular worlds disconnected from the region's churches yet embodying the southern civil religion. The Daughters of the Confederacy led the efforts to memorialize the cause, and they were astoundingly successful. One could study them for lessons on marketing, branding, and lobbying. Religion pervaded their work. The importance of Christianity to their work could be seen in the approved ritual for their meetings. It began with an invocation:

> Daughters of the Confederacy, this day we are gathered together, in the sight of God, to strengthen the bonds that unite us in a common cause; to renew the vows of loyalty to our sacred principles; to do homage unto the memory of our gallant Confederate soldiers; and to perpetuate the fame of their noble deeds into the third and fourth generations. To this end we invoke the aid of our Lord.[17]

The Daughters provided an unmatched crusading zeal to the Lost Cause religion. They preserved oral histories and Confederate relics; served on textbook commissions that only adopted histories sympathetic to the southern cause; produced their own primers for schoolchildren, including one entitled *The Ku Klux Klan or Invisible Empire*; and pressured every former Confederate state to have Confederate Memorial Day as a public holiday. They were especially aggressive in preserv-

---

16 Foster, *Ghosts of the Confederacy*, 81–83.
17 Cox, *Dixie's Daughters*, 1–10; *Ritual of the United Daughters of the Confederacy*.

ing the records of the southern past. They saw them as sacred documents. One Texas Daughter urged her group in 1912 to guard its archives, "even as the children of Israel did the Ark of the Covenant." The "UDC Catechism for Children" worked to instill Lost Cause understandings in the South's white children. Christian tradition has long included catechisms for children to instill religious instruction. They are often the foundation for confirmation classes, and the Lost Cause catechism followed the form used by various denominations. It had six questions for children to master to show their understanding of Lost Cause religious orthodoxy. It was the intention of the catechism modeled on Christian forms to have "a white Christian child growing up with the parallel liturgies in civic and religious spaces," the secular and the sacred spaces, to correlate white supremacist and Christian values as "seamlessly interwoven." Often the same teachers led children in reciting the UDC catechism on Saturdays and the Methodist or Episcopal catechism on Sunday. The Daughters placed the images of Robert E. Lee and Jefferson Davis in virtually every public school in the South, as they invaded a prime secular space with the memory of the sacralized Confederate icons.[18]

The religion of the Lost Cause gave a spiritual gloss to the white South's new segregated racial order in the early twentieth century resting in white supremacy. The religious leaders and organizations who sacralized the Lost Cause normalized its whites-only narrative of the Civil War. By placing a sacred canopy over the secular memory of the Confederacy, its advocates made it almost invulnerable to questioning the memory of the war and the southern social order in general. It did not have to be so. Southern whites used their control of southern cultural institutions and venues to prevent the expression of any historical stories that provided examples of successful and courageous African Americans. Giving religious sanction to the Lost Cause effectively normalized it for generations of white southerners who had no exposure to any other story of the Civil War. In fact, northern whites came to accept the lost Cause narrative as well. When Robert E. Lee was honored in the national Hall of Fame in the nation's Capitol in 1907, it was a victory for North-South reconciliation. The national culture now honored southern soldiers as well as northern soldiers for their military qualities, for bravery in battle. In the process, the causes for which the soldiers fought—the preservation of the Union and African American freedom, on the one hand, and slavery and states' rights to preserve slavery on the other—these causes were downplayed. White

---

18 Cornelia Branch Stone, *UDC Catechism for Children*; Poppenheim, *The History of the United Daughters of the Confederacy*, 11–12; UDC, *Minutes of the Nineteenth Annual Meeting of the United Daughters of the Confederacy . . 1912*, 398.

Americans were regionally reconciled, but at the cost of ignoring the need for reform of society to address issues of social justice related to African Americans.[19]

White southerners in towns from the early to mid-twentieth century viewed sacred and secular differences just as they imagined racial differences. Their persistently differentiating social knowledge, their way of viewing the world, which is a touchstone of secularism in many accounts, was formed in terms of the binaries of spatial segregation. Their social knowledge, their way of thinking about the world, did not move along a line, or within a sliding scale, in which the religious could fade into the secular or the secular could replace the religious. A religious-secular continuum was to southerners like a racial continuum; it was institutionally impossible . . . ." One was either "white" or "black." Despite the racial binary, though, "passing" for white was a reality for many light-skinned African Americans. Despite the theoretical binary, similarly, the southern civil religious functioned to blur the binary between the secular and the sacred, as they intertwined in the rituals, rhetoric, and spatial orientations of the religion of the Lost Cause. Despite white southerners' efforts to maintain the rigidity of racial boundaries, the intertwining of black and white blood among some of the South's people became a metaphor for the blurring of sacred and secular boundaries.[20]

Let me end by flashing forward to the mid-twentieth century, and the civil rights movement that eventually overthrew the legalized system of racial segregation and disfranchisement. The religion of the Lost Cause had declined in the course of the twentieth century, as white southerners embraced the American civil religion, especially as a result of fighting in World War II for such ideals as democracy and equality of opportunity in opposition to fascism. Martin Luther King Jr. was emblematic of the civil rights movement's use of the American civil religion that spoke of those ideals as well as drawing from the religiosity of the historical black church and Gandhian non-violence. But King also tapped into, and transformed, the southern civil religion. He used the language of the late nineteenth-century religion of the Lost Cause, speaking of suffering, of a defeated people, tragedy, honor, the need for virtuous behavior, the need of a defeated people to achieve dignity, and the search for group identity and destiny. He compared traditional southern white values and those of African American civil rights activists in 1963, noting the "the virtues so long regarded as the exclusive property of the white South—gallantry, loyalty, and pride—had passed to the Negro demonstrators in the heat of the summer's battles." King said that the compensation for the physical deprivation of African Americans had been a spiritual maturity, and he hoped to

---

19 Brundage, *The Southern Past*, 1–11.
20 Seales, *Secular Spectacle*, 13.

release "spiritual power" and "soul force" that would redeem the South—the word "redeem" a key one in the evangelical vocabulary.[21]

King's "I Have a Dream" speech in 1965 portrayed a redemptive South that would be the scene for national salvation. Reflecting a traditional southern concern for place, he argued that the nation's transformation would not be in some disembodied location but in a specific locale, the South. The region had been the center of black suffering and of flawed humanity, but ultimately the virtue of black Americans and decent whites would lead to reconciliation. One day "on the red hills of Georgia," black people and white people would "sit down together at the table of brotherhood." In the coming day of redemption, even the state of Mississippi, "a state sweltering with the heat of injustice, sweltering with the heat of oppression, will be transformed into an oasis of freedom and justice." Other civil rights leaders, like King, used sacred language and ritual in their protest, investing it in the secular sites of their demonstrations. Recall the scenes of black protestors kneeling on courthouse steps, courthouses that had been the locales where the religion of the Lost Cause erected its monuments. Courthouses were the centers of the legal underpinnings of racial segregation. The law represented as well an underpinning of secular society untainted by religious authority. Nonetheless, civil rights activists drew from the region's religiosity to redeem this secular icon. Recall as well the scenes of civil rights protestors waving American flags at boycotts of businesses, again economic activity being a foundation of secular society. At those rallies and boycotts, one would likely see a church fan. It was a material symbol of the intertwining of the sacred and the secular, a typical visual icon in the South in the days before air-conditioning. Such businesses as funeral homes and insurance companies would buy large lots of the simple fans and give them to local churches to put on the back of pews along with the songbook and Bible. The presence of the business-sponsored fans in religious institutions gave moral authority to the secular commercial enterprises.[22]

The civil rights story thus represents the possibility of using the intertwined sacred and the secular to challenge authority and change society. It is a powerful story of the transformation of the white southern investment in a redemptive South based in the memory of the Confederacy to a new southern civil religion based in the memory of the civil rights movement as a time when black southerners saw providential meaning in the civil rights movement and the possibility of the South redeeming the nation's tragic racial history. The story suggests the

---

21 King, *Wisdom of Martin Luther King, Jr.*, 77; King, *Why We Can't Wait*, 77.
22 *New York Times*, 28 August 1983, 16.

need for scholarly attention to the complex and conflicting ideological meanings of the secular and the sacred within particular historical contexts.

A scholar of the mass civil rights demonstrations in Birmingham, Alabama, in 1963, entitled his work *Where the Sacred and the Secular Harmonized.* The word "harmonized" in the context of the civil rights movement was insightful. Black freedom songs harmonized verbally and drew from African American heritage, going back to slave spirituals and African American church hymns. But when Fannie Lou Hamer led the singing of freedom songs at rallies in churches and on courthouse squares, she was singing the "gospel of democracy," witnessing not just for religion but for secular political power and voting rights. [23]

Works Cited

Albanese, Catherine L. *Sons of the Fathers: The Civil Religion of the American Revolution.* Philadelphia: Temple University Press, 1977.
Bellah, Robert N. "Civil Religion in America." *American Civil Religion.* Ed. Russell E. Richey and Donald G. Jones. New York: Harper and Row, 1974. 21–44.
Blair, William A. *Cities of the Dead: Contesting the Memory of the Civil War in the South, 1865–1914.* Chapel Hill: U of North Carolina P, 2004.
Bledsoe, Albert Taylor. "Chivalrous Southrons." *Southern Review* 6 July 1869: 109–17.
Blight, David W. *Race and Reunion: The Civil War in American Memory.* Cambridge: Belknap Press of Harvard UP, 2001.
Brundage, W. Fitzhugh. *The Southern Past: A Clash of Race and Memory.* Cambridge, Mass.: The Belknap Press of Harvard UP, 2005.
Butler, Judith. "Civil Religion: Secularism as Religion." *Thinking with Balibar: A Lexicon of Conceptual Practice.* Ed. Ann Laura Stoler, Stathis Gourgouris, and Jacque Lezra. New York: Fordham UP, 2020. 45–53.
Carlson, Peter. "Edward Pollard: Defeated South's White Liar." Historynet.com/edward-pollard-jim-crow-southern-white-liar, 11-8-2018.
Cooke, John Esten. *Stonewall Jackson: A Military Biography.* New York: n.p., 1876.
Cox, Karen L. *No Common Ground: Confederate Monuments and the Ongoing Fight for Racial Justice.* Chapel Hill: U of North Carolina P, 2021.
Dabney, Robert L. *The New South: A Discourse.* Raleigh, N.C.: Edwards, Broughton, 1983.
Flatt, Lester, and Earl Scruggs and the Foggy Mountain Boys. "Preachin', Prayin', Singin'." *The Complete Mercury Sessions.* Polygram Records, 1992. 315-512-64-2.
Foster, Gaines. *Ghosts of the Confederacy: Defeat, the Lost Cause, and the Emergence of the New South, 1865 to 1913.* New York: Oxford UP, 1987.
Heyrman, Christine Leigh. *Southern Cross: The Beginnings of the Bible Belt.* Chapel Hill: U of North Carolina P, 1997.

---

23 Holmes, *Where the Sacred and the Secular Harmonized,* 11.

Holcombe, William H. "The Alternative: A Separate Nationality, or the Africanization of the South." *Southern Literary Messenger*, n.s. 11. February 1861, 84.

Holmes, David G. *Where the Sacred and the Secular Harmonized*. Eugene, Ore.: Cascade Books, 2017.

Jones, Robert P. *White too Long: The Legacy of White Supremacy in American Christianity*. New York: Simon and Schuster, 2020.

Kalra, Ajay. "Bluegrass." *The New Encyclopedia of Southern Culture*, vol. 12. Ed. Charles Reagan Wilson and Bill C. Malone. Chapel Hill: U of North Carolina P, 2008, 24–31.

King, Martin Luther, Jr. "I Have a Dream." *New York Times* 28 August 1983, 16.

King, Martin Luther, Jr. *The Wisdom of Martin Luther King, Jr.: In His Own Words*. New York: Lancer Books, 1968.

King, Martin Luther, Jr. *Why We Can't Wait*. New York: Harper and Row, 1968.

Mathews, Donald G. *Religion in the Old South*. Chicago: U of Chicago P, 1977.

McCardell, John. *The Idea of a Southern Nation: Southern Nationalists and Southern Nationalism, 1830–1860*. New York: W.W. Norton, 1981.

Poppenheim, Mary B. *The History of the United Daughters of the Confederacy*. Richmond: Garret and Massier, 1938.

Seales, Chad E. *The Secular Spectacle: Performing Religion in a Southern Town*. New York: Oxford UP, 2013.

Stout, Harry. *Upon the Altar of the Nation: A Moral History of the American Civil War*. New York: Viking, 2006.

Wilson, Charles Reagan. *Baptized in Blood: The Religion of the Lost Cause, 1865–1920*. Athens: U of Georgia P, 1980.

Wilson, Charles Reagan. "The Modernization of the Lost Cause." *The Enduring Lost Cause: Afterlives of a Redeemer Nation*. Ed. Edward R. Crouther. Knoxville: U of Tennessee P, 2020.

Wilson, Charles Reagan. "Religion of the Lost Cause." *Journal of Southern History* 46 (May 1980): 219–38.

Michael Hochgeschwender
Catholicism in Defense? Roman Catholic Answers to the Quest for Modernity

Abstract: Over the course of two centuries, Roman Catholicism in North America and Western Europe was confronted with the outcomes of a specific form of liberal-enlightened modernity as culturally hegemonic system of ethical and social thought. In opposition to this dominant and established ideology, Roman Catholics adopted a modified and renewed version of medieval social philosophy, Neo-Scholasticism. This seemingly reactionary decision is often characterized as backward and defensive. The essay, however, tries to establish a more nuanced understanding of the Neo-Scholastic criticism of a processual modernity that had to cope with its own inherent problems. In this view, Neo-Scholasticism provided a sound and theoretical rich foundation for a more offensive approach toward a conflicting early modernity.

On a regular basis, textbooks of both, Church History and secular history, provide one more or less coherent answer to the question of how Roman Catholicism answered to the challenges and provocations modernity and modernization brought with them: the Catholic Church as an institution and Roman Catholicism as a social formation based on the doctrines of the Church did actually react defensively. With perhaps the exception of marginalized groups over the course of the nineteenth century, such as, for instance, enlightened Catholicism, the liberal-historicist *Tübingen* school or Catholic modernism of the late nineteenth and early twentieth centuries, the sheer bulk of international Catholicism is presented as overtly reactionary, if not totalitarian, looking backwards to an idealized medieval epoch, strictly anti-liberal and hierarchical. Only with Vatican II (1962–1965) and a renewed theology, had Catholicism found an inherent connection with modernity.[1] Thus, as this standard narrative goes, only the sharp disjuncture, even disconnectedness of a

---

1 John W. O'Malley, *What Happened at Vatican II* (Cambridge: Belknap Press, 2008). See also Peter Neuner, *Der Streit um den katholischen Modernismus* (Frankfurt/Main, 2009). One of the currently most prominent and most dashing representatives of the discourse of discontinuity and the primate of a normative understanding of modernity within the Catholic Church is Magnus Striet, *Für eine Kirche der Freiheit: Den Synodalen Weg konsequent weitergehen* (Freiburg/Br.: Herder, 2022). It is, nevertheless, notable, that his concept of modernity and freedom is very much, and ahistorically so, dominated by eighteenth-century Kantian notions of essentialist human autonomy and thus not necessarily compatible with recent variants of (post-) modern modernism.

modern, post-Vatican II theology from its backward predecessors in the predominantly sinister times of Vatican I (1870) and ultramontanism,[2] made Catholicism compatible with modern times. Moreover, with the *aggionamento* of Vatican II, the marginalized theologies of the Enlightenment, Antonio Rosmini's Ontologism, John Cardinal Newman's anti-scholastic approach, the historicist liberalism of the *Tübingen* School,[3] and, at least in parts, modernism, reclaimed their authority. Thus, the marginalized theologies of the nineteenth century became, after their final breakthrough, the fuel for a rapid modernization of Roman Catholicism. Modernity, within this discourse, means something like a cocktail of thoroughly positively connoted elements: an anthropology built on individual decisions, personal liberty and autonomy, individualized life-styles, a democratic social and political order, an acceptance of a liberal world view, tolerance, and a situational, individualized ethic as well as structural developments such as, for example, industrialization, urbanization, moments of secularization, and mass participation. The question of the social and economic order is, within a liberal modernist framework, left to the free decisions of rational, autonomous actors, based on private property and a – moderate – welfare state approach or, alternatively, in the radical free-market manner of Manchester liberalism or neoliberalism.[4] However, collectivism can also be seen as a possible answer to the crises of modernization.

This narrative is not wrong per se. There can be no doubt about the fact, that, for example, the Catholic Church only started in the 1880s and 1890s to at least accept democracy or the freedom of the press, and only with his 1944 Christmas address, did Pope Pius XII decide to actually promote democratic ideas.[5] This was the result of the totalitarian challenges from National Socialism and Communism. In the following essay, I do not intend to revise the standard narrative on the level of substantial content, but bring some nuance into its one-sided liberal progressivism on the conceptual level. Therefore, I will start with a concise introduction to

---

[2] On the concept of ultramontanism see Gisela Fleckenstein and Joachim Schmiedl, eds., *Ultramontanismus: Tendenzen der Forschung* (Paderborn: Bonifatius Verlag, 2005) and Fr. Jeffrey von Arx, SJ, *Varieties of Ultramontanism* (Washington, DC: Catholic University of America Press, 1998). With regard to the American case cf. Sr. Patricia Byrne, CSJ, "American Ultramontanism", in: *Theological Studies* 56 (1995), 301–26.
[3] Cf. Bradford E. Hinze, "Roman Catholic Theology: Tübingen", in: David Fergusson, ed., *The Blackwell Companion to Nineteenth-Century Theology* (Malden: Blackwell, 2010), 187–213.
[4] On neoliberalism cf. Thomas Biebricher, *Neoliberalismus zur Einführung* (Hamburg: Junius Verlag, 2012) and the inspiring case study by Ariane Leendertz, *Der erschöpfte Staat: Eine andere Geschichte des Neoliberalismus* (Hamburg: Hamburger Edition, 2022), 27–31.
[5] Michael Hochgeschwender, "Waffenbrüderschaft auf Zeit: Der Vatikan, der US-amerikanische Katholizismus und die NATO", in: Werner Kremp and Berthold Meyer, eds., *Religion und Zivilreligion im Atlantischen Bündnis* (Trier: wvt, 2001), 292–306.

the historical setting of ultramontanism and its development from the 1820s to the 1870s. Afterwards, I will focus on the basic assumptions and teachings of Neo-Scholasticism[6] on social issues – as a primary example of rigid Catholic anti-liberalism and of a genuinely Catholic critique of liberal modernity. This is important in order to understand why nineteenth-century Catholics basically repudiated specifically liberal modes of modernity, including free-market capitalism. Subsequently, I will describe in more detail two outstanding Catholic positions repudiating the liberal sociocultural and economic agenda, namely the highly influential and popular multi-volume books written by Fr. Heinrich Pesch, SJ[7] and Fr. Albert Maria Weiss, OP.[8] These two authors represented two different wings of later nineteenth- and early twentieth-century Neo-Scholastic high ultramontanism and were therefore representative for the pluralistic possibilities within the movement. Finally, I will discuss the modes of reception inside American Catholicism with its totally different societal environment and its belated acceptance of the anti-modern doctrines of ultramontanism and Neo-Scholasticism, including some specifically American Catholic answers to the challenges and crises of modernity.

Initially, ultramontanism in Germany and elsewhere started in the 1820s as a bottom-up movement of laypeople that showed marked characteristics of contemporary awakenings in nearly all world religions. Western historians normally tend to focus on Christian, mostly Protestant awakenings, such as the postmillennialism of British and North-American Calvinists, but structurally similar events can be found in Islam, Judaism, Hinduism, and even among Native American religions. It is therefore not really astonishing that Catholicism had its own form of awakening, which, however, took a different shape because of the structures within the Catholic theological and social tradition. In Germany and other European nations, ultramontanism was a result of a wide-spread discontent with the theology and spiritual as well as political practice and the social basis of Enlightenment Catholicism.[9] The Enlightenment was not only, perhaps not even in the first place, occupied by a struggle for liberty and individualism. It was, moreover, struggling for

---

[6] Ralph Del Colle, "Neo-Scholasticism", in: Fergusson, ed., *Companion*, 376–94. See also Fr. Romanus Cessario, OP, *A Short History of Thomism* (Washington, DC: Catholic University of America Press, 2003) and Fr. Gerald A. McCool, SJ, *Nineteenth Century Scholasticism: The Search for a Unitary Method* (New York: Fordham, 1989).

[7] Fr. Heinrich Pesch, SJ, *Lehrbuch der Nationalökonomie*, 5 vols., (Freiburg/Br.: Herder, 1905).

[8] Fr. Albert Maria Weiss, OP, *Apologie des Christentums*, 7 vols., (Freiburg/Br.: Herder, 1907).

[9] Cf. Ulrich K. Lehner and Michael Printy, eds., *A Companion to the Catholic Enlightenment in Europe* (Leiden: Brill, 2013) and Ulrich K. Lehner, *Die katholische Aufklärung: Weltgeschichte einer Reformbewegung* (Paderborn: Schöningh, 2017). With regard to anti-Enlightenment Catholicism before the French Revolution see Darrin McMahon, *Enemies of the Enlightenment: The French Counter-Enlightenment and the Making of Modernity* (Oxford: Oxford UP, 2001).

authority and order, especially in the shape of enlightened absolutism. This specific *gestalt* resulted from its social setting within state bureaucracies and more or less middle-class, bourgeois and aristocratic strata of society. Even before the violent excesses of the French Revolution this social formation – with its focus on and fervor for social disciplining of the seemingly backward world of artisans and peasants, who were, together with the racialized other of early colonialism, the marginalized socio-cultural other inside the emerging nation-state or the princely states of Germany – generated vehement opposition from those marginalized. This marks a significant difference between Catholic ultramontanism and, for instance, the middle-class Protestant awakenings in Britain and the US. Besides, Catholic enlightened absolutism did favor a cooperational model of the relationship between Church and state, predominantly through an intensive collaboration of an episcopate formed more or less by the higher aristocracy and the state governments. As a matter of fact, the Church had become an instrument of the enlightened bureaucracy. This grew into what many Catholic laymen perceived as a lack of genuine spirituality and a reduction of religion to mere utilitarianism. Especially the role of the supernatural, including miracles and direct divine interventions, was effectively reduced. Pilgrimages, once a powerful space for the spirituality and the liberty of the underprivileged classes, were forbidden or at least ridiculed as superstitious and uncivilized, even barbarian. While the emotional discomfort of many peasants and artisans with the seemingly flat and in the end uninspiring religiosity of upper-class Enlightenment Catholicism over the course of the eighteenth century remained unconsidered and unsystematic, a strong feeling of utter neglect was already present. With the French Revolution, the Napoleonic Wars, and romanticism as a spiritual and intellectual counterculture to the dominant and often repressive culture of enlightened bureaucrats, things changed. It was intellectuals and members of the aristocracy who had experienced the violence of the French Revolution. Many of them, such as, for example, Joseph Görres in Germany,[10] had been partisan proponents of the ideas of the Revolution, the Enlightenment, and even Napoleon's expansionism and legal reforms, but now changed their position. They, mostly during the 1820s, helped to form an oppositional movement under the battle cry of *libertas ecclesiae*, or: "A free Church in a free state". In the very beginning this included a plea for a combination of personal liberty, institutional liberty of the Church and an intensified spirituality. New or reinstalled variants of a collectivist devotional culture, such as the adoration of the Virgin Mary, the Sacred Hearts of Jesus and Mary, a staunch belief in miracles, apparitions, and living sainthood, and thus the direct intervention from the sphere of the divine, became significant for

---

10 Monika Fink-Lang, *Joseph Görres: Die Biographie* (Paderborn: Schöningh, 2013).

this new piety. Some of these pious forms had a clear political implication, such as, for example, the cult of the Sacred Hearts of Jesus and Mary, which had been the symbols of the anti-revolutionary forces of the so-called *Chouans* and the "Great Catholic and Royal Army" of the counterrevolutionaries in the Vendée during the struggles, that also took part in the Bretagne in the 1790s. Some Catholic orders, such as the Capuchins, the Redemptorists, and – increasingly important after their re-installation in 1814 – the Jesuits, actively supported not only the new forms of devotional piety but also the political, explicitly anti-revolutionary and anti-enlightened implications of these cults. The so-called *Volksmissionen* became important elements of the renewal of the faith, with its genuinely romantic orientation toward the common man or the common woman, as women were important and highly valuable agents of the movement. They were of such importance that Catholicism was increasingly perceived as an effeminate form of religion in comparison with "manly" Protestantism with its rigid Kantian ethics of obligation and duty (deontology).[11] However, at least until the 1830s, it was the German episcopate and the Popes who were not really convinced by these seemingly democratic impulses from the very social basis of Catholicism. The bishops, many of them still coming from the enlightened absolutist faction of higher aristocracy, adhered to the traditional concepts of the eighteenth century, yet with an anti-revolutionary orientation. Again, it was the political development that made the difference. Not only in Germany but throughout Western Europe the enlightened absolutist state was gradually transformed into an evolving nation state with a strong ideological foundation in liberalism. In Germany, this development was slowed by the continued existence of the small princely states, but this did not preclude the slow and gradual entry of liberal bureaucrats into the establishment of the older enlightened bureaucracy. As both factions remained within the broader context of Enlightenment ideology, they shared a mutual mistrust of the ultramontanist renewal. This mistrust was all the fiercer as they recruited themselves from similar social strata, including parts of the aristocracy, but mainly from a socially upward mobile bourgeoisie. And they did actually share enlightened prejudices with regard to the pious practices of the common people. In addition, they shared a vision of a nationalized, state-controlled Catholic Church. In 1837, the ideological schism between the modern Prussian state and a modernized Catholic Church, more and more oriented toward her own liberty from statist paternalism, led to a divisive clash. The new archbishop of Cologne, Clemens August von Droste-Vischering, a

---

11 On these heavily gendered everyday aspects of devotional culture cf. Olaf Blaschke, "Das 19. Jahrhundert: Ein Zweites Konfessionelles Zeitalter", in: *Geschichte und Gesellschaft* 26 (2000), 35–77.

member of the old higher aristocracy of Westphalia and since 1808 influenced by the social and devotional practice of early ultramontanism, had for a long time been an outspoken enemy of denominationally mixed marriages. He feared, not without reason, that, as in the Rhineland, a Catholic part of Protestant Prussia, these marriages were primarily between Protestant men and socially inferior Catholic women, while the children would be raised as Protestants. He, moreover, disdained post-enlightened Hermesian philosophy and theology and actively tried to oust these liberals from service in the Church. Thus Droste-Vischering became one of the first explicitly ultramontanist members of the German Catholic hierarchy. When the Prussian government decided to arrest the hawkish bishop, ultramontanist intellectuals and pundits all over Germany had their noble cause. Revolutionary-turned-Catholic Joseph Görres with his inflammatory pamphlet *Athanasius* set the tone: *Libertas ecclesiae* became a more prevalent demand than ever before. And the ultramontanists could prove that they had mass allegiance utterly loyal to the awakening. In 1844, for the first time since 1810, the Holy Robe of Jesus was presented to pilgrims in Trier. Supported by the clergy, over 500,000 Germans, predominantly peasants, artisans, mine workers, and romantic aristocrats, together with some ultramontanist intellectuals, flocked to Trier. Liberals, clergymen, and laypeople of all denominations were shocked, and despised this reactionary backlash in harsh and bitter words. Sentiments grew even stronger when about a decade after the apparition of the Virgin Mary in the small French town of Lourdes in 1858, a similar apparition took place in the peasant and mine worker community in the Prussian Saar area called Marpingen in 1867.[12] This time the Prussian state reacted with force. Police shot at the pilgrims, among them many noblewomen from Westphalia, a hotbed of German ultramontanism. The culture wars from the 1860s to the 1890s had reached their point of no return.

At this point, two further developments had already taken place that henceforth framed the ultramontanist movement, both with a starting point in Italy. The first was the involvement of the papacy, the other the rise of Neo-Scholasticism.[13] Hitherto the elitist European episcopate had remained critical with regard

---

12 A detailed and interpretative account is provided by David Blackbourn, *Marpingen: Das deutsche Lourdes in der Bismarckzeit* (Saarbrücken: Echolot, 2007).
13 On the medieval and early modern foundations of Neo-Scholasticism cf. Edward Feser, *Scholastic Metyphysics: A Contemporary Introduction* (Heusenstamm: editiones scholaticae, 2014), Fr. Brian Davies, OP, *Thomas Aquinas's* Summa Theologiae: *A Guide and Commentary* (Oxford: Oxford UP, 2014), Andreas Speer, *Thomas von Aquin: Die* Summa Theologiae: *Werkinterpretationen* (Berlin: De Gruyter, 2005), Hanns-Gregor Nissing, *Dichter und Denker: Thomas von Aquin: Eine Einführung in sein Werk und Leben* (München: Pneuma Verlag, 2022); still helpful are Rolf Schönberger, *Was ist*

to the mass awakenings of ultramontanism, despite the fact that they, contrary to the individualist Protestant awakenings, were strictly institutionalized, ecclesiocentric, and led by the lower clergy. The bishops, however, stood aside. Their class-based bias and their adherence to enlightened principles toward the common people prevented them from taking advantage of the enthusiasm of the pious lower classes. Things changed with conservative popes, beginning with the arch-reactionary Gregory XVI (1831–1846), who, after the experience of the French Revolution, perceived the modern nation state, liberalism, and enlightenment together with free masonry as demonic forces of evil. In his encyclical *Mirari vos* from 1831[14] he strongly condemned the freedom of expression, liberalism, the freedom of religion, and other modern ideas as principally anti-Catholic. Later, in 1839, with his Apostolic Letter *In Supremo Apostolatus*,[15] Gregory XVI also condemned the slave trade which was still relevant in some of the liberal nation states, such as Spain, Brazil, or the United States, hinting at obvious social and economic contradictions in the practice of Western liberalism. Yet Gregory XVI was a man of the *ancient régime* without any broader support among the masses. His successor, Pius IX (1846–1878), was far more adaptable. Having started as a popular reformer in the first two years of his pontificate, the revolution of 1848 and the rise of the Piemontese-Italian nation state with its aggressive stance toward the Papal States (the *Patrimonium Petri*) deeply traumatized him. Therefore he actively sought out cooperation with conservative Catholic forces all over Europe, especially in Austria and France. Moreover, he was keenly aware of the inherent papalism of the ultramontanist movement. Here, the Jesuits and the Redemptorists had taken the lead in supporting the move toward papal infallibility. For the ultramontanist laymen, the Roman Pontiff became a key figure in their struggle against a statist episcopate, somehow similar to the Italian *Pataria* in its eleventh-century coalition with the revolutionary papacy of the Gregorian reform. Nevertheless, this new coalition had its price. The remaining liberals within the ultramontanist movement had to make their decision, whether to go with a distinctively conservative papacy or to cling to the ideas of liberalism. Many of them, such as Ignaz von Döllinger, a world-famous historian and one of the most influential intellectual figures of early ultramontanism, left the movement. Others, among them the formerly Anglican convert John Henry Newman or the American convert Orestes A. Brownson, remained loyal, but not without strong mental reservations. Neither papalism nor the idea that the *Patrimonium Petri* was central to the survival of the papacy

---

Scholastik? (Hildesheim: Bernward, 1991) and Joseph Pieper, *Scholastik: Gestalten und Probleme mittelalterlicher Philosophie* (München: Kösel, ²1986).
14 DH 2730–32.
15 DH 2745–46.

and of Catholicism found their support. But they shared the ultramontanists' criticism of liberalism, the nation state and several aspects of modernity.

The second development was as important as the first one, despite the fact that it somehow contradicted the emotional enthusiasm of the ultramontanist awakening. This was, however, acceptable as enthusiasm among Catholics had never been as decisive as among Protestants. The intellectualist and institutionalist heritage of Roman Catholicism had still been quite influential and lively enough to bind pious devotion into an authoritative framework. Yet Neo-Scholasticism was more than just another ecclesiastical system of thought. It was the heir to medieval and early modern Catholic tradition and had survived its decline in the eighteenth century because of the relentlessly school-based traditionalism of the Dominicans (Thomism), the Benedictines (Thomism), the Franciscans (Scotism),[16] and the Jesuits (Suarezism and Molinism[17]). It was thus, on the one hand, a comparatively heterogeneous and combative tradition, as the different schools were still clinging to their principles. On the other hand, Neo-Scholasticism, which had evolved from the intellectual debate with Cartesianism, Kantianism, and Hegelianism, provided the necessary formal basis for an intellectualist critique of modernity.[18] The home of Neo-Scholasticism was in the seminaries and the schools of the orders in Italy, not necessarily the Roman School, which was more akin to the German *Tübingen School*, but the Italian provincial seminaries and the Jesuit universities. The most prominent early philosophers and theologians of the Neo-Scholastic were Fr. Matteo Liberatore, SJ, Fr. Joseph Kleutgen, SJ, a German who taught in Rome, and Fr. Luigi Taparelli d'Azeglio, SJ. Fr. Liberatore and Fr. Taparelli d'Azeglio became most influential, as they were among the teachers of the later Pope Leo XIII, who was elected in 1878 as successor of Pius IX.[19]

The importance of Neo-Scholasticism lay, besides its enormous intellectualist militancy, in the theoretically rich and multi-layered systematic framework it provided for the analysis of modernity. In stark contrast to post-Cartesian philosophy,

---

[16] See Richard Cross, *Duns Scotus* (New York: Oxford UP, 1999).
[17] Cf. Ken Perszyk, ed., *Molinism: The Contemporary Debate* (Oxford: Oxford UP, 2011). Molinism is, presently, of special importance as many Calvinist theologians and philosophers view it as a possibility to cope with the ever-lasting problem of the coordination of God's prescience, and predetermination and human free-will.
[18] A classical summary of the Neo-Scholastic approach is presented by Fr. Josephus Gredt, OSB, *Elementa Philosophiae Aristotelico-Thomisticae*, 2 vols. (Freiburg/Br.: Herder, 1961).
[19] On the Papal adaptation of Neo-Thomism cf. the encyclical *Aeterni Patris* (1879) (DH 3135–40) by Leo XIII. For the reception of Neo-Scholasticism in Germany see Fr. Thomas F. O'Meara, OP, *Church and Culture: German Catholic Theology, 1860–1914* (Notre Dame: U of Notre Dame P, 1991). See also Elisabeth Keim, *Das Eigentum in der Naturrechtslehre des Luigi Taparelli d'Azeglio* (St. Ottilien: EOS, 1998).

the Neo-Scholastics adhered to epistemological realism in its modestly critical variant.[20] This was the very foundation of any further analysis. It not only allowed for the search for truth as, according to the Neo-Scholastics, the human intellect and ratio were not only aiming at truth. Instead, they insisted that they were actually producing true insights, among them an essentialist reading of human nature as that of a rational animal (*animal rationale*) on the one hand, and a critical mixture of negative and positive knowledge about God with a clear separation between supernatural grace and created nature on the other, as well as a clear distinction between the mysteries of the creed and the knowable truths. This was clearly aimed against any biblical fideism, as prevalent in Protestant evangelicalism, or against conservative fideist traditionalism with its irrational claim of a common *Uroffenbarung* that had informed mankind about God's mysteries. Any religious teaching had to be grounded in an intellectualist, argumentative analysis, a natural theology as *praeambula fidei*. It was the analogous (Thomism)[21] or formal (Scotism) identity of being that served as the safeguard of these distinctions. And being was about order. Therefore, human perception and human intellectual knowledge through essential abstraction were not only possible, as they took part in the broader framework of being, but they were also ordered. Moreover, as human action had to be based on the rational essential and existential analysis of human being, this ordering activity by necessity included moral action and in the following step, political action.

Yet while the metaphysical ontology of Neo-Scholasticism was fundamentally stable, ethical, moral, and political debates could be ignited easily. This resulted from the inherent structure of moral reasoning, which was based on rigid principles, which, however, lost relevance with each step of a practical syllogism because of the inclusion and intellectual deliberation of situational circumstances within this theoretical framework. Moreover, on the ethical level the rather positive intellectualism of the Neo-Scholastics is countered by a moderate skepticism regarding human nature. It not only lacks the ability of any positive knowledge of the mysteries of God's essence, but moreover it tends to narrowly delineate human potential in natural life. This is a result of a theological premise, the teaching about original sin (*peccatum originale*), and of a critical analysis of human history. The

---

20 Cf. Fernand Van Steenberghen, *Erkenntnislehre* (Einsiedeln: Benzinger, 1950), Fr. Joseph Owens, C.Ss.R., *Cognition: An Epistemological Inquiry* (Houston: Center for Thomistic Studies, 1992), Dominik Perler, *Theorien der Intentionalität im Mittelalter* (Frankfurt/Main: Klostermann, 2002), and Rafael Hüntelmann, *Grundkurs Philosophie*, vol. III: *Erkenntnistheorie* (Heusenstamm: editiones scholasticae, 2014).
21 Domenic D'Ettore, *Analogy after Aquinas: Logical Problems, Thomistic Answers* (Washington, DC: Catholic U of America P, 2019).

inherent moderate anthropological skepticism of Catholic theology sharply contradicts the anthropological optimism of many versions of modern liberalism and draws clear boundaries to any attempt to trust human activism without any belief in the centrality of divine grace securing free human actions within a broader framework of human and divine cooperation through the medium of a normative creed. As a matter of fact, any free-willed action has to be based on situational acts of practical prudence adhering to the ontological foundations of values.[22] Thus two possible conclusions made sense: some Neo-Scholastics tried to establish an ethical system of Natural Rights and Natural Law as rigidly deductive as the Rationalist Natural Law systems of the Enlightenment, while others referred to Neo-Scholastic Natural Law teaching as a system allowing for some freedom in deducing moral conclusions for the individual ethical act, which finally led to a sort of case law system.[23] As Neo-Scholasticism was based on an intensive reading of the Aristotelian tradition, it comprised Aristotelian physics and biology but never in a purely dogmatic way. In the end, after a phase of intensive discussion, Neo-Scholastics were, for example, far more able to integrate some forms of Evolutionism into their system than, for instance, Protestant Evangelicals and Fundamentalists.

The ontological analysis of personhood was of political importance. Especially according to especially Neo-Thomists, human persons[24] were essentially oriented toward society as they were not only images of God individually, which gave them dignity and obligations, but also essentially social beings. This was based on their natural inclinations toward life and subsistence, procreativity with regard to the preservation of the species, coordinated activity within a society, and the search for truth. Therefore, any given society had its unshakable basis in this personal order which allowed the criticism of the liberal ideas of contracts and compacts forming society, and any collectivist ideas about society. As a result the idea evolved that a compact, which even according to liberalism was always hypothetical and ahistorical, could serve as a real means for real-world political action, such as, for instance, a revolutionary coup against a legitimate constitution or ruler. Any change had to come in an orderly and gradual manner and within the ethical framework supplied by Natural Law theory. A society and the political

---

[22] Andrew D. Swafford, *Nature and Grace: A New Approach to Thomistic Ressourcement* (Eugene: Pickwick, 2014), which relies heavily on the German Neo-Scholastic theologian Matthias J. Scheeben.

[23] On the theoretical foundations of the Scholastic teachings on Natural Law, see Anthnoy Lisska, *Aquinas's Theory of Natural Law: An Analytic Reconstruction* (Oxford: Clarendon P, 1998).

[24] With regard to the later medieval roots of modern personalism, see the precise analysis by Dominik Perler, *Eine Person sein: Philosophische Debatten im Spätmittelalter* (Frankfurt/Main: Klostermann, 2020).

system based on this ontology was neither the mere addition of self-promoting individuals nor an essentialist body, but the result of a necessary human interaction, a relation.[25] This relational approach again led to a hierarchy of goods, starting with natural individual goods, ascending to the natural common good, the pursuit of beatitude and happiness, which finally led to the supernatural supreme good which was the beatification in God.[26] Thus every social, economic and political system had to primarily follow the idea of the natural common good (*bonum commune*), while the Church was responsible for the true and supernatural supreme good (*bonum summum*). This allowed for both the acceptance of a non-Catholic statehood, but with strong ethical commandments and the postulation of an ultimately necessary Catholic state that would include the *bonum commune* and the *bonum summum*. This ethical reading of the state makes clear why the Neo-Scholastics vehemently opposed the liberal idea of a strict distinction between legal issues of the state and moral, private issues.[27] Moreover, the claim – or the pretense – of deducing intellectual truth made it hard to accept pluralism and freedom of opinion. It took the Neo-Scholastics nearly half a century to find arguments for the latter on the basis of the situational aspects of the practical syllogism. In the fields of practical politics, however, ultramontanist Catholics, even after the Neo-Scholastic turn, found ways to promote democracy without accepting liberal ideological terms. In the later nineteenth and early twentieth centuries in Germany, the Netherlands, Belgium, France, and for some time in Austria, and Italy, Roman Catholic politicians were able to form coalitions with left-wing liberals and social democrats to oust the elitism of nationalist liberal legislations on voting rights, excluding especially the poor and underprivileged.[28] One should not forget that in 1948

---

[25] Cf. Michael Hochgeschwender, "Zwischen Neuscholastik und Amerikanisierung: Das Staatsverständnis des amerikanischen Katholizismus, 1860 bis 1960", in: Michael Kühnlein, ed., *Das Politische und das Vorpolitische: Über die Wertgrundlagen der Demokratie* (Baden-Baden: Nomos, 2014), 261–80 and "Katholische Soziallehre", in: Michael G. Festl, ed., *Handbuch Liberalismus* (Stuttgart: J.B. Metzler, 2021), 281–89.

[26] The natural adaptability towards the *summum bonum* is based on two aspects common to all created nature, specifically of the rational human nature, the *desiderium natural ad Deum*, the natural desire for God as the final truth and the highest beatitude, which follows from the natural inclination toward truth, and the *potential oboediantialis*, a natural observational potency, that ontologically guarantees the rational efforts toward God, despite the natural inability of created intellects to gain any positive knowledge of God's essence.

[27] Cf. Fr. Egon Edgar Nawroth, OP, *Die Sozial- und Wirtschaftsphilosophie des Neoliberalismus* (Heidelberg: F.H. Kerle, ²1962) and Fr. Arthur F. Utz, OP, *Sozialethik*, 4 vols. (Heidelberg: F.H. Kerle, 1958).

[28] See *Lexikon der Christlichen Demokratie in Deutschland* (Paderborn: Schöningh, 2002), s.v. "Christliche Demokratie", and Noel D. Cary, *The Path to Christian Democracy: German Catholics and the Party System from Windthorst to Adenauer* (Harvard: Harvard University Press, 1996). Very important and instructive is Michael P. Fogarty, *Christian Democracy in Western Europe*,

the French Neo-Thomist philosopher Jacques Maritain was a member of the UN committee that prepared the UN Declaration of Human Rights, and that in the mid-twentieth century Neo-Thomist intellectuals, such as Etienne Gilson, Joseph Pieper or Johannes Messner, were able to integrate elements of the liberal discourses, typically from an Anglo-American background, into a Neo-Scholastic framework that was by far more flexible than many observers still believe.

There were, however, some marked differences between liberalism and Neo-Scholasticism, even on practical levels. First, until the mid-twentieth century Neo-Scholastic philosophers avoided the classical discourse on liberal human rights.[29] Instead, they used a narrative of duties and obligations toward other human beings and – even more important – toward God, even though their epistemology and anthropology could have served as a more durable and sound explanation for the very existence of human rights at large. Neo-Scholastic teaching with its reference to a common and universal human nature that was capable of being rationally intelligible allowed – at least in theory – far more for the formulation of universalist human rights than the nominalist and individualist epistemology and anthropology of liberals outside the tradition of French rationalism. Furthermore, according to the Catholic position, human nature is a truly human nature without any regard to its actual functioning. It is sufficient to be potentially rational and potentially self-reflective, or potentially free-willed, to be a human person with all obligations and rights. This was in clear contrast to the liberal idea that only an actually self-reflective, free-willed and rational individual really possessed personhood, which minimized the rights of the disabled, the 'savages', women, children, and fetuses over the course of the nineteenth century. The Catholic doctrine distinguished more precisely between person and personhood. Personhood was subject to developmental processes, while the person, as a naturally and potentially rational and free-willed agent and as the image of God, was a person under any circumstances. Finally, Aristotelian-Thomist anthropology, with its strong emphasis on hylemorphism, i.e. the integral unity of body and soul, managed to escape the intricate problems of a body-mind dualism that very much shaped modern science.

1820–1953 (London: Routledge, 2019) with its stress on the tropes of Christian pluralism and conservatism in opposition to liberal individualism, enlightened centralism, and totalitarian collectivism.

29 Rudolf Uertz, *Vom Gotteswort zum Menschenrecht: Das katholische Staatsdenken in Deutschland von der Französischen Revolution bis zum Zweiten Vatikanischen Konzil (1789–1965)* (Paderborn: Schöningh, 2005). Note, however, that for Latin Americans the history of human rights starts with the Scholastic theologian Fr. Francisco de Vitoria, OP in the early 16th century and not with Hugo Grotius or the Enlightenment, cf. Patricia Seed, *American Pentimento: The Invention of Indians and the Pursuit of Riches* (Minneapolis: University of Minnesota, 2001), 179–81.

Catholics, though, tended to put a strict moral order on the body-soul-relationship, stressing the impact of the rational faculty of human persons to design their own lives in accordance with the likewise rational orders of God. This realist and essentialist ontology was important for Catholics, who were accustomed to follow the ethic axiom *agere sequitur esse*, action follows being. In any case, the obvious reluctance of Neo-Scholastics and other Catholics to use the human rights discourse had political reasons. They perceived the liberal rhetoric as an ideological instrument for spreading disorder and revolution. True authority was seemingly undermined by an anthropocentric and individualist world-view. This search for order, authority, and stability made them prone to authoritarian allurements, despite the attempts of moderate Neo-Scholastics to reformulate the whole theory in a manner closer to the ideas of Anglo-American liberalism.[30]

The second major difference can be located in the concept of individual freedom and political liberty.[31] Contrary to the liberal-enlightened position, Neo-Scholastics never interpreted freedom and liberty as supreme natural values. Both were certainly valuable, but in a completely different interpretation. Freedom was primarily viewed as freedom of the will to act as an agent of one's own to deliberately decide what was morally right through intellectual self-reflection on a free-willed act (*liberum arbitrium*). It was thus about reflection within a given order, not about freedom per se. And freedom was always intrinsically combined with responsibility for any free-willed act. For this reason, freedom had no primordial relationship with political liberty or individual self-determinatio: it was merely instrumental in acting humanly. On the theological level, freedom meant freedom from sin under the guidance of grace. This cooperative relationship of *liberum arbitrium* and grace, the so-called *concursus divinum*, was absolutely decisive for the Catholic theology of the Free Will and the impact of divine grace. It caused an ongoing debate between Jesuit Molinists who preferred a strong impact of the *liberum arbitrium* and Dominican Thomists, who insisted on the sovereignty of God and his grace. This again had no immediate reference to politics. However, it did not exclude a democratic reading. The rather elaborate Neo-Scholastic theory of moral action did, nonetheless, secure an intellectualistic reading of moral theory against any forms of modern emotivism and voluntarism[32] that were assumed to be foundational for the modern liberal human rights discourse.

---

30 See, for instance, Fr. Albert Auer, OSB, *Der Mensch hat Recht: Naturrecht auf dem Hintergrund von Heute* (Graz: Styria, 1956).
31 On the Catholic conception of freedom and liberty cf. the encyclicals *Diuturnum illud* (1881) (DH 3150–52), *Libertas praestantissimum* (1888) (DH 3245–55) by Leo XIII.
32 Alasdair MacIntyre's, *Whose Justice? Which Rationality?* (Notre Dame: U of Notre Dame P, 1988), 326–48, and *Three Rival Versions of Moral Enquiry: Encyclopedia, Genealogy, and Tradition* (Notre

Thirdly, the Neo-Scholastics developed a deeply anti-liberal theory of the state. As already mentioned, they hinted permanently at the flawed reasoning of the early modern, liberal compact theory of the state. In their discourse, the state was the natural result of the human inclination to sociability, and it was an immediate result of God's order written into his creation. According to this reasoning, the state, like the supernatural Church, was a perfect society (*societas perfecta*), which does not mean that the state was always in possession of actual perfection and without any need for change and reform. It just meant that the state had everything available that was necessary to fulfill its natural mission, exactly as the Church with the sacraments had the instruments available to fulfill her supernatural mission. State and Church were parallel perfections and therefore bound to cooperate to serve as instruments toward human perfection under the common good and the highest good. In the end, in a Catholic society they were bound by their nature to reach this aim through cooperation; in a non-Catholic society the state was at least prohibited from trying to somehow weaken the Church.

Fourthly, Neo-Scholasticism in no way shared the liberal idea of the pursuit of happiness, as mentioned in the American Declaration of Independence. This rejection was not only a result of the marked anthropological skepticism of Roman Catholicism; it, moreover, derived from a totally different understanding of happiness. According to the ancient and Scholastic tradition, happiness included two different modes of actualization. One was situational and isolated, the so-called *Felicitas*, the other one, far more important and desirable, was *beatitudo*. *Beatitudo* in itself included two different actualizations, the first comprised an intuitive and natural knowledge at the end of life – that life had been worthwhile – the second one consisted in the supernatural unification with God, or what the Greek Fathers called the *theosis*, the likeness with God. In relation to the multi-faceted variants of *beatitude*, worldly *felicitas*, especially any materialistic understanding of *felicitas*, including consumerism or the pursuit of maximized profits, were merely secondary or even dangerous. Happiness was thus not a byproduct of personal freedom or political liberty; it was inherently linked to a universalist ethical order that was endowed with a certain intellectual truth-value. Interestingly enough, this universalist and intellectualist order was more akin to classical Enlightenment than to post-enlightened, modern liberalism with its voluntarist and emotivist ethics.

In summary: with the active integration of papalism and Neo-Scholasticism, the initially enthusiastic awakening of early ultramontanism was transformed

---

Dame: U of Notre Dame P, 1990) provide an insightful explanation of the emotivist and voluntarist structure of moral arguments in the liberal-enlightened tradition of encyclopedia, not to speak of postmodern genealogy.

into a more rigorous and more intellectualized high ultramontanism. It did not become more politicized as it always had had a political impact, but it turned more toward political conservatism than before. Despite this transformation, ultramontanism never became a totalitarian ideology, nor was it in general a priori anti-modern. It was certainly anti-liberal and anti-enlightened, but not always anti-democratic. Whether or not ultramontanism was able to fit into a democratic structure or practically acted defensively, depended on the socio-cultural and economic circumstances. Furthermore, ultramontanism gained from the Neo-Scholastic perspective a coherent reasonable, intellectualist foundation allowing for a precise analysis of the limits and internal contradictions of liberal theory. Together with Marxism and early twentieth-century Protestant fundamentalism, Catholic ultramontanist Neo-Scholasticism provided an intellectually sound basis for a modern critique of liberal modernity. This criticism was, therefore, never only a defensive measure. It aggressively undermined liberalism's basic theories of justification. Among the most fruitful segments of ultramontanist critique was perhaps the most important and the one with the most eminent practical results: social criticism with its analysis of the inherent injustices of liberal Capitalism.

And this is the point where Fr. Pesch, SJ and Fr. Weiss, OP enter the scene. Both were deeply influenced by high ultramontanism and the impact of the culture wars ignited by nationalist liberals and the Bismarck administration after the First Vatican Council and the definition of papal infallibility as well as Italy's nationalist liberalism's struggle against the Papal States that ended with the military occupation of Rome during the Council.[33] At the height of the Kulturkampf in Germany, in the 1870s, 1,800 Catholic priests in Germany were under arrest, two bishops were in prison, several bishops in exile, and property worth millions of German Reichsmark had been confiscated. This experience of an active suppression through the means of the authoritarian police state shaped the German Catholic milieu, as it shaped Catholic milieus all over Europe. Wherever the liberal nation-state evolved, the Church was under attack. As a result, the majority of German and other European Catholics formed closed milieus with their own organizational structures and a strong anti-liberal sentiment as ideological cement.

During this era, Fr. Pesch and Fr. Weiss actively decided to join Catholic orders that were under the specific surveillance of the government. The Jesuits were even exiled. Nevertheless, the two priests represented different wings of the movement. Fr. Pesch was a so-called social realist (*Sozialrealist*), lacking any romantic fervor

---

33 Cf. Manuel Borutta, *Antikatholizismus: Deutschland und Italien im Zeitalter der europäischen Kulturkämpfe* (Göttingen: Vandenhoeck & Ruprecht, 2010) and Michael B. Gross, *The War against Catholicism: Liberalism and the Anti-Catholic Imagination in Nineteenth-Century Germany* (Ann Arbor: U of Michigan P, 2005).

for the medieval era. Despite being a Jesuit, a member of the perhaps most papalist order in the nineteenth century, he also was a rather secular political economist who had studied with several well-established German economists of the Historical School of Economy, among them Gustav Friedrich Schmoller and Adolf Wagner. They were members of a group of rather conservative economists pejoratively known as *Kathedersozialisten* that tried to solve the social problems of rapid industrialization, pauperism, and exploitation through state intervention. According to their analysis, liberal free-market capitalism, better known as Manchester liberalism, bore the responsibility and the blame for the dramatic poverty of the new working class. In this, they followed the social reformism of British Tories and other European conservatives, favoring a strong and active welfare state over the liberal minimal state or night-watchman state of Manchesterism. Fr. Weiss, OP, in contrast, was a devout social romanticist (*Sozialromantiker*), very much influenced by the social reformer Karl Freiherr von Vogelsang, a convert from Protestantism who, under the influence of Bishop Wilhelm Emmanuel von Ketteler (one of the earliest Catholic ultramontanist social reformers), would become a leading figure in the formative phase of the Austrian Catholic Workers Movement.[34] Other than the social realists, the social romanticists openly despised modernity with its implications of urbanization and industrialization. While they knew that a return to the Middle Ages was impossible, their criticism of modern industrialism and capitalism was far more radical than that of the realists. Fr. Weiss, moreover, basically hated any form of modernity including early modern humanism. He was perhaps among the most idiosyncratic of all Neo-Scholastics with his vitriolic attacks on classical studies, the neo-paganism of the Humanists or Goethe, the foul morals of ancient mythology, and nearly everything else. This was somewhat astonishing, as Fr. Weiss had been trained as a social scientist. Like Fr. Pesch, Fr. Weiss was deeply interested in social and economic questions, but in contrast to the Jesuit, he insisted on a paternalistic attitude of the clerics towards the laymen, harshly condemning any political or social activities outside the control of the Catholic hierarchy.

Perhaps the most relevant difference resulted from their stance toward anti-Semitism.[35] Not only was anti-Judaism an integral and long-standing part of the

---

[34] The distinction between social realists and social romantics is taken from Arno Anzenbacher, *Christliche Sozialethik* (Paderborn: Schöningh, 1997), 132–38.

[35] The topic of Catholic anti-Semitism in the nineteenth and twentieth centuries is still hotly debated. For a supposedly hypercritical account cf. Olaf Blaschke and Aram Mattioli, eds., *Katholischer Antisemitismus im 19. Jahrhundert: Ursachen und Tendenzen im internationalen Vergleich* (Zürich: Orell Füssli, 2000). Less provocative is Uwe Mazura, *Zentrumspartei und Judenfrage, 1870/71–*

Christian tradition; during the 1880s right-wing groups had institutionalized a new variant of anti-Semitism based on essentialist racial attributions and physical characteristics. Besides, social reformers of nearly all political camps had developed strong anti-Semitic prejudices resulting from the imaginary idea that Jewish bankers controlled the international financial system. A sequence of financial scandals over the course of the late nineteenth century involving Jewish bankers had actually fueled this trope. Within the broader field of modern anti-Semites, including nationalist liberals, Socialists, the folkish movements of extreme right-wing nationalism, conservatives, and left- or right-wing social reformers, Catholics had their own residual zone. It is still a matter of heated discussion to what extent anti-Semitism was a definitive marker of Roman Catholicism in this, era but there cannot be any doubt about its influence.[36] Fr. Weiss might be a telling example. On the one hand, he – with his usual acerbity – distinguished himself from the modern, racialized anti-Semitism of right-wing movements. On the other hand, he not only reproduced time-old anti-Judaistic prejudices, but he, furthermore, seemed to accept a culturalist and socio-economic understanding of Jews as perpetrators, who were trying to exploit the non-Jewish masses. He obviously and openly was a foe of any form of Jewish participation in society, while he tended to respect the traditional Jewish orthodoxy.[37] His vitriolic hatred was aimed at a modernist Jewry, as much as he despised modernist Catholicism or liberal Protestantism. In contrast, Fr. Pesch pursued a totally different course, despite the fact that his academic teacher Schmoller was a renowned anti-Semite, and a friend of the Protestant pastor and social reformer Adolf von Stoecker, one of Germany's leading anti-Semites. In Fr. Pesch's texts there are no hints of any form of anti-Semitism. He could sometimes be as vitriolic as Fr. Weiss, but his enemies, whom he eventually dismissed as "blood-sucking vampires" and "hyenas", were capitalists and free-market Manchesterites at large, regardless of their religion or race. He never openly attacked Jews. His criticism focused on liberals and Socialists.

While Fr. Weiss wrote an all-encompassing apologia of Catholic Christianity, Fr. Pesch was far more interested in actual social reform. On the basis of the overall Neo-Scholastic epistemology, metaphysics, and ethics, as sketched above, he drew quite practical conclusions in line with many German *Kathedersozialisten*. His ul-

---

1933: Verfassungsstaat und Minderheitenschutz (Mainz: Grünwald, 1994). With regard to the U.S. see Egal Feldman, *Catholics and Jews in Twentieth-Century America* (Urbana: U of Illinois P, 2001).
36 A theoretical contemplation on the whole debate is provided by Michael Hochgeschwender, "Katholizismus und Antisemitismus", in: Karl-Joseph Hummel, ed., *Zeitgeschichtliche Katholizismusforschung: Tatsachen, Deutungen, Fragen: Eine Zwischenbilanz* (Paderborn: Schöningh, 2004), 31–48.
37 Fr. Weiss, OP, *Apologie*, vol. III, 188–226 and *passim*.

tramontanism was, therefore, compatible with one of the modern strands of political economy. It was neither defensively structured nor anti-modern per se, yet still unequivocally anti-liberal. As a social realist he accepted industrialization and wanted to eliminate its negative results, especially pauperism. In order to reach this aim, Fr. Pesch, in line with the general Catholic tradition and the recent Papal Social teaching, as authentically rendered by Pope Leo XIII in his encyclical *Rerum Novarum* (1891), accepted the economic predominance of private property as a given of Natural Law.[38] He thus theoretically distinguished private property from liberal capitalism. Moreover, Fr. Pesch showed strong sympathy for so-called "state socialism" (*Staatssozialismus*). This meant an active role for the state in securing a minimal status-bound living standard for the poor and the working-class. He, however, preferred voluntary social action by social reformist entrepreneurs in coordination with traditional Church charity to statism. But when the social circumstances made this traditional approach inviable, it was among the scope of duties of the secular government to conduct an active policy with a strong social component. According to Fr. Pesch, even the expropriation of proprietors could be part of these social measures. Besides, Fr. Pesch believed in natural monopolies and opposed any total economization of society. But the most prominent point was to make the state responsible for the active distribution of wealth to the paupers and to safeguard minimal living conditions for working-class families, such as a "family income", a decent education, decent housing, and holidays. This was not about equality, but about the gradual introduction of a living wage (the principle of *suum cuique*) and a well-regulated market. He thus overcame the traditionalist Catholic approach that had very much focused on individual moral amelioration and the individual charity of Catholic businessmen or clerics, shifting the focus towards the state and structural analysis. He, however, never intended to minimize the impact and agency of the Church in social and economic issues. His major theoretical insight consisted of a combination of two concepts: social justice and solidarity. Social justice was deduced from the Aristotelian-Thomist teaching on justice, specifically the term of distributive justice (*iustitia distributiva*), which was now transferred from individual ethics into a solidarist social framework. Solidarism, in turn, originated in a French positivist, Comtean, analysis of the cohesive forces in the social fabric.[39] The positivist analysis had claimed to be non-normative and

---

[38] Cf. Fr. Alexander Horvath, OP, *Eigentumsrecht nach dem hl. Thomas von Aquin, OP* (Graz: Moder, 1929). Fr. Horvath, OP was among the most radical critics of the liberal cult surrounding private property.
[39] On solidarism cf. Herman-Josef Große Kracht, *Gustav Gundlach, SJ (1892–1963): Katholischer Solidarismus im Ringen um die Wirtschafts- und Sozialordnung* Paderborn: Schöningh, 2019) and

purely descriptive, which was misleading, as the underlying theory of society without further reflection demanded social solidarity as a human given. Fr. Pesch took the concept and transformed it, on the theoretical basis of Neo-Scholastic personalism, into a prescriptive formative element of human personhood, deducing this from the essential sociability of any human nature. Personhood, solidarity, social justice, subsidiarity, and the idea that social problems should be solved at the lowest possible level to prevent a sort of maximum-security welfare state, and possibly the rise of totalitarianism, became key notions of the Catholic Social Teaching of the twentieth century.[40] They were even adopted by Socialists and liberals. Social realism for decades served as the dominant mode of social theory in Roman Catholicism. Pius XI, Pius XII and John XXIII as well as John Paul II and Benedict XVI favored it. In modern welfare states such as, for example, West Germany and Austria, social realism became an integral part of the social system. This was, perhaps, the element of ultramontanist thought that was most compatible with liberal modernity, as long as liberalism was able to let go of its radical free-market past.[41]

The fates of social romanticism and Fr. Weiss were different. Like Fr. Pesch, Fr. Weiss was intensively concerned with social reform and the dark sides of liberal capitalism, especially industrial pauperism. Yet, his approach relied heavily on idealized pre-modern concepts, which he translated into the concept of a socially harmonious corporatist state, which would eventually develop into the idea of the *Christlicher Ständestaat*. To the social romantics, social harmony, and an "organic" society were far more important than social participation and solidarity. The state should be organized along the lines of stable profession-based status-groups, the *Stände*, which were supposed to cooperate within the framework of the common good. While the social realists thought in terms of the natural common good, which

---

Hermann-Josef Große Kracht, *Solidarität und Solidarismus: Postliberale Suchbewegungen zur normativen Selbstverständigung moderner Gesellschaften* (Bielefeld: transcript, 2017).

40 Cf. Fr. Pesch, SJ, *Nationalökonomie*, vol. I, viii, 16, 30–31, 70–77, 131–216, 252–82, 351–401. For a recent modernist interpretation see Markus Schlagnitweit, *Einführung in die Katholische Soziallehre: Kompass für Wirtschaft, Politik und Gesellschaft* (Freiburg/Br.: Herder, 2021). Schlagnitweit explicitly denies the argumentative value of Natural Law claims and implicitly abstains from metaphysical epistemology and ontology, respectively from metaphysical anthropology, to allow for a more liberal, freedom- and science-based meaningful reading of the Catholic Social Teaching. Yet he misses a central point: without sober epistemological and metaphysical foundations the truth value of its propositions actually collapses into mere voluntarism based on the authoritative teaching of the Popes. Whether this is more modern than the traditional reading remains open to debate.

41 Cf. Giuseppe Franco, *Von Salamanca nach Freiburg: Joseph Höffner und die soziale Marktwirtschaft* (Paderborn: Schöningh, 2018).

Fr. Pesch and his successors conceived in a pluralist and evolutionary manner, the social romantics favored a more static interpretation. However, even Fr. Weiss with his anti-Judaism and moralistic social harmonism was not only a reactionary. A closer look at his conception of modernity reveals something else. His critique concentrated on elements of modernity that are – in our days – often interpreted as anachronisms in a liberal society, as non-liberal and non-modern relics of former times. Yet, in 1900, they all were seen as genuinely modern and – at least partly – as integral elements of liberalism. Thus, Fr. Weiss vehemently opposed any variety of nationalism, a concept traditionally linked with liberalism. He, moreover, ruthlessly attacked Prussian and liberal militarism,[42] capitalist exploitation,[43] radical consumerism, and a competitive market society, eugenics, and a scientist reductionism without any inclusion of human interests or nature. While denouncing Renaissance humanism and its implications, he very much focused on a Christian, personalist humanism, which, for example, integrated mind and body. Here he could draw extensively on the Papal condemnations of modernity in the encyclicals *Mirari vos* by Pope Gregory XVI from 1831[44] and *Quanta cura*[45] with the (in-)famous *Syllabus errorum*[46] by Pope Pius IX, published in 1864, both condemning nearly every single aspect of liberal modernity. And, finally, he was one of the sharpest critics of slavery. This is quite interesting, as many ultramontanist Neo-Scholastics had been rather weak on this topic. Relying on Aristotle and Thomas Aquinas, they had interpreted slavery as a social evil, but not as a sin. It should be gradually transformed into a system stressing personal freedom, but step by step, with strict reservations based on the idea of social order. Fr. Weiss, however, flatly denied that slavery had any right to exist. In his eyes, slavery was the ultimate abomination of capitalism.[47] To him, individual freedom was of far greater importance than for Fr. Pesch. He also attacked biological racism. This attack included the racist interpretation of polygenesis, which promoted the idea of different humanities that only attributed full humanity to the white race (while still clinging to the idea of the existence of primitive races) and prevented Fr. Weiss

---

42 Fr. Weiss, OP, vol. V., 79–82 and *passim*
43 This common anti-capitalism among a majority of ultramontanist Catholics explains the radicalism of the so-called "Red Chaplains", young Catholic priests in working-class communities, during the Great Strike of the Ruhr area workers in 1889; cf. Herbert Hömig, *Katholiken und Gewerkschaftsbewegung, 1890–1945* (Paderborn: Schöningh, 2003).
44 DH 2730–32.
45 DH 2890–96.
46 DH 2901–80.
47 Fr. Weiss, OP, *Apologie*, vol. II., 184–96, where he even calls capitalism the successor to slavery.

from using biologist and organic terms, such as germs or viruses, for Jews.[48] Many of these points of criticism of contemporary modernity were shared by left-wing liberals and Socialists, who are commonly interpreted as progressive modernists. This should make us aware of the hazard of drawing hasty and perhaps superficial normative attributions with regard to ultramontanist Catholicism. Many elements of Catholic anti-modernism or defensive opposition against liberal modernity are only anti-modern and anti-liberal when they are excluded from the very history of modernity, of which they were actually a part.

In the United States social realism as represented by Fr. Pesch became far more influential than the social romanticism of Fr. Weiss. Many of Fr. Pesch's books, for instance, were translated into English and sold on the American market, as he had been partially and superficially influenced by the discussions on Henry George and Edward Bellamy. This was a result of the different structure of North American society on the one hand, and of American Catholicism on the other. Contrary to many evolving European nation-states, the U.S. disposed of a society that, at least in theory, was more fluid and included more chances of upward mobility. Thus the traditions of aristocratic status-bound societies, of guilds and crafts, the very basis of the romantic *Ständestaat*, were already gone. The character of liberal society as a class-ruled oppressive structure excluding non-bourgeois classes from participation less in theory than in practice (many liberal European states at the end of the nineteenth century still relied on class-based voting rights[49]), was minimized. Moreover, Church and State had already been separated on the federal level in the eighteenth century, and on the state levels in the early nineteenth century. The Catholic Church had actively profited from this development. Consequently,

---

[48] Fr. Weiss, OP, *Apologie*, vol. I, 233–41, vol. II, 226, and vol. V, 30. This strong belief in the essential unity and equality of the whole human race was shared by other Catholic scholars, such as, for instance Fr. Victor Cathrein, SJ, *Die Einheit des sittlichen Bewußtseins der Menschheit*, 3 vols., (Freiburg/Br.: Herder, 1913). These scholars nonetheless distinguished sharply between a racialized inequality which they opposed on essentialist ontological reasons, and a culturalist distinction between primitive and civilized races which they obviously favored. Papal condemnations of race hatred can be found in the encyclical *Ad beatissimi Apostolorum*, in: *Actae Apostolicae Sedis* 6 (1914), 6 and further encyclicals, such as, for instance, *Ardente Cura* by Pope Pius XI. (both are conspicuously missing in DH!). These Apostolic Letters prominently drew from the teaching of Spanish early modern Scholasticism and the Papal Letter *Sublimis Deus* (1537), which quite unequivocally condemned racism and slavery, see Edward Feser, *All One in Christ: A Catholic Critique of Racism and Critical Race Theory* (San Francisco: Ignatius P, 2022), 17–30.

[49] This was, however, not true in Germany where, from 1871 onward, all adult men had the right to vote, from which the Catholic Center Party very much profited. Only in Prussia, the dominant state in the German Empire, a class-based voting rights legislation survived – and many nationalist liberals actively promoted it due to their fear of Catholics and Socialists.

ideas of personal freedom and political liberty did not seem completely outlandish to American Catholics. Yet while the constitutional and legal frameworks in the U.S. were generally favorable to a – in comparison with Europe – more "liberal" development of Roman Catholicism, societal anti-Catholicism was as prevalent as in liberal Europe. As a matter of fact, American society was based on liberal and enlightened ideologies, on Calvinist Protestantism, on free-market capitalism, and on the idea of the superiority of the Anglo-Saxon race. In combination, this complex ideology socially and culturally excluded Catholics, depending on partisan politics and the interest of the two major parties in their own constituency. The Democratic Party was traditionally more favorable towards Catholics, while the Republicans drew the majority of their voters explicitly from liberal and Protestant constituencies. Some founding fathers of the Grand Old party even stemmed from nativist and vehemently anti-Catholic groups, such as for example the Know Nothings. Anti-Catholicism had traditionally been an integral element among the ruling classes of the nation. In contrast to the culture wars in Europe, this was not a matter for the federal authorities. Thus, while there was no active, police-mandated persecution of Catholics in the U.S.,[50] social exclusion was the norm.

As a result, the internal situation of Roman Catholics among themselves and in relation to the political and social system of the U.S. was woefully incoherent.[51] Until the 1820s and 1830s, American Catholicism had been dominated by upper middle-class Gentlemen Catholics, many of them slaveholders in Maryland, Louisiana, Tennessee, or Kentucky. They had a traditional institutional stronghold in the trustees and wardens overseeing ecclesiastical property. This secured the prolonged survival of a bourgeois, enlightened form of liberal Catholicism, very much fixed on the idea of complete integration into the American middle-class. These Gentlemen Catholics, for instance, abhorred emotional and enthusiastic devotional forms of piety, among them pilgrimages, Marian piety, the belief in miracles, the cult of the saints and relics, and so on. Ultramontanism was a latecomer. Only in the 1830s and 1840s did German and especially Irish migrants bring ultramontanist tendencies and devotional practices to the U.S. As they recruited them-

---

50 Manfred Görtemaker, *Deutschland im 19. Jahrhundert: Entwicklungslinien* (Opladen: Westdeutscher Verlag, 1983), 279 argues, that there was no persecution of Catholics in Germany during the 1870s, only a persecution of the Church, yet this drastically underestimates the closely-knit social fabric in the interactions between the Catholic hierarchy and the laypeople in Catholic ecclesiology and it does not take into consideration the social exclusion of Catholics in institutions dominated by Protestants, such as the military, and by liberals, such as the universities.
51 Cf. John T. McGreevy, *Catholicism and American Freedom: A History* (New York: W.W. Norton, 2003) and Michael Hochgeschwender, *Wahrheit, Einheit, Ordnung: Der amerikanische Katholizismus und die Sklavenfrage, 1835–1870* (Paderborn: Schöningh, 2006).

selves predominantly from non-bourgeois classes, the American middle-class Catholics were shocked about the newcomers. At least the Irish migrants, due to their social situation after centuries of persecution and exclusion by the British, were, in a nearly puritan fashion, critical of some of the ultramontanist practices, but all in all, they started to fight the remaining elitist middle-class Catholics. Almost immediately the migrants won the support of the bishops who, until the 1850s, tended to be elitist Enlightenment theologians, but who had a strong interest in getting rid of the ecclesiastical power of the laity. In a decade-long struggle, the majority of migrants overthrew the powerful positions of the gentlemen Catholics. In the 1850s, American Catholicism had turned towards ultramontanism, but it was still critical with regard to papalism. Neo-Scholasticism was no option at this point. And social anti-Catholicism, quite different from the state-oriented anti-Catholicism of the Western European culture wars, over decades ruthlessly endangered the life and property of Roman Catholics in the U.S.[52] A rather complex situation was the immediate result. Even semi-papalist Catholics like the convert Orestes A. Brownson favored integration into the democratic system of the U.S. And predominantly Irish Catholics were willing to act. This integrationist attitude had but a weak theological foundation. However, American Catholics promoted their program, which led to internal frictions between mostly Irish integrationists and many German anti-integrationists even after the definition of papal infallibility in Vatican I in 1870.[53] Interestingly enough, Pope Leo XIII, who was far more diplomatic than his occasionally eccentric and quite authoritarian predecessor Pius IX, and who was involved in coming to terms with the European nation-states, did not intervene until American Catholics tried to actively promote a democratic Catholicism among the anti-ultramontanist *Sillon*-circle in France. In this debate on "Americanism" he took sides only in 1899, when he condemned liberal Americanism.[54] But this was, to the surprise of many, not a wholesale condemnation of a more democratized variant of Catholicism in the U.S. per se. The surprise was unfounded, as in 1893 the Apostolic Delegate to the Columbian World Exhibition, Cardinal Francesco di Paolo Satolli, a strict Neo-Thomist, had enthusiastically declared the future of mankind would depend on the cooperation of the Catholic Bible and the American Constitution![55] The Pope only reprimanded the attempt to spread Americanism, but he actually accepted the necessity to integrate Catholicism into the pluralist and democratic society of the U.S., yet without actively opting

---

52 David H. Bennett, *The Party of Fear: The American Far Right from Nativism to the Militia Movement* (New York: Vintage Books, ²1995).
53 Dogmatic Constitution *Pastor Aeternus* (DH 3050–75).
54 Apostolic Letter *Testem benevolentiae* (DH 3340–46).
55 Peter Tischleder, *Die Staatslehre Leos XIII* (Mönchengladbach: Volksverein, 1925), 331.

for liberalism. One of the most important Americanists, Archbishop James Gibbons of Baltimore was even created a cardinal of the Roman Church. Gibbon was a somehow archetypical American liberal reformer, akin to his contemporary Archbishop James Purcell of Cincinnati. They were politically liberal, stressing integration, yet ecclesiastically authoritarian princes, who suppressed any internal opposition.

However diplomatic the answer of Leo XIII to the Americanist crisis might have been, afterwards Americanism rapidly declined, at least on the official level. And Neo-Scholasticism rose in the American Catholic seminaries, colleges, and universities. After 1899 the theoretically rather weak American Catholic theology was transformed by Neo-Scholasticism into something new and more coherent.[56] But in the end, it was not the Neo-Scholastics who had the most profound impact on the Catholic stance towards liberalism in the U.S., despite the fact that liberal capitalism caused similar social problems to those in Europe. Pauperism, especially during the grave global economic crisis of the 1890s, was as prevalent as in the industrialized nations on the other side of the Atlantic. In the U.S. it was, however, not only the Neo-Scholastic social philosophy that provided the Catholic answer. Here, the leading figure was Msgr. John A. Ryan, who was influenced by Fr. Pesch and his neo-scholastic reading of solidarism as well as by more pragmatic approaches from American social reformers such as Henry George.[57] Msgr. Ryan lacked the sophisticated epistemology and metaphysics of Neo-Scholasticism, but he profoundly understood the problems of the poor, who formed the social basis of American Catholicism. And he was willing to cooperate with reformist liberals, the so-called Progressive Movement. Within the context of early twentieth-century Progressivism, Msgr. Ryan focused on some ideas that already had been reflected on by Fr. Pesch, specifically the idea of social or economic justice as distributive justice.[58] Just like Fr. Pesch, he stressed the importance of private proper-

---

[56] Cf. Markus Faltermeier, "Reconsidering Thomas Aquinas: Natural law in American Catholicism from *Aeterni Patris* to the Progressive Era" (Ph.D.-diss., LMU Munich, 2012).

[57] See, for instance, Gary Dorrien, *Social Ethics in the Making: Interpreting an American Tradition* (Malden: Blackwell, 2011), 185–225, Harlan Beckley, *Passion for Justice: Retrieving the Legacies of Walter Rauschenbusch, John A. Ryan, and Reinhold Niebuhr* (Louisville: U of Kentucky P, 1992, and Michael Hochgeschwender, "Sozialer Katholizismus in den USA", in: André Habisch et al., eds., *Tradition und Erneuerung der Christlichen Sozialethik in Zeiten der Modernisierung* (Freiburg/Br.: Herder, 2012, 186–223.

[58] Cf. John A. Ryan, *Economic Justice: Selections from* Distributive Justice *and* A Living Wage, ed. by Harlan R. Beckley (Louisville: Westminster John Knox Pres, 1996). See furthermore Edward P. DeBerri et al., eds., *Catholic Social Teaching Our Best Kept Secret* (Maryknoll: Orbis Books, 2009). The connections between European and American developments are considered by Sabine Schatz,

ty and its Natural law foundations.[59] And, again like Fr. Pesch, Msgr. Ryan opposed the principle of a total equality of wages. He therefore proposed, together with other Progressivists, an "industrial democracy," i.e. an increased participation of the working-class in the industrial systems would lead to higher wages, the so-called living wages and social change through economic growth, an idea which later would become an integral part of Keynesianism and the New Deal of Franklin D. Roosevelt. Msgr. Ryan even served as an adviser to Roosevelt. This close cooperation between liberal and Catholic reformers in a project of distributive, economic justice within a moderated free-market system led to a totally different setting with regard to liberal modernity: while American Catholics were still stressing the foundational differences, they had far fewer problems cooperating with liberals than the European Neo-Scholastics, which was a result of a certain will to compromise on both sides that was lacking in Europe.[60]

In sum: as the traditional narrative, that denounces ultramontanist and neo-Scholastic Catholicism in its confrontation with liberal modernity in a rather one-sided manner as defensive and even reactionary often misses the problems Catholicism dealt with. Catholics were keenly aware of the dark sides of liberalism. They often criticized aspects of modernity that are defined as anti-modern and anti-liberal today, and they provided modes of spiritual and intellectual empowerment for non-middle-class actors. The whole notion of an anti-modern Catholicism before the Second Vatican Council seems to be based on normative assumptions that are already taken from a liberal worldview. Moreover, these assumptions already stem from a historicist and Hegelian framework[61] that assesses history as a series of linear progressive developments. Any sentence referring to "the spirit of our time", "the necessities of modernity", "offense" and "defense" with regard to modernity, etc., naturally refers to the basic idea that history makes sense in a normative linear progressive understanding. Yet this sense cannot be derived from the anti-metaphysical tendencies at the very foundation of modernism itself. It simply begs the question. The narrative might be correct, but the analysis is deeply flawed.

Das Gift des Alten Europa und die Arbeiter der Neuen Welt: Zum amerikanischen Hintergrund der Enzyklika Rerum Novarum *(1891)* (Paderborn: Schöningh, 2011).
59 For a Neo-Scholastic reflection on private property see Fr. Arthur F. Utz, OP, *Freiheit und Bindung des Eigentums* (Heidelberg: F.H. Kehrle Verlag, 1949).
60 An in-depth analysis of the philosophical controversial subjects and arguments between liberalism and Neo-Scholasticism from the standpoint of a liberal neo-Scholastic is provided by Joseph Des Jardins, "Liberalism and Catholic Social Teaching", in: *New Scholasticism* 61:3 (1987), 345–66.
61 On the guiding historicist framework of the liberal idea of linear progress to modernity see Philipp Sarasin, "More than just another Specialty: On the Prospects for the History of Knowledge", in: *Journal for the History of Knowledge* 1:1 (2020), 1–5.

Such propositions are, therefore, senseless, as their very normativity is based on the narrational exclusion of the dark sides of modernity as anachronistic, atavistic or anti-modern. They thereby eliminate the exact processual understanding of modernity that made modernity normatively so prominent in the beginning, a contradiction in terms. They are of no analytical value. Perhaps recent, more pluralistic and less ideology-driven notions of multiple modernities or a fragmented modernity might be more helpful, at least as long as one can precisely determine what might be outside modernity, as fragmented or multi-faceted as it may be.[62]

Works Cited

Anzenbacher, Arno. *Christliche Sozialethik*. Paderborn: Schöningh, 1997, 132–38.
Fr. Albert Auer, OSB. *Der Mensch hat Recht: Naturrecht auf dem Hintergrund von Heute*. Graz: Styria, 1956.
Beckley, Harlan. *Passion for Justice: Retrieving the Legacies of Walter Rauschenbusch, John A. Ryan, and Reinhold Niebuhr*. Louisville: U of Kentucky P, 1992.
Bennett, David H. *The Party of Fear: The American Far Right from Nativism to the Militia Movement*. New York: Vintage Books, ²1995.
Biebricher, Thomas. *Neoliberalismus zur Einführung*. Hamburg: Junius Verlag, 2012.
Blackbourn, David. *Marpingen: Das deutsche Lourdes in der Bismarckzeit*. Saarbrücken: Echolot, 2007.
Blaschke, Olaf. "Das 19. Jahrhundert: Ein Zweites Konfessionelles Zeitalter." *Geschichte und Gesellschaft* 26 (2000), 35–77.
Blaschke, Olaf, and Aram Mattioli, eds. *Katholischer Antisemitismus im 19. Jahrhundert: Ursachen und Tendenzen im internationalen Vergleich*. Zürich: Orell Füssli, 2000.
Borutta, Manuel. *Antikatholizismus: Deutschland und Italien im Zeitalter der europäischen Kulturkämpfe*. Göttingen: Vandenhoeck & Ruprecht, 2010.
Sr. Patricia Byrne, CSJ. "American Ultramontanism." *Theological Studies* 56 (1995), 301–26.
Cary, Noel D. *The Path to Christian Democracy: German Catholics and the Party System from Windthorst to Adenauer*. Harvard: Harvard UP, 1996.
Fr. Victor Cathrein, SJ. *Die Einheit des sittlichen Bewußtseins der Menschheit*. 3 vols. Freiburg/Br.: Herder, 1913.
Fr. Romanus Cessario, OP. *A Short History of Thomism*. Washington, DC: Catholic U of America P, 2003.
"Christliche Demokratie." *Lexikon der Christlichen Demokratie in Deutschland*. Paderborn: Schöningh, 2002.
Cross, Richard. *Duns Scotus*. New York: Oxford UP, 1999.
Fr. Brian Davies, OP. *Thomas Aquinas's* Summa Theologiae: *A Guide and Commentary*. Oxford: Oxford UP, 2014.

---

62 A lucid and concise discussion of different concepts of modernity is found in Thomas Welskopp and Alan Lessoff, "Fractured Modernity-Fractured Experiences-Fractured Histories: An Introduction", in: Thomas Welskopp and Alan Lessoff, eds., *Fractured Modernity: America Confronts Modern Times, 1890s to 1940s* (München: Oldenbourg, 2012), 1–20.

DeBerri, Edward P. et al., eds. *Catholic Social Teaching Our Best Kept Secret*. Maryknoll: Orbis Books, 2009.
Del Colle, Ralph. "Neo-Scholasticism." *The Blackwell Companion to Nineteenth-Century Theology*. Ed. David Fergusson. Malden: Blackwell, 2010, 376–94.
Des Jardins, Joseph. "Liberalism and Catholic Social Teaching." *New Scholasticism* 61:3 (1987), 345–66.
D'Ettore, Domenic. *Analogy after Aquinas: Logical Problems, Thomistic Answers*. Washington, DC: Catholic U of America P, 2019.
Dorrien, Gary. *Social Ethics in the Making: Interpreting an American Tradition*. Malden: Blackwell, 2011, 185–225,
Faltermeier, Markus. "Reconsidering Thomas Aquinas: Natural law in American Catholicism from *Aeterni Patris* to the Progressive Era." Ph.D. thesis, LMU Munich, 2012.
Feldman, Egal. *Catholics and Jews in Twentieth-Century America*. Urbana: U of Illinois P, 2001.
Feser, Edward. *All One in Christ: A Catholic Critique of Racism and Critical Race Theory*. San Francisco: Ignatius P, 2022, 17–30.
Feser, Edward. *Scholastic Metyphysics: A Contemporary Introduction*. Heusenstamm: editiones scholasticae, 2014.
Fink-Lang, Monika. *Joseph Görres: Die Biographie*. Paderborn: Schöningh, 2013.
Fleckenstein, Gisela, and Joachim Schmiedl, eds. *Ultramontanismus: Tendenzen der Forschung*. Paderborn: Bonifatius Verlag, 2005.
Fogarty, Michael P. *Christian Democracy in Western Europe, 1820–1953*. London: Routledge, 2019.
Franco, Giuseppe. *Von Salamanca nach Freiburg: Joseph Höffner und die soziale Marktwirtschaft*. Paderborn: Schöningh, 2018.
Görtemaker, Manfred. *Deutschland im 19. Jahrhundert: Entwicklungslinien*. Opladen: Westdeutscher Verlag, 1983, 279.
Fr. Josephus Gredt, OSB. *Elementa Philosophiae Aristotelico-Thomisticae*. 2 vols. Freiburg/Br.: Herder, 1961.
Gross, Michael B. *The War against Catholicism: Liberalism and the Anti-Catholic Imagination in Nineteenth-Century Germany*. Ann Arbor: U of Michigan P, 2005.
Große Kracht, Herman-Josef. *Gustav Gundlach, SJ (1892–1963): Katholischer Solidarismus im Ringen um die Wirtschafts- und Sozialordnung*. Paderborn: Schöningh, 2019.
Große Kracht, Herman-Josef. *Solidarität und Solidarismus: Postliberale Suchbewegungen zur normativen Selbstverständigung moderner Gesellschaften*. Bielefeld: transcript, 2017.
Hinze, Bradford E. "Roman Catholic Theology: Tübingen." *The Blackwell Companion to Nineteenth-Century Theology*. Ed. David Fergusson. Malden: Blackwell, 2010, 187–213.
Hochgeschwender, Michael. "Katholizismus und Antisemitismus." *Zeitgeschichtliche Katholizismusforschung: Tatsachen, Deutungen, Fragen: Eine Zwischenbilanz*. Ed. Karl-Joseph Hummel. Paderborn: Schöningh, 2004, 31–48.
Hochgeschwender, Michael. "Sozialer Katholizismus in den USA." *Tradition und Erneuerung der Christlichen Sozialethik in Zeiten der Modernisierung*. Ed. André Habisch et al. Freiburg/Br.: Herder, 2012, 186–223.
Hochgeschwender, Michael. "Waffenbrüderschaft auf Zeit: Der Vatikan, der US-amerikanische Katholizismus und die NATO." *Religion und Zivilreligion im Atlantischen Bündnis*. Ed. Werner Kremp and Berthold Meyer. Trier: wvt, 2001, 292–306.
Hochgeschwender, Michael. *Wahrheit, Einheit, Ordnung: Der amerikanische Katholizismus und die Sklavenfrage, 1835–1870*. Paderborn: Schöningh, 2006.

Hochgeschwender, Michael. "Zwischen Neuscholastik und Amerikanisierung: Das Staatsverständnis des amerikanischen Katholizismus, 1860 bis 1960." *Das Politische und das Vorpolitische: Über die Wertgrundlagen der Demokratie*. Ed. Michael Kühnlein. Baden-Baden: Nomos, 2014, 261–80.
Hömig, Herbert. *Katholiken und Gewerkschaftsbewegung, 1890–1945*. Paderborn: Schöningh, 2003.
Fr. Alexander Horvath, OP. *Eigentumsrecht nach dem hl. Thomas von Aquin, OP.* Graz: Moder, 1929.
Hüntelmann, Rafael. *Grundkurs Philosophie. Vol. III: Erkenntnistheorie*. Heusenstamm: editiones scholasticae, 2014.
Keim, Elisabeth. *Das Eigentum in der Naturrechtslehre des Luigi Taparelli d'Azeglio*. St. Ottilien: EOS, 1998.
Leendertz, Ariane. *Der erschöpfte Staat: Eine andere Geschichte des Neoliberalismus*. Hamburg: Hamburger Edition, 2022, 27–31.
Lehner, Ulrich K. *Die katholische Aufklärung: Weltgeschichte einer Reformbewegung*. Paderborn: Schöningh, 2017.
Lehner, Ulrich K., and Michael Printy, eds. *A Companion to the Catholic Enlightenment in Europe*. Leiden: Brill, 2013.
Lisska, Anthnoy. *Aquinas's Theory of Natural Law: An Analytic Reconstruction*. Oxford: Clarendon P, 1998.
MacIntyre, Alasdair. *Three Rival Versions of Moral Enquiry: Encyclopedia, Genealogy, and Tradition*. Notre Dame: U of Notre Dame P, 1990.
MacIntyre, Alasdair. *Whose Justice? Which Rationality?* Notre Dame: U of Notre Dame P, 1988, 326–48.
Mazura, Uwe. *Zentrumspartei und Judenfrage, 1870/71–1933: Verfassungsstaat und Minderheitenschutz*. Mainz: Grünwald, 1994.
Fr. Gerald A. McCool, SJ. *Nineteenth Century Scholasticism: The Search for a Unitary Method*. New York: Fordham, 1989.
McGreevy, John T. *Catholicism and American Freedom: A History*. New York: W.W. Norton, 2003.
McMahon, Darrin. *Enemies of the Enlightenment: The French Counter-Enlightenment and the Making of Modernity*. Oxford: Oxford UP, 2001.
Fr. Egon Edgar Nawroth, OP. *Die Sozial- und Wirtschaftsphilosophie des Neoliberalismus*. Heidelberg: F.H. Kerle, ^{2}1962.
Neuner, Peter. *Der Streit um den katholischen Modernismus*. Frankfurt/Main: Suhrkamp, 2009.
Nissing, Hanns-Gregor. *Dichter und Denker: Thomas von Aquin: Eine Einführung in sein Werk und Leben*. München: Pneuma Verlag, 2022.
O'Malley, John W. *What Happened at Vatican II*. Cambridge: Belknap Press, 2008.
Fr. Thomas F. O'Meara, OP. *Church and Culture: German Catholic Theology, 1860–1914*. Notre Dame: U of Notre Dame P, 1991.
Fr. Joseph Owens, C.Ss.R. *Cognition: An Epistemological Inquiry*. Houston: Center for Thomistic Studies, 1992.
Perler, Dominik. *Eine Person sein: Philosophische Debatten im Spätmittelalter*. Frankfurt/Main: Klostermann, 2020.
Perler, Dominik. *Theorien der Intentionalität im Mittelalter*. Frankfurt/Main: Klostermann, 2002.
Perszyk, Ken, ed. *Molinism: The Contemporary Debate*. Oxford: Oxford UP, 2011.
Fr. Heinrich Pesch, SJ. *Lehrbuch der Nationalökonomie*. 5 vols. Freiburg/Br.: Herder, 1905.
Pieper, Joseph. *Scholastik: Gestalten und Probleme mittelalterlicher Philosophie*. München: Kösel, 1986.
Ryan, John A. *Economic Justice: Selections from Distributive Justice and A Living Wage*. Ed. Harlan R. Beckley. Louisville: Westminster John Knox Pres, 1996.

Sarasin, Philipp. "More than just another Specialty: On the Prospects for the History of Knowledge." *Journal for the History of Knowledge* 1:1 (2020), 1–5.
Schatz, Sabine. *Das Gift des Alten Europa und die Arbeiter der Neuen Welt: Zum amerikansichen Hintergrund der Enzyklika* Rerum Novarum *(1891)*. Paderborn: Schöningh, 2011.
Schlagnitweit, Markus. *Einführung in die Katholische Soziallehre: Kompass für Wirtschaft, Politik und Gesellschaft.* Freiburg/Br.: Herder, 2021.
Schönberger, Rolf. *Was ist Scholastik?* Hildesheim: Bernward, 1991.
Seed, Patricia. *American Pentimento: The Invention of Indians and the Pursuit of Riches.* Minneapolis: U of Minnesota P, 2001, 179–81.
Speer, Andreas. *Thomas von Aquin: Die* Summa Theologiae: *Werkinterpretationen.* Berlin: De Gruyter, 2005.
Striet, Magnus. *Für eine Kirche der Freiheit: Den Synodalen Weg konsequent weitergehen.* Freiburg/Br.: Herder, 2022.
Swafford, Andrew D. *Nature and Grace: A New Approach to Thomistic Ressourcement.* Eugene: Pickwick, 2014.
Tischleder, Peter. *Die Staatslehre Leos XIII.* Mönchengladbach: Volksverein, 1925, 331.
Uertz, Rudolf. *Vom Gotteswort zum Menschenrecht: Das katholische Staatsdenken in Deutschland von der Französischen Revolution bis zum Zweiten Vatikanischen Konzil (1789–1965).* Paderborn: Schöningh, 2005.
Fr. Arthur F. Utz, OP. *Freiheit und Bindung des Eigentums.* Heidelberg: F.H. Kehrle Verlag, 1949.
Fr. Arthur F. Utz, OP. –. *Sozialethik.* 4 vols. Heidelberg: F.H. Kerle, 1958.
Van Steenberghen, Fernand. *Erkenntnislehre.* Einsiedeln: Benzinger, 1950.
Fr. Jeffrey von Arx, SJ. *Varieties of Ultramontanism.* Washington, DC: Catholic U of America P, 1998.
Fr. Albert Maria Weiss, OP. *Apologie des Christentums.* 7 vols. Freiburg/Br.: Herder, 1907.
Welskopp, Thomas, and Alan Lessoff. "Fractured Modernity-Fractured Experiences-Fractured Histories: An Introduction." *Fractured Modernity: America Confronts Modern Times, 1890s to 1940s.* Ed. Thomas Welskopp and Alan Lessoff. München: Oldenbourg, 2012, 1–20.

Manfred Siebald
Competing Quests for a Hidden God in John Updike's *Roger's Version*

Abstract: As a part of John Updike's Hawthorne trilogy, *Roger's Version* (1986) recreates the plot of *The Scarlet Letter* (1841) through the eyes of Roger Lambert, a divinity school professor. His Barthian theology insists on God's inscrutability, but is challenged by Dale Kohler, a computer nerd, who appears to be theologically conservative and proposes to prove God's existence by making him visible on a screen. However, the pro-and-anti-secularization forces at play in this conflict – science and skepticism vs. religious orthodoxy and missionary zeal – are not always represented by the "usual suspects," the scientist and the theologian. In fact, they form a web as tangled as that which the adulterous and incestuous affairs of the main characters weave. Thus Updike's novel reflects the complex state of American secularization in the 1980s, but intertextually it also comments on the early stages of secularization in Hawthorne's age and in the Puritan era that *The Scarlet Letter* portrays.

In 1999, writing about "The Future of Faith," John Updike called his age an "age of post-faith." His article, which appeared in *The New Yorker*, suggests a number of "reasons for doubt in God's existence": "His invisibility, His apparent indifference to the torrents of pain and cruelty that history books and the news media report, the persuasive explanations that science offers for almost all phenomena once thought mysterious." In his novel *Roger's Version* (1986), while touching only occasionally on the question of theodicy, Updike correlates the other two of these reasons – God's invisibility and human science – and through their interaction creates a complex picture of secularity in the 1980s.

What is "secularity"? In his monumental *A Secular Age*, Charles Taylor distinguishes three understandings of this concept: (a) that public spaces "have been allegedly emptied of God, or of any reference to ultimate reality," (b) that there is a "falling off of religious belief and practice," and (c) that there is "a move from a society where belief in God is unchallenged . . . , to one in which it is understood to be one option among others" (2–3). John Updike's characters in *Roger's Version* mainly reflect the second and third understandings: the tension between believing and not believing and the diminishing relevance of religious rituals, but also the availability of religious and secular options.

The novel has been called "a brilliant narrative of domesticity, adultery, theology, pornography, computer programming, particle physics, and evolution theory" (Schiff, *Revisited* 95). It is told through the mind of Roger Lambert, a former Methodist minister and now a professor of church history at a university (a thinly disguised Harvard) who, in his cynicism, is reminiscent of the satanic physician Roger Chillingworth in Nathaniel Hawthorne's *The Scarlet Letter* (1850). His antagonist is the 28-year-old IT specialist Dale Kohler, whose name suggests a closeness to Arthur Dimmesdale, the pastor and *paramour* of Chillingworth's young wife Hester Prynne and the father of her illegitimate daughter Pearl. He is a computer nerd who asks Roger Lambert for financial support, because he is convinced that he can prove God's existence by making him visible on a screen. His numerous lengthy debates with Lambert on theology and philosophical questions – basically on whether humankind can search for God and find him – fill many pages.

On the level of physical action, Dale has a stormy affair with Roger's wife Esther – at least that is what the unreliable I-narrator[1] visualizes in great pornographic detail – and Lambert himself commits incest with his niece Verna, a behavior that calls into question the sincerity and consistency of his Christian faith. But it is the contested notion of God's invisibility that forms the center of the plot.

For readers of Hawthorne's classic novel, the title of Updike's book suggests that this is only one 'version' of *The Scarlet Letter* – the narrative perspective being that of Roger Chillingworth. 'Arthur Dimmesdale's version' is offered in Updike's *A Month of Sundays* (1975), in which a minister has to spend time in a rehabilitation facility because of his sexual escapades, and 'Hester Prynne's version' is his epistolary novel *S.* (1988), in which the frustrated wife of a wealthy physician escapes to an Ashram in Arizona in search of spiritual enlightenment. When Updike claimed that *A Month of Sundays*, *Roger's Version*, and *S.* form "a trilogy of comic novels based on Hawthorne's *Scarlet Letter*" ("Unsolicited" 858), he told only half the truth. The satirical account of the demasking of a fake guru in *S.*, for example, has its comic elements indeed, but what it says about the religious gullibility of spiritually empty Americans is a rather sad story. All three novels of the *Scarlet Letter* trilogy might as well be called 'tragic' since all of them deal with "American religion and its decay since Puritan New England," as Updike explained in the same article (859).

For our present purpose, the congruence and the dissimilarities between Updike's trilogy and Hawthorne's original novel are of secondary importance – the

---

[1] Although Updike, in an interview with James A. Schiff, bristled at the notion of the narrator being "unreliable" (131), the improbability and unprovability of many of Roger's conjectures are borne out by the mass of textual evidence, e.g., when he himself talks about his "flexible wife's many pictured infidelities with Dale" (301).

critics have extensively commented on these.[2] Let us look at three phenomena that shed light on the state of American secularization in *Roger's Version:* Roger Lambert's commodification and instrumentalization of religious faith, Dale Kohler's ardent but ultimately failing belief in science, and the intertextual implications of the novel.

"A Semblance of a Backbone": John Updike on Religion

An anonymous reviewer in *Publishers Weekly* claimed that in this novel the conflicting ideas are ancient ones: ". . . reason versus faith; science versus religion . . ." Anyone familiar with Updike's numerous statements about his own spirituality and the state of faith in the United States will not be surprised about the presence of these themes in his fiction. He called himself the son of a father "who believed that facts can't be ignored" and who, at the same time, was a "churchgoing man of a certain piety" – two possibly conflicting strains which, the son thought, awkwardly coexisted in him, too (Plath, ed. 181). Because his father was a practising Christian, John "didn't want to be the Updike to cut the thread" and in the 1990s still went to church, albeit infrequently ("Wir wälzten uns"). As he confessed in his memoirs, this subdued, self-effacing credo had a denominational backdrop:

> . . . having been given a Protestant, Lutheran, rather antinomian Christianity as part of my sociological make-up, I was too timid to discard it. My era was too ideologically feeble to wrest it from me, and Christianity gave me something to write about and a semblance of a backbone, and a place to go to Sunday mornings, when the post offices were closed. (*Self-Consciousness* 246).

Remembering his grandfather, who had not been able to hold onto his pastorate for financial reasons, Updike saw his family caught in the Protestant-capitalist nexus postulated and popularized by Max Weber: "It was the inspiring genius of Calvinism to link prosperity and virtue, to take material thriving as a sign of salvation. A failure of economic fortune must be a moral failure: in my mythic sense of my family the stain of unsuccess ate away at my grandfather's life as if in some tale by Hawthorne" (*Self-Consciousness* 191).

One of the vertebrae in Updike's religious backbone was the Swiss theologian Karl Barth, whose works he read (after reading other authors like G. K. Chesterton

---

[2] Most prominently, Adam Schiff has commented on the intertextual relations. See his *Updike's Version* and his *John Updike Revisited.* See also Bingel, Göske, Wagner, and Newman.

and C. S. Lewis) and "who helped [him] to believe" (*Self-Consciousness* 243). Barth is usually counted among the proponents of Protestant neo-orthodoxy and was one of the chief designers of the Barmen Theological Declaration, which, in 1934, asserted the incompatibility of Christian doctrine and Nazi ideology. As Peter L. Berger has shown,[3] he represented the "deductive possibility" of reacting to the pluralizing tendencies in modern societies (as opposed to the reductive and inductive modes) and stood for "reaffirming tradition" (66). Barth's theology counteracted the subjectivist orientation of nineteenth-century liberal theology by insisting on God's being the *totally Other*, who cannot be reached by human efforts – neither by moral nor by cognitive ones.[4]

"Just Repeating the Creed": Roger's Commodification and Instrumentalization of Faith

John Updike's fascination with the Swiss theologian parallels that of Roger Lambert, who prides himself on having been a convinced follower of Barth since his student days – his copy of *The Word of God and the Word of Man* shows the markings of "a young man who thought that here, definitely and forever, he had found the path, the voice, the style, and the method to save within himself and to present to others the Christian faith" (*Roger's Version* [henceforth *RV*] 41). He is so well-versed in Barth's writings that he can quote literally from them (e.g., *RV* 235), and he proudly recites what sounds like a school's or church's 'Statement of Faith': "The God we care about in this divinity school is the living God, Who moves toward us out of His will and love, and Who laughs at all the towers of Babel we build to Him" (*RV* 22).[5]

David Lodge, in his *New York Times* review, called Lambert "a somewhat dilettantish disciple of Karl Barth" (14). And indeed, he does not shy away from using Barth for jokes: "Barth, in this liberal seminary dominated by gracefully lapsed Unitarians and Quakers, was like sex in junior high school: any mention titillated" (*RV* 28). When it comes to providing funds for Dale's project, Roger identifies himself as "[a] Barthian all the way" and assumes that Barth "would have regarded Dale's project as the most futile and insolent sort of natural theology" (*RV* 235).

---

[3] See chs. 3–5 in Peter L. Berger, *The Heretical Imperative* 66–156.
[4] For a detailed discussion of Updike's indebtedness to Barth, see Webb 145–61.
[5] Significantly, the Biblical Tower of Babel was not built "to" God – like an altar for worshiping – but in order to reach heaven and to ensure the builders' lasting fame on earth.

If God is indeed *totaliter aliter*, and if he is experienced as the "God Who flees, the 'Deus absconditus'" (*RV* 221), he is beyond the grasp of the human mind: "What manner of God is He Who has to be proved?" (*RV* 235).

In moments like these, Lambert sounds like a genuine believer, and as a former Methodist minister he seems suited to represent organized religion and personal faith. In Updike's critical view, such representation does not necessarily require a personal conviction: "Just repeating the creed, that's all you ask, you don't have to turn wine into water, but you do ask that they profess what they're being paid, after all, paid to profess ..." (Battiata). Lambert sounds rather jaded when he admits that he was rather manipulative as a pastor, his work being perfunctory and concentrated on the hollow motions of preaching and blessing: "I was much admired, in my pulpit days. Raise the doubts, then do the reassurances. People have no idea what they are hearing, they just want a kind of verbal music. The major, the minor, and back to the major, then Bless you and keep you, and out the door to the luncheon party" (*RV* 278). When he lost his position, his feeling of "liberation from all the conformities expected from ministers" made him ignore Thanksgiving and even Christmas paraphernalia like the Christmas tree (*RV* 99). The rather devastating picture of a religiosity that is limited to certain traditional behavioral patterns and Lambert's unflattering description of church life with its "tribal feasts" (*RV* 91) and "holiday observances" (*RV* 94) are reminiscent of the sentiment of the autobiographical Updike, who in his memoirs confessed to a "hurt hostility, . . . an anti-Christian or at least anti-ecclesiastical bias toward the church itself . . ." (*Self-Consciousness* 156).[6]

But Lambert lambasts not only the superficiality of organized religion and its adherents. As a professor of theology specialized in early Christian heresies,[7] he is "kind of in the religion business" (*RV* 66), as his niece puts it, and teaches students whom he classifies as "the hopeful, the deluded, and the docile" (*RV* 1). And he cynically comments on the futility of theological education in seminaries: "We take in saints and send out ministers, workers in the vineyard of inevitable anxiety and discontent. The death of Christianity has long been foreseen but there will always be churches to serve as storehouses for the perennial harvest of human unhappiness" (*RV* 122).

Finally, whoever argues that a representative of academic theology should be a religious person or even a model of moral comportment, has to conclude that Lambert clearly fails in this respect. According to Updike, Roger "'does have his mo-

---

6 See a similar statement in the interview by Katherine Stephen (Plath, ed. 188).
7 His wife accuses him of keeping an ironic distance to his subject, which makes the historical details of doctrine seem "funny," and the fights about "ridiculous distinctions" a "cruel joke" (218).

ments. You know, ideally, Roger should be a stern atheist; it would make him more of a villain to be an atheist teaching divinity students. But I didn't have it quite in me to make him that, so he, too, has his little epiphanies'" (Battiata). Apart from that, the conservative theological leanings he professes to have are conspicuously out of sync with his situational ethics: his theology is divorced from his morality (de Bellis 49). By insisting on the futility of any intellectual attempts to locate God, he tries to "save within himself and to present to others the Christian faith" (*RV* 41). At the same time, he wants to belittle the respectability of his supposed sexual rival Dale and his computer project, calling it "obscene cosmological prying" (*RV* 235) and "blasphemous" (*RV* 254). There is enough evidence in the long discussions to prove that for Lambert the doctrine of God's inscrutability is more of an argumentative lever to achieve his goals than a personal conviction.

"I'm all for science": Dale's Oscillating Faith

If the outlines of Roger's different roles are somewhat oscillating and hazy, Dale's are even more so. The unappetizing supper he carries to the university's computer lab on the night of his pivotal efforts symbolizes the incongruousness of his personality traits, plans, and impulses in a kind of gastronomic oxymoron: "... a cooling hot-pastrami sandwich in a grease-soaked paper bag, plus a carton of high-fat milk and a pair of broken oatmeal cookies in a plastic envelope" (*RV* 244). This instance of 'objective correlative' suggests that, in Lambert's view, the computer experiment is as unsavory and paradoxical as the food that is supposed to nourish the researcher.

Dale has a fantastic command of information technology, and his knowledge of biology and chemistry is equally detailed – much too specific to be digested at the pace at which he talks about it. As the reviewer of *Publishers Weekly* complained: "... there is more arcane computerology here than readers, including his most devoted, can digest by force-feeding, and probably more theology as well." In the discussions between the scientist and the theologian the reader is drawn into an "intersection of systems of erudition" (Updike, "'Special Message'" 857).

Yet, in spite of his scientific competence, Dale's outlandish attempt to technologically prove God disintegrates incrementally. He may truculently insist, "Facts are facts" (*RV* 9), when he first meets Lambert, but the facts he hopes to uncover refuse to turn up. In the course of the long night at the lab Dale's software "DEUS" does indeed produce something on the screen that resembles a face. As Lambert imagines it (there is no independent witness at hand), "a face seems to stare, a mournful face. A ghost of a face, a matter of milliseconds" (*RV* 263). This image does not match traditional human expectations: It has "long hair but no beard;

the traditional iconography is evidently wrong" (*RV* 263). In addition to this face, Dale has a brief vision of a hand, which the narrator tentatively associates with "a hand nailed limp to the cross" (*RV* 268). All these impressions obviously refer to the countless artistic renderings of Christ's crucifixion, but significantly, the computer image is made the standard by which to measure the veracity of any pictures of Christ's passion.

When Dale has his brief glimpse of the face, his confidence has already dwindled to surmises like "There is something there," and to self-doubts, because what he sees is definitely less than he set out to see, and "not quite enough to base a theology on" (*RV* 265). He begins to fear (in Lambert's introspective words) "that in seeking God along these pathways he takes a wrong turn and encounters a false god" (*RV* 267). He gradually develops a deep skepticism about his abilities, as when he confesses to Lambert: "It's all still so vague in my mind I'm not sure I'm the one should be attempting this; I feel too stupid sometimes . . ." (*RV* 193).[8] And science (as represented by Lambert's neighbor Myron Kriegman) laughs at the fissures and gaps and non-sequiturs in Dale's reasoning.

In his role as a computer scientist – traditionally a fact-and-figure-driven occupation – Dale seems predestined to represent religious doubt and secularization. In his role as a professing Christian, however, he claims that his self-appointed job is to prove the existence of God. Apparently, he never gives a thought to the unbiblical nature of this undertaking: The Jewish Bible and, in accordance with it, Christian theology teach the impossibility of humans' seeing God's face; after all, in the Book of Exodus Yahweh tells Moses: "Thou canst not see my face: for there shall no man see me, and live" (Exodus 33:20 KJV). When Dale boasts: "God can't hide no more" (*RV* 20), he seems to be in direct defiance of this Old Testament injunction and even seems to relish trespassing it.

Thus, Dale's attitude toward God is not that of a devout evangelical believer who stands in awe before an almighty Creator, but his notion of whom he searches is that of an "unseen opponent" (*RV* 261) whom he has to manipulate electronically to make him visible. In fact, he turns God into an object, a mere "something" – a "presence cringing within the mazy electronic alleyways of the computer" (*RV* 267), and he refers to it – in the narrator's spelling – with a capitalized neutral pronoun: "It hates Dale's seeking It, and will extract vengeance if he finds It" (*RV* 267). In fact, God has ceased to be a living, independent subject for Dale, but has been

---

[8] And toward the novel's end he admits: "Maybe the whole thing is too big for me" (315), the theories at the bottom of his experiment seem "hatefully irrelevant and obscure" to him (320), and the "almost-magic" numbers appear as "illusions, ripples of nothingness" (325).

turned into a scientific object, which is "pinned and wriggling on the wall" like the lyrical I in T.S. Eliot's "The Love Song of J. Alfred Prufrock."

This is the more remarkable because his ostensibly conservative discourse in the initial scenes seems to come from a man rooted firmly in the Christian faith. Asked whether he considers himself a Christian, he answers, almost mechanically: "Absolutely. Christ is my Savior" (*RV* 22). Indeed, much of his religious talk sounds like a recital of dogmas – as when he defines the God he wishes to make visible: "There's only one kind of God. God the Creator, Maker of Heaven and Earth" (*RV* 9). And when asked where Christ figures in his attempt to prove God "via natural theology," his answer is quite orthodox, too: ". . . wherever the Creed says He figures, as God made Man, come down to redeem our sins" (*RV* 186).

Almost automatically, therefore, Roger puts him into the corner of fundamentalism. He hates Dale's insufferable "pious smile" (*RV* 6), counting him among the "Jesus addicts" (*RV* 8) and the "do-gooding born-agains" (*RV* 96), and calling him a "Jesus freak" (*RV* 190), who talks in the "insufferable way of evangelists" (*RV* 182–83), and in a "sick-Christian way" (*RV* 331). Fooled by Lambert's unreliable narrative, many reviewers and critics have followed suit and spoken of Dale's "steely fundamentalist fervour" (Nicholas Spice), called him a pious Christian (Wagner 957), "a fundamentalist Christian" (Lodge) or found in him a "born-again Christian's zeal for prayer and biblical quotation" (Schiff, *Updike's Version* 60). For Roger, Dale's eyes show "the missionary light, the will to convert" (*RV* 92), and he has the "extravagant plan to redeem mankind from the intellectual possibility that God is not there" (*RV* 257). He himself claims that he tries to "give God the opportunity to *speak*" (*RV* 232). This plan displays an attitude of presumptuous, almost condescending generosity: Dale seems to think that God is in need of being helped in his self-revelation.

But his apparently missionary project can also be seen as the exact opposite, as a protection against the secularism in himself. Because he is not sure at all of his faith – his lover Esther states that "[h]e's losing his faith" (*RV* 237) [9] – he tries to prove God empirically, in order to obtain something like his own personal certainty. Ultimately, Dale admits that his faith is far from being firm and secure, and what initially appeared to be an apologetic attempt to convince the unbelieving has actually been an attempt at self-healing all along.

In spite of his initial pronouncements, he occasionally admits his preference for non-transcendental thinking: "I'm all for science . . . whatever it can show

---

[9] Daniel Göske considers Dale's religious and psychological degeneration and his scientific downfall to be initiated and accelerated by Roger's machinations (including his manipulative role in providing Dale with the academic grant that, in turn, puts a debilitating pressure on him [158]).

us; I love science, and never meant to get into any of . . . this divinity business" (*RV* 225). De Blessis comments: "Oddly enough, Kohler is shown to lack Lambert's intuitive belief in God's existence; Kohler, by contrast, is a doubting Thomas who demands ocular proof" (*RV* 384). One may discern here what David Ray Griffin has called "a transference of religious devotion from one kind of religious object to another – from one that transcends the world, at least in part, to one that is fully worldly, that is, secular" (Griffin 5). The two objects may look equally prominent at the beginning, but in the long run Dale seems to care more for technological success than for spiritual certainty.

A "Slow Process": Earlier Phases of Secularization

While the novel's plot shows the intrinsic contradictions in the personalities, spiritualities and social roles of both the protagonist and the antagonist to be symptoms of contemporaneous American religiosity, the literary contexts of *Roger's Version* evoke earlier stages of American history: The intertextual connections between a narrative set in 1980s America and one which, in the middle of the nineteenth century, looked back at seventeenth-century New England point to the various stages of secularization in these different phases of American history.

In an interview, Updike remarked that *The Scarlet Letter* is "not merely a piece of fiction, it is a myth by now" – a myth that he wanted to "update" (Schiff, *Updike's Version* 132). Apparently, he had not a revisionist reading of Hawthorne's plot elements and character features in mind, but rather a version of the old "What if?" game that historians love to play: "What if Pearl Harbor had not happened?" or "What if Paul Revere had brought other news?"[10] In Updike's case, the novel asks the question: 'What if Roger, Hester, and Arthur had not lived in the fictional middle of the seventeenth century, but at the end of the twentieth century?'

Updike's source text, *The Scarlet Letter*, takes us to what Mark Noll called "the long life and final collapse of the Puritan canopy" (*America's God* 31–50) and reminds us that secularization in America started as early as in the seventeenth century. The majority of first-generation settlers in Puritan New England presumably were devout and theologically conservative Christians, who clung to their congregationalist beliefs and made them the basis of their ecclesiastical, intellectual and political life – so much so that for a long time their commonwealth was labeled a theocracy. Younger generations of historians have questioned this understanding and maintained that "early America does not deserve to be considered uniquely,

---

[10] See the book edited by Cowley as an example of such informed speculations.

distinctly or even predominantly Christian .... There is no lost golden age to which American Christians may return" (Noll, Hatch, and Marsden 17). The "public spaces" (Taylor) may have been still largely under religious control in early colonial times, but Hawthorne's novel reveals the fissures in the seemingly monolithic edifice of Puritan orthodoxy.

In illustrating what he calls "[t]his slow process of secularization," Emory Elliott lists (a) congregationalism's tendency to create locally divergent forms of church polity; (b) an ensuing gradual waning of ministerial influence on political decisions; (c) the growing number of immigrants who came not because they had a faith which they felt was threatened in Europe, but simply because of a land shortage at home and the prospect of financial gain in the colonies; and (d) "growing religious uncertainties among the young" (255). Reverberations of these developments can be found, for example, in the many specimens of the genuinely American sermonic genre of the Jeremiad. It followed a pattern found in the texts of the Biblical prophet Jeremiah, as he tried to call the people of Israel to repentance: The sermons presented "a rhetorical formula that included recalling the courage and piety of the founders, lamenting recent and present ills, and crying out for a return to the original conduct and zeal" (Elliott 257). That the first generation of Puritan settlers considered it necessary to admonish the next generation in such a way suggests that they perceived what Taylor calls "the falling off of religious belief and practice" (2).

The factors that accelerated the gradual slackening of Puritan rule and led to its final demise were religious movements such as the Great Awakening of the 1730s and 1740s, political ones like the American Revolution with its separation of church and state, and philosophical ones like the Enlightenment, which spawned the theological liberalism that furthered the development of Universalism and Unitarianism in the early nineteenth century and subsequently of Transcendentalism. All this also led to the religious indifference – the "signing off" – which Barbara Packer has found to have increased in the middle of the century.

Roger Lambert does not only echo Roger Chillingworth's version of the plot of *The Scarlet Letter* but is characterized by attitudes in religious matters that are reminiscent of Nathaniel Hawthorne, the author, who has been called "a grimly honest storyteller fascinated by the perversity in human affairs central to his hereditary Calvinism" (Kazin 33). Having descended from staunch Puritans himself,[11] he hovered between a covert Puritan sense of right and wrong and an overt Puritan-bashing. And like his neighbor and colleague Herman Melville, he admitted to

---

11 The uncomfortable fact that one of his ancestors – John Hathorne – had played a part in the Salem witchcraft trials of 1692 made him change the spelling of his family name.

wavering between faith and doubt, between observance and deviance. For example, he confessed to a weakened Christian piety and church-going practice:

> Doubts may flit around me, or seem to close their evil wings and settle down, but so long as I imagine that the earth is hallowed, and the light of heaven retains its sanctity on the Sabbath – while that blessed sunshine lives within me – never can my soul have lost the instinct of its faith. If it have gone astray, it will return again. . . . It must suffice that, though my form be absent, my inner man goes constantly to church, while many, whose bodily presence fills the accustomed seats, have left their souls at home. ("Sunday" 16–17)

Somehow, this is reminiscent of the "very regrettable state of mind" that C. S. Lewis describes in *An Experiment in Criticism:* "The Puritan conscience works on without the Puritan theology – like millstones grinding nothing; like digestive juices working on an empty stomach and producing ulcers" (10). Hawthorne's attitude toward his Puritan ancestors was not altogether negative, but he grinningly appreciated having left them behind: "Let us thank God for having given us such ancestors; and let each successive generation thank him, not less fervently, for being one step further from them in the march of ages" ("Main-Street" 68).

Some Bottom Lines

Roger's Version leaves the reader with an image of secularization in the U.S. in the 1980s, even if the unreliability of the narrator and the fictionality of the plot preclude any objectivity, of course. The narrative deconstruction of old social and spiritual roles, of religious certitudes and assumptions, starts with the old antagonism between religion and science, but ends in a pronounced pluralism of religious and secular positions: The novel suggests that secularization does not necessarily consist in an overt anticlericalism, but can result in self-contradictory modes of thinking and living, and in a habitual religious uncertainty. In 1988, Updike characterized himself as "just one more of the millions of more or less lukewarm, but not quite cold, Protestants that fill this country" (Plath, ed. 208). It is this in-betweenness that marks Updike's fictional world.

– In theological terms, the novel underscores the impossibility of finding any scientific proof of God's existence – after all, Dale's efforts fail, and Lambert's Barthian claim that God is utterly inscrutable is vindicated. Ironically, the project of making God visible turns out to be an intellectual challenge and a competitive effort for Dale, rather than a personal spiritual need or an apologetic project. And science, the very player that used to serve the proponents of secularism in undermining Christian beliefs, is seemingly utilized by Dale in order to save them.

- That means that the fault lines between ideological forces are not as clearly defined as in the past – science and religion are brought into a fickle alliance, with technology becoming the temporary handmaid of religion. Thus, the battleground once fought over by Galileo and the Grand Inquisition is turned into a marketplace, where arguments are traded, and that leads to a stalemate between 'scientific revolution' and 'divine revelation.'
- In the realm of religiosity, the traditional thought patterns and spiritual attitudes have changed places. In the beginning, the scientist seems to be much more devout than the minister, and the minister much more skeptical than the scientist, but as the plot unfolds, they do change places off and on, and in the end none of them prevails.
- Lastly, the plot exposes a marked discrepancy between religious doctrine and practical ethical behavior. The adulterous couples do not live up to the moral precepts inherent in Christian teaching, but that does not put them into a secular bower of bliss. In one of the last scenes, Roger locates his moral existence between "the rotten wood of the old prohibitions" and "our Godless freedoms that become, with daily use, so oddly trivial" (*RV* 348).

As Robert Detweiler says, the novel "reflects secularized Americans' uncertain and conflicting attitudes toward religion" (93). What Charles Taylor calls a "move from a society where belief in God is unchallenged and indeed, unproblematic, to one in which it is understood to be one option among others" (3) has led to a society in which, instead of the clearly distinguishable and assignable attitudes of the theologian and the scientist, we witness a multi-voiced chorus singing the hymns of scientism, atheism, evangelicalism, religious indifference and secular humanism. And they all sing their individuals parts – all at the same time.

Works Cited

Barth, Karl. *Kurze Erklärung des Römerbriefs* [1918, 1921]. Gütersloh: Siebenstern, 1956.
Battiata, Mary. "John Updike, In Restless Pursuit." *Washington Post* 30 Sept. 1986. N.p.
Berger, Peter L. *The Heretical Imperative: Contemporary Possibilities of Religious Affirmation.* New York: Anchor Press, 1979.
Berryman, Charles. "Faith or Fiction: Updike and the American Renaissance." *John Updike and Religion: The Sense of the Sacred and the Motions of Grace.* Ed. James Yerkes. Grand Rapids: Eerdmans, 1999. 195–207.
Bingel, Hanna. *Fictions of Spirituality: Die narrative Verhandlung von Religiosität und spiritueller Sinnsuche in ausgewählten US-amerikanischen Gegenwartsromanen.* CAT 5. Trier: WVT, 2013.
Cowley, Robert, ed. *What If? America: Eminent Historians Imagine What Might Have Been.* New York: Putnam, 2003.

Detweiler, Robert. *Breaking the Fall: Religious Readings of Contemporary Fiction.* Houndsmill: Macmillan, 1989.

Elliott, Emory. "The Jeremiad." *The Cambridge History of American Literature.* Ed. Sacvan Bercovitch. Vol. 1. Cambridge, MA: 1994. 255–78.

Göske, Daniel. "'An essay about kinds of beliefs': Updike's theologische Erzählkunst in *Roger's Version.*" *Spiritualität und Transzendenz in der modernen englischsprachigen Literatur.* Ed. Susanne Bach. Paderborn: Schöningh, 2001. 145–66.

Griffin, David Ray. "Introduction: Postmodern Spirituality and Society." *Spirituality and Society: Postmodern Visions.* Ed. David Ray Griffin. New York: SUNY Press, 1988. 1–31.

Gross, Terry. "Fresh Air with Terry Gross." *Conversations with John Updike.* Ed. James Plath. Jackson: UP of Mississippi, 1994. 207–16.

Hawthorne, Nathaniel. *The Scarlet Letter.* Norton Critical Edition. Ed. Seymour Gross et al. 3rd ed. New York: Norton, 1988.

Hawthorne, Nathaniel. "Main-Street." *The Snow-Image and Uncollected Tales.* Centenary Edition 11. Columbus: Ohio State UP, 1974.

Hawthorne, Nathaniel. "Sunday at Home." *Twice-Told Tales.* New York: NY Publishing Company, 1895. 15–22.

Kazin, Alfred. *God and the American Writer.* New York: Knopf, 1997.

Lewis, C. S. *An Experiment in Criticism.* Cambridge: Cambridge UP, 1961.

Lodge, David. Rev. of *Roger's Version. New York Times* 31 Aug. 1986. https://www.nytimes.com/1986/08/31/books/rogers-version.html, Accessed March 31st, 2023.

Lundin, Roger, and Mark Noll, eds. *Voices from the Heart: Four Centuries of American Piety.* Grand Rapids: Eerdmans, 1987.

Newman, Judie. "Guru Industries, Ltd.: Red-Letter Religion in Updike's *S.*" *John Updike and Religion: The Sense of the Sacred and the Motions of Grace.* Ed. James Yerkes. Grand Rapids: Eerdmans, 1999. 221–48.

Noll, Mark A. *America's God: From Jonathan Edwards to Abraham Lincoln.* New York: Oxford UP, 2002.

Noll, Mark A., Nathan O. Hatch, and George M. Marsden. *The Search for Christian America.* 2nd ed. Colorado Springs: Helmers and Howard, 1989.

Packer, Barbara. "Signing Off: Religious Indifference in America." *There before Us: Religion, Literature, and Culture from Emerson to Wendell Berry.* Ed. Roger Lundin. Grand Rapids: Eerdmans, 2007. 1–22.

Plath, James, ed. *Conversations with John Updike.* Jackson: UP of Mississippi, 1994.

Review of *Roger's Version*, by John Updike. *Publishers Weekly* 8 September 1986. https://www.publishersweekly.com/978-0-394-55435-8, Accessed March 31st, 2023.

Sanoff, Alvin P. "Writers 'Are Really Servants of Reality.'" *Conversations with John Updike.* Ed. James Plath. Jackson: UP of Mississippi, 1994. 181–85.

Schiff, James A. *John Updike Revisited.* New York: Twayne, 1998.

Schiff, James A. *Updike's Version: Rewriting* The Scarlet Letter. Columbia: U of Missouri P, 1992.

Spice, Nicholas. "Underparts." *London Review of Books* 6 November 1986.

Stephen, Katherine. "John Updike Still Finds Things to Say about Life, Sex, and Religion." *Conversations with John Updike.* Ed. James Plath. Jackson: UP of Mississippi, 1994. 186–91.

Taylor, Charles. *A Secular Age.* Cambridge, MA: Harvard UP, 2007.

Updike, John. *A Month of Sundays.* New York: Knopf, 1975.

Updike, John. "A 'Special Message' for the Franklin Library's First Edition Society Printing of *Roger's Version* (1986)." *Odd Jobs: Essays and Criticism.* New York: Kopf, 1991. 856–58.

Updike, John. "Hawthorne's Creed." *Hugging the Shore: Essays and Criticism.* New York: Knopf 1983. 73–80.

Updike, John. "Realism and the Novel: An Interview with John Updike." *Dialogue* 4.4 (1971): 85–92.

Updike, John. *Roger's Version.* New York: Fawcett Crest, 1986.

Updike, John. *S.* London: Penguin Classics, 2006.

Updike, John. *Self-Consciousness: Memoirs.* New York: Fawcett Crest, 1989.

Updike, John. "The Future of Faith: Confessions of a Churchgoer." *New Yorker* 29 November 1999. https://www.newyorker.com/magazine/1999/11/29/the-future-of-faith, Accessed March 31st, 2023.

Updike, John. "Unsolicited Thoughts on *S.* (1988)." *Odd Jobs: Essays and Criticism.* New York: Knopf, 1991. 858–59.

Updike, John. "Wir wälzten uns in heiligen Säften." *Der Spiegel* 4 September 1994. https://www.spiegel.de/kultur/wir-waelzten-uns-in-heiligen-saeften-a-c087c000-0002-0001-0000-000009288597, Accessed March 31st, 2023.

Wagner, Peter. "*Roger's Version.*" *Kindlers Neues Literaturlexikon.* Ed. Walter Jens. Vol. 16. München: Kindler, 1991. 956–57.

Webb, Stephen H. "Writing as a Reader of Karl Barth: What Kind of Religious Writer Is John Updike Not?" *John Updike and Religion: The Sense of the Sacred and the Motions of Grace.* Ed. James Yerkes. Grand Rapids: Eerdmans, 1999. 145–61.

Yerkes, James, ed. *John Updike and Religion: The Sense of the Sacred and the Motions of Grace.* Grand Rapids: Eerdmans, 1999.

Carmen Birkle
Science and Religion in U.S.-American Pandemic Literature

Abstract: In this paper, I discuss the intersection of science, religion, and pandemics. What science and religion share during pandemics is the promise, so it seems, of a way out, of a solution, of a life without the pandemic. I turn to novels revolving around pandemics: Lawrence Wright's *The End of October* (2020), Robin Cook's *Pandemic* (2018), and Connie Willis's *Doomsday Book* (1992). While Wright and Cook focus on fictional pandemics, Willis travels back to the time of the Black Death in 1348. All novels evoke religion, whether as an institution, through representatives, or as a belief system. Moreover, in these novels, the protagonists are (medical) scientists who have given up on any form of Christian religion but constantly have to confront their own doubts and longings for spirituality. Medical science and religion seem to be the two competing forces of support during a pandemic. My reading of the novels has been inspired by Charles Taylor's notion of a secular age.

1 Science, Religion, and Pandemics

The idea of "Religion in the Secular Age" seems to presuppose that we are living in a secular age and wondering, presumably, about the demise of religion. Yet, most scholars emphasize, as does David True, that this label implies that there is simply no "secure and unchallenged position, either religious or secular" (xii) anymore. Rather, this age "is characterized by plural and contested identities" that struggle with each other (True xv). This development is visible – not exclusively but also – in times of crisis, for example, right after 9/11 in the United States with a resurgence of religion, and an increase in the role of religion when we look at cultural clashes and wars, as in the almost traditional conflict in Ireland between Catholics and Protestants or in inner-Islamic confrontations. Pippa Norris and Ronald Inglehart in their 2004 study *Sacred and Secular* "find that in those contexts in which the vulnerability of the populace has been diminished by economic prosperity and social welfare policies intended to relieve distress in hard times, the demand for religiosity has declined. Where uncertainty and, indeed, chaos prevail, the search for solace persists" (Torpey 284).

> As Norris and Inglehart note, religion in the United States remains strongest among the poorest and most vulnerable segments of the society. There is also a regional inflection of religiosity in the United States; the Northeast and the West Coast tend toward irreligion, while the Midwest and South tend toward greater religiosity. A country of some 300 million inhabitants, the United States displays marked divergencies among some of its constituent populations, and some of those groups betray a more "European" set of attitudes toward religion. (Torpey 289–90)

A pandemic is certainly such a moment of chaos. Scholars have also argued that religion has become more of "a private matter" (Taylor 1). Yet this depends on where you look. Even in the United States, where state and church powers are separated, almost all presidential inaugural addresses raise religious issues. For example, in his first inauguration address in 2009, Barack Obama depicted the U.S. as a nation of "Christians and Muslims, Jews and Hindus, and non-believers" (329). The famous Puritan "city-upon-a-hill" model for the United States, used in John Winthrop's sermon "A Model of Christian Charity" (1630), has been claimed by numerous presidents to emphasize American exceptionalism. Overall, as Jonathan Beasley from Harvard Divinity School points out, "28 percent of adults in the U.S. see their faith as having gotten stronger during the pandemic—though that number is strongly driven by white evangelicals, 49 % of whom say the pandemic has strengthened their faith" (Podcast).

However, in fiction, medical scientists seem to have a strong tendency to turn away from religion and, as I will show with reference to Robin Cook's *Pandemic* (2018) and Lawrence Wright's *The End of October* (2020), have been taken aback by religious fundamentalism and its self-righteousness, for example, in the treatment of homosexuality. At the same time, crises such as the current as well as previous pandemics have triggered scientists' reflections on and renewed turn toward some form of spirituality, as Wright's *The End of October* reveals. Connie Willis's *Doomsday Book* (1992) juxtaposes (medical) science and religion in the year 2054 with the experiences of a pandemic in the present and with the Black Death in 1348.

"What does it mean," to speak with Charles Taylor, "to say that we live in a secular age" (1)? While Taylor speaks about Western cultures, Lawrence Wright, for example, also addresses forms of Islam, those of Muslims in Saudi Arabia and Indonesia, whose representatives show a strong personal and public belief. In Western countries, pandemics force people to rethink spirituality and belief. What people are looking for in such crises is religion as both spirituality and institution. Fundamentalists believe that God will save them so that many distrust vaccination or any protective measures such as social distancing, avoiding large gatherings (such as church services), or masking. During a pandemic, the body is "medicaliz[ed]," which, according to Taylor, turns us into "objects of science," that is, "medicalization alters our phenomenology of lived experience" (740), and, in order to maintain control, humans look for scapegoats to be held responsible so that we can "wage war on evil," "battle against axes of evil and networks of terror" (743). Ultimately, "we discover to our surprise and horror that we are reproducing the evil we defined ourselves against" (743). Scientists who believe that "religious [...] views are erroneous" (768) will recognize that they, too, respond "to a transcendent reality" (768), as we will see in *The End of October.* Too much religion or "religious faith can be dangerous" (Taylor 769), as Cook shows in his novel, and, in a worst-case scenario, can lead to "polarization of conflict, even war" (769). But the same can be true for atheists: "Idolatry [for religion or science] breeds violence" (769).

All three novels in their storytelling focus on the intersection of fictional (and real) pandemics, medical science, and religion, and were written before the COVID-19 pandemic. In these novels, the protagonists are (medical) scientists who have given up on any form of Christian religion but constantly have to confront their own doubts and longings for spirituality. Overall, medical science and religion seem to be two competing forces of support during a pandemic.

2 Science and Religious Fundamentalism

Robin Cook (*1940), a medical doctor (who trained at Columbia University and worked at Harvard University) and author, has been known ever since his 1977 novel *Coma* for his many popular medical thrillers. As a doctor, Cook has the necessary knowledge to pack medical expertise, developments, and potential hazards into his gripping fictionalizations of virulent medical questions. *Pandemic* (2018) is based on the recent insight into the genome-editing tool CRISPR/CAS9[1] and subsequent ethical questions, and features the sabotage of a profitable and efficient application of this technology, manipulated through the infiltration of a so-called PERV or gammaretrovirus B, a virus "'known to infect human cells'" (345), into hearts that were artificially grown in pigs and then transplanted into human bodies. While these transplantations are successful, all recipients die as a consequence of this act of sabotage. The protagonist Dr. Jack Stapleton is both a doctor – Chief Medical Examiner – and a detective, who does the autopsies of the victims and follows all the clues until he figures out who the perpetrators are, who themselves,

---

1 CRISPR: Clustered Regularly Interspaced Short Palindromic Repeats; CAS9: CRISP-associated protein 9.

however, have already developed "'both a rapid test to detect the virus in an asymptomatic patient and an ex-vivo method of eliminating it'" (346–47).

While ethical questions are myriad in this novel, religion is very rarely an issue. However, its absence explains why Jack cannot rest until he has found the solution to this case. Its absence reveals the protagonist's position toward any system of belief. The first time Dr. Stapleton's rejection of religion is brought up is in a conversation with one of his colleagues just before an autopsy: "More than anyone at the OCME, Vinnie knew just how irreverent Jack Stapleton could be. Jack was not a religious man after his first wife and two young daughters had been killed in a commuter plane crash. He couldn't imagine a Christian God would let such a terrible thing happen" (21). Personal loss and suffering lead him to question the existence of a benevolent God. This traumatic experience of such evil in the world turns him into an atheist who believes in nothing but science and is unable to accept any theodicy that defends God or providence.

In order to understand whether the current deaths could be the first signs of a pandemic outbreak, he begins to look for parallels with the 1918 influenza pandemic, during which millions of people died because of, as scholars today assume, "'their own immune systems going wild in what is called a cytokine storm'" (36). Stapleton finds clues guiding him to recent heart transplants and to the faked and medically impossible donor stories. Carol Weston Stewart, the initial victim, who dies on the New York subway, supposedly received her heart from a young man who died in a motorcycle accident, which, as Stapleton finds out, just does not make sense. When visiting Carol's parents in search of more information about Carol's heart condition, he encounters Marge and Robert Stewart, and is immediately struck by their "striking and uncanny resemblance to the couple in Grant Wood's painting *American Gothic* [1930], minus the pitchfork" (209). This unfavorable impression of average Americans is a foreboding of what Jack then learns. Carol's father is described as "as stern-looking as his wife and wearing a clerical collar. He had a tight, almost lipless mouth" (209).[2] Long ago, they expelled their daughter from their house. The father's response to Stapleton's question about Carol's health problems unveils the couple's fundamentalist belief in a punishing God: "'It was God's will. We know she had problems with her heart'" (209). Carol's sexual preference as a lesbian turns out to be the reason for this religiously motivated expulsion: "'Her behavior from age thirteen on was an affront to God. Homosexuality is an abomination and a violation of the Seventh Commandment.

---

2 Whether this iconic painting is a dedication to Iowans or a satire of small-scale rural life has never been firmly determined and remains ambivalent. But it certainly evokes "Puritan primness" with the pitchfork as a "devilish motif" (Güner).

We could not have that in our house'" (209–10), is how her father explains Carol's seemingly moral evil (see Pearson 855), which, for them, provoked God's vengeance. The father's clerical collar indicates his religious office. This connection insinuates that Jack Stapleton is facing the quintessential American couple that sees God's hand in Carol's punishment. What Jack does not associate with them, but what can be picked up from the description, is Puritanism, as, for example, presented in Nathaniel Hawthorne's novels and short stories, which are extremely critical of Puritanism. The Puritan Endicott in Hawthorne's "The Maypole of Merry Mount," for example, is described as a "'[s]tern man'" (889), an "iron man" (889). This stern religion does not allow for the merriment, joy, and celebrations of the Merry Mounters. For Carol's parents, her lesbianism is sinful, so that she becomes a "Sinner[] in the Hands of an Angry God" (1741), as Jonathan Edwards would say. Jack does not tell the couple about Carol's death because, as he believes, that "would only harden their self-righteous, narrow-minded indignation about her sexual orientation" (210). The reader is privy to Jack's final deliberations and his aversion "to hyper-religious people, no matter what the religion" (210). His own upbringing was Catholic, which turned him into an "agnostic, wanting to believe there was an organizing, moral force but unsure of what it was. Then, after the catastrophe with his first family, he'd become an avowed atheist, fully convinced a loving God wouldn't kill children or give them neuroblastoma or autism" (210). Jack's development from an imperfect Catholic to an agnostic who doubts, and then an atheist who rejects the existence of God, is confirmed by his meeting with the Stewarts.

3 Science, Religion, and the Human Ego

Lawrence Wright's (*1947) *The End of October* presents a number of characters who grapple with questions of faith and religion during one of the severest pandemics ever. I suggest distinguishing between "'active' and 'latent' religiosity" (Torpey 280) without ignoring their occasional co-occurrence or sequential development. In Wright's novel, characters with different attachments to religion and faith reveal how problematic it actually is to speak of a secular age. Published in 2020, this medical thriller touches upon religion on a number of occasions that are all directly connected to the protagonist Dr. Henry Parsons,[3] a microbiol-

---

[3] Interestingly, Henry Parsons is also the name of Henry Parsons Crowell, founder of the Quaker Oats Company and a respected Christian businessman. This could, of course, be coincidental or intentional.

ogist and epidemiologist as well as "deputy director for infectious diseases" at the Centers for Disease Control and Prevention, in Atlanta (8–9). Upon the outbreak of an unknown disease in a camp in Indonesia, Henry flies there while, simultaneously, terrorists attack Rome with biological warfare. As a consequence, the Italian minister suggests "mass expulsions of Muslims" (9). This first mention of a religion becomes relevant later in the context of the spreading of the virus, although the two incidents are unrelated. Henry's first encounter in Indonesia is with its prime minister, who had "recently taken the hijab, an indication of how far the country was drifting toward religious conservatism" (18).

Henry's official mission as a representative of the World Health Organization ultimately makes it possible for him to visit the camp, which is, as his Indonesian driver tells him, for gay people who have been interned there for their own protection because otherwise they would be tortured and killed by religious extremists in the name of religion (20). The camp inmates' only hopes are prayers and Henry, who, however, is unable to help them. The Kongoli camp gives the unknown virus its name, and Henry's detective work begins once he is out of quarantine and can revive his knowledge of past pandemics. How vast his task is can easily be noted in his thoughts about the "total number of viruses on the planet," which is "estimated to be a hundred million times more than the number of stars in the universe" (55). "Diseases," as he knows, "have a history of stirring up conspiracies" (62), and "the identification of the first victims of the disease – gay Muslims with HIV – was likely to create a pandemic of its own – one of hysteria" (62). Henry is constantly confronted with religious implications. I will first focus on how the virus is actually spread, namely at the huge Muslim hajj; then, I will analyze Henry's and Prince Majid's serious conversation about religion, and briefly look at his wife Jill's and his daughter Helen's beliefs, in order to finally discuss in more detail Henry's atheism and then gradual doubts.

Henry and Prince Majid, a Muslim, head of the Health Ministry and a medical scientist, go to Mecca because Henry's driver in Indonesia, Bambang, has gone to the hajj, one of the main annual Muslim pilgrimages to Mecca in Saudi Arabia.[4] The millions of participants every year, as also discussed in the novel, prove that this event has not lost its relevance both as a religious and a traditional experience. It consists of rituals that need to be followed. In 2020 at the beginning of the COVID-19 pandemic, as well as in the novel, the hajj was not canceled but the numbers were limited. The novel refers to about three million worshippers, and the infected Bambang is among them. Readers look at the scene through his eyes and

---

[4] Each Muslim adult has to participate in it at least once in a lifetime. The hajj is the fifth of the Five Pillars of Islam.

also follow his gradually worsening sickness. For him, his prayers are paramount, and he accepts the pain that is increasing in his body as "a sacrifice" (97). His strong belief makes him thrive on this experience, so that he "felt transported and redeemed, as close to being a pure spirit as he could ever hope to achieve" (97). Even his first vomiting is depicted as purification, and his weakness feels as if he were in a state of tranc, ultimately losing "control over his movements" (99). He is eventually trampled to death while dying from the Kongoli virus.

This active Muslim spirituality and ecstasy are immediately juxtaposed with scientific conversations about the kind of virus that has already spread from Indonesia to Saudi Arabia. Henry's talk with the CDC in Atlanta depicts in detail the different types of influenza, their history, and their components; other pandemics, such as the 1918 Influenza as well as H1N1 (swine flu) are evoked; yet none of them matches the Kongoli virus. Henry does not exclude the possibilities that the virus had either escaped from some lab or had been deliberately produced. Russian officials, including Putin, had already warned that they had produced "'genetic' weapons" (110), and a German experimental scientist, Jürgen Stark, becomes Henry's number one suspect due to his past experiments in South America. Stark embodies the stereotype of the nineteenth-century fictional and unscrupulous German scientist and is the one who plays God; as his name indicates, he is/feels strong.

According to Horst Kruse, the figure of the devilish German medical scientist was one of the most frequently used characters as antagonist and rogue in nineteenth-century American fiction (cf. Washington Irving, "Dolph Heyliger" [1822]; Nathaniel Hawthorne, "The Great Carbuncle" [1837] and "Dr. Heidegger's Experiment" [1837]; Frederic Jessup Stimson, "Dr. Materialismus" [1890]; see also Zacharasiewicz 58–60) (43–94). Henry and Jürgen share a history of experiments conducted in South America when Jürgen manipulated the test and almost all Indigenous people died. Henry was able to rescue a child and adopted Teddy. As in the nineteenth century, the competitors are the cold German and the empathic human(ist) American medical scientist. Kruse explains possible connections to Rudolf Virchow, who supposedly said that he had dissected thousands of corpses and had never detected a single soul ("'Ich habe Tausende von Leichen seziert und keine Seele darin gefunden'" [qtd. in Kurse 89]). Yet, for Kruse, the evil German scientist is a projection of American problems onto European societies (94). While in nineteenth-century fiction, there was no absolutely positive American counterpart, in Wright's novel Henry does fight Stark.

Henry's friend Majid, not just a prince but also a doctor, cannot allow Henry, a non-believer, to have access to patients during the hajj, and asks him "'to honor that Islam is who we are. If you disgrace our religion, it is as if you spit on our soul'" (119). Belief and science are at war, while Henry is trying to offer rational explanations, and Majid is actively praying for guidance and ultimately decides to label Henry a "'true Muslim'" (120) because of his ethics. This scene, presented through Henry's eyes, reveals Henry's own conflicting emotions about religion. He is unable to accept any religion but experiences "intense feelings" such as "contempt," "fear," and "curiosity" (119). He is simultaneously drawn to and repulsed by religious thoughts. Curiosity about what he does not know is in tune with his desire to eliminate anything mysterious, any fear of what religion might tell him that would undo his firm conviction that everything can be explained rationally. The final emotion he recognizes, to his surprise, is "envy" (120). His inner thoughts reveal his latent desire for a more powerful caring force:

> How pleasant to believe that a force outside of one's self cared about human events, a force that could influence the outcome of a dilemma such as this one – if only a person prayed hard enough and persuasively enough to capture the divinity's attention. The concept of holiness meant nothing to Henry, but he recognized that Majid lived partly in the supernatural, where the imaginary had the force of the real, and what felt morally weightless to Henry imposed an awful burden on the conscience of his friend. (120)

Clearly, Henry, even though he honors Majid's religious humanism, feels rationally superior and discards holiness and the supernatural as imaginary but also as strong forces that seem to give moral guidance to those who believe in them. Ultimately, the battle between science and religion is put to rest by Henry's recognition that from now on the chief goal must be "'saving civilization'" (127). As Majid rightly expects, "'the world will blame us [Muslims] for this'" (136) even though they, too, are the victims of this disease. As often during a pandemic, the (Western) world needs its scapegoat, someone to blame politically; it is called "'the Muslim flu'" (165), and conspiracy theories emerge to claim that "Kongoli was a plot. [...] Muslims had created the disease to destroy Christian civilization" (171). Scapegoating is one of the first – and easiest even if misleading – actions in search of a culprit. Henry is the only one who does not cease in his efforts toward finding the real reasons for the outbreak. Henry admits to his daughter Helen that he is an agnostic: "'I'm not religious, you know that,' he said. 'I'm a scientist. I look at the universe as a mystery I'd like to solve. But the more I know about life, the more mystified I am. Why do we exist? We don't know, we may never know. Is there a God?'" (243)

Henry's wife Jill in Atlanta is at a loss how to explain to her children what is happening when the disease finally also ravages the United States. She mourns the fact that she no longer has faith in religion, which she did when she was a child. She misses "the near certainties that she used to feel about God and Heaven when she was her children's ages. [...] Maybe religion was all lies or myths constructed out of the fear of death that she was feeling now" (241). She used to consider religion "superstition" (241). But the situation is different now. The medical and human crisis triggers her desire for spirituality; she experiences "spiritual longing" (241), but she has lost her faith long ago. Meanwhile, Henry has overcome the very simplistic binary of "religion as faith" and "science as knowledge" (Tricomi 1), admitting that science has its limits and revealing that both science and belief are "constructed" (Tricomi 2) and can mean different things to different people, as Helen's response shows. Henry, and of course mostly Majid, reveal that "the secular-religious binary" (Tricomi 5) does not and should not have to be binary, but ultimately religion does not provide meaning for Henry (see Pearson 855). Henry admits to not knowing whether there is a heaven; science just leads him from one door to the next. Helen's answer is striking: "'I believe in Heaven. I think it's in our dreams'" (244); she believes that humans spend half of their life awake on earth, then half of it asleep in heaven, and eventually all in heaven (245). All Henry can say is to rationally call this "'a very elegant theory'" (245). When Helen finally has to bury her own mother, she begins to doubt the existence of a benign God. Curiously enough, she still believes in God's existence, but now God has turned evil. Her belief is a form of "secret rebellion" against her own father. "God was her real father, perfect, caring, present. But that was before. Not anymore. The fact that the sunrise was still beautiful was like God saying, *So what, I don't need people in my world.* My new religion, thought Helen: There is a God, and he hates us" (304–05). For Helen, God is a substitute father, an ideal father, someone Henry could never have been. Just like a father, God has emotions, and, for her, he has turned against humanity. "This is what God did to my mother, Helen thought" (307).

Jill, Helen, and Henry deal with religion and belief in very different ways. While Jill experiences spiritual longing for safety, Helen integrates them into her daily life and establishes a continuity between life and death, and Henry considers them a mystery that he wants to solve scientifically. As it turns out, the religious overzealousness of his own parents, who devoted their lives to a sect and left Henry with his maternal grandparents, has shaped Henry's rejection of religion. Henry is often faced with other people's spirituality, as when his son Teddy sings a song at night when two bears attacks the family's camp. The son makes the bears leave, but their guide tells them the next day that they "'experienced [...] something [...] holy.' [...] 'We will talk about it many times. We will call you the Bear People'" (278).

Spirituality accompanies Henry through his life, but for a long time he remains a mere observer. Yet the pandemic works on him, and he begins to think of praying, which he, at first, rejects as "a sign of his helplessness" (280). More conversations between him and Majid reveal that while he calls himself "'a hardboiled atheist,'" who has, as he says, "'renounced all forms of superstition, including religion'" (284), Majid calls him "'a Muslim'" with "'a very Islamic attitude'" of believing one does not earn the blessings one receives but feels responsible for everything bad that happens (284). For Majid, Henry's secular humanist ethics (Joas 99–101) are the equivalent of a religious belief. Both are subsequently wondering about the difference in the good that believers **and** non-believers do. Why then believe? But Henry takes it a step further and claims that "'when good people do evil, it takes religion to do that'" (285). Majid understands that there must be "'a wound in [Henry] that cannot heal'" (285) to make such a statement. But a lot of evil has been done in the name of religion – be it by Christians or Muslims, or simply fanatics who take the lives of those who do not share their beliefs. Henry finally reveals the wound caused by his parents who followed the leader of a sect to South America. They worshipped him so much that they trusted him with healing their son Henry – who was suffering from rickets, a softening of bones due to lack of vitamin D – but, of course, the leader was unsuccessful and Henry from then on "'a rebuke to the leader's healing powers'" (286). Henry was sent to live with his grandparents, and shortly afterwards all members of the sect took cyanide and died. Reference here is made to the actual historical event at Jonestown, today also called the Jonestown massacre, a mass-murder-suicide of the Peoples Temple in Guyana in 1978 under the leadership of Jim Jones.

Henry's last chance to get home from Saudi Arabia is on an American submarine that takes him on as a doctor to help the sick members of the crew. He clarifies that he does not believe in God but in the evolution of the species that has become, for him, godlike. As he exclaims, "'[a]ll the power we have, all the creativity, all the wisdom! But there is a species of genetic code inside us that wants to blow it all to pieces'" (347). The evil that human beings do, as Henry argues, is genetically encoded and not God's punishment. On the submarine, Henry eventually develops the means to inoculate himself and others so that at least some people are prevented from dying. During his sickness, he feels the urge to pray but he "dread[s] its appeal" (353–54). During his feverish delusions, he begins to see that he could never accept mercy; sin, evil, or condemnation are "theological constructs that had no meaning for him" (354) but he knows that, like Majid, he has to find his own balance between science and religion. In his delirium, he turns to the Qur'an Majid gave him, but continues to see "superstition and wishful thinking" (355) in religion. Yet he takes from Albert Schweitzer's philosophy the idea that "[a]ll life is sacred" (355), which is perhaps a form of secular humanism. He finally prays: "He asked whatever power there was to reunite him with his family. That is all I will ever ask, he pleaded" (356). He is later indeed reunited again with his son Teddy and his daughter Helen but he cannot prevent Jürgen Stark from releasing all kinds of viruses that turn into "the first great biowar" (452). Henry and his children go on board the USS *Georgia* submarine. Henry's last mission is to October Revolution Island in the Russian Arctic, where he discovers dead mammoths as the origin of the Kongoli virus, the dead polar bears who had fed on them, and the Siberian cranes who had taken the virus to China from where it finally spread across the whole world. Henry's final sentence is the admission that "'[w]e're going to say that we did this to ourselves'" (458), implying that had there not been any global warming, the ice would not have melted, the polar bears would not have fed on the carcasses of the mammoths, and the cranes would not have spread the virus. The Kongola virus, thus, turns into "'a harbinger of future crises relating to climate change and the assault on biodiversity'" (WCC and PCID qtd. in Pearson 857).

At the end, Henry and his children find shelter on a "whale-like" submarine "with a fin improbably rising from its head like a metal cross" (299), with the implication that they, together with the crew, will stay below sea level until the world has overcome the human-made diseases or until he has told the world, as did Jonah in the Bible.[5] Indirect reference is also made to the biblical Noah's Ark that allowed several generations and species to survive the flood; here, however, biowarfare is the result of human hubris. The Captain's Gouldian finches are an endangered species who might survive on "'Noah's ark'" (322), as the Captain says. Except for one, they die in Henry's experiment, which, however, helps the crew to survive. Before the flood, God announces to Noah the following: "The end of all flesh is come before me; the earth is filled with iniquity through them; and I will destroy them with the earth" (Genesis chap. VI, 13). Henry already is Noah-like because he has renounced meat; thus, he does not eat "that flesh with blood" (chap. IX, 4), as God instructed Noah after the flood.

4 Religion, Science, and Time Travel

In *Doomsday Book* (1992), Connie Willis, winner of multiple Nebula and Hugo Awards for science fiction, uses the reference to the Middle English great survey book of England and part of Wales from 1086, the *Domesday Book*, to suggest that what readers hold in their hands is—even though fictional—a historically accurate book about history and historical events that are unalterable, like the Last Judgement. The setting is Oxford in 2054 at Brasenose and Balliol Colleges where scientists have invented a way of sending people on time travels through what they

---

5 Jonah does not want to deliver bad news and flees from God to a ship. But it gets into a storm, which can only be stopped if the sailors throw him into the ocean, which they eventually do. Jonah is swallowed by a whale. While inside the whale's belly, Jonah prays to God and is finally spit out after three days. He then goes to Nineveh to announce that the city will be destroyed because of their wickedness if they do not repent.

call the "net." In spite of professional quarrels, Professor James Dunworthy is in charge of sending a young student historian, Kivrin Engle, to the year 1320 to explore what everyday life was like at that time in history. Kivrin travels through this machine right at the moment when an unknown virus causes an epidemic and the machine operator Badri Chaudhuri has already caught the virus, feels sick, and makes a mistake in the configuration so that there is not just a so-called slippage of about four weeks but a delay of 28 years. Therefore, Kivrin arrives at Skendgate, in mediaeval England, in 1348, in the middle of the pandemic of the Black Death. Just before her departure, she got infected, as it later turns out, with the same virus that causes the epidemic in Oxford[6] because this virus is located in the bones of the dead (who died in 1318) dug up at a dig near Oxford. In spite of her immunization against all known viruses, her immunity was not yet fully effective four days before the drop.

In both centuries, the twenty-first and the fourteenth, religion and the epi/pandemic are intimately connected. In both, the scientists neither truly believe in God nor accept the church's religious rituals. In the twenty-first century, the virus wreaks havoc at around Christmas time, and yet people are busy buying presents, practicing carols, decorating public and private places, and performing church rituals. "Despite considerable medical advances, progress is shown to be illusionary, and history is looped in the circle of suffering" (Gomel 412). When routines are disrupted, one American woman complains about not being allowed to travel to a performance she intended to give with her choir at a church outside of Oxford: "'I'm not used to having my civil liberties taken away like this. In America, nobody would dream of telling you where you can or can't go'" (74), to which Mr. Dunworthy's inner response is: "And over thirty million Americans died during the Pandemic as a result of that sort of thinking [...]" (74). Dunworthy's "Pandemic" is a reference to the Influenza of 1918; the current virus is "a Type A myxovirus. Influenza," as Dr. Mary Ahrens confirms (75).

Similar to the discourse on freedom—abused for highly egoistic purposes—stereotypes are used by some for simplified stories trying to explain the outbreak. Since the British Indian Badri Chaudhuri is the first known infected case, Mrs. Gaddson immediately suspects the virus to come from India and calls it the "'Indian flu'" (210) in spite of the fact that Chaudhuri had not left the country and had, like everyone else at the college, been fully vaccinated against all known virus types. Moreover, people flock to the churches, mostly not in order to look

---

[6] I use the term epidemic here since the disease does not spread far beyond Oxford and can be contained after a short period of time. A pandemic travels far and crosses national borders, as the Great Influenza of 1918, the Black Death, and others did.

for protection but, as one priest (from Holy-Reformed) says, to experience the excitement, as in wartime, "'They come for the drama of the thing'" (216–17). Again, Dunworthy is the voice of reason and science: "'And spread the infection twice as fast, I should think [...]. Hasn't anyone told them the virus is contagious?'" (217). In contrast, the priest reads from the scriptures and then frightens the churchgoers into believing that the pandemic has been sent to them by the wrath of God (cf. also Morris 86): "'O God, who have sent this affliction among us, say to Thy destroying angel, hold Thy hand and let not the land be made desolate, and destroy not every living soul. [...] so now we are in the midst of affliction and we beseech Thee to take away the scourge of Thy wrath from the faithful'" (218). The reader follows Dunworthy's interior thoughts, who enters into a sobering dialogue with the sermon delivered by the priest: "'How could God have sent His only Son, His precious child, into such danger? The answer is love. Love.' 'Or incompetence,' Dunworthy muttered" (221). Since Dunworthy is the narrative voice and focalizer in contemporary Oxford, readers tend to accept his perspective as scientifically grounded, also since he is in a constant exchange of information with doctors and other experts. Moreover, he is also a historian and knows exactly what happened during past pandemics and what behavior is necessary to prevent the worst from happening. But just like during the coronavirus pandemic, there are, on the one hand, people who try to abuse the fear of the people for their own profits and, on the other hand, people who are skeptical of science and express anti-elite sentiments. Democracies allow these voices to be heard as well but these voices undermine democracy by questioning the right of democratic governments to put any restrictions on them in order to ensure some protection from the deadly viruses.

Kivrin Engle, the young historian and scientist, sent through the net to 1348, is a believer in science and a recorder of history (it is supposedly through her diary recordings on a chip implanted into her wrist that the twenty-first century can read about her experiences). Almost her first—and last—encounter is with Father Roche, who says the last rites because she is seriously ill upon arrival. Both mention a return, but Father Roche's is back to God, the "'Redeemer'" (108), and Kivrin's is the return through the net back to Mr. Dunworthy. This juxtaposition of God and the scientist reveals the inherent tension in the explanation of what life is about. Kivrin's words in the "Domesday Book" are "Mr. Dunworthy, *ad adjuvandum me festina*" (126; italics in original). Kivrin subsequently recovers, gets to know the people of Skendgate, "'Father Roche and Agnes and Rosemund and all of them'" (578), and only gradually understands that she is in the middle of the Black Death pandemic.

She finds the Norman church and its graveyard with Agnes's grandfather's tomb with the carving "'*Requiescat cum Sanctis tuis in aeternum*'" (224), which, as Kivrin reflects, could have been the grave they had excavated in the dig Kivrin had visited just before her time travel. Father Roche believes that Kivrin is a saint sent by God "'to sinful man,'" but others consider her a witch (225) because she is so different from them and has healing powers. On Christmas in 1320 (as Kivrin still believes), Rosemund, the elder of the two daughters, is about to be betrothed to Sir Bloet, "a fat man in a green velvet kirtle" (307), a custom to get women to reproduce as early as possible, to give birth to "enough heirs that one at least would survive to adulthood, even if its mother didn't" (309). While sometimes awareness hits Kivrin— "They've all died [...] They've all been dead over seven hundred years" (312)—most of the time, she lives with the people on a day-to-day basis and compares, for example, church rituals. Father Roche, too, predicts that "'The Lord will come with fire and pestilence, and all will perish [...], but even in the last days, God's mercy will not forsake us. He will send us help and comfort and bring us safely unto heaven'" (326). For him, Kivrin is the one to do that.

The bishop's clerk is the first to succumb to the plague with the "'bubo and the swollen tongue and the hemorrhaging under the skin'" (385). This is when Kivrin learns that the correct year is 1348 rather than 1320. She actively explains to Father Roche that the clerk has the "'bubonic plague'" (422). For the first time, Kivrin needs to explain to Father Roche that God did not send the Black Death, that God is actually helpless, and that it is "'a disease. It's no one's fault.—God would help us if He could, but He ...' He what? Can't hear us? Has gone away? Doesn't exist? 'He cannot come,' she finished lamely" (423). Kivrin clearly does not believe in God but does not know how to express her disbelief. She rather lets Father Roche assume that she was sent by God to replace him. The easiest explanation for the existence of such a disease was—and still is—as the Oxford of the twenty-first century shows—that it is God's punishment for human sins. Kivrin's knowledge of history and science contrasts with this belief but she is unable to interfere with history and to convey concepts of disease to someone in the fourteenth century. Without any exception, people believed in God's punishment. Kivrin at least can convince some villagers, including Father Roche, to wear a mask. She gradually builds up anger against a God she does not believe in; a God if at all existent who does not help: "You bastard! I will not let you take her [Agnes]. She's only a child. But that's your specialty, isn't it? Slaughtering the innocents? You've already killed the steward's baby and Agnes's puppy and the boy who went for help when I was in the hut, and that's enough. I won't let you kill her, too, you son of a bitch! I won't *let* you!" (493; emphasis in original) This rage against a cruel or ignorant or indifferent God seems to presuppose that God must exist. Kivrin's monologue addressing God, however, is a dead end or a one-way street that does not get a response. She, like the medical scientists in *Pandemic* and *The End of October*, is an agnostic who wants to believe that her rage reaches and moves someone so that things can change for the better. Yet, "[o]nce the plague hit, it acted conclusively. People often died within hours of exposure, within days at most. Deprived of control or hope, the dead and dying ceased to be individuals and became one more body to heap on the pile" (Morris 83). Kivrin is the only one who can help, not heal, but help so that everyone is buried with respect, does not become a body on a pile, a contagious body only, but one with a proper grave—also Father Roche, who is the last one to die in the village: "He hadn't sinned. He had tended the sick, shriven the dying, buried the dead. It was God who should have to beg forgiveness" (533). Kivrin, in spite of all her doubts, is still perceived by Roche as his savior. "'Yet have you saved me,' he said, and his voice sounded clearer. 'From fear.' He took a gurgling breath. 'And unbelief'" (543). Kivrin is invulnerable due to vaccination and can, therefore, be with him until his death. Ironically, the one who is with her in her mind all the time is Mr. Dunworthy (544): "'I knew you'd come,' she said, and the net opened" (578).

Ultimately, Kivrin continues the work which Brother John Clyn started in the 1340s and had to stop at the time of his death. An excerpt from his writing is a form of prologue to the novel, and he emphasizes that what has been experienced, seen, and witnessed, what he remembers and stores in memory, should not be forgotten and, therefore, put into writing. He considers his text an unfinished project to be continued in the future. Here, Kivrin and her voice "corder" (a chip) come in. Religion and science, maybe even for different purposes, preserve the memory of people's wishes and hopes. To keep the past for future knowledge is the opposite of what Kivrin does: she goes back to the past from the future and shows that while science has significantly developed in the meantime, challenges emerge, such as pandemics with unknown viruses, which kill people as they did in the past. Willis's plea to preserve the knowledge of history and to actually make use of it (even when it comes to such a simple preventive measure as mask-wearing) appeals to common sense and a better historical education. However, with more knowledge and the development of medical treatments comes a turn away from a belief in God. Kivrin is at a loss to answer the question why a benevolent God would make humans suffer so much and let young innocent children die such a terrible death. Father Roche's belief that all have gone "home" to God contrasts with Kivrin's scientifically grounded skepticism and disbelief. The Black Death is not God's punishment, a deterministic belief that leaves humans inactive and patiently suffering, but a disease that simply occurs (why it occurs is a fully different concern) and needs to be and can be actively fought with the means available at the respective time. Even though Kivrin is a non-believer, she can help people die with dignity and be properly buried. Even Father Roche, whose name means "stone" and who is the last to die, receives an appropriate burial ritual even if he cannot be put into the frozen ground. But Kivrin, with Dunworthy's and young Colin's help, can ring the bells nine times, as is the custom in that time and age.

5 Religion in a Postsecular Age

What prevents both Dr. Jack Stapleton and Dr. Henry Parsons from believing in a form of Christian religion or, for that matter, any religion, is the evil done in the name of religion. While Carol's parents in *Pandemic* send their daughter out of the house because their fundamentalist fanaticism considers homosexuality a moral evil to be punished by God, Henry's parents are blinded by a cult leader and neglect their son and eventually commit mass suicide. The omnipotent leader instrumentalizes religion to gain and maintain power and demands obedience or dispenses punishment.[7] While the scientist Jürgen Stark in *The End of October* wants power and plays God by trying to undo creation and destroying humanity in order to save the earth, just as the biblical God did when sending the flood, the two scientists of most interest are Prince Majid and Henry Parsons, one a strong believer in Islam, the other an atheist or perhaps an agnostic or secular humanist; one gaining strength from both science and belief, the other denying the existence of a benevolent God in an evil world. Both novels reveal the individual desire and longing for spirituality; both make human destruction of spirituality explicit; both expose that medical science, if not guided by ethics, will destroy the world because some humans strive for omnipotence. The four scientists cover the spectrum from evil atheist (Stark) and humanist agnostic (Parsons, Stapleton) to religious believer (Majid). What this tells us about the West and the East has to remain an open question for now. Similarly, in *Doomsday Book*, Mr. Dunworthy, Kivrin, and other scientists do not believe in the existence of God. While they join the traditional religious Christmas rituals, they focus on the community of scientists who explore history, including medical history, as a usable past to learn from for the future. In all three novels, science and religion battle for the power of explanation, the discourse to reflect on what is happening.

The horror scenario that all protagonists have to deal with is a virus seemingly unknown to those who fight pandemics and yet, in theory, actually known. In *Pandemic*, the virus is human-made, thus known, and can be destroyed. In *The End of October* and *Doomsday Book*, the respective virus is one from history, reemerging due to human interference; in the former of those two novels, the human-enhanced climate change defrosts the mammoths and sets the virus free that origi-

---

[7] Jill longs for protective spirituality; Helen looks for a substitute father and humanized God.

nally killed them so that it is subsequently spread by polar bears and birds. In the latter, a fourteenth-century virus contained in the bones recovered from a tomb at an archaeological site infects the scientists and then a large part of the population around Oxford. Ironically, in this way, history repeats itself, and scientists only learn after the outbreaks which virus they are dealing with and how to eventually contain it. But in their attempts, in all three novels, parallels to former pandemics, most of all the Influenza of 1918, are drawn upon in order to separate what is already known and what is new about the virus. Historical knowledge reveals a continuum, but also the disruptions and mutations in the variations of the influenza (in this case in the twenty-first century) outbreak. These outbreak narratives reveal historical patterns that might help find a treatment.

The belief in a severe God seems to be a simple and deterministic way of explaning the events, except for the one Muslim who is both a believer and a scientist and attempts to reconcile both. In all other cases, the scientists' wrath against "God" because of the suffering that is happening turns them either into agnostics or atheists who much rather explain the world in scientific terms without an active and, in these cases, horribly cruel agent controlling the events. While religion is an important element in all these fictional worlds, it is sometimes reduced to mere rituals, to a support for the rejection of change, to the desire for spirituality, or to ethical humanist engagement. It is, therefore, present in Christian and Muslim societies, in the past and the present, across the world but in variations and often weakened forms. What seems to be desired as explanatory pattern(s) is a synthesis / syncretism of science and religion and not the choice of either religion or science.

Ultimately, the novels simultaneously confirm Charles Taylor's diagnosis of a secular age and Jürgen Habermas's subsequent evocation of a "'postsecular' age" (qtd. in Torpey 291) that refers to secularization and "the [continuing] public significance of religion" (291) as a simultaneous phenomenon in a global world (Habermas 13). Postsecularity is not new, as Hans Joas argues, but the need for the Western world's acceptance of it is (128).

Works Cited

Beasley, Jonathan, Dr. David Jones, and Gloria White-Hammond. "Podcast: Religion in the Time of Pandemic." 12 Mar. 2021. Harvard Divinity School. Web. Accessed 2 Mar. 2022.

Cook, Robin. *Pandemic*. 2018. London: Pan Books, 2019.

Edwards, Jonathan. "Sinners in the Hands of an Angry God." 1741. *American Literature Survey: Colonial and Federal*. Ed. Milton R. Stern and Seymour L. Gross. New York: Viking, 1973. 170–86.

Frankenberry, Nancy K. *The Faith of Scientists in Their Own Words*. Princeton, NJ: Princeton UP, 2008.

Girard, René. *The Scapegoat*. Trans. Yvonne Freccero. Baltimore, MD: Johns Hopkins UP, 1986.

Gomel, Elana. "The Plague of Utopias: Pestilence and the Apocalyptic Body." *Twentieth Century Literature* 46.4 (2000): 405–33. *JSTOR*. Accessed 8 July 2022.

Güner, Fisun. "How *American Gothic* Became an Icon." *BBC Culture*, 8 Febr. 2017. www.bbc.com. Accessed 5 Mar. 2022.

Habermas, Jürgen. *Glauben und Wissen*. Berlin: Suhrkamp, 2001.

Hawthorne, Nathaniel. "The May-Pole of Merry Mount." 1836. *The Complete Novels and Selected Tales of Nathaniel Hawthorne*. 1937. New York: Modern Library, 1965. 882–90.

The Holy Bible. London: Burns Oates & Washbourne, 1914.

Joas, Hans. *Braucht der Mensch Religion? Über Erfahrungen der Selbsttranszendenz*. Freiburg: Herder, 2004.

Kruse, Horst. "'Dr. Materialismus.'" *Schlüsselmotive der amerikanischen Literatur*. By Kruse. Düsseldorf: Bagel, 1979. 43–94.

Morris, Kym. "Time and Self: How Time Travel Reveals What It Means to Be Human." *Popular Culture Review* 22.1 (2011): 79–90.

Obama, Barack. "Inaugural Address, 20 January 2009." *The Complete Collection of Presidential Inaugural Speeches: From George Washington to Donald J. Trump. 1789-2017*. Ed. Tom Phan. Scotts Valley, CA: CreateSpace Independent Publishing Platform, 2017. 326–31.

Pearson, Clive. "Framing the Theological Response to COVID-19 in the Presence of the Religious Other." *The Ecumenical Review* 72.5 (2020): 849–60. *World Council of Churches*. DOI: 10.1111/erev.12577. Accessed 3 Mar. 2022.

Taylor, Charles. *A Secular Age*. Cambridge: Belknap of Harvard UP, 2007.

Torpey, John. "A (Post-)Secular Age? Religion and the Two Exceptionalisms." *Social Research* 77.1 (Spring 2010): 269–96. *JSTOR*. https://www.jstor.org/stable/40972251. Accessed 18 Jan. 2022.

Tricomi, Albert H. *Clashing Convictions: Science and Religion in American Fiction*. Athens: Ohio State UP, 2016.

True, David. Introduction. *Prophecy in a Secular Age*. Ed. David True. Eugene, OR: Wipf and Stock, 2021. Xi-xviii.

Willis, Connie. *Doomsday Book*. 1992. New York: Bantam, 1994.

Wolfe, Gary. K. "Connie Willis: An Introduction." *Journal of the Fantastic in the Arts* 22.3 (2011): 313–14. *JSTOR*. Accessed 8 July 2022.

Wright, Lawrence. *The End of October*. London: Black Swan, 2020.

Zacharasiewicz, Waldemar. *Images of Germany in American Literature*. Iowa City: U of Iowa P, 2007.

Part IV **Re-Framing Theological Issues and Individual Convictions**

William Sweet
Philosophical Pluralism and Religious Faith in a Secular Age

Abstract: I begin with a short statement about the 'problem' of religion in a secular age, and the view that secularism requires not only a separation of religion and politics, but the exclusion of religious discourse from public discourse. Next, I briefly consider one response to this: that religious discourse may have a place in the public sphere because religion contributes to social well-being – but object that this reduces religion to an instrumental value and misses the point of religion and religious faith. I then propose another approach to show that religion and religious discourse have a place in the public sphere. Here, I turn to the recent phenomenon of philosophical pluralism in philosophy. In recent years, there has been increased attention to philosophical traditions that have sometimes been excluded from mainstream philosophical discussion. I give what I believe are the main reasons for this increased attention and argue that people of faith may be able to use this acknowledgement of 'philosophical pluralism' and extend it to argue for a role for religion in the public sphere.

Introduction

What is the place of religion in what has been called "a secular age" (Taylor, 2007)? In an age in which fewer and fewer people profess any religious affiliation or adherence, and where religion at the same time has been accused of being divisive and exclusionary, does it have any place in the public sphere? In this paper I argue that religion still has a place, even in a secular age, and that this place includes a presence in public discussion. I begin with a short statement about the 'problem' of religion in a secular age, and the view that secularism requires not only a separation of religion and politics, but perhaps also the exclusion of religious discourse from public (e.g., political) discourse. While figures such as Jeffrey Stout (2004) and Nicholas Wolterstorff (1997) have offered responses to this, by referring to the arbitrariness of the exclusion or the implausibility of having a shared, neutral public reason, I propose another reason for religious discourse to

---

Acknowledgement: Presented at International Conference 'Religion in the Secular Age' Austrian Academy of Sciences, Vienna, March 24-26, 2022. I wish to thank Professors Waldemar Zacharasiewicz and Herta Nagl-Docekal for the kind invitation, and the participants for their questions and comments.

https://doi.org/10.1515/9783111247878-017

have a place in the public sphere. I turn to the phenomenon of pluralism in philosophy and note some of its basic secular values and commitments. I then argue that we may be able to draw on the model of this secular 'philosophical pluralism' and use it to argue for a role for religion in the public sphere.

1 A Secular Age

Modern democracies are, generally, secular states, and it is no surprise that many, if not all, of us think of ourselves then as living in what Charles Taylor has called, "*a* secular age" (emphasis mine). What does it mean to speak of 'a secular age'?

One of the things that it means is that those of us who live in a modern democracy are in a place and age where religion is largely an option – and that one can live one's life, work, marry, have children, engage in leisure and social activities, participate in politics, and die, without having any connection with religion[1] – although many may still 'observe' the religious holidays in the calendar. Moreover, the public and political authorities in our countries, as well as those agencies that are related to the state, do not, as a rule, advocate for a particular religious tradition – though it may be that some of these authorities have a role in religious leadership (for example, King Charles of the United Kingdom is also 'supreme governor of the Church of England'). While not the case in past eras in most countries, this optional character of religion is one of the factors that makes this particular age a *secular* age. Religion, in its etymological root of 'religare' – to bind – no longer seems to bind us or our nations. As Taylor writes, in a secular context "human beings discover that they just are humans united in societies which can have no other normative principles but those of [what we might call] the MMO [Modern Moral Order]" (Taylor 294) – namely, that human beings "are rational, sociable agents [who have basic rights, and] who are meant to collaborate in peace to their mutual benefit" (Taylor 159) – and that these beings consent to and must follow certain laws or principles, based on reason, for that peace and for society to exist.

Of course, secular states may – and do – differ in their understanding of secularism or of how religion exists within them. There are variations in how, and how far, religion may be present or excluded from the public sphere in secular states – as examples, we might think of India, where religion – Hinduism – is almost always present, and France, where the majority religion, Catholicism, is virtually absent – but

---

[1] Many people in 'the West' indicate a religious affiliation on documents, such as population censuses or tax rolls, while having little or no involvement with their denomination. Yet, as Taylor notes, religion "remains powerful in memory; but also as a kind of reserve fund of spiritual force or consolation." (522)

we are far from the days of 'religious tests,'[2] or expectations that any particular day of the week is an official 'day of rest' for religious reasons.

2 Religion – and Its Place?

Some have argued that religion poses or is a problem in secular societies in a secular age. It is important to understand what one means by 'religion' here. We are all aware that identifying a clear, objective "demarcation"[3] between what is religious and what is not (or what is scientific) is challenging, if not impossible. Still, some clarification of the term is needed.

In this paper, by 'religion' I do not mean religious or ecclesiastical institutions or organisations. I mean religious *faith*, which is a way of seeing the world and a way of living that has a connection to a tradition, and so is conscious of how that faith has been understood in the past – the "premodern conception of 'ordo'" – but also conscious that how it is understood now is not the same as how it was understood in the past. This faith has its expression in various ways (e.g., worship, public prayer, and certain kinds of actions and dispositions) and in various beliefs (e.g., about reality, about morality, but also about how this faith bears on the temporal political community (e.g., education and social and public policy), about how it has been acted on, and on how it has been received, and so on).

These latter features bear on what some have called "the public sphere." For example, Jürgen Habermas writes that, by "the public sphere," "we mean first of all a realm of our social life in which something approaching public opinion can be formed" ("Encyclopedia" 49) or "society engaged in critical public debate" (*Transformation* 52). This is the sense in which I broadly understand the term.

How is, or how has religious faith been expressed in this public sphere?

Some would look to whether and how expressions of faith and religious symbols once had a place in venues of public, coercive (i.e., state) authority – e.g., prayers and religious symbols in legislatures (Quebec [see Beaman]); religious symbols in court-

---

2 For example, in Canada, the closure of most businesses on Sunday was legislated by the 'Lord's Day Act' (1906). This Act was struck down as unconstitutional in the 1985 Supreme Court of Canada case, R. v. Big M Drug Mart Ltd. Still, while today there are almost no 'religious tests,' there has been a push for 'secular tests,' for example, in determining who can enter into certain professions (see, for example, Savulescu and Schuklenk, on who should be admitted to medical schools).
3 While attempts at demarcation between religion or metaphysics and 'science' have been made (e.g., notably by Ayer and Popper) this has been contested by, for example, Laudan.

rooms (Italy);[4] religious attire in government or public educational institutions (France) – but have now been excluded, but also where they have been included – e.g., the swearing of oaths on a holy book in court (Canada), and prayers in Parliament (e.g., UK and Canada). Or we can look at expressions of religious belief made in institutions, schools, hospitals, and the like that may receive some kind of public funding, just as we find expressions in attire or dress made by people from different cultural traditions or sexual orientations. These are not my interests, however.

One may also note religious discourse or religious argumentation that one finds in addresses, sermons, and texts by religious figures, directed to a broad public – e.g., papal social encyclicals and apologies (see Cunningham), speeches by Buddhist leaders on human rights – but also the remarks in public fora of believers, particularly by public officials and parliamentarians.[5] One may note, as well, the expression of religion in reference to conscience on matters of public affairs (e.g., requests for exemptions from certain laws on religious grounds).

The problem, for many (though not all) believers, is that expressions of, or informed by, religious faith appear to be getting squeezed out of the public sphere – e.g., they are no longer welcome or part of that sphere. They are merely permitted, or tolerated, or less – e.g., business leaders scorn Catholic social encyclicals; in some countries the display of religious symbols in public buildings is restricted or covered over; religious exercises at the start of meetings have been discontinued, and so on. While, for a number of non-believers, religion likely still seems to have too visible a place in the public sphere, they, too, would acknowledge that that place is less central than it once was.

Now, some argue that this is what a secular society should do – that is, it should squeeze out or exclude religion from the public sphere and, perhaps, exclude as well (what Rawls called) other comprehensive doctrines. How far this is possible is, however, an issue.

My interest here, then, is whether religious expression can have a place or presence in 'the public sphere' – for example, whether there should be a place for expres-

---

4 See, for example, Catholic News Agency, "Italian judge convicted for shunning courtrooms with crosses," and the decision of the Grand Chamber of the European Court of Human Rights, Lautsi & Ors v Italy [2011].

5 A recent case is that of Päivi Räsänen, a Finnish politician and a former cabinet minister, some of whose writings and remarks on Biblical views of marriage and the family led to her prosecution, in 2021–22, for "incitements against a minority group." According to the state prosecutor, her remarks were "derogatory and discriminatory against homosexuals and violate their equality and dignity. Thus, they overstep the boundaries of freedom of speech and religion and are likely to fuel intolerance, contempt and hatred." While Räsänen was found not guilty, the prosecutor has launched an appeal of the verdict. See "Ex-interior minister Räsänen charged with hate speech," YLE [Finnish Broadcasting Company] NEWS 29.4.2021 https://yle.fi/news/3-11907573 (Accessed March 31st, 2023).

sions of faith, or about issues from the perspective of one's faith, concerning public matters – but also what the obligations or role of public authorities or public power itself, in a secular state, should be – for example, whether the public authority could require respect for, or even lend support for a religion, or whether it could or even should advocate for allowing religious expression in public discussion.

3 Limiting or Excluding Religion from the Public Sphere

What arguments are there for excluding or limiting religious expression in the public sphere? Some argue that expressions of faith simply do not function well in a secular environment. Specifically, religion should have little, if any, place in public discourse, because:

first, religion is not reasonable, and, even if our contemporary concept of reason is rooted (as Jürgen Habermas claims) in a religious approach ("Religion Public Sphere" 16), society must operate according to *public* reason and evidence accessible to all, and not on private ideologies or beliefs;

second, as the late Richard Rorty stated and repeated, expressions of religious faith, by individuals and by institutions, concerning matters of public policy, *or* attempts to justify views on public policy by appeal to such faith, are *"conversation stoppers."*[6] Rorty states that making references to scripture or to faith generally does not allow for a broad public to engage the topic at hand; they are simply assertions and preclude further discussion – perhaps saying more about the speaker's psychology and tastes than the topic at hand;

third, as Rorty and others have also stated, when faith or faith-based claims have been used in the past, they have frequently been harmful (if not otherwise immoral). Religious speech has, they hold, slowed down or interfered with social progress. Religion has also frequently led, they insist, to discrimination and persecution, both by institutions and by individuals: think of Islamophobia and anti-Semitism, the anti-gay, sometimes anti-Christian, etc., remarks made by 'religious people.' Remarks of believers and religious leaders on many public matters can be, as Rorty writes, "not just in bad taste, but ... heartlessly cruel, ... reckless persecution, [... and an] incitement to violence" ("Reconsideration" 143);

---

6 See Rorty "Religion as Conversation-Stopper" and "Religion in the Public Square: A Reconsideration."

fourth, some (such as Richard Dawkins) hold that many expressions of faith are not intelligible,[7] or are without evidence, or are simply false. For example, for Dawkins, "Christian theology is a non-subject. It is empty. Vacuous. Devoid of coherence or content."[8] And it would be pernicious to allow the expression of such "unintelligible" remarks in the public sphere, as it would suggest that what they expressed made some sense;

fifth, the expression of religious belief and the use of religious discourse can be 'exclusionary' – especially the public expression of the views of a majority religion in relation to minorities. Not just religious symbols but religious speech – religious exercises, prayers, sermons, and public expressions of faith – make some feel as though they are not part of the community and that their views are, therefore, not welcome in the public sphere.

And there are other reasons besides.

Finally, some would note that, as the religious faithful carry out evangelization and the propagation of their 'false' beliefs, they also insist on public support (e.g., avoidance of or exemption from taxation of church property), and that appeals to religious conscience have been used to avoid public responsibilities and duties (e.g., serving in the military or providing public service – e.g., jury duty).

In short, there are many who hold that religious expression is a problem, or causes problems, in the (secular) public sphere. It seems counter to the ideal of the public sphere as a neutral place of 'critical public debate.' Thus, while it may not be possible to make such expression illegal, these critics hold that it should be marginalized, excluded, or even ridiculed (see Rorty, "Public Square" 143). Expressions of religious faith should not be given any special protection or exemptions under the law, and perhaps sometimes those who express such faith with harmful intent or effect should be prosecuted for hate speech.

I challenge this view. I will not, however, offer 'solutions,' such as those of John Rawls, who holds that, in order to have a place in public discourse, religious claims should at least be 'translated' into a more neutral language, not requiring any religious understanding.[9] [10] Instead, I claim that religion has a place in a secular age,

---

[7] Dawkins (35) quotes Thomas Jefferson [letter to Francis Adrian Van der Kemp, 30 July 1816]: 'Ridicule is the only weapon which can be used against unintelligible propositions. Ideas must be distinct before reason can act upon them."

[8] Dawkins, in an interview replying to Alisdair McGrath's *Dawkins' God: Genes, Memes, and the Meaning of Life*.

[9] See Rawls, *The Law of Peoples*. On such a limitation as part of a duty of civility, see Rawls, *Political Liberalism* 35; see also 247, n. 36. Rawls later slightly modifies this view to allow, in public discussion, some "reasonable comprehensive doctrines… provided that in due course proper political reasons… are presented that are sufficient to support whatever the comprehensive doctrines intro-

and that religious believers can rightly express and share their religiously-informed beliefs on public matters in the public square.

To support this challenge, I now move to talk about some secular values – specifically, values that are present in a secular discipline, philosophy – and then argue that the recognition of these values, and why a secular discipline has them, gives us a basis for extending not just toleration, but a place for religious belief in the public sphere in a secular age.

4 Pluralism and the Values in (Philosopohical) Pluralism

Many secular societies are pluralistic, and some are multicultural or, at least, intercultural. By pluralistic, I mean that the society recognizes a diversity of religions, ethnicities, genders, values, identities, interests, cultures, and spiritual paths; that this diversity is regarded as broadly beneficial to the community and is a positive force; and that such a society seeks to ensure a peaceful coexistence or at least a mutual toleration among these groups.

Some pluralistic societies are multicultural. Multicultural societies acknowledge and recognize contributions of different religious, ethnic, cultural, and so on, groups – particularly of minority groups – in such a way that these societies usually provide special protections and rights to assist in preserving the identities of these groups, but with none of them as officially normative. (Some worry that this leads to a number of cultural silos that do not interact or interact only minimally with one another [Fleuras 40].) Canada, for example, has followed an official government policy of multiculturalism since 1971, and this appears in its 1982 Constitution.[11] Some pluralistic societies, however, prefer what is called interculturalism, which emphasizes respect, dialogue, and interaction among the various cultures, and does so with the hope of some integration of minority cultures into the society as a whole. Regardless of which model is adopted, diversity is recognized as a fact, and pluralism as a correlative value.

---

duced are said to support" (Rawls, "Public Reason Revisited," 784). But see Rawls, *Political Liberalism, Expanded Edition* 462, where he seems slightly more flexible on this point.

10 Whether religion, understood as a *faith* [personal belief], can be reduced to a set of propositions, religious or otherwise, that could be made subject to public discourse is far from clear. I cannot discuss this here, however, see Sweet and Hart 2012.

11 Section 27 of the Canadian Charter of Rights and Freedoms (Part 1 of Canada's Constitution) reads: "This Charter shall be interpreted in a manner consistent with the preservation and enhancement of the multicultural heritage of Canadians."

(I am not going to argue whether or why secular societies *ought to be* pluralistic, only note that secular societies often *are*, and that there is already, in secular societies, a general recognition that pluralism is valuable.)

At the same time, it is not surprising that many of our academic disciplines are or are becoming progressively pluralistic. This has – perhaps for some time, but certainly increasingly – been true of philosophy.[12] So, when I speak of philosophical pluralism, I am not talking about the pluralism of academic societies or of persons, but of the discipline of philosophy.

This pluralism has long, and often, been a characteristic of philosophy – there is not only a certain pluralism *inherent* in philosophy but, in more recent years, there have been moves to even greater philosophical pluralism. Admittedly, some may disagree with this claim that philosophy is traditionally pluralistic, particularly if they have in mind philosophy in the 20th century Anglo American world. But that there is greater philosophical pluralism in philosophy in the world in the 21st century is undeniable.

Why has this come about? Why have philosophy – and arguably other (secular) academic disciplines – adopted, or have come to adopt, such a pluralism?

My claim is that it is *not* just because this pluralism has *instrumental* value – that is, that it provides philosophers with some knowledge or approaches that they otherwise would not have had, and is not valuable independent of these consequences – which is, in any case, a risky justification. Philosophers are also often interested in other philosophies *for their own sake.* (One of the curious things about philosophy,

---

[12] How have philosophers (in secular societies, and even beyond) been philosophical pluralists? Philosophers of 'the West,' for example, have long drawn on Central European and Middle Eastern philosophers as well as Asian philosophers, and even in the mid-20th century, one could point to the philosophical pluralism that exists when one talks about analytic and continental philosophy, or about the diversity of Anglo-American or continental or phenomenological approaches. In such cases, it is evident that these views do not all share a common ground, or a common understanding, or can be defended by reason because, in many cases, some have said that some of these views have blind spots, or that they just do not see things, or that some things do not follow. For example, the 'analytic' philosopher may be accused of not being able to see something about the nature of human existence, or the person engaged in postmodern thought may be accused of not giving a rigorous, rational argument. In any case, by the end of the 20th century, there had been greater discussion of the approaches of other traditions – traditions from Asia, Africa, and from indigenous peoples, and there have been significant debates and discussions, and some cross-fertilization. Admittedly, authors such as Jonardon Ganeri have called out philosophers in the West for not being as pluralistic and open to diversity as they could be, but the response to this has been positive. See Ganeri "Taking Philosophy Forward." As philosophical pluralists, then, the fact that a 'marginalized philosopher' cannot give an argument that is pleasing to someone on one's own terms is not a sufficient reason for saying that that philosopher should not express those views or that the person should be limited in some way from expressing those views.

and certainly the history of philosophy, is that, while philosophy is interested in truth and wisdom, philosophers generally do not study these various philosophies because they believe them to be true. Many of the claims of many philosophers are not true or right, and yet they are still studied.) My claim is that philosophy has this pluralism in part because of the values and commitments that philosophy has (almost) always had – i.e., that pluralism and the commitment to it are part and parcel of how philosophy is done; that this is a *secular* commitment; and that it is consistency with this and other values that motivates and reinforces philosophical pluralism (and perhaps pluralism in general) – i.e., that it recognizes and acknowledges diverse ways or approaches to doing philosophy.

Thus, rather than being simply instrumentally valuable, other and new philosophies are valuable because, for example:

First, philosophers recognize that other philosophical traditions *need* to be heard in order to be *what* they are, i.e., philosophies; that their exponents need to be heard to be *who* they are – i.e., philosophers; and, perhaps because they recognize that these have arbitrarily or inappropriately excluded certain of them, or those like them, in the past. Recently in Canada and the United States – and, I suspect, throughout the so-called 'West' – there has come to be an increasing interest in the philosophies from African and Indigenous traditions. This builds on the increasing interest (over the past 30 years, for example, in Canada) in Asian philosophies and ways of thinking, as well. Why philosophers have increasingly come to have this interest is, no doubt, influenced by political issues, but their interest in them is not just political;

Second, those who engage in these other traditions seek to and need to express their insights, themselves, and their identities – e.g., mediated through their philosophies – and other philosophers recognize this by listening to and, as appropriate, engaging them. In other words, the awareness of these others not infrequently leads philosophers to want to hear about or from them (see Sweet *Intercultural Philosophy*);

Third, there is a widespread value of, and commitment to, 'openness' (see Wimmer) – perhaps not often as it could have been, but, certainly, increasingly so. Given that there is an awareness that philosophy is inseparable from culture, philosophers recognize that, in order to understand new or different philosophies, they need to engage and to get to know their authors, and so (normally) they believe that they must, first, read these authors on their own terms, recognizing in advance that their 'world views' are likely not one's own. This haslong been a *sine qua non* in the history of philosophy, and it has long been present in comparative and intercultural philosophies as well. Further, the claim has also been made, and there is some agreement about this among contemporary philosophical pluralists, that, for example, Asian or Black or Indigenous philosophers are not obliged to justify their approaches to others, or to translate their views into terms that those in different traditions understand. There would today be some genuine discomfort for philosophers, as pluralists, to say to exponents of other philosophies that 'You can do what you like in your own tradition, but you aren't welcome at the American Philosophical Association.' So, allied with the value of openness is the value of justice; the secular value of justice requires treating philosophers and philosophies with respect. They have an inherent value and dignity.

Fourth, I would suggest that another explanation of this pluralism is that philosophers recognize the importance of 'recognition' – of inclusivity and of the recognition of others as equals – which requires listening to them. This importance of listening is consistent with a feature that the late Alan Gewirth, in *Reason and Morality*, called the principle of generic consistency. To paraphrase Gewirth: that, as we wish to be heard, so – out of logical consistency – we should be ready to hear/listen to others. Thus, one might ask, as a philosopher: Why should I care about the opinion of another? And the answer is: If I care about my opinion, I should also care about their opinions. This reciprocity may inform the manner in which a philosophical view is expressed and, if one wants their voice to be successful or influential, it probably has to adjust and take account of the language, academic tradition, and so on, of one's audience. To the extent that there is a limitation of expression in a pluralistic environment, however, it is when that expression undermines the environment altogether, where order or safety or the expression of other philosophers are undermined. Mutual toleration is a minimum expectation.

Finally, I suggest that philosophers are interested in different philosophies and philosophical approaches simply because *many* have a natural curiosity (and perhaps even a humility) towards new ideas, and a natural desire to seek to know others (in the same profession or vocation), and to know what they know (e.g., whether there are shared values). There are many things that philosophers know that they do not know, and, as they recognize the existence of philosophical diversity, they want to know this diversity. For example, these days, philosophers generally do not put 'rationality' as a precondition to listening, or including someone in discussion, since the conditions for 'rationality' or a common communicative discourse are difficult to define and to justify in a non-question-begging way. Of course, for conversation and discussion to proceed, there must be some shared rules or beliefs (see Mall 77, 78), but this is not a necessary condition for seeing certain views as philosophical.

In short, philosophical pluralism reflects general (secular) values such as equality, inclusiveness / openness, fairness, comprehensiveness, and justice, and this leads to the inclusion of (or to including again) marginalized philosophies and philosophers. This practice of recognition and inclusion and treating others equally does not mean that one must embrace or adopt these philosophies, but that one recognizes that there should be a space for these philosophies within (the discipline of) philosophy.

The point here is not that these are good reasons for philosophers to be philosophical pluralists. My point is simply that many, in the secular discipline of philosophy, already are or profess to be intellectual and philosophical pluralists, and that this simply describes and articulates what it means to be engaged in philosophy in the secular, pluralistic environment of today.

Philosophers listen to other views, *not just* because they basically agree with them, or know that they will learn from them, or because they share a common interest, or find them 'useful,' or because they are 'rational,' *but also* because these views are the views of fellow philosophers, and therefore they should treat their expression with a sense of fairness, equality, and openness, etc., even though they may not agree and even though they may not understand. These values of pluralism – equality, inclusiveness, fairness, and so on – which are also good secular values – lead philosophers to find a place for, or to welcome, marginalized philosophers and philosophers from the periphery, or new philosophies, even non-secular philosophies, on their own terms.

5 For Religion in the Public Sphere in a Secular Age

How does this account of philosophical pluralism bear on the issue of the presence of religion in the public sphere? The values and commitments that are characteristic of the pluralistic and secular practice of philosophy support a place for religion and expressions of religious faith in public debate.

Like philosophy, in many countries of the contemporary West the public sphere – the social world in this secular age – is pluralistic and secular, and it professes to be, like philosophy, open to new ideas. One concern expressed earlier was that some ideas – expressions of religious faith or of beliefs that rest on that faith – simply do not fit in this sphere. Before addressing this and other concerns, let me, parenthetically, make a few comments about the nature of religious expression.

First, it is difficult to say *a priori* that certain expressions are, or are not, expressions of *religious* belief or *religious* discourse: the mere expression of views by a person from a religious tradition does not mean that those views are ipso facto religious; reference in a proposition to a religious text, figure, or event does not obviously make the proposition an expression of a religious belief or part of religious discourse; and some such expressions may not be propositional (but, say, performative). So it is not clear exactly what, in a non-question-begging way, is sought to be excluded from the public sphere.

Second, even when we speak of the propositional character of part of religious faith, it is not obvious that religious faith is reducible to propositions that can be understood independently of their origins – any more than the expression of a *cultural* belief (e. g., about the importance of autonomy, equality, democracy, and freedom; about health and what contributes to it, and so on) can be reducible to other propositions independent of *its* origins.

Third, when it comes to debate over the expression of religious faith in the public sphere, what is curious is that there is relatively little discussion about what the purpose might be of people who wish to express their religious faith and religious beliefs in the public sphere. If one reads the likes of Rorty, one has the impression that it is often or primarily to express bigotry and assert vile homophobic or racist beliefs. But this seems, in fact, far from how religious discourse is normally used. Some expressions of religious belief may seem extreme or rigid but, given the number of times that believers may express their apparently religious views in public settings, it seems implausible that most expressions have this character.

Finally, I would say that there is much, if not a large range of, overlap between propositions expressed by people of various religious faiths and the various moral and descriptive propositions in ordinary language. These statements of religious faith refer to events and persons, make normative claims, and the like – so, while they are distinct from other moral, descriptive, and religious expressions, they are not sui generis and are often about a world that is shared.

Thus, given these comments on the nature of religious expression, are the claims that such expression does not have a place in the public sphere warranted? First, most objections to statements expressed by religious people are not so much that they are religious, but that their contents (or those who express them) are offensive or unintelligible. In the light of the preceding comments on the nature of religious expression, however, it may be that the offensiveness is not a matter of their religious character, and the allegation of an unintelligibility or an inaccessibility of such expression at first glance, is also not obviously sufficient to exclude it from the public sphere. Second, as noted above, many putative religious claims do not seem especially problematic. When a disciple of the Dalai Lama or Martin Luther King or Mahatma Gandhi or a person working in a Salvation Army soup kitchen expresses a view, informed by religious faith, about the injustices of poverty or oppression or discrimination, the view may be dismissed by some, but that is not a sufficient reason to exclude it from the public sphere.

So, given this account of the nature of religious expression, given that it does not seem particularly problematic compared with other forms of expression (e. g., those of a moral character), and also given that those who want to be part of that debate in the public sphere and to be influential in what they are expressing, there is no obvious or a priori reason that such expression might not fit in a pluralistic, open, secular context or that it should be excluded.

One may still object, however, that, even if the concerns raised above are not sufficient to exclude expressions of religious faith or of beliefs that are dependent on that faith, *why include* them, given that, at least in some areas, religious expression seems to put an end to other people's willingness to engage in the discussion? Why encourage – and, indeed, why allow – religious expression in the public sphere?

In line with the account of philosophical pluralism given above, I am not going to argue that such expression should be included because it has an instrumental value or an historical value – e.g., that many secular values and beliefs have often earlier been religious values and beliefs – although both these claims are, I believe, true. Rather, I will give 'secular' reasons, analogous or parallel to the reasons why philosophers include the expression of various philosophies in the discipline of philosophy *qua* pluralistic secular discipline.

A first reason is that religious believers are fellow members of the political community, and, for them to participate, as we expect fellow citizens to participate, they 'need' to be heard. This need may be especially significant insofar as religious faith, in a secular society, is also an indicator of a distinctive culture and tradition; believers need to be able to express their identities and have them recognized; they need to advocate for their views – and, perhaps, to apologize for past views and public harms (e.g., 'colonialism'). Just as philosophers appreciate the needs of philosophers from minority or marginalized traditions as part of the philosophical sphere, in the public sphere one also needs to hear people of faith on their own terms, to try to reserve any antipathy or bias one might have, and to try to understand where they are coming from – their world view – in order to better appreciate what they are saying, and why. The secular values of recognising and responding to the needs of others, as well as recognizing the dignity and value of a fellow citizen, then, require expressions of religious faith being included in the public sphere.

A second reason is that the secular commitment to pluralism, and the importance of recognition and acknowledging distinct identities within the public sphere, are ways of treating fellow citizens, including those who are people of faith, fairly and justly – not expecting them to hide the basis or inspiration for their views or to dissimulate in order to participate in public debate. This means enabling them 'to put their cards on the table' – that is, to express their views, not in a disguised way, but in an open and transparent way. This also, in a way, acknowledges and respects the fact that religious motives have been important grounds for actions and expressions in the public sphere that have made a major contribution to a pluralist and just society in the past (see the examples, again, of Gandhi, King, and Helen Prejean).

Third, values such as openness and inclusivity are inconsistent with the de facto creation of (intellectual) ghettoes – where believers are allowed to hold certain views in private, but are discouraged or forbidden from bringing those ideas, and their identities, cultures, and traditions, into the public square. Indeed, to know who they are, we need to know what their beliefs are, and this again requires hearing their views and even trying to understand them on their own terms. Including religious expression is also a recognition of the equality of the interlocutors – a sign of equal treatment and treatment as an equal – and in keeping with the principle of generic consistency – that, just as one expects a believer to listen to the views of others, including non-believers, so one must allow room for believers to speak and be heard.

Further (fourth), just as philosophers are curious about new or marginalized philosophies, there should be a genuine, secular, pluralistic curiosity in the public sphere about the faith and the beliefs of those of religious faith – some of which beliefs lie at the root of our secular age – and about how and why those who hold them believe that they bear on public issues, e.g., social and public policy and law. The refusal of such curiosity suggests closemindedness and perhaps prejudice.

There are other pluralistic values exemplified in philosophy and other secular disciplines besides that warrant such an inclusion of expressions of religious faith.

Having a place for religious expression in the public sphere and in public discourse, then, is consistent with pluralist secular values, and should not be conditional on these views meeting 'objective' or 'neutral' standards of discourse (see Audi) or on these expressions being easily or readily intelligible to all who encounter them (see Rawls). That being said, given that expression on public matters usually aims at persuasion, it seems to me that most believers would also likely express their views in a way that they thought broadly intelligible or persuasive for an audience that might not share their faith, or in a way that the audience might be receptive to or impressed by the witness and the character, if not the statements, of the believer.

So, in general, secular principles of equality, recognition of identity, the values of authenticity, inclusiveness, fairness, and justice, and so on, found in philosophical pluralism, also seems to require that religious faith have a place alongside the range of expressions of ethnicity, culture, tradition, sexual orientation, and so on, present in a pluralistic society. It does not mean that their interlocutors have to embrace what is being said, or that what is said cannot ever be challenged (though it does suggest that one focus on understanding what the believer is saying before attacking it). Expressions of religious faith have no special exemption from criticism, but neither do they merit any special exclusion from the public sphere.

For those who are concerned that such a view is naïve or optimistic, or underestimates the difficulties caused by some such expression, an illustration of how an unusual or dissonant 'voice' might be present in the public sphere in the secular age has been provided by a paradigmatically secular discipline like philosophy. Philosophical pluralism is a model of not only how such voices from diverse origins can properly be present without philosophy abandoning its claim to be a secular, public discipline, but also how such voices can even be encouraged in public, philosophical discussion. The public sphere can, I would claim, adopt a similar pluralism without abandoning its secularism.

What would it look like, concretely, for expressions of religious faith or views arising out of that faith to have a place in the public sphere?

Arguably, the least that is called for is what John Locke called toleration (see *Toleration*). Locke's view, recall, was that, because we simply do not know the truth or do not have a non-question begging way of determining the truth about many matters of religious faith, we cannot restrict their expression *a priori*. A believer may make an appeal to or based on religious authority; the non-believer to another putative source, but in the absence of a truth evident to most or all, and so long as there is no demonstrable public harm in such expression, toleration and inclusion in the public sphere would be an appropriate minimum response.

Further, given the values of pluralism summarized above, these beliefs could also normally be expressed in public assemblies such as parliaments, city councils, and the like – and also have a presence on the public broadcaster, in newspapers, and in education. Models for the debates or discussions in which they might be expressed might be found in interreligious or ecumenical dialogue (Sweet 2000) or polylogue (Wimmer, Mall) – though they are not restricted to this form. One might also recall that, even in a fairly recent time, such public expression was widespread – think of Martin Luther King's 'Letter from Birmingham Jail,' weighing against discrimination – and there are some instances even today: the various speeches to the United Nations of the Dalai Lama on human rights or, recently, on climate change; of Pope Francis on ecology and the economy (as well as on controversial matters of sexuality). While these expressions are, now, overall less frequent than they once were, and while we do not seem to find many examples of this 'open expression' in daily life,[13] a genuine pluralism in the public sphere does not entail their exclusion.

Just as philosophical pluralism does not lead to a breakdown in doing philosophy, so the presence of religion in the public sphere need not lead to fundamental prob-

---

[13] I recall a visit to the Philippines, in July 2009, and reading a copy of The *Manila Times* newspaper, where, on the front page, it was requested that readers join together in prayer for the recovery of Corazon Aquino, the former President. Many, but not all Filipinos are believers. Many, but not all, Filipinos are Catholic. This religious expression and request might have been rejected by some who saw it. Yet it was regarded as not out of the ordinary that this request should be made in a public space. It is difficult to imagine such public calls to prayer being made by public authorities in secular states today.

lems in that sphere. As noted above, there are models for debates or discussion where religious beliefs are expressed (e.g., ecumenical dialogue), and it seems plausible that this can be extended to the public sphere. And recall that expression does not entail that their views cannot be challenged or debated – that, if they do lead to demonstrable public harm or disorder that undermines the possibility of all 'critical public debate,' just as there are limitations on philosophy's pluralism, there are prima facie grounds for limiting expression here as well. In any event, the present argument is not about freedom of expression, but simply for not limiting expression based solely on its putative origin. Thus, given the example and model of philosophical pluralism that includes even non-secular views, there are good 'secular' reasons for allowing religious faith a place in the public sphere in a secular age.

6 Objections

One can foresee concerns or objections to this proposal, just as there were concerns or objections about religious expression having a place in the public sphere in the first place. I will briefly raise and address a few of the more likely ones.

First, one might object that we do not *need* to hear every 'belief' or religious expression, nor need we feel that we must try to understand religious believers on their own terms. For some expressions of religious belief are offensive, or are hateful, or are ridiculously (and perniciously) false, or unintelligible. So, rather than get caught up in attempting to determine which religious expressions are not problematic, it is better simply to avoid them having a place in the public sphere, period. I would respond that the offensiveness of a religious view, or the distress that it causes, is not sufficient for restricting its expression for the reasons noted earlier – and, particularly if this view draws attention to uncomfortable truth. Moreover, pluralists might note that restriction based on offensiveness may itself be offensive to those who regard it as licit expression or criticism. The problems with putative offensiveness as a limit on expression have long been discussed in the philosophical literature and are too numerous to discuss here.[14] If the objection, however, is that the expression of certain views is harmful – that it constitutes, for example, hate speech – or undermines public order or safety – pluralists may have little or no difficulty restricting that.[15]

---

[14] See, for example, O'Neill, Marshall, Kohl, Greenawalt, or Feinberg. The 'classical' view is found in J.S. Mill, *On Liberty*. Admittedly, a recent strategy has been to define harm in a way that effectively includes offensiveness (see Bell).

[15] The International Covenant on Civil and Political Rights, for example, notes that even freedom of religion (or conscience) can be limited. Article 18, section 3, of that Covenant states that "Freedom to manifest one's religion or beliefs *may be subject* only to such *limitations* as are prescribed

Of course, not all religious views are harmful. But their awareness of the expression that states have restricted in the past might make many pluralists reluctant to be zealous even here. Just as the expression of certain *philosophical* views may offend, so the fact that *religious* expression may offend does not, by itself, obviously 'trump' the need to express and be heard. And, further, given the importance to the speaker of being heard, blanket exclusion of religious expression is not directly warranted.

Second, a critic might say that, even if one allowed religious expression in general, not everyone should use it – for such expression, by persons in authority or of authority, might lead some to think that there was a lack of impartiality in the decisions of these authorities. But, first, judges, for example, are not absolutely impartial; in fact, they need to show partiality for the law and, arguably, for secular values – which may also be religious values. Second, to restrict someone from expressing their religious views does not prevent those views from having an influence on them and, as long as the public decisions they make (as distinct from simply talking about their personal beliefs and convictions) are made in a way that 'plays by the rules' – i.e., have what is considered to be an appropriate justification – then it is not clear why they should normally be prevented from expressing their beliefs. Such expression may even serve a social good (e.g., for others to know that people in authority have such religious views). Forcing one to dissimulate about one's beliefs and their place in one's decision-making does not, however, make the decision any more 'neutral.'

Third, a critic might object that if someone expresses unintelligible or patently false views, there is no warrant for their expression in public debate. At best, they only encumber the discussion; at worst, they distract attention from the issues at hand. In response, however, I would note – but will not argue here – that there is no reason to assume that the canons for truth or proof in religious expression and/or belief are the same as for other beliefs, and so claims of putative unintelligibility or falsehood may be question-begging. I would also note – but, again, will not argue here – that views held, in earlier times, to be unintelligible or false, have in some cases become almost truisms today – e.g., the equality of races, of men and women, of the appropriateness of certain kinds of government to human flourishing – and vice versa (e.g., that 'sciences' such as alchemy, astrology, and phrenology were once held to be true, whereas now they are generally regarded as clearly false or unscientific). Finally, as noted earlier, the study of philosophy is not restricted to the study of only true philosophical propositions – indeed, the study and discussion of

---

by law and are necessary to protect public safety, order, health, or morals or the fundamental rights and freedoms of others" (Emphasis mine). Freedom of conscience, then, is *not* a freedom without corresponding obligations, responsibilities, and limitations.

a wide range of views is consistent with its general pluralistic secular values. So, the putative falsehood or unintelligibility of a belief is no sufficient reason to exclude the believer from uttering it publicly, where it can be addressed. In any case, it does not follow from *the claim* that expressions of faith or of beliefs based on faith are unintelligible, that they are *in fact* unintelligible, and that therefore one has a sufficient reason to exclude such expression from the public sphere.

A final criticism of allowing religious expression in the public sphere is that it is only when there are shared standards for discussion – e.g., these standards being reason and publicly observable evidence – that we can have a 'level playing field' that allows as many individuals as possible to participate and to be understood by others, and that by allowing religious belief in the public sphere, this will undermine the possibility of such a level playing field. In response, one must note that should this standard primarily target the religious believer, and not others who have other comprehensive ethical views and beliefs, there is an inequity. Moreover, excluding religious views from discussion because one fears that they will impede getting a consensus, is, in fact, to impede arriving at a genuine consensus, as one has a priori excluded some of the views in advance. Further, a believer may well be ready to give, in addition, other supports for her religious expression because she seeks to persuade others whom she knows may not share her religious faith – and so religious expression should not be excluded a priori. Finally, it may be that putative 'unintelligibility' of certain (here, religious) beliefs has a role in the public sphere – that it forces others to reconsider the 'level' character of the playing field (and, perhaps, the 'reasonability' of their own assumptions).

In short, any a priori exclusion of religious views or of beliefs based on them is, arguably, arbitrary and questionable. The presence of these views and others like them may be challenging in discussion in the public sphere, may not be well received, and may not seem to contribute much if anything, but this is not sufficient to exclude it from the public sphere altogether. Just as pluralism in philosophy professes (secular) values of openness, inclusion, equality, and so on, so also can the public sphere exhibit such values by not excluding expressions of faith and beliefs based on that faith.

7 Conclusion

Those of us in democracies of the so-called West live in what Charles Taylor and others have called 'a secular age.'

One of the features of our secular age is the apparent reluctance – if not the antipathy – towards having the explicit expression of religious faith in public, and particularly on matters of public debate. This seems to be an implication of the secular view that religious faith is a private affair, should not be present in public institutions, and should not have public support – perhaps much the same as alchemy would not have a place in a university Chemistry Department.

Yet another feature of our secular age is its pluralism. With that pluralism comes, or are professed, certain values and commitments. And this is present in much of the academy including, traditionally, philosophy.

Whether this pluralism in philosophy is justified, it nevertheless exists, and carries with it commitments and values, such as curiosity about and an openness to new philosophies, a recognition that marginalized voices need to be heard, and that inclusiveness and justice should direct our views – while all the same not obliging philosophers to abandon their secular and even rationalistic views.

My claim has been that these 'secular' commitments and values provide a basis for an argument that religious voices should be present and should be able to speak and to be heard on their own terms in the public sphere – perhaps, after the model of ecumenical dialogue. These voices and identities should not be excluded from state-operated media (e.g., public broadcasters) and from public education, and the like. This is a way of treating many of one's fellow citizens with respect, enabling them to be authentic on matters of identity, acknowledging their identities, treating them equally, and so on. It also reminds one of how religious motives and commitments have had an important motive or role for doing good in the past.

Allegations of possible negative consequences of the presence of these voices and beliefs arguably exaggerate potential harms, and, as such, are consequences that can be addressed independently. But, in any event, such consequences should not outweigh the commitment to pluralist secular values: equality, the importance of recognition, identity, justice, inclusiveness, and the like. As the example of philosophical pluralism suggests, diverse, even non-secular, views have a place in philosophy and, by extension, religion can and should have a place in the public sphere in a secular age.

Works Cited

Audi, Robert and Nicholas Wolterstorff. *Religion in the Public Square: The Place of Religious Convictions in Political Debate.* Lanham: Rowman & Littlefield, 1997.

Audi, Robert. "Liberal Democracy and the Place of Religion in Politics." *Religion in the Public Square.* By Robert Audi and Nicholas Wolterstorff. Lanham: Rowman & Littlefield. 1997.

Ayer, A.J. *Language, Truth, and Logic.* London: Victor Gollancz, 1936.

Beaman, Lori G. "Between the Public and the Private: Governing Religious Expression." *Religion in the Public Sphere: Canadian Case Studies.* Ed. Solange Lefebvre and Lori G. Beaman. Toronto: U of Toronto P, 2014. 44–65.

Bell, M. "John Stuart Mill's Harm Principle and Free Speech: Expanding the Notion of Harm." *Utilitas* 33.2 (2021): 162–179.

Cunningham, Erin. "Other times popes have apologized for the sins of the Catholic Church." *Washington Post.* 25 July 2022. https://www.washingtonpost.com/world/2022/07/25/pope-francis-apology-catholic-church-sexual-abuse-scandal/. Accessed 1 August 2022.

Dawkins, Richard. *The God Delusion.* London: Transworld Publishers, 2006.

Feinberg, Joel, *Offense to Others* (volume two of) *The Moral Limits of the Criminal Law,* 4 vols. Oxford: Oxford UP, 1984.

Fleras, Augie. *Canadian Multiculturalism @50: Retrospect, Perspectives, Prospects.* Leiden: Brill, 2021.

Ganeri, Jonardon. "Taking Philosophy Forward." *Los Angeles Review of Books.* 20 August 2018. https://lareviewofbooks.org/article/taking-philosophy-forward/. Accessed 1 August 2022.

Gewirth A. *Reason and Morality.* Chicago: U of Chicago P, 1978.

Greenawalt, K. "Free Speech in the United States and Canada." *Law and Contemporary Problems* 55.1 (1992): 5–33.

Habermas, Jürgen. "The Public Sphere: An Encyclopedia Article (1964)." Trans. Sara Lennox and Frank Lennox. *New German Critique* 3 (1974): 49–50.

Habermas, Jürgen. *The Structural Transformation of the Public Sphere: An Inquiry into a Category of Bourgeois Society* [1962]. Trans. Thomas Burger. Cambridge, MA: The MIT Press, 1989.

Habermas, Jürgen. "Religion in the Public Sphere." *European Journal of Philosophy* 14. 1 (2006): 1–25.

Catholic News Agency. "Italian judge convicted for shunning courtrooms with crosses." 22 Feb 2008. https://www.catholicnewsagency.com/news/11863/italian-judge-convicted-for-shunning-court rooms-with-crosses. Accessed 1 August 2022.

Grand Chamber of the European Court of Human Rights. Lautsi & Ors v Italy [2011] ECHR Application No 30814/06 (18 March 2011). https://hudoc.echr.coe.int/app/conversion/pdf/?li brary=ECHR&id=001-104040&filename=001-104040.pdf. Accessed 1 August 2022.

The International Covenant on Civil and Political Rights. "The Constitution Acts, 1867 to 1982". https://laws-lois.justice.gc.ca/eng/Const/. Accessed 1 August 2022.

Kohl, Uta. "Islamophobia, 'gross offensiveness' and the internet." *Information & Communications Technology Law* 27.1 (2018): 111–31.

Laudan, Larry. "The Demise of the Demarcation Problem." *Physics, Philosophy and Psychoanalysis: Essays in Honor of Adolf Grünbaum.* Ed. Robert S. Cohen & Larry Laudan. Dordrecht: D. Reidel, 1983. 111–27.

Locke, John. *Locke on Toleration.* Ed. Richard Vernon. Cambridge: Cambridge UP, 2012.

Mall, Ram Adhar. "The Concept of an Intercultural Philosophy." Trans. Michael Kimmel. *polylog: Forum for Intercultural Philosophy* 1 (2000). Online: http://them.polylog.org/1/fmr-en.htm. Accessed 1 August 2022.

Marshall, William P. "The Concept of Offensiveness in Establishment and Free Exercise Jurisprudence." *Indiana Law Journal* 66.2 (1991). https://www.repository.law.indiana.edu/ilj/vol66/iss2/1. Accessed 1 August 2022.

Mill, J.S. *On Liberty. Collected Works of John Stuart Mill* 18. Ed. John M. Robson. Toronto: U of Toronto P, 1963-91.

O'Neill, Onora. "Should it be an offence to offend?" https://www.equalityhumanrights.com/en/our-work/blogs/should-it-be-offence-offend, Accessed 1 August 2022.

Pennock, Robert. "Can't philosophers tell the difference between science and religion?: Demarcation revisited." *Synthese* 178 (2011): 177–206.

Popper, Karl. *The Logic of Scientific Discovery* [*Logik der Forschung* (1935)]. London: Hutchinson, 1959.

Rawls, John. *Political Liberalism*. New York: Columbia UP, 1993.
Rawls, John. "The Idea of Public Reason Revisited." *University of Chicago Law Review* 64.3 (1997): 765–807.
Rawls, John. *The Law of Peoples*. Cambridge, MA: Harvard UP, 2001.
Rawls, John. *Political Liberalism, Expanded Edition*. New York: Columbia UP, 2005.
Rorty, Richard. "Religion as Conversation-Stopper." *Common Knowledge* 3.1 (Spring, 1994): 1–6.
Rorty, Richard. "Religion in the Public Square: A Reconsideration." *The Journal of Religious Ethics* 31 (2003): 141–49.
Savulescu, J. and U. Schuklenk. "Doctors have no right to refuse medical assistance in dying, abortion or contraception." *Bioethics* 31.3 (2017): 162–70.
Stout, Jeffrey. *Democracy and Tradition*. Princeton, NJ: Princeton UP, 2004.
Supreme Court of Canada. R. v. Big M Drug Mart Ltd. 1985.
Sweet, William. "Globalization, Philosophy, and the Model of Ecumenism." *South Pacific Journal of Philosophy and Culture* 4 (2000).
Sweet, William, ed. *What is Intercultural Philosophy?* Washington, DC: CRVP Press, 2014.
Sweet, William and Hendrik Hart. *Responses to the Enlightenment: An Exchange on Foundations, Faith, and Community*. Amsterdam/New York, NY: Brill, 2012.
Taylor, Charles. *A Secular Age*. Cambridge, MA: Harvard UP, 2007.
Wimmer, Franz Martin. "Intercultural Philosophy – Problems and Perspectives." *CIRPIT Review* 4 (2013): 115–24.
Wolterstorff, Nicholas "Audi on Religion, Politics and Liberal Democracy." In *Religion in the Public Square*, 1997.
YLE [Finnish Broadcasting Company] NEWS. "Ex-interior minister Räsänen charged with hate speech." 29 April 2021. https://yle.fi/news/3-11907573. Accessed 1 August 2022.

Klaus Viertbauer
Religious Convictions and Public Reason: On the Way to a Two-Stage Epistemology of Religion

Abstract: The paper examines the question whether and to what extent religious convictions can be transformed into normatively binding claims to validity in the process of public opinion formation. For this purpose, the difference between communitarianism and liberalism is recalled in a first step, before it is clarified in a second step how such a transformation of individual religious convictions into universal-normative claims to validity is possible. For this reason, a two-stage epistemology is developed following Jürgen Habermas.

The question of what role religion can play within a secular society proves to be highly complex and multi-layered. Therefore, two discourses have to be strictly distinguished: on the one hand, the discourse of political philosophy on the question of how public opinion is formed in society, on the other hand, the epistemological discourse about the nature of religious convictions. In this paper, I give an overview of the discourse of political philosophy (1) and discuss the epistemological question of how religious convictions can be included in the formation of public opinion (2). Finally, I develop a Two-Stage Epistemology of Religion that is anchored in Jürgen Habermas's work.

1 The Role of Religion in Today's Public

In the following, I outline, on the one hand, three established conceptions within the debate of political philosophy. These are the conceptions of civil religion (i), laicism (ii), and secularism (iii). These concepts can be regarded as being embedded in two paradigms of modern political philosophy: liberalism and communitarianism. While civil religion can be assigned to communitarianism, laicism and secularism are forms of liberalism.

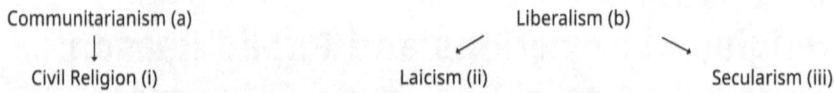

Fig. 1: Communitarianism versus Liberalism

Taking into account the fact that communitarianism, laicism, and secularism have been developed with regard to different national contexts, I will label the concept of civil religion as the US-American, the concept of laicism as the French, and the concept of secularism as the German model. By no means, however, do I intend to narrow down the complex political conditions of these nations by attributing to each of them only one single concept. My point is rather that, in order to understand these concepts, it is necessary to read their arguments in the light of the political situation in the United States, France and Germany.[1] Thus, these concepts can be seen as a heuristic tool that provides a first orientation.

a) Communitarianism

Communitarianism is a paradigm of political philosophy that emerged in the United States in the 1980s and was constituted in opposition to modern liberalism in the form of John Rawls's *A Theory of Justice* (1971). While liberalism, following Kant, seeks universally binding criteria, communitarianism, following Aristotle and Hegel, sensitizes to the constitutive role of the form of life in which a society is embedded. Among the most important books are Alasdair MacIntyre's *After Virtue* (1981), Michael Sandel's *Liberalism and the Limits of Justice* (1982) and Michael Walzer's *Spheres of Justice: A Defense of Pluralism and Equality* (1983). In what follows, Civil Religion is presented as a communitarian interpretation of the relationship between religion and the state.

i) The US Model of Civil Religion

The concept of civil religion was coined in its current form by Robert N. Bellah in the 1960s, presenting it as an interpretive model for the United States of America:

---

[1] By no means do I want to deny the fact that there exist significant alternative approaches. To give just two examples, on the one hand, John Rawls and Richard Rory elaborated a liberal interpretation of the US. On the other hand, Herman Lübbe attempted a communitarian interpretation of Germany.

> While some have argued that Christianity is the national faith, and others that church and synagogue celebrate only the generalized religion of 'the American Way of Life', few have realized that there exists alongside and rather clearly differentiated from the churches an elaborate and well-institutionalized civil religion in America (Bellah 1967, 1).

The concept of civil religion is based on a view of the relationship between the state, the churches and the way they refer to God that is clearly distinguished from laicism and secularism:

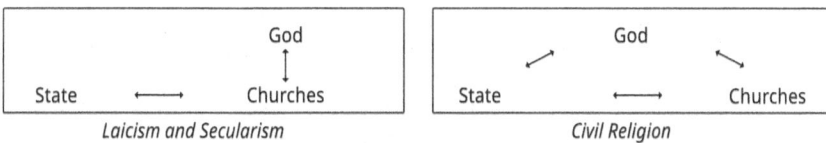

Fig. 2: Laicism and Secularism versus Civil Religion

The most profound difference is the way they refer to God: While in laicistic and secular societies any such reference is made exclusively by the churches, within civil religion, it is also sought by the state. While laicism and secularism threaten to reduce God to a private matter, in civil religion references to God are made in the name of both the state and the churches. People from Europe's secular societies are irritated by American politicians who readily use phrases like "God bless America" or speak of "God's own country". While God is perceived in laicistic and secular societies as an extraterritorial entity whose meaning is only revealed in the realm of religion, the word "God" is undergoing a political reinterpretation in civil religion. The guiding idea here is that the aforementioned new understanding of the reference to God can by no means be traced back to a specific religion but is in principle shared by different communities of faith. Nevertheless, the fact that the form of the reference to God is inspired by that of the Jewish-Christian tradition cannot be denied.

One guiding aim of civil religion is to elaborate a narrative that provides a parallel between the founding of the United States and its role in the world and the history of the biblical people of Israel. More precisely, a decontextualization of biblical narratives occurs, which are first understood as a paradigm and thus as an ahistorical form of thought before they are then projected onto sections of American history:

> Behind the civil religion at every point lie biblical archetypes: Exodus, Chosen People, Promised Land, New Jerusalem, and Sacrificial Death and Rebirth. But it is also genuinely Amer-

ican and genuinely new. It has its own prophets and its own martyrs, its own sacred events and sacred places, its own solemn rituals and symbols. It is concerned that America be a society as perfectly in accord with the will of God as men can make it, and a light to all nations. (Bellah 1967, 21)

According to this view, the biblical Exodus narrative can illuminate the idea of the founding of the United States: one pioneer of such a social, philosophical interpretation of the Exodus is the book *Exodus and Revolution* (1985) by Michael Walzer, who employs the biblical narrative of the Exodus as a paradigm of social revolution:

I shall pay attention, and expound the Exodus as a paradigm of revolutionary politics. But the word 'paradigm' is to be taken loosely here: the Exodus isn't a theory of revolution, and it would make little sense to try to construct a theory out of the biblical story. The Exodus is a story, a big story, one that became part of the cultural consciousness of the West – so that a range of political events have been located and understood within the narrative frame that it provides. (Walzer 1985, 7)

According to Walzer, a revolution prototypically has three moments: while in a situation of oppression, it is first necessary to identify the concrete mechanism of violence, in a second step, a counter-model must be designed that is antithetically opposed to it. Finally, it is necessary to define and jointly initiate measures which, on the one hand, are capable of liberating people from oppression and, at the same time, contribute to the establishment of the counter-model:

We still believe, or many of us do, what the Exodus first taught, or what it has commonly been taken to teach, about the meaning and possibility of politics and about its proper form: first, that where you live, it is probably Egypt; second, that there is a better place, a world more attractive, a promised land; and third, that the way to the land is through the wilderness. There is no way to get from here to there except by joining together and marching. (Walzer 1985, 149)

In the biblical narrative, Egyptian rule can be identified as a mechanism of violence. It is decisive that the enslaved people are by no means a homogeneous group that would allow them to identify themselves in terms of a uniform "we". Significantly, a shared orientation is required in order to first constitute something like a community. Suppose one transfers this idea to the founding of the United States. In that case, Europe could be identified as Egypt, and the common orientation could be reconstructed as an escape from the Old World's religious and monarchical mode of external domination. Against this background, the strong emphasis on freedom in the United States can be explained as a counter-design to Europe. As freedom is given the role of a principle, other values – such as the common good or security – are subordinated to it. In this sense, to address just one of the best-known examples, the Second Amendment to the Constitution can be read as restraining a government from prohibiting its citizens from carrying weapons. To do so would disproportionately interfere with the liberty of its citizens. Finally, the founding act of the United States can be identified with the adoption of the Declaration of Independence. In this regard, the role of the Founding Fathers has been paralleled to that of Moses: just as Moses is not the cause of the Exodus and the taking of the land in the biblical narrative, the Founding Fathers are not to be seen as the cause of the founding of the United States. On the other hand, both Moses and the Founding Fathers take on the role of executors.

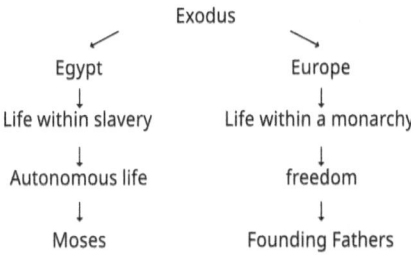

Fig. 3: Exodus as Paradigm

In both cases, an otherworldly authority is being given a decisive role. This transcendent vanishing point is what Robert N. Bellah tries to depict with his model of civil religion. When politicians and clerics speak of God, they use the same term in clearly different ways. In the language game of the politician, God marks a vanishing point that transcends his person on the one hand and is represented by his office on the other. In the language game of believers, God is addressed as a "You", in particular in the form of ritual requests for his assistance that seek to assure the believers of normative action guidelines for existential questions. In short, the reference to God in civil religion constitutes a semantic but by no means a pragmatic agreement between politicians and clerics.

Although Robert N. Bellah's thesis is controversial and the possible references, due to their polyvalence, generate the suspicion that it is a mere projection of biblical narratives without any additional explanatory added value, it is difficult to escape its plausibility, given the references to God in presidential speeches and the way God is interwoven with the country – apparent in the handling of flag and anthem (cf., for example, the replications in Bellah 1978).

b) Liberalism

The concept of a communitarian embedding of religion, as suggested by Robert N. Bellah and Michael Walzer, seems unsuitable for the current situation of Western societies: as John Rawls rightly pointed out, plurality is the main feature of a modern Western society. Therefore, religious communities can no longer be concisely identified with whole civic groups. The idea is rather that people with different religious convictions live peacefully side by side. Consequently, a communitarian interpretation of American society, as outlined by Bellah and Walzer, would seem to make it difficult for Muslims, Hinduists, Buddhists, or atheists to identify with the ethos of the nation they are living in. The liberal interpretation of the relationship between religion and society appears to be a more appropriate approach. Two variants of that interpretation can be distinguished: laicism, which is oriented toward negative religious freedom, and secularism, which is oriented toward positive religious freedom.

ii) The French Model of Laicism

The French model denies the relevance of the question whether religion and the state are compatible, emphasizing that religion is a private matter. Laicity in France is based on the principle of negative religious freedom. A paradigmatic case is the so-called headscarf affair: more than 20 Muslim schoolgirls were expelled from their schools between 1989 and 1996 because they refused to take off their headscarves, which was exaggeratedly interpreted as an attack on the laicity of the state. Thus the executive branch saw the fundamental values of the French Republic openly questioned with reference to religious values. It therefore ruled that religion is a private matter and that the ostentatious display of religious symbols in public must be avoided.[2]

iii) The German Model of Secularism

The third concept strives for an intermediate path, as implemented in the form of secularism that characterizes the German situation – a secularism that is oriented toward positive religious freedom. In Germany the role of religion is regulated in the Grundgesetz (GG) (Constitutional Law) that focuses on individuals rather than

---

2 For further reading cf. Maclure/Taylor 2011.

specific groups in terms of freedom rights. From this perspective, the Grundgesetz addresses believers and their religious convictions under the headings of freedom of faith, conscience, and religion (Article 4 (1) and (2) GG). On the one hand, this places individual religiosity under the protection of the Grundgesetz, while, on the other hand, the Grundgesetz decidedly does not give priority to religion over other fundamental rights, such as freedom of opinion (Article 5(1)), freedom of science (Article 5(3)) or freedom of assembly (Article 8 GG). For many believers, however, religion is not just one option among many, as their religious convictions take the form of worldview propositions that provide an interpretive framework. As long as religions are understood as worldviews, the question arises, on the one hand, whether and, if so, how different religions mutually relate to each other, and, on the other hand, whether or not a religious worldview can recognize the state in its role as arbitrator and moderator. While the theology of religion has addressed the first problem, I turn, in the following part of my essay, exclusively to the second problem, addressing specifically how the implicit primacy of the Grundgesetz (as universal) over religious beliefs (as particular) is criticized. This fundamental debate regularly becomes an issue in our everyday life in situations in which individuals facing conflicting principles of action think they have to choose between religious and state authorities: as examples we might consider the high-profile discussions surrounding circumcision (concerning Judaism), the crucifix in schools (concerning Christianity), or shechita (concerning Islam).

2 The Epistemology of Religious Conviction

In the following, I will sketch an approach based on the German Model of Secularism. I will first propose several general epistemological considerations, with the intention to demonstrate that beliefs are never unambiguously "true" or "false," but merely reflect reality more or less adequately (a). Against this background, I will then address the domain of religious convictions and ask what constitutes their object (b).

a) Epistemical Considerations

While in a first part, I examine what the nature of beliefs looks like (i), in a second part I focus on the more specific question of how the nature of religious beliefs can be characterized (ii).

i) The nature of beliefs

In everyday practice, people are confronted with different, partly consensual, partly conflicting forms of belief. These can take highly diverse forms, such as "I believe that $a^2 + b^2 = c^2$", "I believe that H_2O changes its state of aggregation at 0° and 100° Celsius", or "I believe that Julius Caesar died on 15 March 44 BC." The term belief ultimately goes back to the Greek noun δόξα. In Plato and the tradition referring to him, δόξα first stands for an assumption that, in order to attain the status of knowledge, must be true and requires justification. That is the so-called standard definition of knowledge as justified, true belief (abbreviated: JTB). This definition proves highly problematic in several respects, only three of which can be addressed here:

Firstly, the common view that knowledge as a justified belief is diametrically opposed to belief as insufficiently justified needs to be challenged. Taking a closer look at the above examples we find that a hermetic separation of belief and knowledge cannot be maintained. The justification of a mathematical conviction (e.g., "$a^2 + b^2 = c^2$"), for example, turns out to be incomparably higher than that of a chemical conviction (e.g. "H_2O changes its aggregate state at 0° and 100° Celsius") or even that of a historical conviction (e.g. "Julius Caesar died on 15 March 44 BC"). This difference is not at all due to the beliefs mentioned *per se*, but to the different scientific contexts of mathematics, chemistry, and historical sciences. By no means can the epistemic standards that indicate when a belief counts as knowledge be clarified uniformly and equally for all sciences from an external point of view.[3] Rather, epistemic standards and the methods of their ascertainment need to be discussed within the respective epistemic discourses, for instance, within mathematics, chemistry, and history. Therefore, in scientific work we are never moving in an area where belief and knowledge are clearly separated, but rather in a gray area between these two.[4]

Secondly, the standard definition derived from Plato which defines knowledge as justified, true belief was refuted as inadequate by Edmund Gettier in his paper "Is Justified True Belief Knowledge?" (1963) with reference to the issue of coincidence. Even if a specific belief can be characterized as a justified, true belief according to the JTB provisions, Gettier argues, it is by no means error-resistant. For instance, even banal beliefs such as the one that it is 12 a.m. (true) at 12 a.m. (belief) because my wristwatch reads 12:00 (justified) can be false. Because,

---

[3] This argument was most strongly advocated by Rudolf Carnap in *The Logical Structure of the World and Pseudoproblems in Philosophy* (1928).
[4] This argument is represented in epistemology under the label of "contextualism" by Stewart Cohen (1988; 1999), Keith DeRose (1995; 1999) or David K. Lewis (1979; 1996), among others.

so the punch line, if my watch stopped exactly twelve hours ago at 12 p.m., this belief would be less a matter of knowledge than of coincidence.

Thirdly, the standard definition reduces knowledge exclusively to "knowledge that" and thus to propositional knowledge. Other forms, such as "knowledge how" but also "knowledge by acquaintance" and "knowledge by description" are implicitly excluded. The debate on phenomenological consciousness can exemplify this: as Thomas Nagel points out in his paper "What Is It Like to Be a Bat" (1974), "what-is-it-like-to-be" statements can by no means be arbitrarily translated back and forth from the participant's to the observer's perspective. The idea of what it is like for me to be a bat (V1 for short) merely approximates the idea of what it is like for a bat to be a bat (V2 for short). By no means, however, can V2 be completely reduced to V1. Frank Jackson goes one step further in his papers "Epiphenomenal Qualia" (1982) and "What Mary Didn't Know" (1986), where he develops the thought experiment of Mary, a color researcher, who on the one hand has the sum of all propositional knowledge about colors, but on the other hand is trapped in a black-and-white chamber and has never seen colors herself. The discussion ignites around the question of whether or not Mary receives a genuinely new knowledge at her first sight of colored objects and landscapes. Finally, Joseph Levine identifies an explanatory gap in his article "Materialism and Qualia – The Explanatory Gap" (1983). While statement (i) "Heat is identical with the motion of molecules" can be characterized as fully explanatory, this is precisely not true of statements (ii) "Pain is identical with the irritation of C-fibers" or (iii) "To be in pain is identical with being in a state F." While (i) sufficiently and exhaustively explains our notion of heat with the motion of molecules, this is precisely not the case with (ii) and (iii). Pain can by no means be limited to its causal role for the organism, but also includes a qualitative sensation, which indicates how it is for an organism to feel pain.

ii) The nature of religious beliefs

Religious belief is a highly heterogeneous phenomenon, as can be explained in terms of different epistemic forms. The three best known forms include doxastic (P believes that p), personal (P believes in T), or testimonial (P believes T that p) belief. Religious epistemology is limited to the form of doxastic belief. Along this path, there is coherence with the epistemological debate, as the form S believes p is crucial in either case. While personal and testimonial belief address the relation of a subject to a transcendent other, doxastic belief refers only to a semantic representation. As a representation, terms such as "salvation", "creature", "creator", or "sin" symbolize the propositional side of this relation.

According to the concept of doxastic belief, the status of the relation of self and a transcendent other can be symbolized by the terms "sin" (for a dysfunctional relation) or "salvation" (for a functional relation), and the role of self and a transcendent other by "creature" (for "self") and "creator" (for "other"). Since the meaning of these terms is rooted in the form of life, it manifests itself exclusively in the everyday religious practice of believers. In other words: by loosening themselves in their everyday practice with conceptual pairs such as "sin"/"salvation" or "creature"/"creator", believers by no means refer to certain phenomena which are exclusively accessible to them as believers. On the contrary, the phenomena to which believers refer are equally open to those of other faiths and – to take up a famous wording by Jürgen Habermas – the religiously non-musical. Thus, the difference lies not in the phenomena themselves, but in the attitude with which believers, non-believers and religiously non-musical people refer to them. In other words, the meaning of terms such as "sin"/"salvation" or "creature"/"creator" cannot be defined lexically, but must be read in terms of their performative mode of use.

In his discussion on *Theology and Falsification* (1955) with Antony Flew and Basil Mitchell, Richard Hare explained this fact by introducing the new term "blik".[5] His thought is still informative today: according to Hare, believers, non-believers and religiously non-musical people all possess a blik. The blik cannot be evaluated from an external perspective as "right" or "wrong"; rather, it can only be decided from an internal perspective whether a person loosens himself with his blik "appropriately" or "inappropriately" in everyday practice. A self-selected example can illustrate that: if I loosen with my blik, "Spectacle wearers are out to get me," in my everyday practice, adjusting my behavior accordingly, I will quickly come up against limits. If I flinch, run away or try to entrench myself in the face of anyone wearing glasses, my behavior will be perceived as strange, in the worst case even pathological. Consequently, I loosen myself with my blik in the representational context entirely inappropriately. As a result, I constantly find myself in bizarre situations and being observed by my fellow human beings. While my blik cannot be refuted as "wrong", it leads me to a highly questionable behavior that I will eventually correct step by step.[6]

---

5 The discussion between Richard Hare, Antony Flew and Basil Mitchell is published in the anthology Flew/MacIntyr 1955, 96–108.
6 Among others, this idea was elaborated in detail by Dewi Z. Phillips in *The Concept of Prayer* (1965) and examined on the example of prayer.

b) The paradigm shift from a worldview to a form of life

On my way toward a Two-Stage Epistemology of religious convictions I try to sensistize the changes within both, the social (i) and the individual perspective (ii).

i) The social perspective

Since, based on the principle of the liberal state, freedom of faith, conscience and religion are granted equal status with other individual rights and freedoms, such as freedom of opinion, freedom of the press or freedom of assembly (Art 5 and 8 GG), religious believers often feel completely misunderstood in their practice of faith. This is because religious convictions are modeled by religious believers as a worldview that is not simply one perspective among others, but rather provides an interpretive framework within which other bodies of knowledge about the world can develop their reality-defining power in the first place. This perception poses a serious problem for liberal democracy, as worldviews, churches and religious communities threaten to stand monolithically in opposition to both one another and to the state. Significantly, the confrontation between state and religion has tended to ignite in individual cases.

While Richard Rorty in his paper "Religion as a Conversation-Stopper" (1994) therefore tries to banish religion fundamentally from the realm of the public sphere and regards religion merely as a private matter, John Rawls and Jürgen Habermas strive to build a bridge. Referring to Jürgen Habermas, Rorty argues that today's liberal philosophers believe that we will not be able to maintain a democratic polity if religious adherents are not willing to accept the privatization of religion as a price to pay for guaranteed religious freedom. As Rorty observes, as soon as a citizen introduces religious convictions with a claim to validity in public discourse, the conversation breaks down. Referring to religious convictions in a public debate is, in the eyes of Rorty, comparable to confessing in the same context that one would never have an abortion or that watching pornography is the only thing someone enjoys right now. Statements like these are indeed of personal significance and concern the individual and his or her life. By no means, however, do they represent a matter of public concern. A contrasting perspective is suggested by John Rawls, who elaborates the basis for an equally modern and democratic society in his *Theory of Justice* (1971). On the one hand, Rawls contends that the principles of the modern state cannot be derived from a prior commitment to any comprehensive doctrine. Therefore, in his paper "The Idea of an Overlapping Consensus" (1987), he rejects religious, socialist, but also certain liberal theories as candidates for an appropriate theory of justice. On the other hand, he argues that, since a liberal theory is committed to modern society's pluralism, believers – as long as they formulate their claims to validity in such a way that everyone can comprehend them – must not simply be excluded from public debates. For Jürgen Habermas, this thought ultimately leads to the thesis of a translation of religious convictions into claims to validity that can hope for counterfactual recognition in public discourses. Accordingly, in his talk given when he received the Peace Prize awarded by the German Book Dealers, "Faith and Knowledge" (2001), Habermas makes three demands on religious citizens: firstly, they must be willing to treat the members of other religious group as equal partners in discourse (R_1); secondly, the authority of science must be recognized (R_2); and thirdly, it must be accepted that the principles of the constitutional state are based on profane morality rather than religious doctrines (R_3).

With these rules Habermas appeals to believers to transform their religious convictions from a worldview into a form of life. In this context, a person's religiosity is understood as one (among other) forms of life. For a clarification of that view, the individual perspective of a believer can be referred to as the distinction between *Self*, *I* and *Me*. While in a worldview the *Self* is perceived exclusively through the lens of religion, the form of life models religion in such a way that religion comes into view for the *Self* as Me^R and thus merely as one alongside other forms of life (such as Me^F or Me^B).

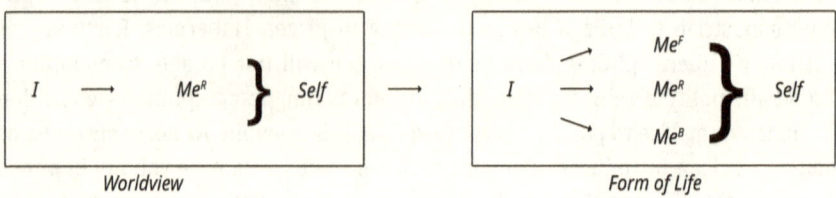

Fig. 4: Worldview versus Form of Life

ii) The individual perspective

The suspicion that a schizophrenic splitting into several independent forms of life may result here can be countered by pointing out the way in which the *I* connects the different forms of life (e.g. Me^R, Me^B or Me^F) to a *Self*. A certain persona (*Self*) may be able, for example, to work as a physicist (Me^B), to live privately in a lesbian relationship (Me^F), and to be active in the church. Thus in no way does Me^R come into conflict with Me^F or Me^B.

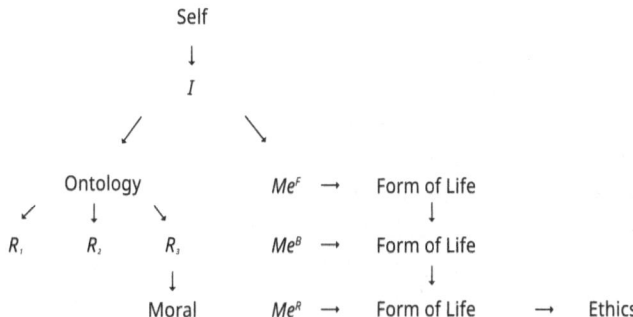

Fig. 5: Self

In distinction to the forms of life, ontology is the commonly shared domain of beliefs, which can be identified with Habermas' three rules (R_1, R_2, R_3). At this point I restrict myself to the first of the three rules and thus to the interpretation of religious freedom.

The scope of the first rule not only covers the explicit exchanges between believers, those who belong to different religious groups and those who are religiously non-musical, but it is implicitly already anchored in our everyday practices. This can be seen specifically in how we interact with each other in diverse contexts: detached from our religious confession, we interact in our everyday lives with female doctors, cab drivers, or waitresses, for example. In this social interaction, a recognition is expressed that identifies the other person as a citizen and that does not tie this to his or her religious confession. On the contrary, it is precisely where such a linkage back to a religious confession occurs and where people are treated differently because of their faith that social interaction is challenged. Only where people are excluded from everyday actions because of their religion is the ontology of the liberal state in the sense of R_1 put to the test.

c) The concept of translation

In this final part, I examine the concept of a Two-Stage Epistemology of Religion and thus split the part into two sections: first I focus on the concept of translation in the work of Jürgen Habermas (i) and, secondly, I illustrate this concept with the example of the translation of Gen 1:27 from a religious into a secular conviction (ii).

i) A formal pragmatic interpretation of translation

Translation (Übersetzung) is a formal-pragmatic claim to validity. Its function becomes comprehensible only as distinct from interpretation (Deutung).[7] In an interpretation, a term T_1 is replaced by a term T_2 in synonym formation. Both terms T_1 and T_2 belong to the same class. In normative questions this class can be identified with Habermas as the language game of morality and distinguished from those language games of ethics.[8] This differentiation is based on the distinction between pragmatics, ethics and morality: pragmatics, ethics, and morality provide three different ways of answering the question, "What shall I do?" While pragmatic discourses relate empirical knowledge to hypothetical purposes and preferences and evaluate the consequences of decisions according to underlying maxims, ethical discourses start with the concrete form of life in which a subject is embedded and seek to provide orientation for a personal way of life. If my bicycle, which I need for my daily commute, has broken down, I am concretely called upon to weigh up reasons that help me decide among several possible courses of action. In the context of a pragmatic discourse, I have to ask myself whether I should either have it repaired, buy a new bike right away, or whether it is advisable to switch to the bus altogether. The situation is different in ethical discourses: when a high school graduate is faced with the question of whether and, if so, which course of study she should take up and whether this should happen in her home town or abroad, she does not weigh up options of equal rank, but asks herself who she wants to be. After all, choosing a course of study and her future career path expresses what constitutes a good life for the high school graduate: whether she wants to earn as much money as possible as a fund manager or to sensitively introduce children and young people to society as a teacher. Moral discourses are completely different: these are concerned with norms that depend neither on subjective ends nor on the goal of a good life.

---

[7] While the concept of interpretation (*Deutung*) was first introduced in the hitherto untranslated paper "Wahrheitstheorien" (1973), that of translation (*Übersetzung*) is a late addition to discourse theory from Habermas in "Faith and Knowledge" 2001.

[8] Habermas distinguished pragmatics, ethics and morality in his essay "On the Pragmatic, the Ethical, and the Moral Employments of Practical Reason" (1991). I will orientate myself on this in the following.

ii) How to translate Gen 1:27: An example

Discussing human genome editing, theologians refer, among other things, to the pericope Gen 1:27, breaking it down into several partial statements for the purpose of a biblical-theological analysis.[9] I limit myself to four possible partial statements: "God is the Creator" (as φ_1), "Man is created in the image of God" (as φ_2), "Man and woman are equal creatures of God" (as φ_3) and "Man is a creature of God" (as φ_4). For the present context, sub-statements φ_2 and φ_4 appear to be of particular interest. Since the partial statements φ_2 and φ_4 contain, with "creature" and "God", two terms whose meaning can be comprehensively spelled out only with reference to the theological language game, a reconstruction of their core statements is necessary. Significantly, no general guideline for such a reconstruction can be provided, since everything depends on the framework of a common compromise shared by believers, people of other faiths and religiously non-musical people. Specifically, validity claims need to be re-formulated until their meaning is understood by believers, dissenters and the religiously unmusical. In the case of φ_2 such reformulations could be "Man is a being endowed with freedom and is obliged to respect freedom" and in the case of φ_4 "Man does not owe his natural suchness to another man". Since, in the translation of T_1 into T_2 only partial aspects (here about φ_2 and φ_4) are matched, what happens here is a form of analogy formation. In this sense T_1 and T_2 show a common intersection (φ_2 and φ_4).

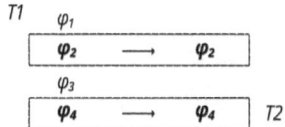

Fig. 6: Analogy

The "translation" is a formal pragmatic claim to validity. The function of translation is to transfer individual terms from one language game to another. To do this, the terms are extracted from one context, reformulated, and inserted into a new context. In our case, this is done from the context of a religious language game into the context of public norm formation. The reformulation takes the form of an analogy. In no way is the meaning of a term with all its (in our case: theological) im-

---

[9] Habermas himself refers to this idea in "Faith and Knowledge" (2001) without elaborating it in detail.

plications comprehensively transferred, but only selected partial aspects of one context are opened up for another.

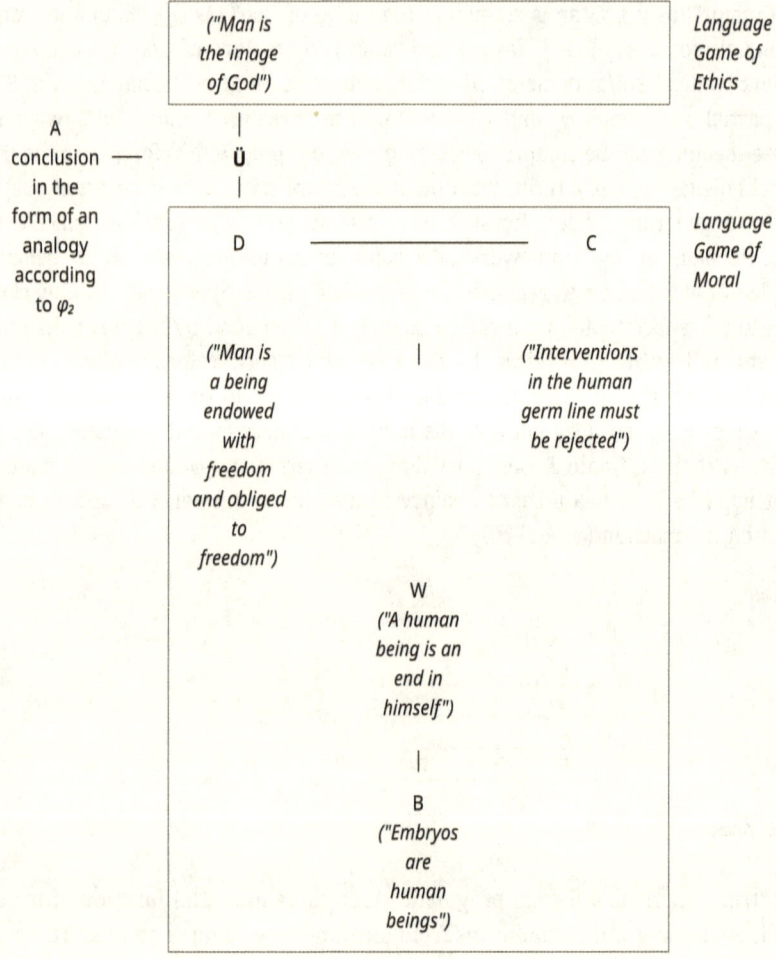

Fig. 7: Translation of Gen 1:27

The translation from "Man is the image of God" to "Man is a being endowed with freedom and obligated to freedom" merely marks the necessary condition for a religious conviction to be treated as a claim to validity by believers, non-believers, and religious non-musicals alike. Whether the translated conviction can then discursively assert itself against potential objections is yet another issue. The concept of translation offers, however, a way to comprehend how secularism enables believers to include their religious conviction in building a public opinion.

3 Conclusion

Finally, I would like to summarize the results: In a first step, I took up the distinction between communitarianism and liberalism, as discussed in political philosophy, assigning civil religion to communitarianism and laicism, and secularism to liberalism. With regard to secularism, I then developed, inspired by Jürgen Habermas, a Two-Stage Epistemology. Elaborating this concept, I proceeded in three steps. First, I explained what constitutes convictions in general and religious convictions in particular; then I discussed the necessity of a paradigm shift from worldview to form of life; and finally, following Habermas' translation thesis, I explained my concept of a Two-Stage Epistemology by introducing the example of Gen 1:27.

Works Cited

Bellah, Robert N. "Religion and Legitimation in the American Republic." *Society* 15.4 (1978), 16–23.
Bellah, Robert N. "Civil Religion in America."*Daedalus* 96.1 (1967), 1–21.
Carnap, Rudolf. *The Logical Structure of the World and Pseudoproblems in Philosophy.* (1928), Chicago: Open Court, 2003.
Cohen, Stewart. "Contextualism, Skepticism, and the Structure of Reasons." *Noûs* 33 (1999), 57–89.
Cohen, Stewart. "How to be a Fallibilist." *Philosophical Perspectives* 2 (1988), 91–123.
De Rose, Keith. "Contextualism. An Explanation and Defense." *The Blackwell Guide to Epistemology.* Ed. John Greco, Ernest Sosa Malden: Blackwell, 1999. 187–205.
De Rose, Keith. "Solving the Skeptical Problem." *The Philosophical Review* 104 (1995), 1–52.
Flew, Antony, Richard Hare, Basil Mitchell. "Theology and Falsification." *New Essays in Philosophical Theology.* Ed. Antony Flew, Alasdair MacIntyre New York: SCM Press, 1955. 96–108.
Gettier, Edmund. "Is Justified True Belief Knowledge?" *Analysis* 23.6 (1963), 121–123.
Habermas, Jürgen. "Faith and Knowledge." (2001) *The Future of Human Nature.* Cambridge: Polity Press 2003, 101–115.
Habermas, Jürgen. "On the Pragmatic, the Ethical, and the Moral Employments of Practical Reason." (1991) *Justification and Application. Remarks on Discourse Ethics.* Cambridge, MA.: MIT Press, 1993, 1–17.
Habermas, Jürgen. "Wahrheitstheorien." *Wirklichkeit und Reflexion.* Ed. Helmut Fahrenbach Pfüllingen: Neske, 1973, 211–65.
Jackson, Frank. "What Marry Didn't Know." *Journal of Philosophy* 83.5 (1986), 291–295.
Jackson, Frank. "Epiphenomenal Qualia." *Philosophical Quarterly* 32 (1982), 127–136.

Levine, Joseph. "Materialism and Qualia – The Explanatory Gap." *Pacific Philosophical Quarterly* 64 (1983), 354–61.
Lewis, David K. "Elusive Knowledge." *Australasian Journal of Philosophy* 74 (1996), 549–67.
Lewis, David K. "Scorekeeping in Language Games." *Journal of Philosophical Logic* 8 (1979), 339–59.
MacIntyre, Alasdair. *After Virtue: A Study in Moral Theory, Second Edition.* Notre Dame, IN: U of Notre Dame P, 1981.
Maclure, Jocelyn, Charles Taylor. *Secularism and Freedom of Conscience.* Cambridge, MA: Harvard UP, 2011.
Nagel, Thomas. "What Is It Like To Be a Bat." *Philosophical Review* 83 (1974), 435–50.
Phillips, Dewi Z. *The Concept of Prayer.* London: Routledge, 1965.
Rawls, John. "The Idea of an Overlapping Consensus." *Oxford Journal of Legal Studies* 7.1 (1987), 1–25.
Rawls, John. *A Theory of Justice.* Cambridge, MA: Harvard UP, 1971.
Rorty, Richard. "Religion as a Conversation-Stopper." *Common Knowledge* 3 (1994), 1–6.
Sandel, Michael. *Liberalism and the Limits of Justice* (1982). Cambridge: Cambridge UP, 1998.
Walzer, Michael. *Exodus and Revolution.* New York: Basic Books, 1985.
Walzer, Michael. *Spheres of Justice: A Defense of Pluralism and Equality.* New York: Basic Books, 1984.

Christoph Irmscher
Scientists Who Believe: From Louis Agassiz to Katharine Hayhoe

Abstract: Arguing with fellow evolutionist Asa Gray in 1860, Charles Darwin explained that there was "too much misery in the world" for him to believe that the world had been created by a benevolent God. Against the background of Darwin's challenge to religion, this essay reviews three scientists who found ways of reconciling science with religion, inspired in different ways by Gray's theistic optimism. Examples range from Darwin's main antagonist Louis Agassiz, who felt that God's plan for the world was fully legible and that it was the scientist's duty to teach the public how to read it properly, to the geneticist Francis Collins, the past director of the National Institutes of Health, who contends that belief in God is a rational choice, to climate scientist Katharine Hayhoe, chief scientist of the Nature Conservancy, for whom the Bible contains practical advice for ecologically responsible living. What never occurred to Agassiz or Darwin and what Collins never considers—namely that the world as we know it might end—has become real possibility for Hayhoe.

Several years ago, I published a new biography of Louis Agassiz (1807–1873), once the most famous scientist of the nineteenth century, still remembered today for the term he popularized, "the Ice Age," for the natural history museum at Harvard University he founded and filled with specimens, his pioneering scientific fieldwork, and, less favorably, his visceral racism, now under renewed scrutiny.[1]

Agassiz, born in Switzerland in 1807, at the foot of the Bernese Alps, was a minister's son. He resisted his father's wish that he become a preacher or a doctor and escaped to universities in Germany, completing his Doctor of Philosophy at the University of Erlangen-Nuremberg and, as a concession to his father, his medical degree at the University of Munich (he never laid hands on a patient).

As a scientist, he quickly rose to fame, widely admired for his encyclopedic work on fossil fish, which attracted the attention of the famous Alexander von Humboldt, and perhaps even more so for his studies of glaciers, which involved spending increasing amounts of time high up in the mountains, where he sur-

---

[1] Irmscher, *Louis Agassiz*; Harvard University is facing a lawsuit over its alleged exploitative use of two out of the fifteen daguerreotypes made for Louis Agassiz in 1850, among the earliest images featuring enslaved people; Marcelo, "Court: Harvard Can Be Sued For Distress Over Slave Photos."

rounded himself with an army of assistants and admirers. Although he was not the first to notice that glaciers had moved in the history of their existence, he was the most efficient propagator of the theory that the earth had, during its long history, been covered at least in part by vast sheets of ice.

Thanks to Humboldt's mentorship, Agassiz, weighed down by debts he had incurred over his ambitious publication projects and his crumbling marriage, received the invitation to deliver the prestigious Lowell lectures in Boston. He arrived in 1846 and never left. Harvard created a new professorship just for him —and the "foreign professor" soon became a legendary figure, especially admired by the Boston literati. It seemed as if he had his hands in everything. He created the first seaside laboratory in the history of American science, fundraised for his museum, taught students how to do fieldwork, and encouraged citizens to send him fish for a great new work on American ichthyology.

Charles Darwin, who became Agassiz's great nemesis, knew that when it came to the facts of natural history there was no one who knew more than Agassiz, whose encyclopedic interests spanned everything from embryology to ichthyology to geology. The publication of Darwin's *On the Origin of Species* (1859) led to a great rift between the two men. In Chapter XI ("Geographical Distribution"), Darwin had the temerity to thank Agassiz, mockingly, for having provided him with precisely the scientific insights that allowed him to formulate a theory that Agassiz would have rejected. Referring to the now disproven theory that representatives of the same species living "at distant points" in the world could be explained by the assumption that "the same species must have been independently created at several distinct points," Darwin joyfully concluded: "we might have remained in this same belief, had not Agassiz and others called vivid attention to the glacial period, which ... affords a simple explanation of these facts." Agassiz's concept of the "Ice Age," which stipulated that the surface features of continents had been drastically reshaped by glacial activity, offered a beautiful and cohesive explanation as to why species had migrated and could now be found in different parts of the world—not because God had created them there in separate acts of divine fiat, as Agassiz would have argued, but as the result of geological action.[2] If Darwin had intended this passage as a deliberate slight, it worked, as Agassiz's furiously annotated copy of *Origin* attests.[3]

Louis Agassiz was not the churchgoing kind, as the Bostonians quickly noticed.[4] Yet the science he practiced seemed predicated on the belief that everything

---

[2] Darwin, *On the Origin of Species* 365–367.
[3] Agassiz's marginalia are discussed in Gould, *I Have Landed* 314–18.
[4] Henry Wadsworth Longfellow, quoting Horace, deemed him a "sparse and infrequent worshipper of the Gods," Longfellow, Journal, 11 June 1848.

in nature had been created for a purpose, that science, properly pursued, would give you access to the divine. Let us take a look at one of the few surviving Agassiz manuscripts *not* concerned with scientific matters, an explication of Psalm 8, lines 3–4: "When I consider thy heavens, the work of thy fingers, the moon and the stars, which thou hast ordained, what is man, that thou art mindful of him?"[5]

This is a pretty wild text, almost ecstatically written. It is certainly not an endorsement of the psalmist's position. For Agassiz, the psalmist's humility before God was a thing of the past, rendered unnecessary by the progress of modern science. The skies today, says Agassiz, no longer look the way they did to King David. "We cannot if we would, we would not if we could, put out of mind the knowledge which the intervening centuries of study and observation have established." Astronomy, for example, has lent more splendor to the universe than it ever had before: "There is now seen an order more extensive and perfect in the positions and motions in the heavenly bodies than the Psalmist could have dreamed of." If God's wisdom is infinite, so is that of modern man who comprehends it all, and when Agassiz says "man," he really means "scientist": "The mind of man profoundly considered is as vast and stupendous a creation as an outward firmament of worlds." The stars in the skies cannot understand the nature of their own existence; the scientist, however, can.

Agassiz provides an example from contemporary science, the astronomer Urbain Le Verrier (1811–1877), who in 1846 had, through the power of mathematical deduction alone, predicted the existence of Neptune, a planet that can contain up to sixty Earths. Listen to how Agassiz sets up the story:

> A young astronomer in Paris sits down with his slate and pencil. He ascertains just the amount of various Irregularities in the motions of Uranus, not accounted for before et[6] then he reckons by a process which to the common and uneducated mind is utterly incomprehensible and amazing, reckons by figure and algebraic operations how large must that disturbing body be, how distant its orbit, and just where it ought to be found on any given day and hour.

Le Verrier had not spent a minute peering at the sky, concentrating instead on the sheet of paper before him. Yet, once he did look up from his figures, his prediction was found to be entirely accurate, as Agassiz insists: "The wondrous tube is pointed to the spot and so there it is a little twinkling star, yet a world, one of our family, and compared with which for vastness of size and orbit, this earth is but a child's

---

5 Louis Agassiz, "VIII Ps. 3.4. *When I consider Thy heavens* . . .," Louis Agassiz Papers, Houghton Library, Harvard University, MS Am 1410 (142).
6 Agassiz substitutes French "et" for "and."

bauble." Vast it is, yet the human mind—which is a copy of the divine mind—can see and grasp it: "this mind of man, perverted, dwarfed and misused as it is, is a higher creation, a more astonishing display of God's power and skill, a more signal expression of his attributes than the material worlds with which that mind deals."

God's skill? Louis Agassiz's God was not the unpredictable judge of human conduct Calvinists like his father had imagined. If God's attributes are power and skill, turn to the scientist for the most perfect manifestation of divinity. If God planned the world, the scientist could figure it out: "The world is the geologist's puzzle-box; he stands before it like the child to whom the separate pieces of the puzzle remain a mystery till he detects their relation and sees where they fit, and then his fragments grow at once into a connected picture beneath his hand."[7] To Agassiz, the world was fully knowable. The former pastor's son had become a kind of preacher, too, the Jonathan Edwards of natural history—with the crucial difference that Agassiz did "the"—the Jonathan Edwards of natural history not want to convert Americans to Christ but to science.

Darwin shared that confidence in the power of science. In *On the Origin of Species*, he argued that the kind of science he was advocating—which, unlike Agassiz's science, did not insist on a fixed order in nature and the immutability of species—was going to do away with an attitude toward nature in which we stare at it like "the savage at a ship." Darwin certainly also had a finely developed sense for the role of wonder in nature—"grandeur" is the keyword in the very last paragraph of *On the Origin of Species*.[8] Yet the suffering that he also saw in nature made it difficult for him to assume the presence of a benevolent God who oversees it all. "I own that I cannot see," he wrote to his friend and collaborator, the Harvard professor Asa Gray (1810–1888), "as plainly as others do, & as I shd wish to do, evidence of design & beneficence on all sides of us. There seems to me too much misery in the world." No benevolent God would have created a world in which cats, cruelly, relentlessly, play with mice.[9] Asa Gray, a nimble-minded botanist as well as a devout Presbyterian, did not agree with his Harvard colleague Agassiz. A believer in, and vigorous defender of, evolution, he also believed that Darwin's theory—the key for understanding change in nature—above all confirmed God's wisdom and goodness. Darwin acidly responded that while Gray was keen on observing the raindrops that nourish the Earth, he was more interested in those that fall into the ocean.[10]

---

7 Agassiz, "America the Old Word," in Agassiz, *Geological Sketches* 11.
8 Darwin, *Origin* 485, 490.
9 Darwin to Gray, May 22 [1860], Darwin Correspondence Project, DCP-LETT-2814.
10 See Gray, *Darwiniana* 128–29; Darwin to Asa Gary, September 26, 1860, Darwin Correspondence Project, DCP-LETT-2930. For more on Darwin's correspondence with Gray, see Irmscher, *Agassiz*

Modern scientist-believers rarely want to make a religion of science, as Agassiz did. And they cannot afford to let themselves be swayed by suffering, as Darwin did. (Significantly, it is animal suffering, not human suffering that unsettles Darwin in this letter). And so they find themselves returning, again and again, to Asa Gray's position, sometimes explicitly so.

Take one of the most famous contemporary scientists in the US to have outed himself as a devout believer, the physician-geneticist Francis S. Collins (born 1950). Born on a farm in the Shenandoah Valley, he grew up homeschooled, spending his free time milking cows and shucking corn.[11] He served as professor of internal medicine and human genetics at the University of Michigan, where he was known as the "gene hunter" for his pioneering technique of "positional cloning" to pinpoint disease-related genes. His research groups have been responsible for the discovery of the genes associated with cystic fibrosis, neurofibromatosis, Huntington's disease, and Hutchinson-Gilford progeria syndrome, a rare form of premature aging. From 1993 to 2008, Collins led the National Human Genome Research Institute, which culminated in April 2003 with the mapping and finished sequence of the three billion DNA letters that make up the human genetic instruction book. From 2008 to 2021, he was director of the National Institutes of Health (NIH), its longest-serving leader. His appointment was not uncontroversial. "One can only hope," wrote Sam Harris, a well-known defender of secularism, in the *New York Times*, that Dr. Collins' convictions "will not affect his judgment at the institutes of health."[12] But Collins also faced criticism from religious organizations. Especially toward the end of his NIH tenure, he was relentlessly pummeled for defending the use of fetal tissue in biomedical research, his alleged involvement in funding "gain-of-function" research in the Wuhan Lab of Virology, and his allegedly "un-Christian" attacks on unvaccinated Americans: "Francis Collins might want to re-read his Bible."[13] Collins remained undaunted. He served through three different administrations, using his influence and the wide respect he enjoyed to secure large budget increases, which he funneled into programs related to brain health and addiction research and the development of COVID-19 therapies and vaccines.

Collins came to Christianity via his science, impressed by the faith some of his patients displayed and on the wings of his dissatisfaction with the many things sci-

---

134–45; Irmscher, introduction to Agassiz, *Introduction to the Study of the Natural History* 13–5, 20–21.
11 Dhruv Khullar, "Science, Faith, and Francis Collins," accessed July 7, 2022.
12 Sam Harris, "Science Is in the Details," accessed July 7, 2022.
13 John West, "Francis Collins' Rhetoric About the Unvaccinated Is Anything but Christian," accessed July 7, 2022; John G. West, "The Tragedy of Francis Collins's Model for Science-Faith Integration," accessed July 7, 2022.

ence could not explain. In his accessibly written 2006 bestseller *The Language of God*, translated into 24 languages, Collins extols the existence of the Moral Law, which makes humans want to be good, or mostly good, to each other: "It is the awareness of right and wrong along with the development of language, awareness of self, and the ability to imagine the future, to which scientists refer when trying to enumerate the special qualities of *Homo sapiens*."[14] Then there is the wonder that attaches itself to some simple facts, such as that if the rate of expansion after the Big Bang had been the tiniest bit smaller, the universe would have re-collapsed.[15] There is, contends Collins, nothing in science that renders the existence of God implausible, and there is much that makes His existence necessary. Like Agassiz, Collins believes in the knowability of the world and rejects the argument used by the proponents of Intelligent Design that there is irreducible complexity in Nature. Like Agassiz, too, Collins feels he needs to recruit Americans for science, a task rendered more difficult, ironically, by the fact that, when it comes to a hot button issue like evolution, many Americans would rather side with the creationist Agassiz on evolution than with Darwin. "This book argues that belief in God can be an entirely rational choice," Collins writes in the introduction to his book, "and that the principles of faith are, in fact, complementary with the principles of science."[16] If there is suffering in the world, this is not God's fault but that of imperfect humans, the leaky vessels of God's will: "It is humankind, not God, that has invented knives, arrows, guns, bombs, and all manner of other instruments of torture used during the ages."[17] God would want the human mind to know the world, which is why Collins encourages his evangelical fellow Christians to embrace evolution. There is no need, says Collins, to choose between the cathedral and the laboratory: "The God of the Bible is also the God of the genome."[18] The latter statement especially reveals that this quest for the harmony between science and faith—the need to believe in a God who wants us to be good and is good to us in turn—is a very personal one for Collins, who sees Asa Gray as one of his spiritual mentors, one of the architects behind the concept of "theistic evolution" that resolves the dilemma that has haunted him: "This perspective makes it possible for the scientist-believer to be intellectually fulfilled and spiritually alive, both worshipping God and using science to uncover some of the awesome mysteries of His creation."[19]

---

14 Collins, *Language of God* 23.
15 Collins, *Language of God* 71–4.
16 Collins, *Language of God* 3.
17 Collins, *Language of God* 43.
18 Collins, *Language of God* 211.
19 Collins, *Language of God* 201.

Unlike Collins, the climate scientist Katharine Hayhoe was a believer first and then became a scientist. Born in Canada, Hayhoe is the chief scientist for the Nature Conservancy and a climate ambassador for the World Evangelical Alliance. American Evangelicalism had found its way to certain forms of environmental advocacy long before Hayhoe arrived on the scene. Since 1993, the Evangelical Environmental Network (EEN) has made its mission to support evangelical Christians "in their effort to care for God's creation, to be faithful stewards of God's provision, to get involved in regions of the United States and the world impacted by pollution, and to advocate for actions and policies that honor God and protect the environment."[20] What is often referred to as "creation care" went global with the "Jamaica Call to Action" issued by the Lausanne Movement (inspired by the American evangelist Billy Graham) and the World Evangelical Alliance in 2012. Whatever the differences between the churches, the two "primary conclusions" of the "Jamaica Call" seem to provide some common ground for the environmental initiatives that have come out of churches and communities that would normally tend to the conservative end of the political spectrum: (1) that scripture mandates stewardship of the Earth and (2) that the current environmental crisis is "pressing, urgent, and ... must be resolved in our generation."[21] The biblical justification usually comes from Genesis 2:15: "And the LORD God took the man, and put him into the garden of Eden to dress it and to keep it."

Hayhoe is a member of the board of the EEN and, we may assume, shares its theological commitments. What is new about her public advocacy is the importance she assigns to science in the fight for ecological survival. Humans are the primary agents and beneficiaries of "creation care," while non-human nature often appears as the object of the transformative work Christians need to undertake to preserve it. Hayhoe is less concerned with theological doctrine; for her, both human and non-human life are equally worth preserving—she knows that, as Rachel Carson pointed out long ago, the non-human world may carry on, in some form, without humans in it but not vice versa. If faith allows us to confront the facts about the world we live in without fear, science enables us to take the actions needed for our survival. When Hayhoe turns to the Bible, it's characteristically not the Old Testament but St. Paul she invokes: "God has given us a spirit of power, which enables us to act, instead of being frozen and paralyzed," she says, paraphrasing a passage from Paul's second letter to Timothy (2 Timothy 1:7).[22] Hayhoe thus confronts a basic problem that has

---

20 See "EEN: Mission & History," https://creationcare.org/who-we-are/, accessed July 3, 2022.
21 "Creation Care and the Gospel: Jamaica Call to Action," https://lausanne.org/content/statement/creation-care-call-to-action, accessed July 3, 2022.
22 Hayhoe, *Saving Us* 83.

stymied evangelical environmentalism, the anti-science attitude of many of her fellow evangelicals, which she believes is not determined by faith but by political ideologies that have attached themselves to evangelicalism and perverted its essence. "I'm a Christian and I believe that if you are someone who takes the Bible seriously, then you already care about climate change."[23]

Hayhoe's recent book, *Saving Us: A Climate Scientist's Case for Hope and Healing in a Divided World*, which I have been summarizing here, contains, like Collins's book, much that is personal and anecdotal. Most of the anecdotes are of the anecdotes are not about herself but about others she has encountered during her lecture tours: Matt the farmer from Iowa, who has embraced soil management; Gladys, a mother of six from Tanzania who switched from kerosene to solar lamps and is now selling them across the region; Tom the engineering professor from the south of England who rejects the idea that science can know for sure that the climate is changing but loves to knit and has other sustainable habits (salvaging cast-off furniture, refusing to use a car) that ultimately make him Hayhoe's ally, despite the fact that after an earlier encounter she had "devoutly" hoped she would never see him again.[24] Hayhoe's goal is not a theoretical one. She is not interested in extolling science, as Agassiz does, and she is not worried about reconciling science with faith, as Collins is. In all fairness, Collins himself has engaged in a fair amount of activism, too, and with renewed vigor post his NIH tenure, partnering with an organization like "Braver Angels," dedicated to bringing "Reds & Blues together to find common humanity."[25] My point here is mainly that the need to act does not provide a theoretical basis for his attempt to reconcile science and faith, while in Hayhoe's case it definitely does. For Hayhoe, a scientist who believes is a scientist who acts. She wants to make a practice of the hope, she says, in a book full of practical advice, ways in which we may overcome our distrust of data and of each other. Moving the world to net-zero electricity? You just have to believe it is possible. And do not forget to wash your laundry on cold.

What did not occur to Agassiz or Darwin, and what Collins, concerned with sorting out his spiritual conflict, does not consider—namely that the world as we know it might end, rendering all our debates and differences moot—is a real possibility for Hayhoe. But it is one that her faith does not allow her to accept either. In a way, then, Hayhoe, too, returns to old Asa Gray, affirming her interest in the raindrops that nourish the earth, though she does add a new element to it: it is up to us to make sure that the rain continues to fall.

---

23 Hayhoe, *Saving Us* 18.
24 Hayhoe, *Saving Us* 177, 161, 227.
25 See Dhruv Khullar, "Faith, Science, and Francis Collins"; https://braverangels.org/ (Accessed March 31, 2023).

Works Cited

Agassiz, Louis. Louis Agassiz, "VIII Ps. 3.4. *When I consider Thy heavens . . .*," Louis Agassiz Papers, Houghton Library, Harvard University, MS Am 1410 (142).

Agassiz, Louis. *Geological Sketches.* Boston: Houghton Mifflin, 1866.

Agassiz, Louis. *Introduction to the Study of Natural History.* Edited and annotated by Christoph Irmscher. Cham, Switzerland: Springer/Birkhäuser, 2017.

Carson, Rachel. *Silent Spring.* 1962. Boston: Mariner, 2002.

Collins, Francis S. *The Language of God: A Scientist Presents Evidence for Belief.* 2006. New York: Free Press, 2007.

Darwin, Charles. *On the Origin of Species: A Facsimile of the First Edition.* Cambridge, Mass.: Harvard University Press, 1964.

Darwin Correspondence Project. Cambridge University. https://www.darwinproject.ac.uk/, Accessed March 31st, 2023.

Gould, Stephen Jay. *I Have Landed: The End of a Beginning in Natural History.* New York: Harmony, 2002.

Gray, Asa. *Darwiniana: Essays and Reviews Pertaining to Darwinism.* 1876. Edited by A. Hunter Dupree. Cambridge, Mass: Belknap, 1963.

Harris, Sam. "Science Is in the Details," *The New York Times.* July 26, 2009. https://www.nytimes.com/2009/07/27/opinion/27harris.html?_r=1&scp=1&sq=science%20is%20in%20the%20details&st=cse, Accessed March 31st, 2023.

Hayhoe, Katharine. *Saving Us: A Climate Scientist's Case for Hope and Healing in a Divided World.* New York: One Signal/Atria, 2021.

Irmscher, Christoph. *Louis Agassiz: Creator of American Science.* Boston: Houghton Mifflin Harcourt, 2013.

Khullar, Dhruv. "Faith, Science, and Francis Collins." *The New Yorker.* April 7, 2022. https://www.newyorker.com/news/persons-of-interest/faith-science-and-francis-collins, Accessed March 31st, 2023.

Longfellow, Henry Wadsworth. Longfellow, Journal, 11 June 1848, Longfellow Papers, Houghton Library, Harvard University. MS Am 1340 (201).

Marcelo, Philip. "Court: Harvard Can Be Sued For Distress Over Slave Photos," *AP News*, https://apnews.com/article/education-lawsuits-connecticut-massachusetts-norwich-4dbd345707f1-de398413f966146a45f5, Accessed March 31st, 2023.

West, John G. "Francis Collins' Rhetoric About the Unvaccinated Is Anything but Christian," *The Stream*, September 29, 2021, https://stream.org/francis-collins-rhetoric-about-the-unvaccinated-is-anything-but-christian/, Accessed March 31st, 2023.

West, John G. "The Tragedy of Francis Collins's Model for Science-Faith Integration," *Evolution News & Science Today* (a publication associated with the creationist Discovery Institute). October 18. 2021, https://evolutionnews.org/2021/10/the-tragedy-of-francis-collinss-model-for-science-faith-integration/, Accessed March 31st, 2023.

David Staines
Northrop Frye and Marshall McLuhan: Two Canadian Christian Thinkers

Abstract: Northrop Frye and Marshall McLuhan, two major Canadian thinkers, did much to fashion Canadian understanding of Canada and the world. Both men were also devout Christians, one an ordained United Church minister and a left-wing Protestant, the other a deeply conservative Catholic convert. For Frye, the Bible was the summit of his scholarly attention; for McLuhan, religion was in the background of his writings, though it clearly played a major role in his thinking. Frye – at Victoria College in the University of Toronto – and McLuhan – just down the street at Saint Michael's College in the University of Toronto – had their religious beliefs stand behind their literary theories, making their Toronto the centre of critical investigation and study.

In 1995 I published *Beyond the Provinces: Literary Canada at Century's End*, with the following dedication: "To the Memory of Northrop Frye (1912–1991) and Marshall McLuhan (1911–1980)." This pairing was not a coincidence. In the final decades of his life, Frye was a beloved father figure to me from his time as Charles Eliot Norton Professor at Harvard, where he stayed in Leverett House (when I was Assistant Dean there), and the years afterward. McLuhan, one of my teachers at the University of Toronto, remained an indelible presence in my life; I invited him to Harvard several years later to deliver a lecture, which was later published as "Canada: The Borderline Case." I was privileged to know both these men with an intimacy I cannot exclude from this paper. Unlike a more traditional academic paper, these reminiscences offer a portrait of the men and the works they created. These major thinkers, who did much to fashion our understanding of Canada and the world, became national and international celebrities; they shaped much of our Canadian experience both as we understand it in our country and as others have come to understand us.

Frye and McLuhan, like most Canadians, did not like biographies. Deeply suspicious of the biographical method, Frye demurred when approached by a willing biographer: "He was uncertain about his suitability for a full-length book. He'd already warned off biographers by claiming that he had led an uneventful life" (Ayre 2). John Ayre's biography of Frye was published in 1989, less than two years before his death; it remains the sole biographical study. McLuhan's life became the subject of biographies, though only after his death.

Born in Sherbrooke, Quebec, Frye was raised in Moncton, New Brunswick, then travelled in 1929 to Victoria College in the University of Toronto, where he received, four years later, his BA in English and Philosophy, receiving Gold Medals in both subjects. He then entered Emmanuel College, Victoria's theological college, where he was ordained a United Church minister in 1936. He also received an MA from Oxford University in 1940.

Frye's maternal grandfather was a Methodist preacher, and his daughter, now married, lived the devout life of a pastor's daughter. "The form, particularly of the evangelical impulse, survived intact through Cassie to her son Northrop. Although he would bitterly reject the fundamentalism, even in rebellion he would carry on its central aspects of left-wing Protestantism" (Ayre 19). Frye rejected his mother's literal fundamentalism, as he later reminisced to his good friend Roy Daniells on April 1, 1975:

> In early adolescence I suddenly realized, with an utter and complete conviction of which I have never lost one iota since, that the whole apparatus of afterlife in heaven and hell, unpardonable sins, and the like was a lot of junk. There remained, of course, the influence of my mother, and the fact that I had already agreed to go on to college as a church student. My mental processes were pretty confused, but restructuring them by hindsight I think they were something like this: if I go though {sic} the whole business of revolting against this, I shall be making a long and pointless detour back to where I shall probably come out anyway, and will probably have acquired a neurosis besides. I think I decided very early without realizing it at the time, that I was going to accept out of religion only what made sense to me as a human being. I was not going to worship a god whose actions, judged by human standards, were contemptible. (Ayre 45)

A left-wing Protestant, then, rooted in Christian principles, Frye often conducted funeral services for his colleagues and friends, asking the Lord to grant peace and serenity to those who had passed away.

Born in Edmonton, Alberta, McLuhan grew up in Winnipeg, Manitoba, in a nominally Baptist family. Although he went to the University of Manitoba planning to become an engineer, he read his way out of engineering and into English literature, receiving his BA in 1933 in English and Philosophy – graduating in the same subjects and in the same year as Frye and receiving the University Gold Medal in Arts and Science – and his MA in 1934 in English. He then attended Cambridge University where he obtained his second BA in 1936, his MA in 1940, and his PhD in 1943 with a dissertation on "The Place of Thomas Nashe in the Learning of His Time."

Through his reading of G.K. Chesterton and Hilaire Belloc in the early 1930s, he converted after two years of prayer to Catholicism. He wrote his brother Maurice on April 11, 1936: "Had I come into contact with the Catholic Thing, the Faith, 5 years ago, I would have become a priest I believe" (McLuhan, *Letters* 82). On

March 25, 1937, with Hopkins scholar, John Pick, as his godfather, he was baptized into his chosen faith.

Devoutly disciplined in the practice of his religion and henceforward a daily communicant at mass, he kept his religion well in the background of his writings, although it played a major role in his thinking. "I deliberately keep my Christianity out of all these discussions lest perception be diverted from structural processes by doctrinal sectarian passions. My own attitude to Christianity is, itself, awareness of process" (*Letters* 384). After teaching for one year at the secular University of Wisconsin, he went to Saint Louis University for seven years, then spent two years at Assumption University, before accepting an offer in 1946 to join Saint Michael's College in the University of Toronto, only a few steps from Victoria College. And the first people to have McLuhan and his wife Corinne to dinner when they arrived in Toronto were Northrop Frye and his wife Helen.

Both Frye and McLuhan began publishing articles in the 1930s. As undergraduate editor of *Acta Victoriana*, Frye contributed articles and editorials, writing "some of the most acerbic editorials which have appeared in the magazine" (Ayre 80). Starting in the fall of 1930, McLuhan wrote several articles on such contemporary writers as Yeats, Eliot, and Pound, who "resurrect visions of an older and a better time, when men and women lived more intensely and in deeper communion with each other and with the world" (Marchand 33).

Apart from his continuing work in *Acta Victoriana*, Frye's first published article was "Wyndham Lewis: Anti-Spenglerian" in the *Canadian Forum* of June 1936, where he wrote of Lewis's criticism being dominated by Spenglerian concepts. And Oswald Spengler was one of a few thinkers and writers who continued to influence Frye's thinking: "In my opinion Spengler has a permanent place in twentieth-century thought" (Frye, "*The Decline of the West* by Oswald Spengler" 8).

"G.K. Chesterton: A Practical Mystic," McLuhan's first published article in January 1936, studied a major figure in his conversion to Catholicism. A close reading of Chesterton's poetry and prose, the article posited Chesterton as "A Practical Mystic": "In an age of shallow optimism, of crumbling creeds and faltering faith, he has walked securely and widely, boisterously praising life and heaping benedictions upon decadents" (McLuhan, "*G.K. Chesterton*" 464). McLuhan's seven subsequent articles and reviews appeared from 1938 to 1941 in *Fleur de Lis*, Saint Louis University's literary magazine, whose editors announced in their opening issue of 1937: "with the decline of Protestantism and the rise of innumerable anti-christianisms, drowning western civilization will soon be forced to clutch at Catholicism" (Marchand 55). Finding his intellectual home in this Jesuit University, McLuhan, a converted Catholic and a conservative thinker, was ready to denounce the godless world outside his academic walls by enunciating the truths of Thomas Aquinas and other thinkers of the Middle Ages.

Frye's first book, *Fearful Symmetry: A Study of William Blake* (1947), a detailed exploration of Blake's complex poetry and criticism, proposes that the poet's prophecies reshape the biblical myth of the creation, fall, redemption, and apocalypse; the book moves beyond Blake himself to the role of myth and symbol in various literary genres, a concept of all his subsequent books. But Blake, whom he had been studying in a seminar, was not his ultimate focus, as Frye admitted to his cousin in 1934:

> No great poet, with the very doubtful exception of Shakespeare, has, since the rise of Christianity, been able to write without the inspiration of the Christian religion behind him, and consequently he is forced to give expression to the deepest religious impulses of his age. Hence in every period there is one supreme poet who expresses the very essence of that period's attitude to Christianity. In English literature such were Chaucer, Spenser, Milton, Dryden and Blake to their various times. (Ayre 103–104)

For McLuhan, Blake was simply a heretic.

The perennial focus of Frye's investigations was not Blake, however, but the Bible. Although he "confessed that everything he has learned from either Blake or his evangelical Methodist background" (Ayre 4), it is this evangelical background that haunted him from his earliest years to the summit of his career, his final two books on the Bible, *The Great Code: The Bible and Literature* (1982) and *Words with Power: Being a Second Study of "The Bible and Literature"* (1990). Even as early as *Fearful Symmetry*, he states: "The Bible is therefore the archetype of Western culture, and the Bible, with its derivatives, provides the basis for most of our major art" (*Fearful Symmetry* 109). McLuhan continued in the nineteen-forties (and afterwards) to write traditional criticism, for example, in his essays on Keats and Poe, Kipling and Forster, confessing to Malcolm Muggeridge in 1974 that "all of my life has been devoted to teaching and cultivating literary values" (*Letters* 507).

At the University of Wisconsin, he realized that he could not reach his students directly through literature, the students being more conversant with comic books than with the novels of Charles Dickens:

> I confronted classes of freshmen and I suddenly realized that I was incapable of understanding them. I felt an urgent need to study their popular culture: advertising, games, movies. It was pedagogy, part of my teaching program. To meet them on their grounds was my strategy in pedagogy: the world of pop culture. Advertising was a very convenient form of approach. (Stearn 268)

As a consequence, his first book, *The Mechanical Bride: Folklore of Industrial Man* (1951), studies a mass of advertisements, comic strips, and newspaper front pages to show the connections among them, attempting "to set the reader at the center of the revolving picture created by these affairs where he may observe the action that is in progress and in which everybody is involved. From the analysis of that action, it is hoped, many individual strategies may suggest themselves. But it is seldom the business of this book to take account of such strategies" (*The Mechanical Bride*, v). In this way, he developed his method of explorations of "probes" of popular culture, this bridging his interest in literature with his students' interest in popular culture. He seeks only to look, to watch, and to observe. *The Mechanical Bride*, as Frye noted, "reflects the perspective of a country committed to observing rather than participating in the international scene" ("Criticism and Environment," 19). The book is, McLuhan confided to his mother, "really a new sort of science fiction, with ads and comics cast as characters. Since my object is to show the community in action rather than *prove* complex implication, it can indeed be regarded as a new kind of novel" (*Letters* 217).

McLuhan wrote two more books which cemented his reputation as a visionary theorist. *The Gutenberg Galaxy: The Making of Typographic Man* (1962) argues that every new medium of communication alters entirely the outlook of the people who use it. Arguing in a radial rather than a linear style and with the close reading of the New Critic, he shows that every technology creates a new human environment, and technological environments, which are not merely passive containers of human beings, but active processes, reshape people and other technologies, too. This second book won the Governor General's Award for Non-fiction, and the chair of the selection committee was Frye himself.

His third book, *Understanding Media: The Extensions of Man* (1964), studies the effects of the communication networks on people who are becoming victims of the electric age all about them. McLuhan recognizes that it is the artist who has the singular ability to observe the true nature of our world: "The artist is the man in any field, scientific or humanistic, who grasps the implications of his actions and of new knowledge in his own time. He is the man of integral awareness" (65). The artist has the highest level of participation in the probing of contemporary reality: "these two uniform ways of backward and forward looking are habitual ways of avoiding the discontinuities of present experience with their demand for sensitive inspection and appraisal. Only the dedicated artist seems to have the power for encountering the present actuality" (70).

The artist is the only person living in the present of a situation. Others are driving the car, looking out the rear-view mirror at what is in the past and assuming they are staring directly at the present; they remain unaware that they are securely lodged fifty years behind. The artist, as McLuhan told his students, is the passenger in the car, staring resolutely at what is taking place around him or her. For this reason, the artist is often regarded as avant-garde when there is no such term; all that exists are those staring at the past and those few who view life as it is happening now.

McLuhan's fame led to his appearances in the 1960s on campuses around the world, the covers of major magazines, and offers of academic and other jobs, for he was a theorist, people were convinced, who understood contemporary reality. He was lionized by the media, then in time discarded when someone else assumed his or her transitory importance. He was a true innocent, not in the sense of being unknowing or ignorant, but in the sense of being unaware of the designs of some of those around him.

> Frye's primary charge against McLuhan is that he had become a cult figure. McLuhan had disingenuously, at best, allowed his name and ideas to be associated with business people and media celebrities, politicians and advertisers; he had sold out to the non-literate, or more precisely the anti-literary, audience. By catering to data chaos, he had betrayed his humanist roots. (Powe 127–8)

But this "cult figure," a person lifted up by the media, was certainly not the beloved professor who catered to the questions of his many, many generations of students over the years.

The last time I saw McLuhan was in the summer of 1979 in Los Angeles. At a dinner party he and I attended were guests from the business and educational worlds, and much of the evening found McLuhan responding to them, offering advice, playing the role of media visionary. At the end of the evening, I was anxious to leave, exasperated at the other guests' easy acceptance of the mythic figure and disappointed at my own inability to connect with the man I was so fond of. McLuhan wanted to walk me to my car, and although I declined his invitation, he insisted. When we were outside, he confided to me, his left arm around my shoulders: "I want to thank you for being here this evening. It is always so much easier for me at this kind of evening when someone who knows me is also present. It makes the evening possible to endure." Still and always the innocent, caught up in a web not completely of his own making. He remained until his death the visionary both created by the public who needed visionaries and later rejected as other visionaries were sought. He lived the role created for him with as much grace as possible.

The recipient of nine honorary degrees, Marshall McLuhan died on December 31, 1980.

In the last year of McLuhan's life, Frye wrote: "it is perhaps time for a sympathetic rereading of *The Gutenberg Galaxy* and *Understanding Media* and a reabsorption of McLuhan's Influence" ("Across the River and out of the Trees" 11–12). And in 1981, he ended his address on "The Double Mirror" with the statement, "as my late friend and much beloved colleague, Marshall McLuhan used to say, man's reach should exceed his grasp, or what's a metaphor?" ("The Double Mirror" 41).

In early 1981, shortly after McLuhan's death, I drove down to Toronto, for my mother was having a small private Sunday brunch with Northrop and Helen Frye and Corinne McLuhan. Their conversations, sad and mournful as befitted the occasion, reflected the simple fact that Corinne was totally at home in the presence of Toronto's other great literary theorist and his wife.

While McLuhan was touring the world as an invited speaker throughout the 1960s into the 1970s, Frye was busy writing books, including *T.S. Eliot* (1963), *The Return of Eden: Five Essays on Milton's Epics* (1965), *A Natural Perspective: The Development of Shakespearean Comedy and Romance* (1965), and *Fools of Time: Studies in Shakespearean Tragedy* (1967). The seventies saw him leave for Harvard as Charles Eliot Norton Professor of Poetry; the title of his talks and subsequent book was *The Secular Scripture: A Study of the Structure of Romance* (1976). The very title, *The Secular Scripture*, suggested another scripture, which had been haunting him since his undergraduate years at Victoria College.

In 1982 Frye published *The Great Code: The Bible and Literature*, which has been republished in at least nineteen other languages, including Chinese, Japanese, and Korean; the companion volume appeared eight years later. As Frye openly admits, The *Great Code* "attempts a study of the Bible from the point of view of a literary critic ... not a work of Biblical scholarship, much less of theology: it expresses only my own personal encounter with the Bible." He further confessed, "My interest in the subject began in my earliest days as a junior instructor, when I found myself teaching Milton and writing about Blake, two authors who were exceptionally Biblical even by the standards of English literature" (*The Great Code* xi-xii). Arguing that the Bible is best read as a unity, he shows how it is the fundamental element in the imaginative experience of western culture, indeed the single most important influence in the imaginative tradition of western art and literature. And the volumes' translations into so many languages are further proof that the Bible transcends even western culture. For Terry Eagleton, Frye's writings are "the work of a committed Christian humanist (Frye is a clergyman), for whom the dynamic which drives literature and civilization – desire – will finally be fulfilled only in the kingdom of God" (93).

"The code is the tale that tells the story of individual apocalypse; it is the path encrypted in the imagination that could offer a way out of the darkening maze of history: and the imagination has been with us from the beginning of time" (Powe 238). In these two books Frye asserted the centrality of the Bible "from the point of view of a literary critic," and in these books he achieved the major goal of his life. At the same time, "Frye's critical ideology also tended to make a religion of literature, a religion that McLuhan, who already had one that he considered perfectly satisfactory, most heartily detested" (Marchand 114).

Frye became the singular eminence of the 1970s and 1980s, being invited around the world to give public lectures. He came to fulfill the role McLuhan had developed in the 1960s. Then, as with McLuhan, Frye's lustre began to diminish in the 1980s as the media found other people to lionize ... for a time. Yet according to Robert D. Denham's *The Reception of Northrop Frye*, "the demise of Frye's influence, like the rumours of Twain's death, have been very greatly exaggerated" (x), and the book provides concrete evidence of the continuing and growing interest in Frye's criticism.

The recipient of thirty-eight honorary degrees, Northrop Frye passed away on January 23, 1991.

Although McLuhan would jokingly tell his students in the 1960s that "at Victoria College, the truth shall make you Frye," there was no bitter animosity between Frye and himself. They were respected colleagues who followed different but complementary paths in their literary worlds. Alvin A. Lee, the general editor of the *Collected Works of Northrop Frye*, recalls,

> I personally observed them in social gatherings together and they were always amiable and collegial with each other. I also discussed the work of each with each of them separately and always came away with the sense that they respected each other though they were doing very different things and thinking in very unlike ways – and that they disagreed on some things. Norrie was more than willing to learn, and did, from his colleague Marshall ... when these lively, brilliant men came together to articulate things there was always a good deal of mutual respect and learning from each other. (Powe 37)

And Frye himself said about his relationship with McLuhan:

> Marshall was an extraordinary improviser in conversation; he could take fire instantly from a chance remark, and I have never known anyone to equal him on that score. I also feel, whether I said it or not, that he was celebrated for the wrong reasons in the sixties, and then neglected for the wrong reasons later, so that a reassessment of his work and its value is badly needed.
>
> I think what I chiefly learned from him, as an influence on me, was the role of discontinuity in communication, which he was one of the first people to understand the significance of. (Nevitt 126)

A final personal anecdote. It was the summer of 1976, and I was putting together a book titled *The Canadian Imagination: Dimensions of a Literary Culture*. All the essays had been submitted except for one, McLuhan's "Canada: The Borderline Case." I came back to Toronto to see McLuhan and wonder where my essay was; he informed me that since I was back – if only for a time! – we could work on it together. I was dumbfounded and crestfallen, for I was about to go to England for research for much of the summer, the trip financed by a research grant. That evening, over drinks with the Fryes in their home, I lamented my plight. Frye replied succinctly that the book would be immeasurably better if it contained McLuhan's essay. I reluctantly agreed; I returned to Toronto later to watch McLuhan pen his own complete essay; I did not go to England.

Why did both these literary theorists refuse to take up other academic posts? Frye, the most informed and respected critic of Canadian literature, would not leave Victoria College in the University of Toronto, even though his lecturing took him around the world, and he had been offered many other academic positions away from Toronto. McLuhan, the most knowledgeable proponent of the new media and the recipient of many other academic offers away from Toronto, always returned from his world travels to Saint Michael's College in the University of Toronto. "With the publication of The Gutenberg Galaxy in 1962, McLuhan's reputation, already firmly established on the basis of The Mechanical Bride (1951) and his work with Explorations achieved world-wide proportions, and he found himself in receipt of offers of professorships from American and Canadian universities at a salary far in excess of what he was receiving at St. Michael's College" (Harris 134).

As a reviewer, Frye saw himself initially "as a nurse, that is, as somebody bringing along a culture that was not yet wholly mature but showed so many signs of it" (Cayley 135). By the 1970s, he was giving to "our writers some strong and honest assurance that they were at last out of the parish and standing with their peers on high, new ground" (Ross 123). Outside of Canada was equally important to Frye's vision and understanding: "it is of great importance to the United States to have a critical view of it centred in Canada, a view which is not hostile but is simply another view" ("Conclusion" 321). "You tend to get lost in a country as big as the United States," he commented, "and you have to be frantically aggressive to make much of a sense of your individuality. But in Canada there's a small enough community responding to you – I'm thinking roughly of the cultured, intellectual community – so that you do not get known as a person, or any rate identified as a person ... Canadians have been obsessed with communication, which took itself out in building bridges and railways and canals in the nineteenth century and in developing very comprehensive theories of communication, like Innis's and McLuhan's in the twentieth century. I suppose I belong to some extent in that category" (Cayley 123–24). Frye respected and loved his teaching position in the University of Toronto, where he was an observer on the rest of the world.

For McLuhan, the same understanding was equally true. In 1952, he wrote about Canada's artistic outlook. The Canadian, "located between two great communities, the English and the American," he wrote, "is provincial to both. He would, therefore, be in a superb position to develop habits of critical insight if the development of such habits were not paralyzed by colonial timidity or Scottish caution" ("Defrosting Canadian Culture" 95). Twenty-five years later, he wrote in the same vein: "Sharing the American way, without commitment to American goals or responsibilities, makes the Canadian intellectually detached and observant as an interpreter of the American destiny." He concluded, "The low-profile Canadian, having learned to live without such strongly marked characteristics, begins to experience a security and self-confidence that are absent from the big-power situation" ("Canada: The Borderline Case" 227, 247). McLuhan respected and loved his teaching position in the University of Toronto, where he was an observer of the rest of the world.

Both Northrop Frye and Marshall McLuhan elected to stay in Canada where they were vital participants in their country's evolution as well as distinguished witnesses of major events outside their country. And both men, one a United Church minister, the other a conservative Catholic, had their religious beliefs stand behind, one overtly, the other not overtly, their literary studies and theories, making their Toronto the centre of Canadian and world attention.

Works Cited

Ayre, John. *Northrop Frye: A Biography.* Toronto: Random House, 1989.
Cayley, David. *Northop Frye in Conversation.* Concord, ON: Anansi, 1992.
Denham, Robert D., ed. *The Reception of Northrop Frye.* Toronto: U of Toronto P, 2021.
Eagleton, Terry. *Literary Theory: An Introduction.* Minneapolis: U of Minnesota P, 1983.
Frye, Northrop. "Across the River and out of the Trees." *University of Toronto Quarterly* 50 (Fall 1980): 1–14.
Frye, Northrop. "Conclusion." *Literary History of Canada: Canadian Literature in English.* 2nd edition. Volume 3. Ed. Carl Klinck et al. Toronto: University of Toronto Press, 1976.
Frye, Northrop. "Criticism and Environment." *Adjoining Cultures as Reflected in Literature and Language.* Ed. John X. Evans and Peter Horwath. Tempe: Arizona State University, 1983. 9–21.
Frye, Northrop. *The Decline of the West* by Oswald Spengler." *Daedalus* 103 (Winter 1975): 1–13.
Frye, Northrop. "The Double Mirror." *Bulletin of the American Academy of Arts and Sciences* 35 (December 1981): 32–41.
Frye, Northrop. *Fearful Symmetry: A Study of William Blake.* Princeton: Princeton UP, 1947.
Frye, Northrop. *The Great Code: The Bible and Literature.* New York: Harcourt Brace Jovanovitch, 1982.
Frye, Northrop. *Words with Power: Being a Second Study of "The Bible and literature."* Toronto: Penguin, 1990.
Harris, Robin S. *English Studies at Toronto: A History.* Toronto: U of Toronto P, 1988.
Marchand, Philip. *Marshall McLuhan: The Medium and the Messenger. A Biography.* Toronto: Vintage Canada, 1989.
McLuhan, Marshall. "Canada: The Borderline Case." *The Canadian Imagination: Dimensions of a Literary Culture.* Ed David Staines. Cambridge: Harvard UP, 1977.
McLuhan, Marshall. "Defrosting Canadian Culture." *The American Mercury* (March 1952): 91–7.
McLuhan, Marshall. "G.K. Chesterton: A Practical Mystic." *Dalhousie Review* 15 (January 1936): 455–64.

McLuhan, Marshall. *The Gutenberg Galaxy: The Making of Typographic Man.* Toronto: U of Toronto P, 1962.
McLuhan, Marshall. *The Letters of Marshall McLuhan.* Selected and edited by Matie Molinaro, Corinne McLuhan, William Toye. Toronto: Oxford UP, 1987.
McLuhan, Marshall. *The Mechanical Bride: Folklore of Industrial Man.* New York: Vanguard, 1951.
McLuhan, Marshall. *Understanding Media: The Extensions of Man.* Toronto: McGraw-Hill, 1964.
Nevitt, Barrington with Maurice McLuhan. *Who was Marshall McLuhan?* Toronto: Comprehensivist, 1994.
Ross, Malcolm. "Northrop Frye." *University of Toronto Quarterly* 41 (Winter 1972): 170–3.
Stearn, Gerald Emanuel. *McLuhan: Hot & Cool.* New York: Dial Press, 1967.

Part V **Religion in Poetry, Music and Visual Media**

Alois Woldan
Religious Aspects of Ukrainian Poetry – The Case of Vasyl' Stus

Abstract: This paper is devoted to Vasyl' Stus, one of the most famous Ukrainian poets of the 20th century. It examines religious aspects in his poetry, which appear in different contexts, which are delved into via a selection of examples. Religious motifs are to be found in quotations from prayers and liturgical formulations appealing directly to the Lord. Biblical citations and messianic stylizations indicate a strong sense of the poet's prophetic mission. Descriptions of churches in Kyiv evoke allusions to the city's historic and religious past. With the help of religious motifs the author reflects on his tragic situation by referring to ideas of existential philosophy. All these motifs contribute to a perception of Vasyl' Stus not only as a poet, but a martyr for his country, Ukraine.

Vasyl' Stus (1938–1985) is one of the most significant Ukrainian poets of the second half of the 20th century. His death in a Soviet labor camp makes him a symbol of the repression of the Ukrainian spirit as well as of the unbroken will to fight against that repression. A major part of his works could not be published during his lifetime and was only released after his death. Stus is seen today as a martyr for all that is Ukrainian, with numerous papers written on him. The University of Donetsk (now evacuated from there) bears his name.

Stus grew up in poverty in Central Ukraine.[1] He studied at the Donetsk State Pedagogical University (Donetsk was called "Stalino" at the time) and was a teacher in elementary schools for many years before he was admitted for his doctorate studies at the National Academy of Sciences in Kyiv. However, he was expelled in 1967 for participating in a demonstration. Up to this time Stus had written numerous poems, critical essays and reports, but his opportunities for publication were drastically reduced following his expulsion. His first volume of lyrics could only appear outside the USSR. The poet became more and more a political dissident who, in open letters, fruitlessly supported victims of repression. In 1972 he was arrested for the first time and was sentenced to five years of detention camp and three years of exile. In 1979 he returned to Kyiv where he became active in the Ukrainian Helsinki Group. In the same year he was arrested for a second time and this time sentenced to 15 years of prison camp, which the poet served in the

---

[1] For Stus' biography cf. Achilli 1–3; Pavlyshyn 585–586; Stus 1986: 149–162.

Urals. Even in prison camp the poet did not refrain from some form of resistance and died of the consequences of a hunger strike in 1985. At the same time in Moscow Gorbachev was proclaiming Perestroika. In 1989 Stus's remains could be taken to Kyiv, his funeral becoming a massive demonstration with thousands following his coffin.[2]

Although Stus had little opportunity to publish, his works of mainly lyrical character are very extensive – five collections put together by the poet himself and consisting of more than 1,000 poems mostly written in prison, and distributed through underground channels. Many of his texts could not be smuggled out and were destroyed by the authorities. In the 1990s the first edition of his works in six volumes was published[3] and after the year 2000 a further release was made, which, however, was discontinued after four volumes.[4]

Religious themes and motifs play a major role in Stus's poetry, especially in the texts written after his first arrest and later in the prison camps. They appear in varying forms and in diverse contexts, which I would like to delve into via a selection of examples. These range from prayer and liturgical formulations, biblical citations and messianic stylizations to descriptions of churches in Kyiv and the lyrical speaker's reflection on the situation in which a clear existential notion exists and the subject's imprisonment is expressed in a world of evil. In the selection of examples, I must limit myself to a few of the most illustrative ones. The poet's complete works contain many more such motifs.[5]

1 Prayer and Liturgical Forms

The poem "Tam, za bezkraiem, tam, za horoju" (III/2, 90) begins as love poetry with the longing for that unattainable you, formulated from the perspective of a female lyrical speaker (one could imagine Stus' wife writing her thoughts to her imprisoned husband). The second part, which is connected to the first through the motif of a snowstorm, becomes an appeal to God, connecting liturgy with individual experience:

---

[2] Natalia Shostak analyzed the significance of this funeral in the building of the Ukrainian nation. Cf. Shostak 12–15.
[3] Vasyl' Stus. *Tvory: u chotyr'och tomach, shesty knyhach.* L'viv: Prosvita, 1994–1998.
[4] Vasyl' Stus. "Zibrannia tvoriv: u dvanadtsaty tomach." Kyïv: Fakt, 2007–2009.
[5] A series of further motifs can be found in Volians'ka 1987.

Slava, Bozhe,	Glory to you O Lord,
za purhu zametil'nu,	for the storm that blows away,
skoro cholod ruky moï skuje.	since cold binds my hands.
Ja vidchula	I felt
voliu Tvoiu vsesyl'nu.	your almighty will.
Ja vstupaju, Bozhe,	I am entering, O Lord,
v tsarstvo Tvoie. (III/2, 90)⁶	in your Kingdom.

The motif of the snowstorm, well known in Russian literature, is initially a symbol of negative power capable of endangering people, and then reframed as an element of divine providence: where the cold paralyzes people's ability to act, divine almightiness takes over. In this manner a terrible fate can be accepted and compensated for. The word "volia", used here as meaning God's will, is considered to stand for human freedom in Ukrainian. This double meaning points to an acceptance of God's will by people, thus leading to their individual fulfillment and betterment, which is characteristic of Christian personalism.⁷ In Ukrainian poetical tradition since Shevchenko the concept of "volia" is connected with the concept of "dolia" in the sense of "fate" – for Stus human fate is always overridden by God's will, making it possible for one to accept even the hardest turns of fate.

A similar constellation between the lyrical speaker and his wife can be found in a short four-line poem that contains paraphrases of the Lord's Prayer:

Shche vydyt'sia: dalekyĭ kraĭ chuzhyĭ,	One can still see: the foreign distant land,
i v n'omu zhinka, zdumana zygzycia,	over there, my wife lost in thought,
shepoche sprahlo: Bozhe, khaĭ sviatyt'sia,	she whispered devotedly: hallowed be God,
o, naĭ sviatyt'sia kraĭ dalekyĭ miĭ.⁸	Yes hallowed be my distant foreign land.

The distance to the beloved can be spanned with the words of the Lord's Prayer "hallowed be thy name" by making "hallowed" the foreign and hostile expanse separating the two. Once again these lines, as also in the cited example above, speak of a faith in God's purpose, thus making bearable the difficult situation of separation.

---

6 All of Stus' quotations according to the edition *Tvory: u chotyr'och tomach, shesty knyhach*. L'viv: Prosvita 1994–1999. Vol. I/1, 2: 1994; Vol. II: 1995; Vol. III/1, III/2: 1999.
7 Roksolana Verbova examined these aspects as the central concept in Stus' convictions. Verbova, Self-improvement, 5–10.
8 This poem has not been included in *Tvory: u chotyr'och tomach, shesty knyhach*. 1994–1998, it is quoted after Stus, Vasyl'. *Poeziï*. Ed. by Mychaĭlyna Kotsiubyns'ka. Kyïv: Radianks'kyĭ pys'mennyk 1990, 118.

A longer text that reflects the existential situation of the lyrical speaker is formulated as a prayer following no particular scheme but rather expressing the personal discourse between the lyrical speaker and God.[9] It begins with the plea "O Bozhe, tyshi daĭ!" (II, 112) "Oh God, give peace!" and concludes in the same way.[10]

O Bozhe, tyshi daĭ! O bozhe, tyshi!	Oh God, give peace!" Oh God, peace!
Tsia samookupatsiia dushi,	This self-obsession of the soul,
otsia obluda liudianosti, mozhe,	this deception of humanity is
strashnisha za zlochynstvo [...] (II, 112)	perhaps worse than a crime [...]

It is an unusual appeal to God – no other religious formulation of this type is known – but it is an extremely important one as the prayer's form shows. While all petitions in the Lord's Prayer are of equal rank, this petition for peace has priority over all others. Being at peace becomes the location to experience God, creating a situation in which the soul is freed of its concentration on itself, its "self-obsession". In the text itself this formulation "Oh God, give peace" appears three more times, becoming more intensive, and further new dimensions of peace become clear.

[...] Tyshi daj!	[...] Give peace!
Zupynu. Abo zhe – samopovertannia[11]	Stop. or – your own return
do rozdorizh. Znachy spravzhnishi mezhi	at the crossroads. Set better boundaries
mizh smertiu i zhyttiam, mizh dnem i nichchiu,	between death and life, between day and night,
mizh pravdoiu ĭ brekhneiu. Ta naĭpershe –	Between truth and lie. Most importantly
daĭ tyshi, Hospody. (II, 112)	give peace, Lord!

According to Karl Jaspers, people faced with fundamental decisions must refer back to their own existence. Not only the talk of boundaries thus makes this plea for peace a borderline situation;[12] from here a path also leads to God according to Christian existentialism.

---

[9] This form of discourse is also an element of Christian personalism. Cf. Verbova, "Self-Improvement", 6.
[10] Agnieszka Korniejenko points out the significance of leitmotifs in Stus' poetry. 1996:20 f
[11] The term "samopovertannia", actually "returning to oneself", in analogy to forms such as "samookupatsiia" / "self-occupation", are one of numerous neologisms characteristic of Stus' poetical language. Cf. Shevel'ov, 368; Volians'ka 413.
[12] This term is often used by interpreters to characterize the poet's convictions. Cf. Plachotnik 6; Rubchak 338, Pachlovs'ka 69.

2 Biblical Stylizations, Messianism

In a number of texts the poet deals with his mission sent by God, thus expressing the author's strong sense of mission. The source of the poetry in a divine commandment is emphasized through biblical quotations and paraphrases. The following scene is reminiscent of prophets being called upon or also the legitimation of Jesus as the Son of God by a voice from the heavens.

Vel'mozhnyĭ son mene zdolav,	A commanding dream came over me,
i tut naraz pochuv ia:	and shortly after I heard:
Hospodniĭ holos prolunav:	The voice of the Lord droned:
miĭ synu! Aliluĭia!	my son! Hallelujah!
Terpy strasnu steziu konan',	You shall endure the path of death,
spiznaĭ smertel'ni chary	get to know the deadly magic,
dorohy dobr i pochezan',	the path of goodness and of wrongdoing,
svavillia i pokary.	of obstinacy and punishment.
Khoch tiazhko dushu berehty	When it is also hard to preserve the soul
pid nebom tsym poludnim,	under this heaven in zenith
a treba ĭty, a treba ĭty	one must go, one must go
shchosviatom i shchobudnem. (III/1, 130)	every holiday, and every day.

The downside of being called upon to be a prophet is suffering. Prophets being called upon in the Old Testament led to a path of suffering and even more so the calling upon of the Messiah in the New Testament. In the same way the lyrical speaker in this text is well aware of following the same path which, in a biblical sense, is a path of temptation. Along this path obstinacy poses the greatest danger – by possibly distracting from the true goal and ruining the mission. The destined path to be taken, the preservation of the soul, the acceptance of suffering: these are all concepts that can repeatedly be found in Stus' poems.[13]

The idea that the poet is also a prophet and religious leader for his people is especially present in literature of Polish Romanticism and was referred to there as "messianism" because the leader had to suffer for his people but then finds salvation. This idea can also be found in Ukrainian Romanticism[14] with Taras H. Shevchenko, its greatest representative who, in a similar manner to Stus, had an effect

---

[13] Cf. Achilli 263; Natalia Pachotnik emphasizes the relationship between the motif of the prophet and the foreshadowing of a tragic fate. Cf. Pachotnik 64.
[14] A central document of Polish Messianism, Adam Mickiewicz' *Księgi Narodu Polskiego /Book of the Polish People* (1834), was translated a few years later into Ukrainian and adapted for Ukrainian circumstances by Mykola Kostomarov.

through his biography as well as his works. Stus adopts many of Shevchenko's ideas in his texts and sees himself in the role of a prophet,[15] although he knows that this will have a tragic ending. The biblical Golgotha appears many times in his texts, for example: "Tsia Bohom poslana Holhofa / vede u padil, ne do zir" (Stus III/1, 36) "This Golgotha sent from God leads into a valley, not to the stars". The use of the word "padil" is in this case inseparably connected to the concept of "the valley of tears" ("padil sloz") making use of yet another biblical image.

In a longer poem, in which the lyrical speaker justifies his path to his mother, and may give no false reasons, the source of the mission is clearly named as God's will and it is stressed that the poet is the chosen one: "tse voliu Bozhu / ia buv na sebe, nache krest, pryĭmyv" (III/2, 65) "That is the will of God / that I have loaded upon myself, like a cross". Equating God's will with the cross bearing down on the poet's shoulders brings the suffering of Jesus to mind, referring once again to the sacrifice that the messianic destiny of the lyrical speaker calls for.

A climax in the biblical messianic diction is reached in a short text that appeared in a newspaper at almost the same time as the news of the poet's death[16] and is considered to be a type of testament.

Jak dobre te, schcho smerti ne bojus' ia	How good it is, that I am not afraid of death
i ne pytaiu, chy tjazhkyĭ miĭ khrest,	and do not question, if my cross is heavy,
shcho pered vami, suddi, ne kloniusia	that I do not bow before you judges
v peredchutti nedovidomych verst,	with the premonition of unimaginable expanses,
shcho zhyv, liubyv i ne nabravsia skverny,	that I lived, loved, and accepted no evil,
nenavysti, prokl'onu, kaiattia.	no hate, no curse, no regret.
Narode miĭ, do tebe ja shche vernu,	My people, to you I will yet return,
iak v smerti obernus' ia do zhyttja	as in death I turn to life
svoïm strazhdennym i nezlym oblychchiam.	with my suffering countenance, without falsity.
Jak syn, tobi dozemno uklonius'	As a son I bow deeply before you
i chestno hlianu v chesni tvoï vichi	and look with honesty into your honest eyes
i v smerti z ridnym kraiem poridnjus'.	and will become one in death with my homeland.
(III/1, 45)	

On the one hand the poet emphasizes his fearless stance in the face of lethal danger yet explicitly turns to his people with the message of his resurrection. The meaning of an individual's life for the national community becomes evident, and reference to the resurrection invokes traditions of messianism. The suffering appearance similar to an icon in which godly traits emerge from behind the

---

15 For the intertextual references between Shevchenko and Stus cf. Shevel'ov, 382; Volians'ka 417. Pliushch 297. Equally often parallels between both poets have also been drawn based on the common denominators of their biographies. Cf. Shostak 10.
16 Cf. Volians'ka 414.

human ones[17] is reminiscent of the Passion of Jesus, of the impression of the savior on the veil of Veronica. The last lines of this poem make the connection between the son with his people and country with recourse to common roots. The tie between the messianic poet with his folk and land culminates in the death of the lyrical speaker: in death he will become one with the land of his birth, entering and merging with a greater community, a "natio" / "nation" defined by being born there. (The root "rid" in the adjective "ridnyĭ" / "native" and in the verb "poridniuvaty" / "to become one" emphasizes birth as the common origin). In hardly any other text does the poet make clearer the interrelationship between the fate of an individual and patriotic messianism as well as between the biblical and national ideas than in this short text.

3 Churches and Places in Kyiv

Religious themes in the lyrics of Vasyl' Stus are also addressed via sacred buildings, especially the churches of Kyiv. In this context, one must keep in mind the major significance of the city of Kyiv in Ukrainian tradition, where the city remains the religious center. Kyiv is a type of earthly Jerusalem that guarantees the close link between the (Ukrainian) nation and the (orthodox) religion[18] even when Kyiv was dominated during Soviet rule by an ideology that was hostile to religion and church. Right at the beginning of *Palimpsests* there is a text in which the view from the barred windows of the prison in Kyiv allows for a view of the church of St. Iryna and begins with the words:

Tserkva sviatoï Iryny	The Church of the holy Iryna
krykom krychyt' iz imly.	cries with a scream from the fog.
Mabut', tobi vzhe, miĭ synu,	Perhaps you my son already,
zashpory v dushu zaĭshly.	had the icy cold enter your heart.
Skil'ky nabylos' tuhy!	So much grief has collected!
Chym ïï rozvedu?	With what can I make it disperse?
Zhinku lyshyv na naruhu,	My wife I have left in shame,
mamu lyshyv na bidu.	my mother in poverty.
[...]	[...]
Kyïv za hratamy, Kyïv	Kyjiv is behind bars, all of Kyjiv
ves' u kvadrati vikna.	all of Kyjiv within the square of the window.

---

[17] Leonid Pliushch points out the superimposition of the human face and icons in further texts by the author. Cf. Pliushch 296.
[18] This connotation of the city of Kyiv is also purported by Shevchenko, whose texts form a substantial basis for Stus' "Palimpsests". Cf. Pliushch 297.

Pochid pochavsja Batyïv	The military campaign of Batu has begun
a chy orda navisna?	is the city still in the shadow of the horde?
Morokom horlo ohorne -	The throat is captured in darkness -
ani tobi prodychnut'.	you can no longer breathe.
Zdrastuĭ, bido moia chorna,	Be welcomed, my black misery,
zdrastyĭ, strasna moia put'.	be welcomed my path of passion.
III/1, 33	

It should be noted, however, that this church disappeared long ago, when the city was conquered and the church destroyed in the 13th century. Even the chapel that was built on the same location was torn down in the 1930s (cf. Achilli 272). On this basis the visual impression is replaced by an acoustic one since the church can no longer be seen but can be heard. The church's voice becomes the lyrical speaker's partner in a dialog from prison in which one of the city's most important historical dates, the conquering of Kyiv by the Mongolians and Tartars in the year 1240 is remembered. The parallels are obvious: it is no longer the Golden Horde of the 13th century that has established itself as a power over Christian Kyiv but rather a different but equally non-Christian force in today's world. The superimposition of the past and present stands in harmony with the overall title of the collection, "Palimpsests". The tragic history of the city and the entire country correspond to an equally grievous history of the lyrical speaker: the violence his wife and mother experienced matches the violence the church went through, and the ordeal the lyrical speaker has gone through is a synecdoche for the suffering of his people.[19]

Any description of the city's Christian tradition based on its sacred architecture cannot go without mentioning Saint Sophia's Cathedral, which is one of the oldest and most important of the churches in Kyiv and was modelled upon the Hagia Sophia in Constantinople. This church not only characterizes the area of Kyiv but is also a metonymy of its history (Shevel'ov 1987:383). The bell tower of Saint Sophia's Cathedral, a central feature of Kyiv's old city becomes contaminated by the prison walls in one poem; once again the "great" history of the city and the lyrical speaker's private ordeal of suffering become superimposed on one another.

Uzhe moie zhyttia v inventari	My life is already in the inventory book
rozbite i rozpysane po grafach.	broken up and listed in tables.
Tse kondaky tvoï i tropari,	These are your hymns, litanies,
tse kara, tse z otrutoiu karafa.	this is the punishment, the jug with the poison.
Nad tseĭ tiuremnyĭ mur, nad tsiu zhuru	Over these prison walls, this hardship

---

[19] In his interpretation of this poem Alessandro Achilli refers to the representative function of the church emphasized by the similar sounds of "Iryna" and "Ukraina" – as well as the identification of the lyrical speaker with the city of Kyiv. Achilli 272.

i nad Sofiïvs'ku dzvinytsju znosyt'	and over the bell tower of the Saint Sophia Cathedral
mene miĭ duch. Nekhaj-no i pomru –	my spirit carries me. Should I also die –
ta vin za mene vidtonkoholosyt'	it will certainly sound on for me
try tysjachi propashchych vechoriv,	three thousand evenings lost
try tysjachi svitankiv [...]	three thousand times the dawn [...]
(III/1, 47)	

Even when life up to that point had been broken and divided up amongst the files of the judiciary, the free spirit that not even prison can break can rise above the walls of imprisonment to reach the heights of the bell tower, where taking over the function of the bell allows its sound to bring alive a destroyed past. Once again, the lyrical speaker resorts to the religious tradition of the city where the poet is imprisoned to make use of it for his own situation. Once more the story of the individual is integrated into the city's global history.

In another poem the "blessed Sophia appears" as a herald of the city of Kyiv, to then appear in the faces of familiar people:

[...]	
blahoslovenna svinula Sofiia,	Blessed Sophia appears,
i halaktychnyĭ Kyïv bronzovie	and the galactic Kyjiv glistens in bronze
u merekhtinni naĭdorozhchych lyts'.	in the light of the most familiar faces.
[...]	
A ty uzhe – po toĭ bik, ty – za hrannju,	Yet you are already on the other side, beyond that border
de vydyvo hoĭdaietsia khystke.	Where one only sees vague shadows.
Tam – Ukraïna. Za mezheiu. Tam.	Over there is the Ukraine. Beyond the border. There.
(III/1, 32)	

Here a link is established between the religious dimension of the city and its human qualities; Kyiv is the city where those people with the closest ties to the lyrical speaker live. The fate of the speaker – imprisonment and banishment – has separated him from those on the other side of a border that is hardly discernible anymore. Yet there, paradoxically, is said to be Ukraine, on the other side of the border, in Kyiv symbolic of the entirety of Ukraine. Ukraine encompasses both: culture, history and human closeness on the one hand, and distance, loneliness and the reality of the penal camp on the other.[20]

---

[20] Shevel'ov points out the ambivalence of Stus' image of Ukraine in the tradition of Shevchenko: Ukraine is a paradise, one that has however been plundered. Shevel'ov 382. Similarly in Stus' works Rubchak differentiates a familiar, home-type ("ridna") Ukraine from a foreign ("chuzha") Ukraine. Rubchak 337.

The Dnipro River is also equally essential in Kyiv's cityscape as it is for its mythological and literary symbolism. In one of the poems it partakes of the sacredness of the city by becoming symbolic of the Lord's index finger:

Khaj mnoiu vyshumovuiut' vitry,	May the forests rustle above me,
mohyly tuzhat' i Dnipro dalekyĭ	the burial mounds await and the distant Dnipro
v nyz'ki basy vsyliaie chliupit sviĭ.	directing its roar to deep basses.
I bezohliadno-holi nebesa	And the heavens naked and vast
Baĭduzhe zadyvliaiut'sia u deko,	indifferently gaze at the leaf,
a ia skazhu: to ie Hospodniĭ perst.	but I say: that is the finger of God
(III/1, 157)	

The lyrical speaker's vision arises from the loneliness of the steppe in an existentially rather than culturally caused situation. As the river is approached, the surrounding natural landscape is marked with religious symbols thus making a connection to the cultural sphere. The river running vertically rather than horizontally is understood to be "the finger of the Lord"[21] as a sign of the sacred character of the countryside. This corresponds to the cultural connotation of the Dnipro, which has always had a sacred character because its entirety partakes of the city's holiness, notwithstanding the specific religious-traditional ritual of sanctifying water at Jordan's holiday that is also connected with it.

4 Existential Dimension

The religious themes in Stus' poems also imply individual metaphysical testimonies, as compared to the mentioned usage of common religious phrases and symbols.[22] Talk of God climaxes in the polemic of a God who is not present and remains silent while allowing all the world's suffering. Both of these arguments are well known in the tradition of European theology and philosophy and are frequently linked to the problem of the theodicy. It is typical of how Stus sees God that appearances are made only in the company of humans, with hardly any abstract or theoretical thoughts only about God.

As is the case in an early poem in which a blind mother with emaciated hands searches for her son in an image but finds neither him nor God:

---

21 The Finger of the Lord is a symbol that signifies the tragic fate of the lyrical speaker just as the cross and persecution do. Cf. Plachotnik 2004: 66.
22 The influence of western European existential philosophy especially that of Jean Paul Sartre und Albert Camus on Stus has often been pointed out. Cf. Pachlovs'ka 2000: 68–70; Pliushch 300; Rubchak 316.

I til'ky maty snya vzhe ne chuie,	Already the mother can no longer hear her son,
vzhe bil' ïi starechyï spopelyvsj.	her aged pain has already become ashes.
Vona sama. Vona slipa – svichadom	She is alone. Blind – in the mirror
osinn'ogo pomerzloho stavka.	of the frozen autumn pond.
I vyskhla vyzhovkla ïi ruka	And her parched, yellow hand
shche obrazy obmatsuie nerado.	touches the images of saints, without pleasure.
Bo de tam syn? De boh? Nema obokh.	Where is then there my son? Where is God? Both do not exist.
I smert' obsila pustku, nache l'och.	And death has filled the emptiness like a hole.
(I/1, 194)	

God is spoken of in the suffering of the mother who has lost her son, but God is not there and is replaced by death. The association between the mother searching for her son and the Mother of God who lost her only son becomes clear; the mother in the poem also becomes a biblical mother of pain. Only God, who could ease that pain, is missing – a clear quarrel with God[23] in the sense of the theodicies mentioned. These lines, however, also clearly show that God appears only in the context of humans even if he – as deus absconditus– cannot be found.

Similar symbols can be found in a short text which, like many others, describes the reality of the penal camp, giving a short genre-picture of the everyday life of the prisoners:

Shche dosvitok. Hospod' shche spyt'.	The day is still dawning. The Lord is still sleeping.
Zitkhaie v'jazen' kolo mene	The prisoner next to me groans
i motoryshno tak krychyt',	cries out in fright,
okrytyï snom. V vikni gluchomu	Still shrouded in sleep. In the mute window
na den' zaïmaiet'sia zoria.	dawn starts off into the day.
(III/1, 177).	

A strange and striking image: the Lord God in the cell sleeping next to the prisoner who is not awakened by the surrounding noises. An image that fluctuates between the humanness of God who shows his solidarity with the prisoners yet also his passiveness in not hearing. The sleeping Lord calls to mind the biblical story of the storm at sea with Jesus initially sleeping in the boat (Mk 4.38). In Stus' text the Lord's awakening to save them is missing. The glaring contradiction of crying out and silence remains.

Experience of God is also inseparable from the experiences of the penal camp. One of the short verses written in such a camp begins with the words:

---

23 The conflict with God that Stus has in this and other texts is in the tradition of Shevchenko. Cf. Rubchak 344.

Nemaie Hospoda na tsiï zemli:	The Lord God does not exist on this Earth:
ne sterpiv Boh – z-pered ochej tikaie	God couldn't stand it – he fled right before our eyes
aby ne bachyty neliuds'kych kryvd,	so as not to watch inhuman torment,
dyiiavol's'kych tortur i okrutenstva.	Diabolical torture and atrocities.
V kraju potvornim ie potvornyï bog –	In the land of monsters there is a God of monsters
pochvar volodar i vladyka liuti	lord of abominations und the ruler of torment
[...]	
[...] Pan-Boh – pomer.	The Lord God has died.
(III/1, 72)	

This very anthropomorphic God, who runs away from the suffering of his own creations, in the following lines makes room for another god, written in lowercase in the text, a monster who is in command over all agony, the ruler befitting of the world of a penal camp. The true God, however has not run away; he is dead. With such a formulation reminiscent of Nietzsche, a climax in the polemic with God and the resistance to a God who allows great injustices, is reached. The rarely used spoken form for God "Pan-Boh" ("Lord God") only emphasizes the extent of the loss. The contradiction between a good God and the reality of the camps, thus equating him with a ruler of atrocities, results not only in the death of God but again also leads to the problem of theodicy.

God who is not there. God who sleeps. God who remains silent. God who is dead. All of these images are part of a controversy with God led by the poet in the biblical tradition of Job. This accusation is, however, only the side of his faith in God, which allows him to accept his intended path of suffering.

Even amongst the poems written before the author spent time in prisons and camps, a text can
be found with an analysis of human existence that comes to a very pessimistic conclusion.

Otak zhyvu: iak mavpa sered mavp,	So I live: like an ape among apes,
holom pohrishnym iz tavrom zazhury	with a brow of sin and the flaw of worry
vse b'iusia ob tverdi kaminni mury,	I continually lash out at the wall of stone,
jak ïchniï rab, jak rab, ja nyshchyï rab.	like their slave, me the lowly slave.
[...]	[...]
O Bozhe pravednyï, vazhka dokuka –	O true God, a difficult task
sliporozhdennym rozumom zbahnut':	to be fathomed with comprehension born in blindness:
ty v ts'omu sviti – lish kavalok muky,	in this world you are merely a piece of suffering.
oterplyï i rozridzhennyï, mov rtut'	blunt and diluted, like mercury.

From an extremely pessimistic image of the conditio humana with emphasis on the absurdity of human existence (cf. Achilli 2018:131) the argument in this text, albeit with limited means of a possible knowledge of God, leads to another one.

God is reduced to the suffering, be he its origin or its quintessence. This concept that moves that person to the foreground as the one who has had to bear such suffering calls to mind the existential philosophy of Camus.

The experience of prison confirms such an image of God as the source of violence and suffering:

Tjuremnych vechoriv smertel'ni alkoholi,	Deadly alcohol of the prison evenings,
tjuremnych dosvidkiv slipa,	blind mercury of the interrogation,
jak blyzna, rtut'.	like a wound.
A sto merciv, obsivshy sertse, zhdut',	And hundreds of the dead, who have taken seat in my heart, wait,
moieï smerti, a svoieï voli.	for my death, upon their will.
[...]	
[...] koly Boh	[...] Since God
postav, jak ljutyĭ bych	scourge and despotic ruler
i mozhnovladtsia	
(III/1, 94)	

The evenings of imprisonment are likened to deadly alcohol. Combined with the memory of so many dead that this world of unfreedom has claimed the situation evokes an image of God in which He appears as both a grim scourge and a despotic ruler. God as the almighty tool of repression that in the end demands the death of humans. Such a thought is the expression of deep despair and a complete rejection of belief in a good God, which is in line with theodicy. On the other hand, this reflection results from life in penal camp in which the conditio humana becomes perverted into conditio inhumana.

The close relationship between mankind and God and the necessity of human existence in order to speak of God can be seen in texts in which God within a person is described in an unusual way:

V meni uzhe narodzhujet'sia Boh	God is already born in me
i napivpam'iatnyĭ, napivzabutĭj,	is half remembered, half forgotten,
nemov i ne v meni, a skraiu smerty,	as if not in me, but rather on the fringe of death,
[...]	[...]
Ja z nim udvoch zhyvu. Udvoch isnuiu,	I live with him together, together I exist,
koly nikoho. I hrymyt' bida,	when no one is there. And misfortune drones,
mov kanonada. Vin oporiatunok,	like the thunder of canons. He is salvation.
ja zh bilousto movliu: poriatuĭ,	I speak with white lips: save me,
miĭ hospody. Oporjatyĭ na myt',	my Lord. Save me for a moment,
a dali ja, ohovtanyĭ, vriatuiu	and I will continue myself, obediently, to save
sebe samoho sam. Samoho – sam.	myself. Me myself.
(I/1, 195)	

Here the incarnation of God is spoken of, a Christian image that radically leads back to the lyrical speaker who thereby himself appears as a man-God. The divine in humans, as is typical of Stus, becomes perceptible in the borderline situation of a deadly threat yet at the same time brings salvation. That very salvation on the other hand can be achieved by the person himself if he has recognized the divineness within himself.[24] The tension between divine and human activity, between being saved and saving oneself leads to an estrangement that many interpretations see as surrealistic[25] but in any case reflects the poet's imagery and thoughts that are accessible only with difficulty.

The same concept of God within a person is found in an image in which the person becomes immersed in God and God in the person: "Nablyz' mene Bozhe, i v smert' uhorny, / pirnu ja u tebe, ty – v mene pirny"[26] "Bring me closer, oh God, enshroud me in death, / I immerse myself in you and you immerse yourself in me". This form of intensive penetration of humankind and God is more reminiscent of a mystical concept than a canonical one. It is once again experienced as death nears, evoking the divine in mankind and the humanness in God. Experiencing God when human existence has become extremely brittle and fragile: that too is a Christian concept that Stus expresses based on his experience, in his own manner and using his poetical language. When this poem ends with a conventional religious expression – "Lysh' ty mene, Hospody-Bože, prosty!" / "But may you, Lord, forgive me" – then the lyrical speaker returns once more to this Christian-existentialist tradition.

5 Conclusion

The national and international reception that Vasyl' Stus received oscillated between two poles (cf. Korniejenko 1996, Pavlyshyn 2010): the reference to his biography as a martyr of the Soviet regime and the emphasis on his poetry. These make him one of the most significant representatives of Ukrainian literature in the 20th century and also ascribe to him a significant role in world literature. In the 1970s Stus became known in Western Europe and the United States as a civil rights ac-

---

24 The path to God, that originates as awareness within each person, is typical of the Gabriel Marcel's thoughts. Cf. Verbova, "Self-Improvement", 8.
25 For this poem Mateusz Mościszko sees no possibility of a religious interpretation. For him this text is a "poem full of absurdities". Mościszko 2019, 98.
26 This poem has not been included in *Tvory: u chotyr'och tomachj, shesty knyhach.* 1994–1998, it is quoted after Stus, Vasyl'. *Poeziï*. Ed. by Mychaĭlyna Kotsiubyns'ka. Kyïv: Radians'kyĭ pys'mennyk 1990, 119.

tivist, a Ukrainian dissident and prisoner of conscience, with Amnesty International also active in his cause. Little notice was taken of his poetry, not even when the first European volume of his lyrics was published in Brussels in 1970. In Soviet Ukraine Stus was only known in opposition circles and among his former companions. His texts were hardly ever made public, except for those that were published underground.

After his death and in the phase of Glasnost and Perestroika that began shortly thereafter, a few of Stus' texts were published in Ukraine. Literary and critical works followed which, however, mostly made the author's tragic fate paramount. The scholarly study of the poet's work remained more in the hands of foreign experts with groundbreaking works appearing in the USA, Canada and Australia. It was only when the first edition of his works was published (1994–1999) that discussions of the literary works of the poet intensified in Ukraine. Today, most experts are of the opinion that the two sides of Vasyl' Stus, his biography and his works, cannot be viewed in isolation from one another. However, since the year 2000, emphasis in Ukraine has moved to his biography. Stus is seen as a pioneer in the fight for freedom of Ukraine, as an example of patriotism and the willingness to make sacrifices, as a martyr for his country. In the present state of war that has threatened the existence of the Ukrainian nation since February 2022, this second view continues to prevail.

Works Cited

Achilli, Alessandro. *La Lirica d Vasyl' Stus: Modernismo e intertestualità poetica nell'Ucraina del secondo Novecento.* Firenze: Firenze UP, 2018.

Korniejenko, Agnieszka. "Wstęp". Korniejenko, Agnieszka. *Poezija Wasyla Stusa. Wstęp, wybór i tłumaczenie artykułów Agnieszka Korniejenko.* Kraków: UNIVERSITAS 1996, 7–26.

Mościszko, Mateusz. "Surrealistyczny obraz piekła w poezji Wasyla Stusa: Na podstawie zbioru *Wesoły Cmentarz.*" *Slavia Orientalis* LXVIII 1. 2019, 89–99.

Pachlovs'ka, Oksana. "Ukraïns'ki shistdesiatnyky: filosofiia buntu." *Suchasnist'* 4. 2000, 65–84.

Pavlyshyn, Marko. "Martyrology and Literary Sholarship: The Case of Vasyl Stus." *Slavic and East European Journal* 54. 4 (Winter 2010): 585–606.

Plachotnik, Natalia. "Profetychni motyvy v poezii Vasylia Stusa." *Slovo i chas* 4. 2004: 62–6.

Pliushch, Leonid. "Vbyvstvo poeta Vasylia Stusa." *Vasyl Stus. His Life and Works, Recollections and Essays by his Contemporaries* (in Ukrainian). Ed. Osyp Zinkewych and Mykola Francuzenko. Baltimore-Toronto: V. Symonenko Smoloskyp Publishers, 1987. 285–301.

Rubchak, Bohdan. "Peremoha nad prirvoiu: Pro poeziiu Vasylia Stusa." *Vasyl Stus. His Life and Works, Recollections and Essays by his Contemporaries* (in Ukrainian). Ed. Osyp Zinkewych and Mykola Francuzenko. Baltimore-Toronto: V. Symonenko Smoloskyp Publishers, 1987. 315–51.

Shevel'ov, Jurii. "Trunok i trutyzna: Pro "Palimpsesty Vasylia Stusa." *Vasyl Stus. His Life and Works, Recollections and Essays by his Contemporaries* (in Ukrainian). Ed. Osyp Zinkewych and Mykola Francuzenko. Baltimore-Toronto: V. Symonenko Smoloskyp Publishers, 1987. 368–401.

Shostak, Natalia. "To Whom Does a Poet Belong? The Reburial of Vasyl' Stus (1989) as a Ritual of Cultural Appropriation." *Spaces of Identity* 2.3/4 (2002): 7–18.

Stus, Vasyl'. *Poeziï*. Ed. Mychailyna Kotsiubyns'ka. Kyïv: Radianks'kyĭ pys'mennyk, 1990.

Stus, Vasyl'. *Vybrani Poeziï. Angliïs'kyĭ pereklad Jaropolka Lasovs'koho. Vstupna stattja Juriia Sevel'ova.* Miunchen: Ukraïns'kyĭ Vil'nyĭ Universytet, 1986 / Vasyl Stus. Selected Poems. Translated and edited by Jaropolk Lassowsky Introduction by George Y. Shevelov. Munich: The Ukrainian Free University, 1986.

Stus, Vasyl'. *Tvory: u chotyr'och tomachj, shesty knyhach*. L'viv: Prosvita, 1994–1998.

Stus, Vasyl'. *Zibrannia tvoriv: u dvanadtsaty tomach.* Kyïv: Fakt, 2007–2009.

Verbova, Roksolana. "Personalists'ki ideï u tvorchosti Vasylia Stusa." *SKHID* 3.143 (May-June 2016): 63–8.

Verbova, Roksolana. "Self-Improvement through the Prism of God's Cognition in the Poetry of Vasyl Stus." *SKHID* 3.167 (May-June 2020): 5–10.

Volianks'ka, Ljudmyla. "Proshchaĭ, Ukraïno, moia Ukraïno, chuzha Ukraïno, naviky proshchaĭ!" *Vasyl Stus. His Life and Works, Recollections and Essays by his Contemporaries* (in Ukrainian). Ed. Osyp Zinkewych and Mykola Francuzenko. Baltimore-Toronto: V. Symonenko Smoloskyp Publishers, 1987. 402–23.

Federico Celestini
Gustav Mahler's Symphonic Transcendence and Its Counterparts

Abstract: Siegfried Lipiner (1856–1911) became a sort of mentor to Gustav Mahler, who always respected his literary and philosophical advice. Lipiner was just twenty years old when he published the poem *The Unbound Prometheus* (Der entfesselte Prometheus) in 1876 and managed to send the work to Nietzsche and Wagner, who actually read it and held it in high esteem. Mahler's early Nietzsche reception was clearly influenced by Lipiner's religious-metaphysical conception of tragedy. However, to assume that this is reflected exactly in his music would be a hasty conclusion. Artistic entities cannot be traced back to unambiguous contents, but have their own dynamics, in which discursive elements and philosophical ideas can be reconfigured or even subverted. This will be demonstrated by means of an overview of Mahler's first five symphonies.

1 Siegfried Lipiner

On 19 January 1878 the young Siegfried Lipiner gave a remarkable lecture at the "Reading Association of German Students" (Leseverein der Deutschen Studenten) in Vienna titled "On the Elements of a Religious Renewal in the Present Age" (Über die Elemente einer religiösen Erneuerung in der Gegenwart). Lipiner was born into a Galician-Jewish family in Jaroslav in 1856. Lipiner and Gustav Mahler must have met at the University of Vienna around 1877, when Mahler enrolled there. Lipiner began his writing career at an extremely early age and became a sort of mentor to Mahler, who always respected his literary and philosophical advice. After Mahler's marriage, their long-standing friendship soured, probably because of Lipiner's opposition to Alma, and their relations were severed until 1909, when the two friends were reconciled.[1]

Lipiner was just twenty years old when he published the poem "Prometheus Unbound" (Der entfesselte Prometheus) in 1876 and managed to send the work to

---

[1] A detailed account of Lipiner's life and his relations to Mahler can be found in Lengauer, de la Grange 123–127, and Hefling.

Nietzsche and Wagner, who actually read it and held it in high esteem.[2] Lipiner's poem was clearly also a tribute to Nietzsche, who had an unbound Prometheus printed on the title page of his *Birth of Tragedy*. In the third section of the poem, the Titan encounters a figure named the "Dulder," (the sufferer), who is unmistakably recognizable as Christ by his attributes suggestive of the Passion. Prometheus immediately recognizes his affinity with the sufferer and calls him "brother" and "comrade of my torment."[3] The sufferer transforms into a ruler and informs Prometheus that as the Lover, Sufferer, and Creator, he will judge Prometheus. Prometheus kneels before Christ, acknowledges his greatness, and is thus empowered to bring redemption to humanity in the form of a new life after death. Although the image of Prometheus kneeling before Christ is not very Nietzschean, it nevertheless vividly reflects Lipiner's religious-metaphysical conception of tragedy.

Lipiner's differences with Nietzsche initially went unnoticed or, in Nietzsche's case, they were not brought to the fore. Some members of the Reading Association, who formed a circle of friends around Engelbert Pernerstorfer and held the intellectual leadership within the association, wrote a collective letter in October 1877, in which they congratulated Nietzsche on his 33rd birthday to which the latter replied with thanks.[4] Lipiner, who had enclosed a personal accompanying note, was thus able to initiate a correspondence with Nietzsche, which, however, did not last very long, due to divergences in character as well as in content.[5] Lipiner was also esteemed by the physician and natural philosopher Gustav Theodor Fechner, with whom he studied at Leipzig University. During this time, he came into contact with Erwin Rohde and Johannes Volkelt, among others, and shortly afterwards with Paul Natorp in Strasbourg. The latter wrote an obituary in the *Kunstwart* and pre-

---

[2] See Walter 190 f.; McGrath 69; Venturelli, 455 f.; Lengauer. Nietzsche's positive, even enthusiastic reaction to reading Lipiner's work can be found in a letter to Erwin Rohde from 28 August 1877 (Nietzsche 277 f.).

[3] Lipiner, *Der entfesselte Prometheus* 108.

[4] The collective letter was signed by Siegfried Lipiner, Max Gruber, Victor Adler, Sigmund Adler, Heinrich Braun, Engelbert Pernerstorfer and Seraphin Bondi. See McGrath 69 f.

[5] McGrath attributes the break in the correspondence to the importunity of Lipiner's persistence, who repeatedly and ultimately unnervingly tried to persuade Nietzsche to visit the Salzkammergut in the summer of 1878 (McGrath 70 f.). However, the break was more likely to have been caused by reasons related to the publication of *Menschliches, Allzumenschliches*. Lipiner, who was sent a complimentary copy by the publisher at Nietzsche's request, wrote the philosopher a 32-page (!) letter, which has not been preserved. From other letters of Nietzsche, however, it is clear that Lipiner criticised *Menschliches, Allzumenschliches* and joined the close confidantes of Wagner who noted the "negative influence" of the "Jew Paul Re" on Nietzsche. See Celestini, *Die Unordnung der Dinge*, 59–63. See on Lipiner and Nietzsche also Lengauer, Hödl and Hefling.

faces to the posthumous publication of Lipiner's dramas *Adam* and *Hyppolythos*.[6] Lipiner withdrew from the public eye in the early 1880s and first became a librarian, then later the Director of the Library of the Austrian Parliament (Bibliothek des Reichrates) in Vienna. In 1891 he converted from the Jewish to the Protestant faith. It was not until 1894 that he received his doctorate, with a dissertation on "Homunculus, a study of Faust and the philosophy of Goethe" (Homunculus, eine Studie über Faust und die Philosophie Goethes), which seems to have been lost. The project of a large-scale, four-part drama *Christus*, for which *Adam* was conceived as a prelude, remained unfinished.[7]

2 Lipiner's Religious Concept of Tragedy

In his aforementioned lecture for the "Reading Association", Lipiner recognised humankind's fundamental need for transcending empirical reality, which was ignored by the positivist and materialist tendencies of his time, and was disappointed by the institutionalised churches. Lipiner calls this need religious as soon as it manifests itself in feelings. But it becomes art when it presents itself in contemplation, and metaphysics when it provides itself with a rational framework.[8] According to Lipiner, no matter what the form of expression, the need for transcendence takes on a special urgency when faced with the idea of death, and feeds on the desire for imperishability and, consequently, for resurrection.[9] Lipiner is confident in this respect, despite what he sees as problematic conditions in his time. Combining thoughts of Schopenhauer, Wagner and Nietzsche, he evokes a new culture in which art and religion unite in tragedy:

> Tragedy is religion, and in the presence of tragic art man becomes religious. For in tragic art he sees himself, sees how he negates reality and as phenomenon joyfully passes away – joyfully, for precisely in this passing away, and only in it, does he feel what cannot pass away, and as a man dying away, he feels his resurrection as God [Gott].[10]

Lipiner adds the dimension of transcendence to ancient tragedy, thus making the tragic annihilation of the self a prerequisite for eternal happiness and immortality through resurrection in God. He makes the connection with the Prometheus poem

---

6 Natorp, "Dichtungen eines Vergessenen" and Natorp, "Geleitwort".
7 Castle.
8 Lipiner "Über die Elemente / On the Elements" 117.
9 Ibidem 127.
10 Ibidem 137.

in a central passage of his speech. Here he distinguishes between "banal" pantheism, in which nature, viewed superficially, is seen as divine, and "true" pantheism, in which nature is experienced from within. Similarly, the tragic transformation occurs from within. Thus, according to Lipiner, the human ceases to live as an individual being in order to experience being "Pan". Filled with this sense of the divine and the immortal, the human, as a tragic hero, attains a higher self, and becomes divine. The mortal human should kneel before himself as an immortal being. Even the proudest opponent of God, the true son of Prometheus, is here willing to praise the deity because he himself has become one. At this moment "death and time are overcome", and pain is "deprived of its sting and hell of its victory".[11] After Lipiner committed himself to Kantian philosophy, to Friedrich Albert Lange, Johann Karl Friedrich Zöllner and Gustav Theodor Fechner, he quoted several lines from Malwida von Meysenbug, a long-time and close friend of Wagner and Nietzsche, in which he recognized the core of his own thoughts, and which were also to become relevant to Gustav Mahler:

> I felt that I was praying as I had never prayed before, and now I recognized what actual prayer is: contemplation, out of the isolation of individuation, into the consciousness of unity with all that is; kneeling down as the perishable and rising up as the imperishable.[12]

Lipiner's synthesis of Schopenhauer, Wagner, and Nietzsche begins with the question of individuation, which is seen by all three authors as the origin of human unhappiness, but in doing so blurs important distinctions that, moreover, led to the break between Nietzsche and Wagner in 1878. The metaphysical being of "things in themselves" longed for by Lipiner is conceived by Schopenhauer as "will" ("Wille"). Schopenhauer, however, does not see this as a pleasing instance of redemption, but rather a "blind urge", a "dark, dull drive" from which it is necessary to redeem oneself. Schopenhauer – and therein lies his pessimism – knows no redemption of the world, but only redemption from the world, achieved through resignation. This attitude of resignation was foreign to Nietzsche, even at the time of his book on tragedy. But Lipiner's religious reading is also incompatible with Nietzsche's conception of tragedy. In *The Birth of Tragedy*, individuation is not depicted as a consequence of the objectification of metaphysical will, but as a cultural-historical case, namely the process of subjectivation triggered by the step

---

[11] Ibidem 137; 139.
[12] Ibidem 149 f. The quote comes from Meysenbug 2nd Vol. 114 f.: "Ich fühlte, dass ich betete, wie ich nie zuvor gebetet hatte, und erkannte nun, was das eigentliche Gebet ist: Einkehr, aus der Vereinzelung der Individuation heraus, in das Bewusstsein der Einheit mit Allem, was ist; niederknien als das Vergängliche und aufstehen als das Unvergängliche."

into civilisation. In the tragedy, Nietzsche recognises the encounter between the Apollonian self, constituted this way, and the instances of Dionysian otherness that originated in Asia. Accordingly, tragedy, in Nietzsche's view, confronts us neither with religious, nor with metaphysical questions, but with the aesthetic experience of a violation of the self, staged in tragedy. This violation of the self assumes cultural-political relevance in view of the collective and cultic dimension of the proceedings of the tragedy.[13] The provision of either a German-nationalist or another political-cultural identity is contradicted by Nietzsche's conception of tragedy as a violation of the Self. The German nationalistic students' enthusiasm for Nietzsche in Vienna was thus the result of a misunderstanding. While Nietzsche's first book was still characterised by metaphysical language and terminology, by the time Lipiner and his friends were devoted to him, he was in a phase of clarification and revision, reconfiguring his thoughts and increasingly distancing himself intellectually and emotionally from Schopenhauer and Wagner and their positions.

3 Mahlers's Symphonic Narrative and Lipiner's View of Tragedy

Mahler experienced the collective enthusiasm for Nietzsche in the Reading Association until it was dissolved at the end of 1878 by government decree. Afterwards he remained in close contact with the main figures of the so-called Pernerstorfer circle.[14] His early reception of Nietzsche was thus influenced by Lipiner's synthesis. However, to assume that this is reflected exactly in his music would be a hasty conclusion, as firstly, the elements of this synthesis form a precarious equilibrium in which minimal shifts can have significant consequences. Secondly, artistic entities cannot be traced back to unambiguous contents, but have their own dynamics, in which discursive elements and philosophical ideas can be reconfigured or even subverted. I would like to demonstrate this by means of an overview of Mahler's first five Symphonies.

Lipiner's extension of the tragic process through a triumphant conclusion corresponds to a narrative that can be described by the formula *per aspera ad astra*. Even if Lipiner thinks primarily of drama, in accordance with his poetic activity,

---

13 For more on this see Celestini, *Nietzsches Musikphilosophie* 47–64.
14 The multinational Habsburg state saw the spread of German nationalist sentiments, as practised by the Leseverein, as a politically threatening development and decided to take repressive measures. On Mahler's contacts with the Pernerstorfer circle after the dissolution of the Leseverein, see McGrath 118–123.

and of music drama in the sense of Wagner, this narrative also corresponds to the symphonic tradition of the 19th century, as shaped in particular by Beethoven's influential Fifth and, above all, Ninth symphonies. Thus, when Mahler developed the idea of realizing Lipiner's religious conception of tragedy as a symphonic narrative, he by no means had to turn the symphonic tradition upside-down. Rather, the task would be to turn the conventional "happy end" into a recognizable and believable symphonic manifestation of transcendence. In his First Symphony, Mahler accomplishes this task by sharpening the polarity between catastrophe and fulfilment, to the point of drastic explicitness. In the context of his discussion of Mahler's music, Theodor W. Adorno calls the key moments of this narrative *Zusammenbruch* (collapse) and *Durchbruch* (breakthrough).[15]

Of Mahler's symphonies, the first is closest to Beethoven's model. As in Beethoven's Ninth Symphony, the moments of tragic collapse and apotheosis-like breakthrough are found in the finale, although in Mahler's case, anticipations of both are already heard in the first movement. In the first part of Mahler's Finale, the traditional dualism of sonata form escalates into a drastic opposition between the main theme group in F minor (bars 1–174) and the secondary theme group in D flat major (bars 175–237). In contrast to the symphonic tradition of the 19th century, this opposition is not reconciled after the development section (bars 238–427). The diversity of these expressive worlds, just like that of the styles and idioms expressed during the course of the symphony, is *not* brought to a unity or synthesis in the finale. The finale, and thus the entire symphony, culminates in the jubilant overcoming of the tragic collapse by the solemn brass chorale in D major (bars 623–656), which is followed in the coda by a veritable apotheosis clearly marked in the score as "Triumphant" (bars 657–731).

4 Mahler's Symphonic Shaping of Transcendence

Symphonic transcendence appears in the finale of Mahler's First Symphony as a fracture of the immanence of form because of the breakthrough, whose religious connotation is clear in the choral character of the music. Mahler himself commented on this to his friend Natalie Bauer-Lechner as follows: "But my D major chord should sound as if it had fallen from heaven."[16]

In his First Symphony, Mahler exposed, as it were, the "theme" of the shaping of a symphonic narrative disposed around the polarity of catastrophe and fulfil-

---

15 Adorno 215f.
16 Bauer-Lechner 9.

ment. In the symphonies that followed, this theme is varied, sometimes with considerable modifications. Nevertheless, it always remains recognizable. In the Second Symphony, the narrative scheme *per aspera ad astra* is further developed and additionally strengthened with respect to both the dramaturgical design and the compositional means employed. The polarity of collapse and breakthrough, which in the First Symphony is basically limited to the finale, characterizes the entire Second Symphony. Here, the "outcry of despair," a clash between a B-flat minor chord and the C of the low strings, is already heard in the third movement (bars 465–468). In the first movement, violent orchestral outbursts anticipate the third movement's explosion (bars 291; 325–328), which returns at the beginning of the finale. Here, however, arpeggio figures in the trumpets and trombones add a breakthrough element to the orchestral scream (bars 5–6; 9–10). While the strings and woodwinds hold the dissonant chord for nine measures, the brass arpeggiate the underlying consonant triad. In this way, the transformation of the breakdown into a breakthrough is advanced. Military signals and birdcalls seem to indicate the arrival of the *a cappella* chorus in triple pianissimo, announcing the resurrection with a text by Friedrich Gottlieb Klopstock.[17] A triumphant apotheosis, which surpasses that of the First Symphony through the use of the chorus and solo voices, concludes the movement and the entire work "With the highest display of power" – as marked in the score.

The Second Symphony shows both an intensified realization of the idea of transcendence and closer proximity to Lipiner's thoughts. For Mahler's compositional idea of the apotheosis-like breakthrough as a transformation of the tragic collapse corresponds perfectly to Lipiner's vision of a tragic transformation in which the human ceases to live as a mortal, in order to become a divine being.

5 Transcendence as Synthesis: Mahler's Third Symphony

With the first two symphonies, Mahler confronts us with two related forms of symphonic transcendence, which differ, however, primarily in their relationship to the opposing moment of tragic collapse. In the Third Symphony, even greater differences emerge. In this work, stylistic pluralism and centrifugal tendencies reach a degree that is extraordinary even for Mahler. The cosmic dimension aspired to is al-

---

[17] Friedrich Gottlieb Klopstock, *Die Auferstehung* (Geistliche Lieder 1758). With additions by Mahler, who composed the text himself from the third stanza onwards.

ready evident in the layout of the symphony, as shown in the sequence of movements with their original titles in the handwritten score:

Mahler's Third Symphony
Original titles for the movements from the handwritten score[18]
1. Introduction: Pan awakes
    follows immediately
    Summer marches in ("Bacchus procession")
2. What the flowers in the meadows tell me
3. What the animals in the forest tell me
4. What man tells me
5. What the angels tell me
6. What love tells me

The pantheistic element in the symphonic conception, which leads to the stylistic pluralism of the work, as well as the explicit reference to Pan in the introduction, make the connection to Lipiner obvious. The influence of Lipiner's Leipzig teacher Gustav Theodor Fechner is also palpable in the symphony's cosmological conception. At the same time, the design of the breakthrough in the Finale, with the mitigation of the symphonic apotheosis embedded in an *adagio* Finale, shows a modified compositional realization of the traditional narrative. The final apotheosis appears in the *adagio* Finale of the Third Symphony as an instance of synthesis of the disparate rather than one of transcendence.

6 Questioning Transcendence through Humour and Metamorphosis: The Fourth and Fifth Symphonies

The Fourth and Fifth symphonies show even more profound modification of the symphonic narrative, whose fundamental polarity between *Zusammenbruch* and *Durchbruch* however remains perceptible. In the Fourth Symphony, Mahler dispenses with the sonification of symphonic transcendence in the Finale, creating a work strikingly different from those that preceded it. Mahler calls it "Humoreske," like most of the Wunderhorn songs and individual movements of the earlier symphonies. But for the first time, the final movement, *Das himmlische Leben*, is also conceived humorously. In the Fifth Symphony, the situation is even more com-

---

[18] Quoted from Floros 75.

plex. The polarity between collapse and breakthrough already shapes the second movement, with the breakthrough again sounding in the form of a chorale apotheosis in D major at the end of the recapitulation. After the experience of the earlier symphonies, it is, however, surprising that the breakthrough is withdrawn in the coda, by the return of the main theme group in A minor, which has a stormy, even infernal character through sharply dissonant *sforzati*. The return of the breakdown themes in bars 544–556 confirms the impression that the breakthrough at the end of the recapitulation was by no means decisive.

Although all the elements of the familiar narrative are present, the peculiar configuration of the breakthrough, as a result of its positioning in the second movement, and its withdrawal in the coda, creates an entirely new situation. The second movement concludes the first part of the symphony. An unusually long *scherzo* movement opens the second part. The famous Adagietto follows, and a *rondo* Finale, in which the chorale theme is secularized, as it were, into song and dance, and the teleological orientation peculiar to metaphysical logic is replaced by the post-metaphysical notion of circular movement, closes the work enigmatically.[19]

7 Musical Elaboration of Philosophical Ideas: A Preliminary Conclusion

Lipiner's thoughts on the renewal of religious ideas and his dramatic works surely made a deep impression on Mahler. Nevertheless, I would not consider them to be "the programme" of Mahler's symphonies. Idioms, characters and types of movements that refer to extra-musical spheres such as calls, signals, marches, dances, and chorales are common in Mahler's symphonies and easily recognizable. By including these in a symphonic movement, extra-musical meanings associated with musical figures are subjected to musical treatment. At the same time, musical processes that capture such figures laden with extra-musical meanings thereby take on semantic relevance. Thus it becomes possible to unfold a kind of thinking that has a metaphysical or even a post-metaphysical quality in the medium of music. In Mahler's case, this is due to the relationship between his music and the thoughts of Lipiner, Schopenhauer, Wagner, and Nietzsche. What seems most important to me here is that the music is by no means limited to the representation of those philosophical contents but is able to reconfigure and change those

---

[19] For a detailed analysis of this symphony and a discussion of the Nietzsche-like aspects see Celestini, "Gustav Mahlers Fünfte Symphonie".

contents thanks to the musical logic that unfolds in the course of compositional processes.

Works Cited

Adorno, Theodor W. "Mahler. Eine musikalische Physiognomik." *Die musikalischen Monographien*. Frankfurt am Main: Suhrkamp, 1971 (*Gesammelte Schriften*, 13). 149–319.
Bauer-Lechner, Natalie. *Gustav Mahler in der Erinnerung von Natalie Bauer-Lechner, mit Anmerkungen und Erklärungen von Knud Martner*. Ed. Herbert Killian. Hamburg: Wagner, 1984.
Castle, Eduard. "Die Welt als Mythos. Siegfried Lipiner und sein Kreis." *Deutsch-Österreichische Literaturgeschichte*. Vol. 4: *Von 1880 bis 1918*, Wien: Fromme, 1937. 1560–70.
Celestini, Federico. *Die Unordnung der Dinge. Das musikalische Groteske in der Wiener Moderne (1885–1914)*. Stuttgart: Franz Steiner Verlag, 2006 (Archiv für Musikwissenschaft – Beihefte, 56).
Celestini, Federico. *Nietzsches Musikphilosophie. Zur Performativität des Denkens*. Paderborn: Wilhelm Fink, 2016.
Celestini, Federico. "Gustav Mahlers Fünfte Symphonie." *Gustav Mahler. Interpretationen seiner Werke*. 2nd Vol. Ed. Peter Revers and Oliver Korte. Laaber: Laaber-Verlag, 2011. 3–51.
de la Grange, Henry-Louis. *Gustav Mahler. The Arduous Road to Vienna (1860–1897)*. Completed, revised and edited by Sybille Werner. Turnhout: Brepols, 2020.
Floros, Constantin. *Gustav Mahler 3. Die Symphonien*. Wiesbaden: Breitkopf & Härtel, 1985.
Hefling, Stephen. "Siegfried Lipiner's 'On the Element of a Renewal of Religious Ideas in the Present'." *Mahler im Kontext / Contextualizing Mahler*. Ed. Erich Wolfgang Partsch and Morten Solvik. Wien: Böhlau, 2011. 91–114.
Hödl, Hans G. "Nietzsche in Österreich. Prometheische Religion: Siegfried Lipiners poetische Nietzsche-Rezeption." *Verdrängter Humanismus – verzögerte Aufklärung*. Vol. 4: *Philosophie in Österreich (1880–1920). Anspruch und Echo. Sezession und Aufbrüche in den Kronländern zum Fin-de-Siècle*. Ed. Michael Benedikt, Endre Kiss and Reinhold Knoll. Klausen-Leopoldsdorf: Verlag Leben – Kunst – Wissenschaft, 1998. 379–96.
Lengauer, Hubert. "Siegfried Lipiner: Biographie im Zeichen des Prometheus." *Die Österreichische Literatur. Ihr Profil von der Jahrhundertwende bis zur Gegenwart (1880–1980)*. Ed. Herbert Zeman. Graz: Akademische Durck- und Verlagsanstalt, 1989. 2nd Vol. 1227–46.
Lipiner, Siegfried. *Der entfesselte Prometheus. Eine Dichtung in fünf Gesängen*. Leipzig: Breitkopf & Härtel, 1876.
Lipiner, Siegfried. "Über die Elemente einer Erneuerung religiöser Ideen in der Gegenwart / On the Elements of a Renewal of Religious Ideas in the Present." Trans. Stephen Hefling. *Mahler im Kontext / Contextualizing Mahler*, Ed. Erich Wolfgang Partsch and Morten Solvik. Wien: Böhlau, 2011. 115–51.
McGrath, William J. *Dionysian Art and Populist Politics in Austria*. New Haven: Yale UP, 1974.
Meysenbug, Malwida von. *Memoiren einer Idealistin*. New ed. Berlin: Schuster & Loeffler, 1917.
Natorp, Paul. "Geleitwort zu Siegfried Lipiner." *Adam: Ein Vorspiel / Hippolytos: Tragödie*. Stuttgart: Verlag von W. Spemann, 1913. 3–13.
Natorp, Paul. "Dichtungen eines Vergessenen. Siegfried Lipiner." *Kunstwart. Rundschau über alle Gebiete des Schönen. Monatshefte für Kunst, Literatur und Leben* 25/3 (1912): 209–10.
Nietzsche, Friedrich. *Sämtliche Briefe*. Vol. 5. München: Dt. Taschenbuch-Verl.: Berlin [u. a.]: de Gruyter, 1986.

Venturelli, Aldo. "Nietzsche in der Berggasse 19. Über die erste Nietzsche-Rezeption in Wien." *Nietzsche-Studien. Internationales Jahrbuch für die Nietzsche-Forschung* 13 (1984): 448–80.

Walter, Bruno. *Thema und Variationen. Erinnerungen und Gedanken.* Frankfurt am Main: Fischer Verlag, 1947.

Jörg Türschmann
Serial Baroque in the TV Show *American Gods*

Abstract: *American Gods* (2017–2021) tells of how people's faith makes the gods real. The old gods of vanished cultures and from other continents have previously embraced the American way of life. But now they are gathering to fight the new deities of globalization, new technologies and new media. These allegorical protagonists are accordingly called "media," "new media," and "technology." The streaming series *American Gods* is of course the product of this new communication culture and corresponds to the cherished paradoxes of self-referential art in the baroque age. It deals with the transatlantic relationship as it is shown between the Old and the New World. But it is also about the US itself, because *American Gods* was released during the presidency of Donald Trump and the new deities can be interpreted as the allegories of his mediacracy.

1 Human Gods and Divine Humans

Gods do not really have a home, except in heaven. So the title of the TV show *American Gods* is misleading in a way. But in some ancient cultures, the gods sometimes have been said to dwell among us in human form. In this respect, *American Gods* does not offer a Christian image of the world of gods, but an encounter of ancient and new gods in America. The characters are all human in form, even if they behave strangely and have superhuman abilities. They are a rare case of obvious allegories in an audiovisual narrative. Thus *American Gods* is part of a long tradition of allegorical narratives that has existed since antiquity, when gods embodied human characteristics.

In antiquity, the Greeks were known to have regarded many gods as representatives of human qualities, and this kind of polytheism was adopted by the Romans. It is certainly Rome's contribution to the cultural history of Europe that some authors conceived the gods of the Greeks as personifications in the form of literary characters. Lucan, Virgil, Lucretius and Ovid are certainly the most important authors of this period and made the personifications of Fama and Fortuna common protagonists of their literary works. Omitting important predecessors, examples from later periods are the very popular *Le Roman de la Rose* in the High Middle Ages and the works of Petrarch and Dante in the Early Renaissance. The Baroque period continued this tradition in the 16th and 17th centuries. The Spanish allegorical novel *Criticón* written by the Jesuit Baltazar Gracián is certainly a very famous example from the early modern period of world literature. Actually, we probably think of allegorical images more in terms of painting or sculpture such as the Pietà, the Justitia or images of the Republic, frequently embodied by female figures.

Dante's *Divina Commedia* has meanwhile become a point of reference in some television series (Türschmann, "La repetición como figura herética"). The Manicheism of Hell and Paradise seems to be particularly suitable for staging the confrontation between good and evil on television. Nevertheless, it is surprising that such a complex literary work, written in verse, is sometimes even explicitly cited in a popular narrative genre such as a television series. Perhaps it is an attempt to turn the protagonists of a series into adversaries in a world stylized as a paradigm of human existence by the grace of God. Thus, gods and men never meet in such cases, but men remain among themselves. Their conflicts are only culturally enhanced by the reference to a highly esteemed literary work. The situation is a different one in the case of *American Gods*: here, the gods remain largely among themselves. Although there are many explanations of the origins of the various gods, the only thing through which humanity influences the fate of these gods is their individual history as migrants to America.

As it happens, *American Gods* is the work of an immigrant: British author Neil Gaiman wrote the fantasy/ mythology-steeped 2001 book on which the series is based after he moved to America.

> The narrative depicts a quintessentially American rite of passage: the road trip. An unlikely pair – ex-convict Shadow Moon (Ricky Whittle) and fast-talking Mr. Wednesday (Ian McShane) – go on a journey that traverses the nation's highways and byways. Most of the characters they meet are gods who were brought into the U.S. by immigrants from all around the world, and many of those deities have fallen on hard times (Ryan).

And what they bring to America are not only their divine properties but also set pieces from the cultures they come from. This means that these ancient gods may have familiar names, such as Odin, but their historical origin counts even more than their divine power. This is somewhat contradictory because gods exist outside of history in their respective cultures. Hence, these old gods who immigrated to America in the course of time are also representatives of human destinies. They are now fighting for people to believe in them again. In the last consequence, this means that the Americans should become conscious of their cultural roots, by again finding the faith in the gods, from whose cultures the American population possibly originates.

2 What Is Told

The three seasons of *American Gods* (USA, 2017–2021; p.: Starz) recount how people's faith makes the gods real. The Old Gods of vanished cultures and from other continents have previously embraced the American way of life. But now they are gathering to fight the new deities of globalization, new technologies and new media – the gods of American capitalism. Showrunners Bryan Fuller and Michael Green conceived the series based on the novel by English author Neil Gaiman. The staging of the first season is particularly spectacular and has delighted critics. The TV show refers implicitly, among others, to the old Spanish Baroque tradition of having allegorical figures embody abstract concepts such as truth, love or evil. This cultural heritage has long become the basis of the relationship between *Neo-Baroque and Contemporary Entertainment* (Ndalianis). That is why the New Gods in the series are called "Media," "New Media," and "Technology." And *American Gods*, of course, belongs to these new media and thus corresponds to the cherished paradoxes of self-referential art in the baroque age. But the *American Gods* series is also about the US itself, because the TV show was released during the presidency of Donald Trump and the new deities can be interpreted as the allegories of his mediacracy. Bryan Fuller, one of the showrunners, explained his feelings after Trump became president: "The powerlessness that I felt after the election is offset in some small way by being able to work on this show and have a multicultural, multifaith exploration of what it is to be an American citizen at a time when we're in huge conflict with ourselves" (quoted by Ryan).

The plot of the series is simple: the Old Gods gather to fight against the New Gods who want to take over the world. Among the multitude of gods, trolls and other mythological figures, a few stand out. The main characters are the Old God Odin (Ian McShane) and his bodyguard Shadow Moon (Ricky Whittle), who in a sense takes over the function of Hermes, the messenger of the gods. It is a pact with the devil between the two, because Shadow Moon hopes to meet his deceased wife again in the beyond. The first season is like a road movie. The two protagonists visit various Old Gods on their journey through the U.S., in order to win them over. However, on the trip Shadow Moon also encounters the New Gods, who want to seduce him, especially the goddess of the new media, who is also the spokeswoman of the New Gods and who is played by Gillian Anderson, very well known for her acting in the series *The X-Files* (USA, 1993–2018; p.: Fox). Then there is a nerd, who stands for the digital media in particular. Another important protagonist is the Old Goddess Bilquis – a goddess of love identified with the Queen of Sheba, who devours her victims with her vagina during the sex act. She appears in the episodes of the first season again and again, independently of the other gods in individual scenes. Only in the last episode of the first season is she also seen together with the other gods. The presence of this goddess in the first episode – superfluous as far as the narrative is concerned – foreshadows a problem common to all female protagonists among the deities, but ultimately to all characters:

> In the second season of *American Gods*, for example, Bilquis, the Queen of Sheba, will have a more important role than in the book, where she dies very soon. Despite this concern, there is no radical transformation in the role of female characters or in the structure of their myths, because the creators do not set their work in the mystical structures of the imaginary but in the synthetic [...] (Pérez-Amezcua and Junco 20).

The eight episodes of the first season end with a feast for all participants at the estate of the Goddess Easter. On this occasion, the arrival of spring is to be celebrated, but the new gods disrupt the festival.

3 Historical References

Of course, the series is a U.S. production and has to do with America for that reason alone. But there is also a clear reference to the early history of the continent. The first episode begins with the story of a Viking ship that in 813. p. n. e. sailed to the coast of North America. Indigenous people force the Vikings to retreat by firing a series of arrows. The Vikings make several blood sacrifices to the god Odin in order for him to give them the wind they need to return home, which eventually happens. The second episode begins with a story that takes place on a slave ship in 1697. The slave Rob Okoye prays to the god Anansi, who appears before all the slaves and tells them of the terrible fate that awaits them in America. Anansi encourages them to break out and set fire to the ship, which they do. In the process, everyone on the ship dies except Anansi, who turns into a spider and arrives safely on land. – During the last ice age, a tribe crosses at the beginning of the fifth episode the Bering Land Bridge with the symbol of its god Nynyunnini. Similar to the events from the first episode, it encounters the local native people and gods, who do not allow them to enter the territory. The tribe begins to lose faith. Nynyunnini dies and is forgotten.

At the beginning of the sixth episode, there is a reference to the present-day situation: a group of Mexican immigrants, who are trying to enter the United States illegally, pray to Jesus, who appears and tries to protect them. Border police kill him. Another example of a more recent historical reference is in the seventh episode: the Goddess Ibis tells the story of Essie, a young Irish woman sentenced to deportation, who leaves gifts to Irish elves in exchange for happiness. On a ship bound for America, she seduces the captain and persuades him to take her back to London. There she becomes a thief; however, she is caught by the police after forgetting to leave a gift to the elves. The pregnant woman is again deported to America, this time successfully, where she marries the owner of the property she works on and who leaves her a farm after his death. Essie continues to leave gifts to the elves.

4 The Staging of the Power of Faith

The following example from *Jurassic Park* (USA, 1999; dir.: Steven Spielberg) shows how entertaining meta-filmic self-reflexivity can be during a film: "Objects in mirror are closer than they appear." These words can be read in small letters on the rearview mirror of a safari car in which the protagonists flee from an escaped T. Rex. Angela Ndalianias rightly points out that "[t]his detail is extraneous to the film's concerns, and the text is not meant for anyone within the narrative space" (Ndalianis 166). Since the dinosaur can also be seen in the rearview mirror, the attentive film viewer can understand this mirror image, which is very much also accessible to the characters in the car, as an iconic reference to the electronic genesis of the T. Rex. In this respect, the inserted text can be seen as an ironic interweaving of the narrative world with the world of the spectator. For the audience, the existential threat to the characters in the film corresponds to the real fascination created by a computer animation that was extraordinary at the time of its creation. In terms of cultural history, the affinity of metalepsis with the Baroque, Romantic, and Postmodern eras, which focus on the conundrum of the relationship between illusion and reality, is repeatedly pointed out as important for the overall cinematic construction. One of the most complex examples of this idea can be found in *Elisa, vida mía* (*Elisa, my life*; E, 1977; dir.: Carlos Saura), where explicit allusions are made to the *Theatrum mundi* and baroque literature of Spain's 'Golden Age' in the 16t[h] and 17th centuries. In this way, this film is a compendium of possibilities of metalepsis, as the narratologist Gérard Genette describes them in individual forms for theater, literature, and film (Genette 76).

Basically, two things are characteristic of metalepsis (Türschmann, "Die Metalepse"): the equal status of subject and mirror image, of frame and image, and the impression of an immediate contact between two worlds through the seemingly physical crossing of the boundary between them. As with the touch of the fingers in Michelangelo's *Creation of Adam*, the seemingly immediate physical contact between author or viewer and creature is the reason for the fascination the filmic metalepsis evokes. And this can be represented within a film, as in film comedy in the case of the broken mirror replaced by a 'real' person as in films with Max Linder, Harry Langdon or the Marx Brothers. Or as in *American Gods*, where a New God, the "Technical Boy", asks an artificial intelligence developer, the so-called "CEO" (S2E8; 22:45–23:04): "What do you think happens if you touch a god?" CEO: "I don't know ... like Michelangelo ... a flash of light." Technical Boy: "Like the Sistine Chapel."

It is worth recalling the above statement: *American Gods* shows how people's faith makes the gods real. Therefore it can be argued that this TV show is a metalepsis on the border between human imagination and actual occurrences. However, this crossing of the border is itself only a staging within the cinematic fiction of *American Gods*. It is not about the deception of fictional characters who leave fiction and enter the world of the viewer. The gods enter the world of the people in the fictional world, but they never address the real viewers of the television series. And Odin's son Shadow Moon, a human being with emerging divine capacities, is also the only person in the fiction who perceives the presence of the gods. Therefore the first season resembles a coming-of-age drama and a *Bildungsroman*, because at the end, Shadow Moon puts aside his doubts and declares that he believes in gods.

5 Allegories of U.S. Media Hegemony

With the recognition of the existence of the gods, Shadow Moon acknowledges that humans and gods can meet. To put this message in a broader context, it is striking that the medium of film has always presented a metaphysical sphere in which the adventures of the countless heroes present themselves as real. This is often announced in the opening credits of countless films, in which the production companies introduce themselves with the image of the globe or the Goddess Europe. Columbia Pictures shows a woman holding a torch, reminiscent of an ancient goddess. Universal Pictures makes particularly clear the claim to enter an extraterrestrial sphere. The logo shows the globe, entwined with the company's lettering.

Anyone who mentions the logo of a U.S. film company must inevitably think of the book by Paul Virilio entitled *War and Cinema: The Logistics of Perception* (Virilio). Virilio's thesis is that all media technology has a military origin. In this context, the logos of U.S. film companies express America's claim to dominate the world, at least in terms of the media. Much of this is certainly true when one thinks of the influence of Hollywood cinema and the spread of the Internet. What does this finding mean for the possible reference in the *American Gods* series to the Trump era between 2017 and 2021, which coincides with the three seasons of the series? Obviously, the New Gods represent the simulation of reality in the social media. Trump's media strategy, as we know, was extremely simple: he provoked with the help of tweets and fake news on Twitter. By doing so, he always guided the public debate and forced his opponents to react. This is what the New Gods do to the Old Gods, who had made themselves comfortable in the US. The Old Gods of traditions, different immigrants, and different ages must unite in order not to lose their supremacy. The question is whose side Shadow Moon is on, because at the end of the first season, he believes in all the gods. But it is implied that he himself will take up the fight against the New Gods. At the end of the final season, he will sacrifice himself for his father Odin, who will thus be resurrected and resume the fight against the New Gods:

> The news of the premature end to the often-troubled series is not altogether unexpected, and follows the Season 3 finale on March 21 [2021]. That season-ender saw Whittle's Shadow Moon seemingly killed after a vigil at the mythical Tree of Life for his seemingly deceased and estranged father, Mr. Wednesday/Odin, played by McShane. A pivotal point in Gaiman's book, the incident set up American Gods' fourth season with Wednesday taking advantage of Shadow Moon's sacrifice for Wednesday's own resurgence in the battle against the New Gods (Patten).

This return of Odin does not happen as predicted. The production conditions and the disputes between the responsible artists and producers were too serious for the project to continue.

6 To Whom It May Belong

All in all, the high production costs were not the only reason why the series was not continued. As with most TV shows, the decisive factor was the number of viewers. It is certainly normal for audience interest to wane over time. *American Gods*, however, was unusual from the start because it deals with a religious theme. The TV show is not just a fantasy version of countless other series aimed primarily at a teenage audience to express the fears of adolescents about their awakening sexuality. Instead, *American Gods* is full of allusions to cultures and historical events all over the world and at all times of humankind. Thus, the technically elaborate images and sounds are the *mise-en-scène* of the gods' modes of appearance. But they serve less to create tension on the level of the plot. The spectacular passages have something statuesque about them and almost seem like rituals, which are supposed to bring the respective deity closer to the believers, as at a mass. Therefore, it should not be forgotten that *American Gods* is fundamentally about the encounter between good and evil, between tradition and innovation, between heaven and hell, when the Old and the New gods confront one another.

American Gods is a recent TV show, which is why there is little systematic research on it apart from short posts on blogs giving details about the actors or the production conditions or promoting the TV show. It may be interesting to take a closer look at the reception of the series in Europe. Of course, this is not possible because of Amazon, which streams the series and does not publish the audience figures. But there is at least a vague indicator of the different reception in Europe. The Bosnian Wikipedia entry for the series is strikingly long, summarizing in detail the episodes of the first season (*"Američki bogovi* (serija)"). And as far as this can be researched, there is only one detailed scholarly study, in Turkish (Yanat Bağci). In her essay, the author also describes the plot of the TV show, in part in great detail, pointing out some aesthetic peculiarities, but also some scenes that are crucial to her argument. Ultimately, this study is largely limited to reproducing the plot based on the characteristics of the protagonists, and in this respect is similar to the Bosnian Wikipedia entry.

The Turkish author accurately describes some impressive scenes of the TV show, for example in the second episode of the first season, when the demigod Shadow Moon stands in a supermarket among many TV sets that suddenly turn on by themselves. The face of "Media" (Gillian Anderson) appears, who tries to win him over with attractive images and multiple self-dramatizations, including as Lucille Ball aka Lucy Ricardo. Media says (S1E2; 25:51–26:13): "I'm all sorts, Shadow. This screen is the altar. I'm the one they sacrifice to. Then to now. Golden Age to Golden Age. [...] Time and attention, better than lamb's blood." The Golden Age, then, is one that recalls the *Edad de Oro* of Spain's Baroque era and many other similar epochs. On television Media addresses television, which is also the medium of *American Gods*. The stars belong on the altar of which Media speaks. They are known to be "gods" to their fans: "The star participates in all the world's joys, pities all its misfortunes, intervenes constantly in its destiny. [...] the star seems to exist at the solar center of the movies [...]" (Morin 8). That is why, in *American Gods*, Media aka Gillian Anderson features the familiar motif of Marilyn Monroe as the air from the subway shaft lifts her skirt. (S1E5; 38:20–39:45) – It is evident from the description of this and other scenes that the message is very simple: (media) tradition must be respected, and the new media replace valuable interpersonal contacts by wasting the time and attention of the audience. The Turkish author does not explicitly subscribe to this moral of the story, but neither does she comment on it from a proper distance.

Is it a coincidence that these texts mentioned above were written by authors from the eastern regions of Europe? Showrunner Fuller commented: "I don't think people will be very interested in the show if they've never even considered religion before. It's not for the apathetic" (quoted by Ryan). The World Value Survey has presented a map based on a survey from 2017–2021, which reflects the results of a survey in relation to the belief in hell (Strauss). Bosnia-Herzegovina (71.2%) and Turkey (90.6%) have by far the highest affirmation ratings when people there are asked if they believe in hell and Satan. In connection with the authors' Bosnian and Turkish origin, it is not specifically important that the series is about hell. But the inhabitants of the countries where many respondents answered in the affirmative are particularly religious. This connection between the religious subject of *American Gods* and scholarly interest in certain cultures could only be confirmed by means of a comprehensive investigation and is, of course, highly speculative in this preliminary form.

But such a conclusion fits well with the observation that Latin American telenovelas are also particularly popular in Eastern Europe (Salgueiro). And because TV viewers there appreciate the telenovela so much, Latin American artists even attract the attention of the Eastern European academic audience: "Who would think that a genre so criticized by Latin American intellectuals would be the one which would open us the doors to the image market [in former Yugoslavia] and, even more so, who would believe it would be so well liked. The saying goes well: 'nobody is a prophet in their own land'" (Salgueiro, in: Hisse). Conversely, Turkish series with romantic love stories are particularly popular in Latin America, especially in Chile (Gurk). This is because traditional gender roles are conveyed in both cases, and love stories are told that often end with a wedding and a religious blessing.

The possible relationship between the U.S. audience in the period of Trump's presidency and the release of *American Gods* certainly prompts conjecture simply because of the same time period. Blogs often contain very personal but sometimes remarkable statements like the following: "It's a show about America's enthusiasms and errors, its character and characters, that comes alive as a series of dreamlike vignettes – a tone poem about a nation and the battle for its beliefs. It works for the material: America, after all, is a pretty weird place" (Suderman). Or: "This isn't really drama as most of us would understand it: it's just a succession of Top Trumps superheroes, each with their own set of outrageous skills, manipulated into a series of exquisitely realized vignettes [...]" (Delingpole). The allegorical series characters ("vignettes") and the 'values' represented by the Republicans should actually be a good fit, because religion and tradition are represented by both the Grand Old Party and the Old Gods, who are the likeable figures in the TV show. However, Trump uses social media to propagate precisely these values and to discredit his political opponents because of their supposed moral and political failings. He is not afraid to harness the new media for his own purposes. Therefore, for him, there would be no contradiction between the Old and New Gods. Nor is it the case that only the technical innovations of the digital media count and the old traditions are no longer important because, after all,

America is to become 'great *again*'. The nationalism shared by societies in which church and family are the ideological foundations of their traditional culture also shapes the idea of a restored U.S. The main difference from the Old Gods, however, is perhaps that they come from ancient cultures outside America and therefore represent a diversity of beliefs and religious practices that does more justice to the presence of many religions in the U.S. than many previous TV productions.

> Despite what some critics say, religion has always been on TV in many different ways and has become, in the decade since 2000, an important part of TV's landscape, marking shows as realist, as relevant, and as 'quality TV.' Granted, the range of religious representations is still limited, being almost exclusively Christian. But the increasingly conflicted ideas and slowly growing diversity of religious representation reflect the changing patterns of religiosity in America (Lagerwey 10).

Therefore the new media stand for a paradox: although they have been significantly developed in the U.S. and are used all over the world, in the TV show they possibly stand for Christianity in its exclusive evangelical interpretation. This is a remarkable finding because it would imply that pop culture icons represent a religious and ideological monoculture.

7 Final Observations

However, the plot of *American Gods* is not the central point. Much more important is the spectacular aesthetics, which is particularly evident in the first season, perhaps because the financing of the TV show was even more generous then. *American Gods* is basically a television series that deserves to be seen on the big screen. But the small size of the TV picture is compensated for by the great picture and sound quality, even if one point of criticism is that the quality of the brilliant picture dazzles:

> The colors are comic-book supersaturated; the definition is so high you almost want to turn off your HD just so you can be spared those crater-size skin pores; no candle can be lit without a microscopic journey to the tip of the match, thence to the struck flame and the molten red wax, which is terribly pretty, though nothing we haven't seen in *Breaking Bad* and, before that, *Requiem for a Dream* plus, of course, in every scene of everything ever by Paolo Sorrentino. Aren't we due some kind of lo-fi backlash soon? (Delingpole)

The aesthetic of *American Gods* demands from the viewer the attention and time that Goddess Media speaks of, though this practice may not be novel. But in Fuller's and Green's TV show faith in art and creation does not give way to distraction. However, this is only possible in the same way as in the cinema, even if one is watching at home with the help of the TV screen or even on the cell phone display. The series therefore only partly resembles the 'excesses' of the new media in that the dialogues and flashbacks, explained with intertitles, make it different from an ordinary fantasy series. The linguistic and historical information is indispensable, because otherwise many unusual protagonists would be incomprehensible. Thus the TV show characterizes what has been also repeatedly claimed about the allegorical novel since antiquity: there would be no plot, but only a sequence of allegorical images in the form of personifications. This statement, which is often meant as criticism, is only partly true. The loose-leaf collection of pictures or photos in the old-fashioned historical form of a folding booklet (*leporello*), already mentioned above with a quote as "a series of dreamlike vignettes," in which the gods explain their actions and characteristics, is a media offering to curiosity that differs from many other TV shows. *American Gods* invites, in fact, the viewer to perform the ritual of religious contemplation in a certain way and in a new guise.

Works Cited

"*Američki bogovi* (serija)." *Wikipedia* 29 Dec. 2021. https://bs.wikipedia.org/wiki/Ameri%C4%8Dki_bogo vi_(serija), 19 Aug. 2022.

Delingpole, James. "*American Gods.*" *The Spectator* 13 Mai 2017. *https://www.spectator.co.uk/article/seri al-offenders*, 21 Aug. 2022.

Genette, Gérard. *La Métalepse: De la figure à la fiction*. Paris: Seuil, 2004.

Gurk, Christoph. "Türkische Serien in Lateinamerika: Großer Herzşmerz." *Süddeutsche.de*. 21 Jan. 2021. https://www.sueddeutsche.de/medien/tuerkei-serien-lateinamerika-telenovela-1.5181624?reduced=true, 19 Aug. 2022.

Hisse, Bianca. "*Europa del este en romance con la telenovela latinoamericana* (Installation and Durational Performance in Collaboration with María Luisa Sanín Peña; Galerija Miroslav Kraljevic, Zagreb, Croatia February 2020)." *Bianca Hisse*. n.d. https://biancahisse.com/europa-del-este, 21 Aug. 2022.

Lagerwey, Jorie. "Are You There, God? It's Me TV: Religion in American TV Drama 2000–2009." Ph.D. U of Southern California, 2009.

Morin, Edgar. *The Stars: An Account of the Star System in Motion Pictures*. Den Haag: Mouton & Co., 1961.

Ndalianis, Angela. *Neo-Baroque Aesthetics and Contemporary Entertainment*. Cambridge, MA, London: MIT Press, 2004.

Patten, Dominic. "*American Gods* canceled at Starz: No Season 4 But Maybe a TV Movie." *Deadline*. 30 March 2021. https://deadline.com/2021/03/american-gods-canceled-no-season-4-starz-neil-gai man-1234724166/, 19 Aug. 2022.

Pérez-Amezcua, Luis Alberto, and Ethel Junco. "Myths of Femininity in *American Gods.*" *Journal of Comparative Literature and Aesthetics* 43.4 (2020): 15–27.

Ryan, Maureen. "'Gods' Riffs on Faith, Fantasy: Myth and Culture Mix in Starz Series." *Variety* 335.15 (2017): 24.
Salgueiro, Ramón. "Europa del este en romance con la telenovela latinoamericana." *Casqui* 87 (2004): 66–71.
Strauss, Simon. "Das geteilte Europa: Warten auf die Strafe Gottes." *FAZ.NET*. www.faz.net. 18 Aug. 2022. https://www.faz.net/aktuell/feuilleton/debatten/in-rumaenien-und-polen-glaubt-die-mehrheit-noch-an-die-hoelle-18250419.html, 21 Aug. 2022.
Suderman, Peter. *"American Gods." Reason.com*. 1 Aug. 2017. https://reason.com/2017/08/01/american-gods/, Aug. 2022.
Türschmann, Jörg. "Die Metalepse." *montage/av* 16.2 (2007): 105–12.
Türschmann, Jörg. *"El cartero siempre llama dos veces:* La repetición como figura herérica en cine y televisión." *Cine global, televisión transnacional y literatura universal: Estéticas hispánicas en el contexto de la globalización*. Ed. Matthias Hausmann and Jörg Türschmann. Frankfurt am Main: Peter Lang, 2022: 123–38.
Virilio, Paul. *War and Cinema: The Logistics of Perception*. London, New York: Verso, 1989.
Yanat Bağci, Yelda. "Mitoloji, tanrilar, medya ve yeni media: *American Gods* dizisi üzerine bir çözümleme." *The Turkish Online Journal of Design, Art, and Communication* 11.3 (2021): 1148–61.

List of Contributors

Ruth Abbey is a Professor and Chair of the Department of Humanities and Social Sciences at Swinburne University in Australia. She is the author of *Nietzsche's Middle Period*; *Philosophy Now: Charles Taylor*; *The Return of Feminist Liberalism*; and *Human All too Human: A Critical Introduction and Guide*. She is the editor of *Contemporary Philosophy in Focus: Charles Taylor*; *Feminist Interpretations of John Rawls*; and *Cosmopolitan Civility*. She has published a number of articles and book chapters, ranging from topics such as contemporary liberalism, to conceptions of marriage, to animal ethics. She has also served as the Editor in Chief of *The Review of Politics*.

Carmen Birkle is a Professor of North American Literary and Cultural Studies at Philipps-Universität Marburg. She was president, vice president, executive director, and international delegate of the German Association for American Studies and currently serves as treasurer for the European Association for American Studies. She is Dean of the Faculty of Foreign Languages, Literatures, and Cultures at Philipps-Universität (2017–23). Apart from being the author of two monographs – *Women's Stories of the Looking Glass* (1996) and *Migration—Miscegenation—Transculturation* (2004) – and of numerous articles and (co-)editor of 15 volumes of essays and special issues of journals, she is also General (Co-) Editor of the journal *Amerikastudien / American Studies* (open access). Her current work on a monograph is situated at the intersection of American literature, culture, and medicine in the 19th and early 20th centuries. Moreover, her contribution to a larger interdisciplinary project on "Geschlecht—Macht—Staat" focuses on female presidents in U.S.-American TV series. A monograph on Muriel Gardiner and the edition of Gardiner's correspondence are projects gradually taking shape.

John D. Caputo, the Watson Professor of Religion Emeritus (Syracuse University) and the Cook Professor of Philosophy Emeritus (Villanova University), is an American philosophical theologian who works in the area of "weak" or "radical" theology, drawing upon hermeneutic and deconstructive theory. His next book, *What to Believe?* is scheduled to appear in 2023. His most recent books are *Specters of God: An Anatomy of the Apophatic Imagination* (2022); *In Search of Radical Theology: Expositions, Explorations, Exhortations* (2020); *Cross and Cosmos: A Theology of Difficult Glory* (2019); *Hermeneutics: Facts and Interpretation in the Age of Information* (2018) and a second edition of *On Religion* (2019). *The Essential Caputo* (2018) is a collection of his work from the early 1970s to the present time. In his major works he has argued that interpretation goes all the way down (*Radical Hermeneutics*, 1987), that Derrida is a thinker to be reckoned with by theology (*The Prayers and Tears of Jacques Derrida*, 1997), that theology is best served by getting over its love affair with power and authority and embracing what Caputo calls, taking a phrase from St. Paul, *The Weakness of God: A Theology of the Event*, 2006), which won the American Academy of Religion award for excellence in the category of constructive theology, and that God does not exist, God insists (*The Insistence of God: A Theology of Perhaps*). His papers and correspondence are housed in the Simon Silverman Phenomenology Center at Duquesne University (Pittsburgh, USA).

Federico Celestini is Professor of Musicology and Head of the Music Department at the University of Innsbruck. He studied in Rome at the University "La Sapienza" before completing his Ph.D. and Habilitation in Musicology at the Karl Franzens University in Graz, Austria. Celestini has been awarded several fellowships and guest professorships, e. g. from the British Academy (University of Oxford), the Riemenschneider Bach Institute (Cleveland), the Alexander von Humboldt Foundation (Freie Universität Berlin) and the Mellon Foundation (University of Chicago). From 2011 to 2022 Celestini was Co-Editor of *Acta Musicologica*, the peer-reviewed journal of the International Musicological Society. He is director of the Gustav Mahler Research Centre in Dobbiaco and a member of the Austrian Academy of Sciences. His publications include books on Haydn's piano sonatas, on Viennese modernism, on music aesthetics and on Nietzsche's music philosophy.

Michael Hochgeschwender, born 1961, is professor for North American History and Cultural Anthropology at the *Amerika Institut* of the Ludwig-Maximilians-University at Munich. He studied Catholic Theology and History in Würzburg and received his Ph.D. from Tübingen University in 1996 (*Freiheit in der Offensive: Der Kongreß für kulturelle Freiheit und die Deutschen*). He was awarded his habilitation from University of Tübingen in 2003 and served as Deputy Chair for Contemporary History in Tübingen as well. In 2004 he went to Munich University. Among his publications are *Wahrheit, Einheit, Ordnung: Der amerikanische Katholizismus und die Sklavenfrage, 1835–1870* (Paderborn: Schöningh, 2006), *Amerikanische Religion: Evangelikalismus, Fundamentalismus und Pfingstlertum* (Frankfurt/Main: Suhrkamp, 2007), *Der Amerikanische Bürgerkrieg* (München: C.H. Beck, 2010) and *Geburt einer Nation: Die Epoche der Amerikanischen Revolution* (München: C.H. Beck, 2016). His major fields of study are History of American Religion and the histories of the Revolutionary and the Civil War Era. He currently works on Paleo-Indian history.

Christoph Irmscher is Distinguished Professor of English and Director of the Wells Scholars Program at Indiana University Bloomington. His many books include *Louis Agassiz: Creator of American Science* (2013) and *Max Eastman: A Life* (2017).

Professor **Maureen Junker-Kenny** is Fellow emerita of Trinity College Dublin where she taught Theology, Ethics and Philosophy of Religion in a nondenominational Department, having moved there from the University of Tübingen in 1993. Her publications include *Habermas and Theology* (London 2011); *Religion and Public Reason: A Comparison of the Positions of John Rawls, Jürgen Habermas and Paul Ricoeur* (Berlin/Boston 2014); *Approaches to Theological Ethics. Sources, Traditions, Visions* (London 2019); co-ed. (with K. Viertbauer), *European Journal of Philosophy of Religion*, Special Issue 2019, "Habermas on Religion"; *Self, Christ and God in Schleiermacher's Dogmatics. A Theology Reconceived for Modernity* (Berlin/Boston 2020); *The Bold Arcs of Salvation History. Faith and Reason in Jürgen Habermas's Reconstruction of European Thinking* (Berlin/Boston 2022); "Vom ‚paulinischen Christentum' zum ‚Anderen der Vernunft' im nachmetaphysischen Denken", in: *Theologie und Glaube* 112 (2) (2022) 135–150; ed., *Etudes Ricoeuriennes/ Ricoeur Studies* 13/2 (2022), "Ricoeur and the Question of Religion". Research interests: Schleiermacher and theology in Modernity; religion and public reason; Habermas; Ricoeur; approaches to philosophical and theological ethics; biomedical ethics.

Irene Kajon is professor emerita of Moral Philosophy at Sapienza – University of Rome. She also taught Jewish Religion and Thought at Pontificia Università Lateranense (Rome) from 2009 to 2020. Her current research in the field of philosophical anthropology, in dialogue with Jewish and Christian sources and with art and literature, concerns the idea of humanism today. Her books include *Fede ebraica e ateismo dopo Auschwitz* (Perugia: Benucci, 1993); *Profezia e filosofia nel 'Kuzari' e nella 'Stella della redenzione'. L'influenza di Yehudah Ha-Lewi su Franz Rosenzweig* (Padova: Cedam, 1996); *Contemporary Jewish Philosophy. An Introduction* (London: Routledge, 2nd ed. 2010); *Ebraismo laico. La sua storia e il suo senso oggi* (Assisi: Cittadella Editrice, 2012).

Brendan Moran is Professor of Philosophy at the University of Calgary. His work principally focuses on modern and contemporary European philosophy. His publications include two books on Walter

Benjamin's philosophy, two co-edited books on Benjamin, Franz Kafka, and Giorgio Agamben, and articles and book chapters on Benjamin, Kafka, Heidegger, Levinas, Foucault, Agamben, Laruelle, Salomo Friedlaender, and Seloua Luste Boulbina. Much of his work concerns the relationship of philosophy, politics, and literature. Current interests include the relationship of time with justice; this extends to the philosophy of decolonization and issues of justice in academia. A book on Benjamin's justice and a co-edited volume on Benjamin and Political Theology are currently in progress.

Ludwig Nagl, Ao.Univ.-Prof. i.R., Department of Philosophy, University of Vienna, Austria. 1970/71 Assistant Professor, Millersville State University, Lancaster, Pennsylvania, USA; 1987 Visiting Scholar, Department of Philosophy, Harvard University, Cambridge, Mass., USA; 1993 Guest Professor, Department of Philosophy, University of Jena, Germany; 1996 Visiting Scholar, Minda de Gunzburg Center for European Studies, Harvard University, Cambridge, Mass., USA; 2011 Visiting Professor, University of St. Petersburg, Russian Federation. Selected publications of relevance to the presented paper: *Toward a Global Discourse on Religion in a Secular Age. Essays on Philosophical Pragmatism*, Vienna-Zurich, 2021; *Das verhüllte Absolute. Essays zur zeitgenössischen Religionsphilosophie*, Frankfurt a. M., 2010; *Religion nach der Religionskritik* (ed.), Berlin, 2003; *Essays zu Jacques Derrida and Gianni Vattimo "Religion"* (ed.), Frankfurt a. M., 2001; "Symposium zu Charles Taylor, ‚A Secular Age'" (ed.), *Deutsche Zeitschrift für Philosophie*, 2/2009, pp. 288–327. For a complete list of Ludwig Nagl's publications see http://home.phl.univie.ac.at/ludwig.nagl/

Herta Nagl-Docekal is University Professor (retd.), Department of Philosophy, University of Vienna, Austria; full member of the Austrian Academy of Sciences; membre tit., Institut International de Philosophie, Paris. Vice-President of FISP, The International Federation of Philosophical Societies (2008–2013). Visiting Professor at University of Utrecht (The Netherlands), Frankfurt am Main, Konstanz, Free University Berlin (Germany), University of St. Petersburg (Russian Federation). Dr. honoris causa: University of Basel (Switzerland). Her work was translated in the US, Japan, France, Hungary, Italy, Latvia, the Czech Republic, and the Russian Federation. Selected publications: *Artificial Intelligence and Human Enhancement. Affirmative and Critical Approaches in the Humanities* (co-ed. with W. Zacharasiewicz, Berlin 2022), *Transatlantic Elective Affinities. Traveling Ideas and their Mediators* (co-ed. with W. Zacharasiewicz, Vienna 2021), *Innere Freiheit. Grenzen der nachmetaphysischen Moralkonzeptionen* (Berlin 2014), *Feminist Philosophy* (Cambridge, MA, 2004), *Continental Philosophy in Feminist Perspective* (co-ed. with C. Klinger, University Park, PA, 2000), *Der Sinn des Historischen* (ed., Frankfurt a. M. 1996). http://home.phl.univie.ac.at/herta.nagl/

Sami Pihlström is Professor of Philosophy of Religion at the University of Helsinki, Finland. He is currently the President of the Philosophical Society of Finland, the President of the William James Society, and a Vice-President of Institut International de Philosophie (I.I.P.). He has published widely on pragmatism, realism, transcendental philosophy, philosophical anthropology, and the philosophy of religion. His recent books include *Pragmatic Realism, Religious Truth, and Antitheodicy: On Viewing the World by Acknowledging the Other* (Helsinki University Press, 2020), *Why Solipsism Matters* (Bloomsbury, 2020), *Pragmatist Truth in the Post-Truth Age: Sincerity, Normativity, and Humanism* (Cambridge University Press, 2021), *Toward a Pragmatist Philosophy of the Humanities* (SUNY Press, 2022), and *Humanism, Antitheodicism, and the Critique of Meaning in Pragmatist Philosophy of Religion* (Lexington Books, forthcoming 2023). He is a member of Academia Europaea, I.I.P., the Finnish Academy of Science and Letters, and the Finnish Society of Sciences and Letters.

Gertrude Postl. Professor of Philosophy and Women's and Gender Studies at Suffolk County Community College, Selden, NY, USA. Research focus: feminist philosophy, especially the intersection between body, language, and representation (Luce Irigaray, Julia Kristeva, Hélène Cixous), and issues of reading/writing, author, and text (Roland Barthes and Jacques Derrida). Recent publications include: *Hélène Cixous. Das Lachen der Medusa zusammen mit aktuellen Beiträgen* (co-edited with Esther Hutfless and Elisabeth Schäfer, Vienna: Passagen, 2013); entry on "Language, Writing, and Difference," *The Routledge Companion to Feminist Philosophy* (London, New York: Routledge, 2017); "'Life as a Narrative.' Julia Kristeva and Hannah Arendt," in: Brigitte Buchhammer (ed.), *Freiheit – Gerechtigkeit – Liebe; Freedom – Justice – Love. Festschrift zum 75. Geburtstag von Herta Nagl-Docekal* (Vienna: LIT Verlag, 2019); *Feminist Philosophy. A Close Encounter with the Work of Herta Nagl-Docekal* (co-edited with Brigitte Buchhammer, Vienna: LIT Verlag, 2022).

Manfred Siebald is a retired professor of American Studies in the Obama Institute for Transnational American Studies at Johannes Gutenberg University, Mainz. After receiving his Ph.D. from Philipps University, Marburg, he completed his habilitation in Mainz. He taught as Clyde S. Kilby Professor of English at Wheaton College, Illinois, at Georgia State University in Atlanta, and at York University, Toronto. His major research areas have been the intersections of literature and religion in the U.S.A., American church history and hymnology, but also popular culture (especially detective fiction and music). Among his publications are the monographs *Auflehnung im Romanwerk Herman Melvilles* (1979), *Dorothy L. Sayers* (1989, ^{2}2007), and *Der Verlorene Sohn in der amerikanischen Literatur* (2003). He has also edited and co-edited several other books, contributed numerous articles to periodicals, encyclopedias, and essay collections and from 1991 to 2002 was assistant editor of the journal *Amerikastudien/American Studies*.

David Staines is the former Dean of the Faculty of Arts and now Professor of English at the University of Ottawa. He has authored and/or edited more than twenty books on Medieval Culture and Literature and Canadian Culture and Literature. In 1998, he received the Lorne Pierce Medal from the Royal Society of Canada for outstanding contributions to Canadian criticism, and in 2011, he was awarded the Order of Canada and the Order of Ontario for his services to Canadian literature. His most recent book is *A History of Canadian Fiction* (2021).

Professor **William Sweet** is Jules Léger Research Chair in the Humanities and Social Sciences and Professor titulaire in Philosophy at St. Francis Xavier University, Nova Scotia, Canada. Sweet studied the history of philosophy, principally at l'Université d'Ottawa (Ph.D); political theory at the Université Paris 1-Sorbonne (D.E.A.); and epistemology of religion at the Centre Sèvres (Paris), l'Université Saint-Paul (D.Phil.), and the University of South Africa (D.Th.). He is a Past President of both the Canadian Philosophical Association and the Canadian Theological Society. He currently serves as a Vice President of the Council for Research in Values and Philosophy (Washington), and was a member of the Steering Committee of FISP (Fédération Internationale des Sociétés de Philosophie) from 2003 to 2018. He is the author and/or editor of some 30 books, has taught as a Visiting Professor at universities in China, Poland, Taipei, and India, and has lectured on six continents. He was elected a Fellow of the Royal Historical Society in 2013 and of the Royal Society of Canada in 2017, and a Membre titulaire of the Institut international de philosophie (Paris) 2021.

Jörg Türschmann is professor for French and Spanish Literature and Media at the Department of Romance Studies, University of Vienna. He is the deputy head of department, the co-director of the Vienna Center for Canadian Studies, and a member of the commission "The North Atlantic Triangle" of the Austrian Academy of Sciences. His research interests are 19th century novels, film philosophy and transnational relations between Argentine, French, German and Spanish literatures and cinema. He has edited books on semiotics, film theory and transnationality in cinema and television. His most recent publications are *Culturas del Transporte en América Latina* (deSignis, 2021), *TV-Serien aus französisch- und spanischsprachigen Kulturräumen* (Springer, 2022). *Cine global, televisión transnacional y literatura universal* (Lang, 2022).

Klaus Viertbauer (b. 1985) serves as Assistant Professor at the Catholic University of Eichstätt in Germany. His area of specialization includes philosophy of religion. In particular he has published two monographs on Søren Kierkegaard (*Gott am Grund des Bewusstseins?*, 2017) and Jürgen Habermas (*Religion und Lebensform*, 2022).

Charles Reagan Wilson is Professor Emeritus of History and Southern Studies at the University of Mississippi and former director of the Center for the Study of Southern Culture. He is general editor of the 24-volume *New Encyclopedia of Southern Culture* (2006–2013) and coeditor of the *Mississippi Encyclopedia*. Much of his work has been on religion in the American South, including *Baptized in Blood: The Religion of the Lost Cause, 1865–1920* (1981), *Religion and Public Life in the South* (2005), and *Southern Missions: Religion of the American South in Global Perspective* (2003). His most recent books are *The American South: A Very Short Introduction* (2021) and *The Southern Way of Life: Meanings of Civilization and Culture in the American South* (2023).

Alois Woldan, born in Linz, Austria, in 1954, studied theology and Slavonic and Comparative Literature at the University of Innsbruck. Scholar in Voronesh, Russia; lecturer at the University of Linguistics in Moscow; Ph.D. in Slavonic and Comparative Literature, University of Innsbruck; Assistant Professor at the Slavonic Department of the University of Salzburg; lecturer in German and Austrian culture at the University of Wrocław/Poland; full Professor of East Central European Studies at the University of Passau, Germany; full Professor of Slavonic Literatures at the University of Vienna; retired in 2020. Fields of study: history of Polish and Ukrainian literatures, literatures in Austrian Galicia, translation of poetry from Polish and Ukrainian into German. Important publications: *Der Österreich-Mythos in der polnischen Literatur.* Wien: Böhlau Verlag, 1996; *Europa Erlesen: Lemberg.* Klagenfurt: Wieser Verlag, 2008; *Beiträge zu einer Galizienliteratur.* Frankfurt a.M.: Peter Lang, 2015.

Waldemar Zacharasiewicz is Emeritus Professor of American Studies at the University of Vienna. He chairs the commission "The North Atlantic Triangle" of the Austrian Academy of Sciences. He is also a member of Academia Europaea and an International Fellow of the Royal Society of Canada. His main research interests have been travel literature and imagology, the study of transatlantic migration, and the literatures of the American South and of Canada. Among his publications are a monograph on the theory of climate in English literature and literary criticism (1977), two book-long studies on *Images of Germany in American Literature* (1998 and 2007), a collection of his essays entitled *Imagology Revisited* (2010), and a volume on T*ransatlantic Networks and the Perception and Representation of Vienna and Austria between the 1920s and 1950s* (2018). Of relevance to the topic of his essay are two collections of essays: *Transatlantic Exchanges: The American South in Europe—Europe in the American South*, co-edited with Richard Gray (2007), and *Cultural Circulation: Dialogues between Canada and the American South*, co-edited with Christoph Irmscher (2013).

Index of Authors

Adler, Sigmund 338
Adler, Victor 338
Adorno, Theodor W. 109, 118, 126, 342
Agassiz, Louis 15, 297–302, 304
– Biography of ~ 297
– and Calvinism 300
– criticized by Darwin 300 f.
– and concept of the "Ice Age" 298
– mentored by Humboldt, Alexander von 298
– as minister's son 297
– and Old Testament 299
– and racism 297
– and readability of the world 297
– and reading of Psalm 8 15, 299
– and vastness of the human mind 299
Amalric, Jean-Luc 135
Arendt, Hannah 115
Augustin, St. 64, 125

Barth, Karl 9, 12, 225 f.
Beethoven, Ludwig van 16, 342
Bellah, Robert 14, 181, 280–284
Benjamin, Walter 6, 89–104, 126
Berger, Peter L. 226
Berger, Zackary Sholem 61
Blake, William 15, 310, 313
Bondi, Seraphin 338
Braun, Heinrich 338
Brod, Max 98, 102
Brownson, Orestes A. 199, 215
Buber, Martin 2–4, 21, 23, 27–33, 53, 59–62

Carlson, Thomas 56, 183
Carnap, Rudolf 56, 286
Carson, Rachel 168, 303
Chekhov, Anton 171
Chesterton, G. K. 225, 308 f.
Cicero 3, 21 f.
Clement, William Dean 47
Collins, Francis S. 15, 297, 301–304
– attacked by the religious right 301
– Career of ~ 301
– as defender of evolution 302

– and faith as a rational choice 297, 302
– justifies suffering 302
– and vaccine advocacy 301
– *The Language of God* 15, 302 f.
Comte, Auguste 210
Cook, Robin 12, 237–239
– *Pandemic* 12, 237–241, 250, 252

Dabney, Robert L. 183
Darwin, Charles 15, 297 f., 300–302, 304
– and animal suffering 300 f.
– and controversy with Gray, Asa 297, 300
– vs. design in nature 297, 300
– *On the Origin of Species* 298, 300
Davis, Jefferson 183, 186, 188
Dawkins, Richard 79 f., 83, 262
Derrida, Jacques 6, 93, 102, 146
Detweiler, Robert 234
Dewey, John 4, 48, 53–55, 57, 59–61
Doggett, D. S. 185
Döllinger, Ignaz von 199
Dostoevski, Fyodor 119, 170

Eagleton, Terry 313
Elias, Norbert 75 f.
Elie, Paul 167, 176
– *The Life You Save May Be Your Own* 167, 176;
    see also O'Connor, Flannery
Eliot, T. S. 119, 230, 309, 313
Elliott, Emory 232
Emerson, Ralph Waldo 166

Faulkner, William 165–167
– *The Sound and the Fury* 165–167
Fechner, Gustav Theodor 338, 340, 344
Fiorenza, Francis Schüssler 125
Flatt, Lester 179 f.
Foessel, Michaël 130
Fortier, Jeremy 75 f., 82
Frankl, Viktor 41 f., 48
Freud, Sigmund 10, 152, 154–156
Frey, Daniel 123
Friedlaender, Salomo 102

https://doi.org/10.1515/9783111247878-025

Frye, Northrop   15, 307–316
Fuchs, Eduard   93

Gandillac, Maurice de   91
Gilson, Etienne   204
Goethe, Johann Wolfgang von   98 f., 101, 208, 339
Gordon, Peter E.   92
Görres, Joseph   196, 198
Grady, Henry   187
Graham, Billy   303
Gray, Asa   297, 300–302, 305
– as Darwin's correspondent   297, 300
– and design in nature   297, 300
– and God's goodness   297, 300
– as spiritual mentor of believing scientists   297, 301 f.
Gregor/Gregory XVI, Pope   199, 212
Grimm, Jacob and Wilhelm   92
Gruber, Max   338

Habermas, Jürgen   1 f., 7 f., 14, 64, 92, 95–97, 123–131, 133 f., 137 f., 151, 157, 253, 259, 261, 279, 288–293, 295
Hahn, Hans   56
Hamer, Fannie Lou   191
Hampe, Michael   55
Harrington, Austin   129
Harris, Sam   301
Hawthorne, Nathaniel   12, 223–225, 231–233, 241, 243
Hayhoe, Katharine   15, 297, 303–305
– and Gray, Asa   305
– and non-human life   303
– and practical approach to environmentalism   15, 297, 303 f.
– vs. science denial by fundamentalists   15, 304
– *Saving Us*   15, 304
– Hegel, Georg Wilhelm Friedrich   7, 27, 109, 115–117, 126 f., 132, 135 f., 146, 148, 171, 200, 217, 280
Hobbes, Thomas   74–76
Holcombe, William   181
Honneth, Axel   95 f.
Horkheimer, Max   6 f., 93–95, 109 f., 114, 118–120, 126

Humboldt, Alexander von   297 f.
Husserl, Edmund   141, 143 f., 147

Jackson, Stonewall   183, 185 f.
James, William   4, 35, 37–39, 48, 53–58, 64 f., 171
Jaspers, Karl   5, 70, 170, 324
Joas, Hans   246, 253
Johannes Duns Scotus, OFM   125
Jones, Charles S., Jr.   186 f.

Kafka, Franz   6, 90, 98, 101 f., 119
Kant, Immanuel   2–4, 6–9, 21–33, 42 f., 45, 53–56, 58, 60, 62 f., 109–114, 117 f., 120, 123, 125–128, 130–132, 135 f., 138, 141, 145, 147 f., 171, 280
Kierkegaard, Søren   10, 146, 165, 170, 172 f., 175
King, Martin Luther, Jr.   11, 72, 81, 189 f., 268 f., 271
Kleutgen, Joseph, SJ   200
Klopstock, Friedrich Gottlieb   343
Kraft, Werner   102
Kraus, Karl   6, 104
Kristeva, Julia   9 f., 151–160

Lactantius   3, 21 f.
Lange, Friedrich Albert   340
Langthaler, Rudolf   126, 130, 134
Le Verrier, Urbain   15, 299
Lee, Robert E.   183 f., 188
Leo XIII, Pope   200, 205, 210, 215 f.
Levi, Primo   41 f.
Lévinas, Emmanuel   4, 42, 59
Lewis, C. S.   226, 233, 286, 309
Liberatore, P. Matteo, SJ   200
Lincoln, Abraham   80, 181
Lipiner, Siegfried   16, 337–345
Longfellow, Henry Wadsworth   298

Macarthur, David   55
Mahler, Alma   337
Mahler, Gustav   16, 337, 340–345
Marcel, Gabriel   10, 170 f.
Maritain, Jacques   204
Martin, David   71 f.
McLuhan, Marshall   15, 307–316
Messner, Johannes   204

Metz, Johann Baptist   96, 125
Meysenbug, Malwida von   340
Milton, John   36, 47, 310, 313
Molina, P. Louis de, SJ   200, 205
Monroe, Bill   180
Morus, Thomas   173
Murphey, Murray G.   56

Natorp, Paul   338f.
Neurath, Otto   56
Newman, John Henry   199
Nietzsche, Friedrich   16, 27, 95, 332, 337–341, 345
Noll, Mark   231f.

O'Connor, Flannery   10, 165–169, 176
– Everything That Rises Must Converge   167
– "Good Country People"   168
– "The Fiction Writer and His Country"   168
– *The Habit of Being: Letters*   168
– "The Life You Save May Be Your Own"   176
– "The Regional Writer"   166

Peirce, Charles Sanders   10, 37f., 63, 165, 171
Percy, Walker   10, 165–167, 169–176
– *Lost in the Cosmos: The Last Self-Help Book*   170
– *Love in the Ruins*   169, 173
– *Signposts in a Strange Land*   170f.
– *The Last Gentleman*   169f., 173
– *The Message in the Bottle*   170, 172
– *The Moviegoer*   167, 169f., 172f.
– *The Second Coming*   169
– *The Thanatos Syndrome*   169, 173–175
Percy, William Alexander   169, 172
– *Lanterns on The Levee: Recollections of a Planter's Son*   169
Pernerstorfer, Engelbert   338, 341
Pesch, P. Heinrich, SJ   11f., 195, 207–213, 216f.
Peukert, Helmut   125
Pieper, Joseph   199, 204
Pinker, Steven   5, 69f., 73–84
Pius IX, Pope   199f., 212, 215
Pollard, Edward   183
Pröpper, Thomas   138
Putnam, Hilary   4f., 53–65
Putnam, Ruth Anna   55, 65f.

Rawls, John   4, 14, 53, 81f., 127f., 260, 262f., 270, 280, 284, 289
Reichenbach, Hans   54
Richmond, Virginia   185f.
Ricœur, Paul   123f., 131–137
Rochlitz, Rainer   91
Rohde, Erwin   338
Roman, Sébastien   131, 133f., 137
Rorty, Richard   62f., 146, 261f., 268, 289
Rosenzweig, Franz   23, 59
Rosmini, Antonio   194
Rousseau, Jean-Jacques   180
Royce, Josiah   49, 63, 171
Ryan, John A., Msgr.   12, 216f.

Sartre, Jean Paul   44, 170, 330
Satolli, Francesco di Paolo, Cardinal   215
Schlette, Magnus   55, 57, 59
Scholem, Gershom   6, 102f.
Schopenhauer, Arthur   16, 339–341, 345
Schwarz, Benjamin   60
Scruggs, Earl   179f.
Shakespeare, William   115, 310
– *Romeo and Juliet*   115
Shevchenko, Taras H.   323, 325–327, 329, 331
Smith, Wilfred Cantwell   64f.
Spengler, Oswald   309
Spratt, Leonidas   181
Stus, Vasyl'   16, 321–327, 329–331, 334f.
Suárez, P. Francisco, SJ   200

Taparelli d'Azeglio, P. Luigi, SJ   200
Taubes, Jacob   92
Taylor, Charles   1, 4f., 7, 10, 53–55, 69–84, 109, 119f., 165, 167, 175f., 223, 232, 234, 237–239, 253, 257f., 274, 284
A Secular Age   1, 5, 7, 53f., 83, 119f., 167, 176, 223, 258
Teilhard de Chardin, Pierre   169
Thomas von Aquin, OP   125, 198, 201f., 210, 212, 216, 309
Tracy, David   125
Tumulty, Peter J.   59

Updike, John   12, 223–228, 230f., 233
– *A Month of Sundays*   224
– *Roger's Version*   12, 223–231, 233

Volkelt, Johannes 338

Wagner, Richard 16, 208, 225, 230, 337–342, 345
Waldron, Jeremy 74, 80
Walzer, Michael 14, 280, 282, 284
Warren, Robert Penn 166
Weber, Max 59, 133, 225
Weiss, P. Albert Maria, OP 11, 195, 207–209, 211–213
Wendel, Saskia 130

Willis, Connie 12f., 237f., 247, 251
– *Doomsday Book* 12, 237f., 247–252
Winthrop, John 181
Wittgenstein, Ludwig 4, 38, 43, 53f., 56f., 59, 61f., 64, 143, 146
Wolterstorff, Nicolas 61, 257
Wright, Lawrence 12, 237f., 241, 243
– *The End of October* 12, 237–239, 241–247 250, 252

Zöllner, Johann Karl Friedrich 340

Index of Subjects

Absolute, The   4, 23, 32f., 36, 39, 62, 102, 110, 117, 148
Adagio   344
Aestheticism   175
African Americans   11, 165, 173, 180, 183f., 188f.
Agnosticism   40f., 44, 114, 168
American Dream   11, 165f.
– Questioning of the ~   11, 165
American Revolution   180f., 232
American South   11, 165–173, 179–191
Angel of history   90, 96
Antinomy of practical reason   126f.
Apollonian   341
Artist   159–161, 174, 176, 311, 355, 357
Atheism, atheist   23, 38f., 44, 60, 93, 114, 143, 234, 242
Aufklärung   55, 195; see also Enlightenment
Autonomy   23, 128, 132, 193f., 268
Axial Age   5, 70–73, 78, 82, 84, 125

Baroque, Neo-Baroque   17, 349, 351, 353, 356
Behaviorism, behaviorist   10, 165, 171, 174
Believer, non-believer   1–3, 6f., 14, 21, 47, 64, 80, 109, 112–114, 118–120, 182, 238, 246, 260f., 263, 268–272, 283, 285, 288–291, 293–295, 301, 355
Bible   15, 61, 80, 123, 148, 168, 186, 190, 215, 229, 247, 297, 301–304, 307, 310, 313
– *Book of Exodus*   229
– *Jeremiah*   232
– *Letter of St. Paul to Timothy*   303f.
Bible Belt   165
Biblical monotheism   7, 123–125, 135
Birmingham, Alabama   191, 271
Black Death   13, 237f., 248–251
Bluegrass music   179
Breakthrough (*Durchbruch*)   17, 138, 194, 342–345

Canada   259f., 263, 265, 303, 307, 314–316, 335
– Canadian experience   307

– Canadian literature   2, 315
Capitalism   11, 99–101, 118, 195, 207f., 210–212, 214, 216, 351
Catastrophe   90, 98, 241, 342
Categorical imperative   111, 127
Catholic, catholicism   11–13, 16, 69, 142, 167, 170–172, 186, 193–217, 237, 241, 259f., 271, 307–309, 316
Character   10, 12, 23, 29, 32, 36, 45f., 53, 99–102, 112, 115–117, 123, 127, 136, 166, 169f., 172f., 175, 213, 223, 231, 241, 243, 258, 268, 270, 274, 311, 322, 330, 338, 342, 345, 349–354, 357
Chorale   342, 345
Christ   144, 166, 213, 229f., 300, 338
Christianity   9, 61f., 73, 80f., 125, 141f., 147, 186f., 209, 225, 227, 281, 285, 302, 309f., 358
Civil religion   11, 14, 165, 179–183, 185–187, 189f., 279–281, 283, 295
Civil rights movement   11, 72, 81, 179, 189–191
Civil War, American   11, 165f., 179–181, 183, 188
Class, classless   75, 77, 172, 186, 188, 196, 199, 208, 210, 212–215, 217, 292, 310
Collapse (*Zusammenbruch*)   17, 55, 211, 231, 342f., 345
Communication   104, 131, 311, 314f., 349
Communitarianism   14, 279f., 295
Compassion   64, 95; see also Pity
Compositional process   346
Confederate battle flag   183f.
Confederate States of America   179, 181, 185
Confession   15, 113, 175, 291
Conservative   16, 92, 98, 181, 184, 199, 201, 208f., 223, 228, 230f., 303, 307, 309, 316
Consolation   90f., 258
Constellation   97, 323
Convalescence   99
Cosmos   15, 29, 36, 89, 99, 102, 104, 112, 170, 176
Creation care   303
– embraced by evangelicals   303

- Influence on scientists 303
Creationism 302
- and Agassiz, Louis 302
- Americans and ~ 302
- and creation care 302 f.

Death 6, 12, 25, 28, 31, 92, 114, 117, 133, 143, 169, 174, 185, 227, 240 f., 243–245, 251, 281, 307, 312–314, 321, 324–327, 331–335, 338–340, 353
Defeatism of reason 128
Democracy 11, 14, 57, 59, 76, 79, 81, 134, 137, 147, 181 f., 189, 191, 194, 203, 217, 249, 258, 268, 289
Deus absconditus 227, 331
Dignity 111, 158, 189, 202, 251, 260, 266, 269
Dionysian 341
Divine 2, 6, 10, 30, 33, 36, 40, 45, 48, 60–62, 65, 81, 89, 91 f., 100–103, 125, 129, 144, 153, 158, 160, 184, 196, 202, 205, 234, 298–300, 323, 325, 334, 340, 343, 349 f., 354
"Dixie" 183 f.; *see also* American South
Dogmatic scientism 4, 53 f.
Dystopia 10, 12 f., 165, 170, 173 f.

Eastern Europe 357
Emotivism 205
Enemy 93, 132, 198
Enlightenment 10, 55, 77 f., 80–82, 113, 118, 135, 141, 147 f., 152, 156–158, 160, 194–197, 199, 202, 204, 206, 215, 224, 232; *see also* Aufklärung
Entertainment 9, 156, 159, 180, 351
Environmentalism 15, 79, 303 f.
- embraced by evangelicals 15, 303 f.
- and Hayhoe, Katharine 15, 303 f.
Ethics 2, 13, 23 f., 26–28, 30, 32, 46, 48, 55, 61, 64, 95, 97, 126, 130–132, 135, 145, 181, 197, 206, 209 f., 216, 228, 244, 246, 252, 292
Euthanasia 174
- Advocated ~ 174
Evangelical Environmental Network (EEN) 15, 303
Evangelical Protestantism, Evangelical Protestants 11, 179–180, 182
Evangelicalism 201, 234, 303 f.
Evidentialism 38 f.

Evil 3 f., 9, 13, 16, 25–27, 32, 35 f., 38–41, 44–46, 49, 63, 79, 81, 111, 126, 136, 142, 168 f., 185, 199, 212, 233, 239–241, 243, 245 f., 252, 322, 326, 350 f., 355
- The problem of ~ 3 f., 26 f., 35 f., 38–41, 44–46, 49, 63, 243
Evolution 15, 246, 302
Existential 16, 40, 43, 54, 57 f., 132, 170, 201, 283, 321 f., 324, 330, 333, 353
- crisis 16
- question 57, 170, 283
Extraterritorial 2, 7 f., 123 f., 131, 137 f., 281

Fact-value dichotomy 56, 59
Faith 1 f., 4, 9 f., 12 f., 25–28, 44, 53 f., 59–62, 65, 70, 83, 97, 102, 112–114, 125 f., 129, 144 f., 147, 151–156, 160, 180–182, 197, 223–228, 230, 232 f., 238 f., 241, 244 f., 257, 259–263, 267–272, 274 f., 281, 285, 288–293, 301–304, 308 f., 323, 332, 339, 349–354, 358; *see also* Religion as an "option"
- Rational faith 24 f., 27, 113, 130
Fate 6, 89–91, 97–104, 142, 211, 323, 325, 327, 329 f., 335, 350, 352
Feeling 5, 27 f., 79, 110, 115 f., 118, 196, 227, 244, 339, 351
Fideism 38 f., 201
Finale 17, 342–345, 355
Finiteness 7, 109 f., 114, 117, 119 f.
Forgiveness 103, 116, 144, 153–156, 158–160, 251
Frankfurt School 7, 109, 126, 130
Freedom 10, 14, 30, 42, 82, 89, 98, 103, 125, 127 f., 132, 136–138, 156, 158, 181, 184, 188, 190 f., 193 f., 199, 202 f., 205 f., 211 f., 214, 234, 248, 260, 263, 268, 272 f., 282, 284 f., 289, 291, 293 f., 323, 335
French Revolution 71 f., 91, 195 f., 199
Fullness (Charles Taylor) 1, 5, 84, 120
Fundamentalism 15, 151, 207, 230, 238 f., 308

Germany 11, 28, 175, 195–198, 200, 203, 207, 209, 211, 213 f., 280, 284, 297
- German nationalism 341
Gods, old vs. new ~ 17, 349–352, 354–359
Good will 23 f., 26–28, 132, 136

Index of Subjects — **373**

Grief   7, 109, 114, 117, 327
Guilt   89, 99–101

Happiness, unhappiness   6, 23–25, 27f., 89, 99–101, 104, 111, 116f., 127, 135f., 203, 206, 339, 352
Healing   6, 15, 89–92, 103f., 230, 246, 250, 304
Health   104, 240, 242, 268, 273, 301
Hedonism   173
Hero   183–185, 340, 354
Heterologue   61f.
Highest good   24, 111f., 114, 117, 127f., 136, 206
Historical materialism, historical materialist   6, 92f., 95
History   2f., 5f., 13, 17, 24, 26f., 32, 36, 41, 44, 48, 64f., 69–74, 76, 81–83, 89–95, 97f., 104, 113, 125f., 128f., 133–135, 138, 144f., 153, 155, 157, 175, 180, 186–188, 190, 193, 195, 201, 204, 213f., 217, 223f., 231, 242f., 247–253, 265, 281, 286, 297f., 300f., 303, 313, 328f., 349f., 352f.
Holocaust   3, 35, 41f.
Homologue   61
Hope   6–8, 15, 24f., 28, 56, 72, 78, 80, 89, 91–93, 95, 98, 103, 109–111, 114, 118, 123f., 126–128, 131, 135f., 138, 144, 147, 166, 185, 228, 242f., 251, 263, 290, 301, 304, 351
Humanism   9f., 39, 43, 47–49, 60, 78, 81f., 151f., 155–159, 165, 167, 175, 208, 212, 234, 244, 246
– Exclusive ~   120, 167, 169, 173
Human rights   71, 82, 204f., 260, 271
Humour   344
Hypothesis   4, 48, 53, 58, 79, 148f., 151

Ideology   16, 124, 131, 133f., 137f., 174, 182f., 193, 197, 207, 214, 218, 226, 313, 327
Immanent frame   1, 4f., 53f., 79f.
Immortality   24, 101, 339
Imperishability   339
Individuation   340
Injustice   6f., 45, 83, 89, 93, 95f., 110, 142, 144, 181, 190, 207, 268, 332
Intercultural philosophy   265
Interpellate   93

Intimate revolt   10, 151, 156–160
I-You-relation   60–62

Jamaica Call to Action   303
Jeremiad   232
Jewish faith   209, 339
Jewish philosophy   2, 4, 53, 59, 62f.
Job (biblical character)   26, 45–48, 63, 229, 312, 332
Judgement (judge, Last Judgement)   6, 89, 91–94, 100, 103, 127, 133, 181, 247, 260, 273, 300, 326
Justice, injustice   2, 6f., 13, 21, 30, 33, 45, 47f., 53, 55, 60, 83, 89, 93, 95f., 99, 101–104, 109f., 114, 129, 142, 144, 147, 181, 189f., 205, 207, 210f., 216f., 266, 268, 270, 275, 280, 289, 332, 358

Kantian philosophy   340
Killing   13, 77, 91f.
Kunstwart (journal)   338

Laicism   14, 279–281, 284, 295
Language acquisition   171
Lausanne Movement   303
Law   1, 27, 54, 74, 81, 103, 112, 127f., 153, 155, 183f., 190, 202, 258, 260, 262, 270, 273, 284
Leipzig University   338
Liberalism   11, 14, 75, 194f., 197, 199f., 202, 204–208, 211f., 216f., 232, 262f., 279f., 284, 295
Liberty   151, 194–197, 205f., 214, 272, 283
Library of the Imperial Council (Bibliothek des Reichrates)   339
Literature   9f., 12, 15–17, 41f., 46, 96, 151f., 154, 156–160, 172, 237, 272, 308, 310f., 313, 323, 325, 334, 350, 353
Louisiana   167, 173–175, 214
Love   7, 32, 62, 109, 114–117, 131, 144, 154f., 173f., 179, 226, 230f., 249, 304, 322, 338, 344, 351, 357

Manifest destiny   181
Marxism, marxist   6f., 92, 94, 109, 114, 207
Meaning   3f., 6f., 9, 21–23, 27, 33, 35–44, 46–49, 57, 65, 89f., 103f., 118f., 127f., 130,

135–137, 142, 147, 152–160, 170 f., 179–181, 184, 190 f., 245 f., 262, 281 f., 288, 293, 323, 326, 345
– Meaning-making 3, 35–38, 40–43, 48 f.
Media 2, 9, 16, 156, 158, 166, 275, 311 f., 314, 349, 351, 354, 356–359
Medium of communication 311
Medical science 237, 239, 252
Messianic, messiah, messianism 6, 81, 89–93, 95–104, 321 f., 325–327
Metalepsis 353
Metamorphosis 344
Migration 12, 17, 214 f., 232, 298, 350, 352, 355
Military call 343
Mitleid see Pity; Compassion
Modernity 1, 5, 11, 22, 54, 63, 70, 79 f., 96, 119, 124 f., 141, 145, 147, 193–195, 200, 207 f., 211–213, 217 f.
Molinism 200
Moral law 15, 23–28, 30, 111, 127, 136, 302
Moral progress 5, 69 f.
Musical logic 346
Muslim hajj 12, 242

National Human Genome Research 301
National Institutes of Health (NIH) 15, 297, 301, 304
National Socialism, National Socialists 175, 194
Nature 5, 24–26, 43, 55, 63, 65, 69, 76, 79 f., 95, 99–102, 112, 115, 128, 153, 166, 171 f., 201–204, 206, 211 f., 229, 264, 267 f., 279, 285–287, 299 f., 302 f., 311, 340
Natural law 202, 210 f., 216 f.
Nature Conservancy 297, 303
Neo-Baroque see Baroque, Neo-Baroque
Neo-Scholasticism 193, 195, 198, 200–202, 204, 206 f., 215–217
New media 17, 223, 315, 349, 351, 356–359
New South 183, 186 f.
Nonscientific knowledge 55
Now-time (Jetztzeit) 91, 97, 103

Pan 332, 340, 344
Pandemic 12 f., 237–245, 248–253
Pantheism 340
Phenomenological suspension 141, 144, 147

Physician 15, 165, 170–171, 174 f., 186, 224, 301, 338
physis 99, 153
Pity 95; see also Compassion
Pluralism 4 f., 13 f., 53, 55, 63, 65, 82, 203 f., 233, 257 f., 263–267, 269–272, 274 f., 280, 290, 343 f.
Politics, political 9 f., 53, 60, 75, 97, 101 f., 132, 151, 203, 205, 214, 257 f., 282
Postmetaphysical thinking 123–125, 128, 134
Postulate 8, 24, 35, 46, 58, 112, 117, 123, 126, 136
– Postulates of pure practical reason 112
Practical reason 8, 23 f., 27 f., 56–58, 62, 111–113, 125–127, 129, 135 f., 292
Pragmatism 2, 4, 35–38, 41–43, 45, 48, 55–57, 60, 63, 171
Pragmatic method 35, 37, 40, 42
Procedural democracy 137
Proletariat 99
Prometheus 16, 337–340
Prophecy 94
Protestant, protestant faith 11 f., 179 f., 186, 195 f., 198–202, 207, 209, 214, 225 f., 233, 237, 307 f., 339
Protestant Reformation, protestantism 180–182, 197, 208 f., 214, 308 f.
Psalm 8 15, 299
Psychoanalysis 9 f., 151 f., 155 f., 158, 170
Public sphere 1, 13 f., 257–263, 267–272, 274 f., 289
Puritanism, puritan, puritans 12, 181, 215, 223 f., 231–233, 238, 214, 241

Race relations 183, 209, 212–214
Racism 72, 169 f., 212 f., 297
Radical 7 f., 10, 12, 40, 45, 124, 128, 132, 136, 138, 143, 148, 151, 158, 161, 168, 174 f., 194, 208, 210–212, 334, 352
Rationality 55, 57, 126, 130, 136 f., 145, 152, 205, 266
Reading Association of German Students (Leseverein der Deutschen Studenten) 337
Realm 8, 10, 30, 32, 91, 96, 100, 124, 126, 129, 157–160, 234, 259, 281, 289
Reason, practical reason 2, 6–10, 13 f., 17, 21, 23–29, 31 f., 38, 42, 44, 46 f., 49, 56 f., 74 f.,

Index of Subjects — 375

81 f., 84, 90, 93, 96, 101, 109–111, 114, 118, 120, 123–133, 135–138, 141, 144–147, 151, 153 f., 158–160, 198, 205, 213, 223, 225, 240, 244, 249, 257–259, 261–264, 266–269, 272–274, 279, 292, 311, 314, 326, 338, 352 f., 355
Recognition   10, 13, 40, 72, 100 f., 131, 135, 156, 170 f., 175, 244, 263 f., 266, 269 f., 275, 290 f., 354
Reconciliation   30, 72 f., 103, 116, 188, 190
Reconstruction   7, 73, 124 f., 184, 202, 293
Redemption, redeem   6, 23, 29, 31, 89, 92 f., 96, 103, 190, 249, 310, 338, 340
Reformed humanism   157 f.
Religion as an option   4, 53 f., 58, 223, 234, 258, 285; see also Faith
Religion of the Lost Cause   179, 182–190; see also Confederate States of America
Religion, purely moral   7, 109 f., 113
Religion and science   233, 251
Religion and suffering   3 f., 35–49, 100 f., 125, 129, 144, 240, 251, 253, 300–302, 330–333
Religious belief   4 f., 12, 14, 53, 56–58, 60, 62, 79 f., 112, 165, 167, 223, 232, 246, 260, 262 f., 267 f., 272, 274, 285, 287, 307, 316
Religious convert   2, 16, 167, 199, 208, 215, 230, 307–309, 339
Religious epistemology   287
Remembrance   6, 89 f., 94–97, 104
Representation   16, 32, 156 f., 166, 169, 227, 287, 345, 358
Resignation   111, 340
Resonance   80, 119 f.
Respecting the other   63
Resurrection   124, 135, 166, 185, 326, 339, 343
Retribution   89, 103
Revolution   28, 70, 72, 76 f., 153, 196, 199, 204 f., 234, 247, 282
Rhythm   99, 101, 153, 180
Ritual   8, 11, 21, 57, 81, 123–126, 129, 131, 138, 181–185, 187, 189 f., 223, 242, 248, 250–253, 282 f., 330, 355, 359
Rondo   345

Sacred   10 f., 91 f., 124, 153 f., 158–160, 179 f., 182–191, 196 f., 237, 246, 282, 327 f., 330
Sacrifice   82, 155, 243, 326, 335, 355 f.

Saint Paul   303
Satire, satiric   169, 224, 240
Saving   94, 244, 334
Scherzo   345
Science   1, 12, 15, 22, 35, 53–55, 57 f., 61, 82, 94, 111, 124, 132, 135, 141, 143, 171, 204, 223, 225, 228, 230 f., 234, 237–241, 244–247, 249, 251–253, 257, 259, 273, 285 f., 290, 297–304, 321
– Denial of ~   141
– extolled by Agassiz   15, 297–302, 304
– Ignorance of Americans   224, 302
– and religion   2, 9, 12, 23, 30, 53, 124 f., 128, 130 f., 141, 145, 147, 151, 234, 237–239, 241, 244, 246, 252 f., 260, 285, 289, 339
– Scientist   10, 12 f., 15, 83, 208, 212, 223, 228 f., 234, 237–239, 242–244, 249, 252 f., 297, 299–304
Scientism   53, 55–57, 171, 234
Science fiction   247, 311
Secular age   1 f., 4, 10, 13, 21 f., 33, 35, 44, 53, 63, 123, 169, 171, 175, 237 f., 241, 253, 257–259, 262 f., 267, 270–272, 274 f.
Secularism   43, 47, 82, 152, 179, 182, 185, 189, 230, 233, 257 f., 271, 279–281, 284 f., 295, 301
Secularization   12, 14, 17, 90, 92, 151, 194, 223, 225, 229, 231–233, 253
Self-instrumentalization   128
Self-legislation   128, 132
Semiotic   153–155, 157 f., 160, 170 f.
– Semiotic/symbolic   8, 95 f., 124, 130, 133–135, 137, 153, 155, 157, 160, 185, 329 f.
– Semioticians   171
Signification   10, 137, 152–156, 159 f.
Slavery   71, 74, 77, 81, 181 f., 188, 212 f.
Social imaginary   130 f., 133 f., 137
Social teaching   210 f., 216 f.
Society of the Spectacle   9, 151, 156 f., 159–161
Solidarity   8, 123, 128 f., 210 f., 331
Sonata form   342
Space   8, 11, 29, 31, 56, 59, 65, 83 f., 89, 101, 129, 133 f., 138, 141, 144, 157, 160, 167, 169, 179, 182, 184 f., 188, 196, 223, 232, 266, 271, 353
Spirit   7, 65, 109, 115–119, 142, 148, 153, 182, 184, 217, 243, 303, 321, 329

Index of Subjects

SS radical dedication (to racist concepts) 175
Sublimation 156, 159 f.
Suffering 3, 6, 16, 26, 35–49, 92–95, 100 f., 125, 132, 136, 144, 167, 185, 189 f., 246, 248, 251, 253, 300–302, 325 f., 328, 330–333; *see also* Sacrifice
Supernaturalism 9, 141 f., 144 f., 147 f.
Symbol 27, 125, 131, 133, 135, 171, 180, 18 3, 186, 190, 197, 259 f., 262, 282, 284, 310, 321, 323, 330 f., 352
Symphony 342–345
Symphonic narrative 16, 341 f., 344

Technology, technological 99, 118, 228, 234, 239, 311, 349, 351, 354
Theodicies 3, 35 f., 38–40, 42, 44–46, 48 f., 331
Theodicism vs. antitheodicism 46 f.
Theology 2 f., 6–9, 13, 23, 35, 61 f., 92–94, 109 f., 114, 120, 123, 125, 129, 135, 141–144, 148, 158, 180 f., 193–195, 198, 200–202, 205, 216, 223 f., 226–230, 233, 262, 285, 288, 313, 330
– of hope 7, 109 f., 114, 120, 135
Thomism 195, 200 f.
tikkun (mending) 6, 103
Timothy *see* Bible: *Letter of St. Paul to Timothy*
Toleration 80, 263, 266, 271
Torah 97
Totalitarian regime 7, 110
totaliter aliter 61, 227
Tradition, traditionalism 5 f., 8, 13, 16, 22, 27, 36, 38, 49, 56, 65, 70 f., 123, 129, 135, 137, 159, 165, 179 f., 183, 187 f., 195, 200, 202, 204–206, 209 f., 213, 216, 226, 257–260, 264–267, 269 f., 281, 286, 313, 323, 326–332, 334, 342, 349, 351, 355–357
Tragedy 16, 184, 189, 301, 313, 337–342
Transcendence 5, 8, 16, 24, 44, 53, 60, 71 f., 79 f., 120, 138, 144, 146 f., 337, 339, 342–344

– Transcendental illusion 42 f., 49
– Transcendental rationality 141, 145, 147
Transference, countertransference 231, 154
Transience, transient 89, 99–103
TV series 17, 349–352, 354–359

Ukraine 16, 321, 329, 335
Ukrainian literature of the 20th century 321, 323, 334 f.
Ultramontanism 11, 194–196, 198 f., 206 f., 210, 214 f.
United Church 15, 307 f., 316
United Daughters of the Confederacy 187 f.
University of Vienna 337
Utopia 7 f., 71, 123 f., 130 f., 133–135, 137 f., 173 f.

Vienna 35, 40, 143, 168, 171, 173 f., 257, 337, 339, 341
Violence 5, 72–84, 91, 131 f., 143, 151, 173 f., 183, 196, 239, 262, 282, 328, 333
– reduction 5, 69, 73, 75–83, 189
Virtue 23–26, 65, 71, 75, 99–103, 110 f., 127 f., 183, 189 f., 225, 280
Virus 13, 213, 239 f., 242 f., 246–249, 251–253

Waltz melodies 173 f.; *see also* Vienna
Western civilization 309
Will (*Wille*) 7, 22–28, 30, 36, 38, 41, 46, 48 f., 54, 57–59, 62, 78 f., 83, 91, 94 f., 104, 110 f., 114, 116, 118, 123 f., 127, 130–132, 136, 148 f., 151, 153, 166, 170, 174, 181, 190, 194 f., 200, 205, 217, 225–227, 229 f., 233, 238–240, 242, 244–247, 250, 252, 262, 267, 269, 272–274, 280, 282, 285, 288 f., 292, 301 f., 308 f., 313, 321, 323, 326 f., 329, 333, 337 f., 340, 352, 355 f.
– to believe 48, 54, 58
– to meaning 41, 48

www.ingramcontent.com/pod-product-compliance
Lightning Source LLC
Chambersburg PA
CBHW031751220426
43662CB00007B/362